The Apartheid State in Crisis

THE
APARTHEID
STATE
IN CRISIS

Political Transformation in South Africa, 1975–1990

ROBERT M. PRICE

New York Oxford
OXFORD UNIVERSITY PRESS
1991

Oxford University Press

Oxford   New York   Toronto
Delhi   Bombay   Calcutta   Madras   Karachi
Petaling Jaya   Singapore   Hong Kong   Tokyo
Nairobi   Dar es Salaam   Cape Town
Melbourne   Auckland

and associated companies in
Berlin   Ibadan

Library of Congress Cataloging-in-Publication Data
Price, Robert M.
The apartheid state in crisis :
political transformation in
South Africa, 1975-1990 /
Robert M. Price.
p. cm. Includes bibliographical references and index.
ISBN 0-19-506749-5 (cloth) — ISBN 0-19-506750-9 (pbk.)
1. South Africa—Politics and government—1978–
2. South Africa—Politics and government—1961-1978.
3. Apartheid—South Africa.
I. Title. DT1963.P75 1991
320.968—dc20   90-7871

9 8 7 6 5 4 3 2

Printed in the United States of America
on acid-free paper

For Mimi

Preface

I began to write this book in early 1986, when South Africa was in the throes of insurrectionary upheaval. Although I perceived that a political transformation of historical proportions was underway, one that would eventually produce an end to white minority rule, I comprehended only dimly the mode by which the ruling white oligarchy would agree to relinquish its monopoly of political power. My intent was to write about political transformation "in progress." I sought to explain how a political regime, which until only recently had appeared to be utterly self-confident and invincible, if not invulnerable, had been thrown on the defensive, losing its sense of purpose and initiative. And, I sought to show that a long-term process was underway through which the power balance between the white supremacist state and its opponents was gradually shifting toward the latter. I endeavored to lay before the reader the specific dynamics of that process; to elucidate and reveal the relationship between political, social, and economic forces that shape the nature of South African political change and drive it forward.

I completed the book manuscript in early 1990, when the pace of change, ongoing for approximately fifteen years, quickened appreciably. The ascendance of F. W. de Klerk to the South African presidency, and his early actions in office, suggested to virtually everyone that the process of change was moving toward the negotiating table. In light of these developments, this book represents the "background to negotiations." It provides an explanation of how and why South Africa's ruling political oligarchy decided to negotiate the country's political future with individuals and organizations that for over thirty years it had sought to silence or destroy. It also provides signposts to help illuminate what will probably be a lengthy and rough path to a negotiated settlement. For the ongoing process of political transformation shapes the negotiating positions of the South African protagonists, affects their relative power, and influences what they will and will not compromise. This examination of more than a decade of change in South Africa also foreshadows future developments should negotiations break down short of an agreement. Lacking a crystal ball, I am unable to predict precisely when the current movement toward negotiations will be matched by results, or what the exact terms of a political settlement will be.

The material set forth here was developed in the process of teaching a course on South African politics at the University of California at Berkeley. As such, I owe a debt to the students at Berkeley, especially to the undergraduates, who continually challenged me to hone my arguments, to "prove" my points, and to organize my presentation in a coherent manner. I am also indebted to the staff at Berkeley's Institute of International Studies, and especially to the institute's director, Professor Carl G. Rosberg, Jr. They provided essential support and assistance that greatly facilitated the research and writing of this book. The Carnegie Corporation of New York, and the John D. and Catherine T. MacArthur Foundation, through grants to the University of California, also provided crucial support.

My good friends and colleagues John Marcum and Michael Clough have been a constant source of ideas and information on matters South African, and they have served as invaluable sounding boards as I sought to come to terms with the drama and uncertainty of the unfolding South African reality. The same can be said of two of my graduate-students-turned-colleagues, Pearl-Alice Marsh and Gay Seidman. Ken Jowitt, my colleague and companion in Berkeley's political science department, has engaged me in discussion and debate on a daily basis. He has helped me see the comparative and general aspects of the political forces at work in South Africa.

I owe the greatest of debts to the community of "progressive" South African journalists and scholars. Finding themselves in the midst of a monumental political upheaval, threatened with a myriad of censorship regulations, and potential targets of state repression, these individuals chronicled and analyzed a revolution in progress. There has probably never been a revolutionary experience whose grass-roots reality has been so thoroughly documented as the South African insurrection of 1984–86. Through their "monitoring groups"—alternative press, academic publications, newspaper commentaries, clipping services, and the like—they have created an invaluable corpus of empirical data and analytic writing on the South African process of change. Without their work I could not have written this book.

Finally, thanks to Erik, Matty, Daniel, and Mimi. Writing this book has meant absences. There were my trips away from home—and my far more numerous, they might say continuous, "mental absences" as I worked out the next sentence, paragraph, or chapter while simultaneously trying to carry on a conversation. They have tolerated my intermittent and incomplete presence with understanding, if not always with the best of humor. In truth one cannot, after the fact, make up for being absent or preoccupied. I can only hope that the quality of this work will in some way compensate my family for what I have denied them in the process of its writing.

Berkeley   R.M.P.
May 1990

Contents

Illustrations

Tables

The Apartheid State in Crisis

Introduction

This book is about political change. Its major thesis is that in a decade and a half, roughly from 1975 to 1990, South Africa underwent a profound political transformation. Yet most knowledgeable observers of the Republic of South Africa would dispute this assessment. They would undoubtedly point out that the most essential feature of the South African political system during this period was the control of the state by a small racial minority, and the correlative exclusion from political participation and access to state power of the country's black majority. They would also likely point out that between the establishment of the modern South African state in 1910 and the last decade of the twentieth century, there was little significant alteration in this basic reality of white control and black exclusion. Finally, they would probably argue that even the steps taken by President F. W. de Klerk in early 1990—in particular the legalization of the African National Congress (ANC) and the release from prison of Nelson Mandela—did not change this basic fact of political life. They would be right on all counts.

Political Change and the South African State

The problem that arises in most assessments of political change in South Africa is that they focus on the formal aspects of the political order—the structures of governance; the set of legal rules, political norms, and established institutions that together constitute the regime. Political change is said to occur when there is a transition from one ruling group to another, when government institutions are fundamentally redesigned, and/or when one constitution is replaced by another embodying different basic principles. None of these things occurred in South Africa during the period under discussion, and therefore observers used terms that connoted stasis to describe the extraordinary political turmoil that was occurring— "turbulent stability," "violent equilibrium," "dynamic stability." But an analytic focus on aspects of the political process other than the formal arrangement of power reveals a different story; one suggesting that the foundation of the white monopoly

3

of power was being eroded, bringing closer the day when minority rule will give way to a form of government based upon the previously disenfranchised majority.

The foundation upon which the formal political order rests can be thought of as a "substructure" of domination—social interactions, cultural norms, economic activities, and informal power relationships that create the basis for compliance with the prescriptions of the ruling group. Changes in this underlying structure are often the precursor of and condition for alteration in the political system's "superstructure," the formal system of power. Basic alterations in the former, the substructure of power, can be thought of as involving political *transformation,* and can be distinguished from political *transition,* the movement from one formal arrangement of power to another. Transformation prepares the way for transition.

The relationship between transformation and transition presents considerable analytic difficulty because the linkage between substructure and superstructure is loosely coupled. Shifts in the foundation or substructure will not necessarily be immediately reflected in corresponding alterations at the formal or superstructural level. Nevertheless, these shifts in the underlying foundation of the political order ought to be viewed as representative of significant political change, which over the long run will lead to a transition at the formal or constitutional level. Whether one sees the South African situation between 1975 and 1990 as characterized by stasis or change depends, then, on one's analytic focus. Examined at the level of formal power arrangements, stasis was the overriding South African reality, but viewed at the level of the underlying system of domination, change is what is notable. Comprehending the political transformations of the 1980s provides a basis for understanding the dynamics and shape of the transition process that will probably characterize the South Africa of the 1990s.

My point can perhaps be clarified by use of an analogy drawn from the physical world. A volcanic eruption produces change, often dramatic change, in the landscape. The eruption is a product of unseen geological changes occurring deep beneath the surface of the earth—rock becomes superheated, gases build, and a magma of gas and molten rock push upward. Sometimes these underground geological changes produce venting and tremors noticeable on the earth's surface. They are signs of the underlying geological changes taking place, and they are also harbingers of a future transforming volcanic eruption. They may also involve alterations in the earth's structure that relieve pressure and thus delay or prevent an eventual volcanic cataclysm.

In this book I will be examining the changes in South Africa's "political magma"—much as the geologist studies volcanic activity—so as to better understand why, how, and when political changes occur within society's formal arrangement of power. As with the student of volcanic phenomena, my attention will be drawn to political "venting" and "tremors"—in particular, rebellions and insurrections— both as signs of underlying change and as events that shape the nature of future eruptions. Of course, with social phenomena—unlike natural ones, such as volcanoes—events can be shaped by purposeful action. A ruling group can use government policy to shape or prevent changes in both the formal political order and the underlying substructure of domination. These efforts may not achieve their intended purpose but they will nevertheless impact on the change process. In my analysis of the trajectory of change in South Africa, therefore, Pretoria's policies and the way in which they interact with, shape, and are shaped by the sociopolitical forces pushing for change will be a major consideration.

Structural Incompatibilities in White Minority Rule

Since the end of World War II, the South African system of white supremacy has been increasingly undermined by fundamental incompatibilities built into its system of racial rule. As the country's economic system became increasingly industrial, it came to depend on an ever larger and more urbanized black proletariat. In South Africa as in every other society, the social conditions of industrial production and urban life create a milieu conducive to collective organization and political activism. Thus everywhere that industrial modernization has occurred, erstwhile peasants have shed their passivity and launched ever more effective demands for political inclusion.

This universal process contains for the South African system a special problem. For in the South African case the proletariat is largely black, and its demand for inclusion thus threatens the political control of a white minority that, since the seventeenth century, has guaranteed itself a position of economic and social privilege by virtue of its monopoly of political power. One can say, then, that there exists a basic incompatibility between the social and political forces inevitably set loose by the process of industrial modernization and the South African system of rule by a racial minority. Much of the political history of South Africa since World War II can be interpreted as a series of efforts by the ruling oligarchy to maintain its power in the face of this intensifying incompatibility. The state in South Africa has, in essence, been attempting to hold back one of the more ubiquitous historical processes.

The ability of the South African ruling group to resist "the tide of history," as it were, has been made more difficult by another incompatibility that has been built into the regime of racial rule for more than four decades. Since the defeat of nazism there has been general agreement in the international community on the odiousness of a political system based upon racial classification and stratification. South Africa's political system of white supremacy and especially the apartheid order that was constructed after World War II, has been incompatible with this normative consensus. South Africa is unique among world states in that it explicitly and legally enshrined racial classification, stratification, and domination as the primary *principle* of its political and social order. This uniqueness has also been its vulnerability. Official racism has bedeviled South Africa's international relations, as efforts by the state to maintain its internal order place a strain on its external relationships. It is quite common for states of the contemporary world to coerce their populations without experiencing an adverse effect on their global relations, but the incompatibility between South African white supremacy and global norms has denied the South African state this luxury.

The incompatibility of industrialism and racial rule has defined South Africa's dominant political cleavages, and scripted the roles of its main political protagonists. Marx and Engels saw the process of capitalist industrialization as splitting

society "more and more into two great classes directly facing each other. . . ."[1]
The class struggle, they believed, would be the engine of political and historical
change. But the ability of evolving capitalist democracies to absorb ever larger
segments of the working class into the community of national citizenship robbed
political life of the dichotomous conflict that Marx and Engels had envisioned.
Perhaps only in South Africa, a society formed by settler colonialists along strict
racial lines, has industrialization produced a politics characterized by a single great
divide or cleavage. Like the peasants of Western Europe, the African population
was proletarianized as it was drawn into the settlers' increasingly industrial economy. But in contrast to Europe, the settler society's racial barriers, designed to
protect the privileged interests of colonists from the more numerous indigenous
African population, also served to block the inclusion of the new proletariat in the
political system of the settler. As a result, by the beginning of the last quarter of the
twentieth century the politics of South Africa was overwhelmingly defined by a
white racial oligarchy locked in conflict with an increasingly unified black opposition. The dialectical struggle between these two forces—pressure for change by the
black majority, on the one hand, and the government's countereffort to maintain
white control, on the other—constituted a change "dynamic" that drove the South
African political and social system toward transformation.

The Marxian conception of political transformation is societally endogamous.
The engine of change, the dialectical class struggle, is viewed as within a self-
contained social system. But in the modern era any particular society is situated
politically, militarily, and economically within a global interstate system. The significance of this for the process of radical or revolutionary change is aptly drawn by
Theda Skocpol in her seminal work on social revolution entitled *States & Social
Revolutions*:

> If our aim is to understand the breakdown and building-up [sic] of state organiza-
> tions in revolutions, . . . we must . . . focus upon the points of intersection be-
> tween international conditions and pressures, on the one hand, and class-structured
> economies and politically organized interests, on the other hand. State executives
> and their followers will be found maneuvering to extract resources and build
> administrative and coercive organizations precisely at this intersection. Here, con-
> sequently, is the place to look for the political contradictions that help launch social
> revolutions.[2]

How a state is situated in the international system has a powerful effect on the
resources available to it for avoiding social situations conducive to radicalism and
revolution, as well as for resisting efforts by domestic opponents to alter the political
status quo. At the same time, domestic sociopolitical upheavals can affect the
situation of a state within the global interstate system. They can, among other
things, affect the flow of resources into and out of the state.

The external incompatibility of South Africa's system of racial rule created a
special intensity to the interactive process between domestic events and international reaction. Rather than a dialectic, South Africa during the last quarter of the
twentieth century has been subject to a "trialectic" of change. The interaction of

three elements—growing domestic opposition to racial rule, efforts of the state to preserve white minority control, and international pressure—gave rise to a process of debilitating economic crisis and intensifying political conflict that placed immense pressure on the South African state.

Mode of Political Transition

Once it has occurred, fundamental political change, like a revolution or a great war, seems in hindsight to have been inevitable. In retrospect, the way in which the old order topples as a result of the erosion of its sociopolitical foundation seems clear. But the analysis of the erosion of the foundations of a political order *prior* to a transition in the formal political system, as is the case with this study of South Africa, offers no such clarity or certainty.

The question of *when* basic changes in South Africa's constitutional arrangement will occur is often of primary interest to contemporary observers. It is also the question least likely to be accurately answered. The analyst of political "eruptions" has even less ability to provide a precise answer to the "when" question than the physical scientist trying to predict the exact date of a volcanic episode. To those who want to know precisely *when* the new order will emerge, it is sobering to remember that just six weeks before the czarist autocracy was overthrown in the February Revolution, Lenin expressed doubt that "we, the old, [will] live to see the decisive battles of the coming revolution."[3]

If we set aside the "when" question as simply technically beyond our capability, the question of *how* alterations in a system's foundation will lead to a change in its formal structure cannot be avoided. For only if we have a conception of the mechanism by which substructure and superstructure are linked can we comprehend which shifts in the foundation are relevant to eventually producing a fundamental alteration in the formal system of power relations. Only by grasping intellectually the likely mode of political *transition* can we understand how the analysis of an eroding political foundation, which is the substance of this book, relates to fundamental political change.

For observers of South Africa, specifying the mode of transition has been a perplexing endeavor. Because the demographic imbalance between the races seemed to rob white supremacy of its viability, an imminent end to white minority rule has been a not infrequent prediction among the mostly liberal academic observers of the South African scene. But these confident expectations about inevitable change were belied by the apparent insolubility of an essential question: How would the white ruling oligarchy, with a professional and loyal military and all the modern technologies of physical and social control at its command, be led to relinquish its political power and thus the guarantee of its privileges?

The many different scenarios of change that observers have projected onto South Africa's future, and their predictive weakness, reflects this perplexing intellectual dilemma. The fatal analytic flaws in two oft-discussed scenarios for how political transition would occur—ruling-group collapse through either economic sanctions or external invasion—are relatively easy to detect. The first scenario, which holds that comprehensive international economic sanctions will rapidly destroy the South

African economy, leading to the capitulation of Pretoria and the introduction of majority rule, exaggerates the role of the international economic factor in the South African process of change. The South African economy is linked to the global economy by dozens of countries and thousands of business firms. It would take a common will and active coordination among this myriad of states and corporations to cut South Africa's worldwide economic links. It would also require them to devote considerable resources toward monitoring global economic transactions, as well as ground, air, and maritime routes so as to ensure that their collective action is not undermined by actors attracted by the premium prices that sanctions-busting would yield. This scenario is rendered highly implausible, then, by both the complex international linkages of the South African economy and the unwillingness of many relevant actors to exercise the level of coercion and coordination that would be necessary to make it work. This does not mean that international economic pressure is irrelevant to the South African change process. Even partial sanctions have an effect—on the policies adopted by Pretoria, on the strength of the opposition to minority rule, and ultimately on the foundation of white political supremacy—but that effect is neither immediate nor direct. Moreover, it is interwoven with a complex set of domestically based processes.

The second scenario relies on external military rather than economic power to force the end of white supremacy in South Africa. Here, the military forces of one or more industrialized countries, or more often, some joint African military command, has been suggested as the means to produce Pretoria's capitulation. However, there is not the slightest evidence that industrial countries would engage the South African Defence Force (SADF) in an effort to transform South Africa domestically. And the imbalance between the militaries of African countries and the SADF, as well as the inability of the former to cooperate sufficiently, makes this scenario even less plausible than the first. It is true that the development and modernization of the militaries of Angola and Zimbabwe in the 1980s shows that military balances are not fixed. Moreover, South Africa's inability to replace lost jet planes, a consequence of the international arms embargo, renders its superiority in the air vulnerable. But challenging Pretoria's regional military hegemony is a very different matter than invading South Africa and forcing its unconditional surrender.

A third mode of political transition, one of the more common in the late twentieth century, involves the rapid collapse of a ruling oligarchy that is under attack by massive popular demonstrations. Iran in 1979, the Philippines in 1986, and Eastern European countries in late 1989, are examples of this type of political transition. In the case of the Philippines, the collapse of the Marcos regime was attributed by observers and those involved to the mobilization of "people power."

The mass political mobilizations of black opposition in South Africa throughout the 1980s suggested to many that Pretoria, like so many other ruling oligarchies during the period, would succumb to mobilized "people power." But the critical feature of Ferdinand Marcos' downfall as well as of the collapse of the shah and the East European Leninist regimes was not the power of mass populism. Rather it was the unreliability of the regimes' security apparatus.

The rapid collapse of a ruling oligarchy under mass pressure occurs when internal divisions within the state's security forces render them unreliable agents for the repression of popular uprising. Sometimes the army collapses through defeat in external war, as in Russia in 1917, and other times it is riven by the deep sociopolitical conflicts that characterize the larger society, as occurred in Iran in 1979 and the Philippines in 1986. In either case, if an oligarchy under mass pressure finds itself without its shield against popular anger, a period of rapid power deflation followed by political transition is often the result. China in 1989 illustrates the opposite condition: a cohesive and loyal military, willing to use its firepower against unarmed civilians, can sustain a ruling oligarchy in the face of the most massive popular demonstrations. But when a ruling elite is reluctant to order the troops to shoot the people for fear that they themselves will become targets, as the shah apparently believed; or when the order is given and refused, as happened to Marcos in the Philippines, and apparently Erich Honecker in East Germany; or when there is nobody to receive the order because the army has disintegrated, as happened to Batista in Cuba, then there is nothing for the ruling group to do but step aside.

This type of outcome is unlikely in South Africa. The racial nature of the conflict there ensures the loyalty of the predominantly white army against popular black revolt, and defeat in war—such as sapped the czarist army's ability to defend the Russian autocracy—is difficult to imagine. Yet in the long term, as manpower shortages force reliance on black soldiers, and if declining political morale makes the white conscript unreliable, the cohesiveness and loyalty of the security forces might well become problematic.

A fourth transition scenario involves armed resistance by an externally based but domestically active liberation movement. The most common version of this hypothesis has Umkhonto we Sizwe, the military wing of the ANC, confronting and neutralizing the South African security forces in a war of national liberation. This would allow the African National Congress to replace the existing regime of white supremacy, much as the collapse of the Kuomintang in China in 1949, in the face of the People's Liberation Army, led to a takeover by the Chinese Communists.

In recent years the significance of revolutionary armed force in producing a transition to majority rule in South Africa has been viewed with increasing skepticism. And this skepticism has come from surprising quarters. ANC and South African Communist Party theoreticians have openly questioned the suitability of South Africa's geographic and political terrain to support guerrilla insurrection,[4] and they have accorded reduced significance to an armed seizure of power.* Another source of doubt about the "armed takeover" scenario has come from Soviet experts, who have joined liberal academics in the West not only in their skepticism about the military capability of the ANC, but also in suggesting that continued pursuit of armed resistance may be counterproductive.[5] Well before F. W. de Klerk was named President of South Africa and negotiations became a possibility, Soviet experts viewed a negotiated settlement as a *political* alternative to armed force, and the continued pursuit of the latter was seen as making the former less likely.

---

*It should be noted that the ANC has never considered armed resistance the sole or even primary means of accomplishing the overthrow of the regime of white supremacy. Its position differed from that of the critics of armed force, however, in that it saw a role for it along with other means of undermining Pretoria.

Developments during the 1980s make it clear that Pretoria is unlikely to be pushed aside by a successful war of national liberation. Umkhonto we Sizwe has shown neither the will nor the capacity to take on the SADF, despite considerable advances politically and organizationally, and despite a dramatic increase in the number of small unit military actions within South Africa's borders. The considerably increased political challenge launched by the black opposition during the 1980s did not include the development of a significant military challenge to the South African state. The scenario of political transition through military victory can, therefore, probably be grouped with the scenarios of collapse via economic sanctions, external invasion, or popular demonstrations and filed under "wishful thinking." But the idea that armed resistance has *no* significant role to play in producing political change, or that it is counterproductive to that end, is an entirely different matter. As with another form of force, economic pressure, its relevance may be as one element in a process that creates the conditions for a negotiated transition to a new political order.

If white rule is unlikely to be brought down through Pretoria's military defeat by revolutionaries or by economic pressure, and if internal regime collapse is only a remote possibility, it follows that if a transition to a new political order occurs it will be through a negotiated settlement. But how the South African adversaries get to the point of successfully negotiating a political transition toward majority rule is a complicated matter.

Negotiations and Political Transformation

In contemporary discussions of South Africa there exists a misleading tendency to dichotomize force and negotiations; the latter is offered as a peaceful and *political* alternative to the violence of the former. Unfortunately such a dichotomy is analytically misleading because it suggests the two are unrelated except as mutually exclusive alternatives. But, in fact, force is often a prerequisite for meaningful negotiations. Most wars end not by the utter collapse of one side, but by negotiations. The negotiated phase of conflict resolution is often simply the end of a path paved by violence. Armed conflict, by imposing costs on the combatants, alters their political positions until these converge enough to allow for agreement by negotiation. This is the essential meaning of the Prussian general Karl von Clausewitz's seminal observation that "war is politics by other means."

Risks, Perceptions, and Majority Rule

A situation conducive to successful negotiation requires that one or both adversaries shift their positions so that there exists an area of overlap. Within what might be termed a "zone of agreement," compromises can then be arrived at that result in a resolution of the conflict. In respect to political change, an actor's position will shift when he alters his assessment of the future risks that adhere in the status quo compared to the risks he believes are contained in some projected situation of change. In insisting upon white minority control, Pretoria and the white South Africans that support it have been calculating that the political status-quo is less threatening to their futures than a system that allows for majority rule. Pretoria can be expected to negotiate a shift to majority rule only when its risk calculus is reversed; that is, when government officials or the constituencies on which they rely calculate that whites will be poorer and less secure attempting to maintain a regime of white supremacy than they would be in a system in which blacks might gain political control.

The implications of the above logic are clear: that which reduces the material welfare of whites and/or threatens their physical security, and does so in a way that ties these costs to efforts to maintain minority control, will make a negotiated transition to majority rule more likely. A weakening economy and what the South Africans call political unrest are the two primary mechanisms for producing this outcome. The former results in declining material standards of life and a lack of confidence about future prospects; the latter, including insurrectionary activity (strikes, boycotts, demonstrations, riots), armed conflict, and urban/rural sabotage not only threatens physical safety but contributes in general to an overall decline in the quality of life.

The reverse of the above argument is usually advanced: a negotiated solution to the South African situation is more likely to come about in an environment of economic prosperity that is free of violent threats. This premise holds that an expanding economic pie eases the process of change because it obviates the need for resource redistribution, thus making a new order more palatable to whites. Our discussion of the conditions necessary for successful negotiation pinpoints the fallacy in this line of thinking. The "change by way of growth" argument assumes that there already exists a predisposition on the part of the authorities to abandon political control by a racial minority. Expanding resources would simply facilitate movement within an already existing zone of agreement. When the commitment to majority rule on the part of the governing group does not exist, or when those in power are in fact committed to maintaining the status quo, as has been the case, there is no reason for prosperity to spur a movement toward majority rule. This is the pointed lesson, as is frequently noted, of the experience of the 1950s and 1960s, when unprecedented growth and prosperity coincided with the imposition of the harsh apartheid form of white supremacy.

The argument that political peace will be conducive to negotiating an end to white rule has greater initial plausibility than does the "change through prosperity" notion. Armed resistance, sabotage, and general turbulence, particularly when they involve civilian casualties, are usually thought to harden attitudes within the target population, rallying support for the state. A version of this argument is frequently made about the ANC's pre-1990 commitment to armed struggle. The use of violent tactics, especially when they involve "soft" (civilian) targets, are said to (1) drive whites toward Pretoria; (2) generate support for harsh security measures; and (3) increase white fears of the black opposition, consequently making it more difficult to break whites away from support for a system of white supremacy.

In the short term, there is little reason to question the proposition that the increased use of force by a liberation movement, particularly when it produces civilian casualties, hardens resistance to change. But the medium- to long-term response to armed resistance and political unrest may well be quite different. The negative reaction that insurrectionary violence produces in the target population presumes that the status-quo forces are capable of providing increased security against its opponents. But if it turns out that this presumption is misplaced—if, over time, security instead declines; if the physical dangers and psychological stress imposed by violence, sabotage, and other disturbances increase despite the state's countermeasures, then the desire for personal security, for ending the continuing danger, can produce a willingness to consider coming to terms with the revolutionaries. We will, in the course of this book, see this dynamic at work in South Africa.

In sum, I have argued that the precondition for negotiations leading to fundamental political change in South Africa is an extended period of economic decline and political unrest. Over time a situation of economic, physical, and psychological deterioration is likely to impact on strategically important constituencies. Support for the political status quo will consequently erode among elements considered vital by the ruling elite, including segments of its security forces. The government's capacity to control will deteriorate as the costs of security escalate beyond the financial capabilities of a deteriorating economy, and its self-confidence will collapse as the resources and policy options to turn the situation around are perceived as exhausted. This process of decline and disaffection will lead to a gradual shift, over time, toward a position where negotiations for some form of fundamental political change, such as majority rule, is deemed acceptable. It is the general thesis of this book that since the mid-1970s South Africa has experienced the unfolding of precisely this process.

Notes

1. Karl Marx and Friedrich Engels, *Manifesto of the Communist Party,* reprinted in Lewis S. Feuer, ed., *Marx & Engels* (Garden City: Anchor Books, 1959), p. 8.

2. Theda Skocpol, *States & Social Revolutions* (Cambridge: Cambridge University Press, 1979), p. 32.

3. Quoted in E. H. Carr, *A History of Soviet Russia,* 4 vols. Vol. 1: *The Bolshevik Revolution: 1917–1923* (London: Macmillan, 1950), p. 69.

4. See Tebogo Kgobe, "Is South Africa Suited for Guerrilla Warfare?" *The African Communist,* no. 117, second quarter; 1989, passim.

5. See, for example, the article in *Pravda* (August 20, 1989, p. 4) by Boris Asoyan, a high-level official in the African Directorate of the Soviet Foreign Ministry. See also the unpublished paper by A. A. Makarov, another senior Soviet foreign ministry official, entitled "South Africa: Its Domestic Situation and Prospects of Development," presented at a meeting on U.S.–Soviet Policy Toward Africa, sponsored by the American Friends Service Committee and held at Bloomsbury University, Pennsylvania, in April 1990. See also the report by Gleb Starushenko entitled, "Problems of Struggle Against Racism, Apartheid and Colonialism in The [*sic*] South Africa," presented at the Second Soviet–African Conference held in Moscow on June 24–26, 1986, published in the *Proceedings* of The Africa Institute, pp. 3–25. For a summary of the changing Soviet analysis of the South African situation, see Winrich Kuhne, "A 1988 Update on Soviet Relations with Pretoria, the ANC, and the SACP," *CSIS Africa Notes,* no. 89, September 1, 1988, passim.

1

Backdrop:
The Securing of White Supremacy

Apartheid as Ends and Means

Apartheid originated as an ideology of race relations that took hold within the Afrikaner intellectual and political elite in the mid-1940s. With the 1948 electoral victory of the Nationalists, the party of the Afrikaner community, the ideology evolved and was implemented in an elaborate system of laws and administrative regulations. A single principle—the complete separation of black and white races in South Africa—underlay both the ideology and the institutional system it spawned. After 1948, government domestic policy was directed at enforcing race separation in every conceivable sphere: interpersonal relations, social and economic organization, residential patterns, and the political organization of the state. In pursuit of the latter objective, the government planned to create ten separate states for the African population out of the old native reserves, which covered some 13 percent of the country's land area. In this manner, the Afrikaner elite hoped to eliminate Africans from the South African heartland altogether, except as foreigners in search of temporary employment.

To understand the evolution of apartheid doctrine and practice, it is important to recognize that for the Afrikaner political leaders the endeavor of "separation" upon which they had embarked had both consummatory and instrumental significance. Something possesses *consummatory significance* when it represents an ultimate goal or value, or when its achievement is so closely linked with the realization of some other ultimate purpose that the two are inseparable. Something has *instrumental significance* when it is an agent or tool for the accomplishment of something else; it is significant only as a means to an end. These analytic concepts allow us to distinguish two different types of commitments that actors have toward social objects. The same object can, of course, be valued in a consummatory sense by some actors and instrumentally by others, and a single actor can simultaneously perceive both consummatory and instrumental significance in a given object.

In comprehending apartheid—its nature, purposes, and evolution—it is useful

13

to keep three things in mind. First, apartheid never existed as a full-blown and fully worked out sociopolitical design. Rather, its particulars developed around the core principle of race separation, as South Africa's Afrikaner governing group sought to respond to domestic and international challenges as it saw them. Second, as the historical context facing the ruling group changed over time, the mix of consummatory and instrumental significance attached by the governing elite to the apartheid project could be and was modified. Third, apartheid's instrumental purpose incorporated a number of components whose relative salience for policymakers shifted as the historical context changed and the governing elite's perception of key challenges and threats was consequently refashioned.

Apartheid as Ultimate Goal

The consummatory significance of apartheid in the history of Afrikanerdom lies in its connection to two closely related things. The first is what C. Dunbar Moodie, in his seminal work *The Rise of Afrikanerdom,* calls the Afrikaner civil religion;[1] the second is what by the mid-twentieth century had become a collective obsession among the Afrikaner ethnic community—the maintenance of their group identity. At the heart of this civil religion is the notion of Afrikaners as God's chosen people with an ordained calling or mission. "God created the Afrikaner People with a unique language, a unique philosophy of life, and their own history and traditions," stated a leading Afrikaner nationalist in 1944, "in order that they might fulfill a particular calling and destiny here in the southern corner of Africa."[2] Afrikaner doctrinal writings do not go very far in spelling out the nature of Afrikanerdom's national calling, except insofar as understanding it to be simply vigilance in the maintenance of its cultural uniqueness.[3] Thus, J. C. van Rooy, chairman of the Afrikaner Broederbond during the 1940s, defined his people's divine mission this way: "We must stand guard on all that is peculiar to us and build upon it . . . to continue with the struggle to maintain our language and culture."[4]

Apartheid—the doctrine and practice of complete group separation—can be seen as the operationalization of this Afrikaner national calling. If, as Moodie has said, the purpose of the Afrikaner on earth "was to remain true to his express particularity,"[5] then "apartness" was a necessary corollary. The genetic mixing and cultural diffusion that were seen as the natural concomitant of intergroup contact would erode unity and identity among the *volk,* thus undermining its God-given mission. Separation, then, becomes within this logic an ordained enterprise. It also follows that within the domain the Afrikaner defines as his own, his political sovereignty is divinely required. As van Rooy stated in 1944: "The Christian republican state is the only constitutional form for the proper completion of our calling."[6]

Apartheid as Means

Since the South African government accompanied the implementation of apartheid with very heavy use of ideological rhetoric, many observers of the South African scene have focused on its ideological aspects—what I have called its consummatory significance. There is, however, another aspect of apartheid that is equally if not more important for the unfolding of South African politics—what I have termed its instrumental significance. Apartheid offered to the Afrikaner elite a method for overcoming its most basic political challenge—a challenge built into the very structure of the South African sociopolitical system: how to maintain in perpetuity the domination of a white minority over a vastly more numerous black majority. Simple demographic realities had always raised very serious doubts about the viability of white supremacy on the southern tip of Africa, but for the white political leadership this problem was particularly vexing in the aftermath of World War II. The global political currents set loose by the war contained potentially serious consequences for white South Africa's domestic and international security.

The domestic security threat lay in the forces of mass nationalism that spread, in the early postwar years, throughout the non-Western world, undermining the foundations of European colonial domination. In sub-Saharan Africa, the late 1940s saw the birth of anti-colonial movements in Ghana and Nigeria that shattered the assumed stability of these two bastions of British rule. By 1959, when South African Prime Minister Hendrik F. Verwoerd announced his separate development policy, namely, the creation of black homelands that would eventually become independent states, the process begun in Ghana had permeated virtually every colony in sub-Saharan Africa, and the entire enterprise of European colonialism on the continent entered its eleventh hour. Seen from Pretoria the specter of European political retreat from Africa in the face of mass politicization and mobilization was something that could not be ignored with equanimity. Left unchecked, the forces of modern mass nationalism might well be the ingredient that the African National Congress needed to emerge as an irresistible force in South African politics, spelling doom for white rule. Indeed, in the early postwar period the Afrikaner leadership could find considerable basis for such a fear.

During the war years profound changes had occurred in the structure of the South African economy and society, with ominous implications for the future of white domination. For South Africa, World War II represented a time of economic growth. The military efforts of the Western allies stimulated demand for South African–produced munitions, armored vehicles, and minerals. At the same time, the German occupation of much of Europe cut South Africa off from many imports, protecting her fledgling firms from international competition. The result was expanded production, especially within South Africa's manufacturing sector. Between 1939 and 1945 output of manufacturing industries grew by 116 percent.[7] Growth of the manufacturing sector was accompanied by a shift in the South African labor force toward a more skilled, stable, and urban-based African working class. Between 1940 and 1950 the number of Africans employed in manufacturing rose from about 147,000 to 267,000, an increase of 81 percent.[8] During the same period, the number of African residents in South Africa's urban areas more than doubled, increasing from approximately 900,000 in the late 1930s to 1,890,962 in 1951,[9] raising the proportion of urban Africans from about 14 to 22 percent.[10]

The new National Party (NP) government took a dim view of these economic and social developments. The "overrunning of cities" and "indiscriminate squatting in urban areas" was how the Department of Native Affairs annual report for 1949–

50 described the wartime African urbanization.[11] Verwoerd, then the new minister of native affairs, declared that "White South Africa is now being overrun by a black stream."[12] The government's concern with what it termed the "flood of Bantu" into the cities was in part a response to economic interest groups. The viability of South African mining and agriculture, which since the beginning of the century depended upon a plentiful supply of cheap African labor, was being threatened by the rapid growth of the urban manufacturing sector. The availability to Africans of more stable, skilled, and attractive employment in the cities threatened the supply of African labor to mining and agriculture, at least at the traditionally low wage rate paid by those sectors. Consequently, mining and agricultural interests, in order to preserve their access to cheap labor, clamored for the introduction of laws that would inhibit the movement of Africans to the urban areas. The draconian apartheid measures adopted by the government to reduce and control rural-to-urban migration of Africans and to channel the supply of African labor to specific sectors and industries ("canalization") were thus interpreted by many scholars as a response to the economic interests of this alliance of "gold and maize."[13]

The significance of economic considerations notwithstanding, apartheid policy also grew out of clear political and security concerns. A desire to reassert and sustain white minority, and especially Afrikaner, control over a situation characterized by dramatic and potentially volatile social transformation oriented the actions of the National Party in the early years of its rule. Prior to the momentous 1948 general election the Sauer Commission of the National Party stated that "the fundamental basis of [the party's] policy . . . is the maintenance and protection of the white race. . . ."[14] In its preelection report the commission introduced the term "apartheid" to popular political discussion and presented a blueprint for the implementation of apartheid policies after the party's electoral victory. It responded directly to the socioeconomic transformations of the 1940s, reporting: "The Party realizes the danger of the flood of Africans moving to the cities and undertakes to protect the white character of our cities."[15] A year later, the Department of Native Affairs described African urbanization as threatening because it promised "unrest" and "general disorder."[16] According to Dr. Verwoerd, it was not "safe to allow the free movement of Natives over the whole of South Africa. . . . [W]e want planning to keep South Africa white."[17]

From the standpoint of the maintenance of white supremacy, the significance of African urbanization was not simply a matter of numbers. Rather, the urban environment and the more stable working class that it encompassed provided a social and cultural medium for the more effective organization of African opposition to white domination. This "law" of Marxian sociology—that the conditions of urban working-class life provide the social basis for political organization and heightened consciousness—was clearly manifest in the South Africa of the 1940s. The decade witnessed a spate of strike activity and the organization of industrial unions with African membership. In 1940 there were about twenty African trade unions, claiming a membership of only 26,000. Five years later, African trade unions numbered 119, and had a membership of 158,000, encompassing 40 percent of the African work force in commerce and manufacturing.[18] These organizational advances coincided with a dramatic rise in the militancy of workers. In the six years between 1940 and 1945 there were some 220,205 man-days lost to strikes by African workers; an average of 4.2 days per striker. In contrast, in the ten-year period from 1930 to 1939, only 71,078 man-days were lost due to strike action; an average of 2.7 days per striker.[19]

It should be noted that in the special and peculiar situation of South Africa, worker organization and militancy is never purely an economic matter. The state-supported systems of labor control and repression, along with the social segregation and racial discrimination that are a central feature of every African worker's reality, ensure that worker militancy is unlikely to remain focused for very long on narrow bread-and-butter issues. A push to improve wages and working conditions rapidly confronts and must challenge much of the edifice of white supremacy. Moreover, it is the South African white community's utter dependence on black labor that represents the weakest link in its system of power and privilege, for that dependence affords Africans potential leverage over whites. However, it is only through organization, which can by imposing discipline produce truly collective action, that this potentiality can be transformed into reality. That is why the organization of African workers has always been viewed by South Africa's white rulers as politically portentous.

Along with the development of African trade union organization, the war years witnessed the expansion and militant transformation of directly political organizations. From the vantage point of the emergent leadership of the National Party, the most important of such organizations were the South African Communist Party (SACP) and the African National Congress. During this period, the former began drawing membership from the African working class, and it played a leading role in the organization of African trade unions.[20] The ANC underwent a transformation from an organization oriented to the tiny African middle class, and working within the severe restrictions of the South African legal order, into a mass organization dedicated to militant collective action: strikes, boycotts, civil disobedience, and noncooperation.[21] The SACP and ANC not only increased their relevance and role in respect to an urban mass base, but African politics of the 1940s was also characterized by the strengthening of the relationship between the two organizations.[22]

The aftermath of World War II was no more propitious for South Africa's international posture than for its long-term domestic political stability. In the wake of the fight against nazism, South Africa, with its sociopolitical system based upon racial classification and domination, did not constitute a very attractive friend or ally for the Western powers. And it was to these Western industrial states that South Africa looked. They were its main trading partners, importing South African minerals and selling it manufactured goods; they were the prime source for the new technology and capital needed for South African industrial expansion; and perhaps most important, they were the hoped-for source of diplomatic and military support in the event of Communist subversion or attack from without. In addition, in a general cultural sense white South Africans (and Afrikaners in particular) self-consciously identified themselves as part of—indeed, as a bastion of—Western civilization. "We shall remain the outpost of western civilization . . . on the southern tip of Africa, *inter alia,* for spreading civilization through the rest of Africa," stated Dr. Verwoerd in his maiden speech as prime minister in 1958.[23] But in the aftermath of World War II, South Africa's system of racial supremacy threatened to turn the country into an international pariah rather than an outpost.

It was not simply that the principle of race supremacy, once accepted as the foundation of European relations with the rest of the world, was now rejected. The process of rapid decolonization and the Cold War context in which it took place added a practical impetus to the "moral wedge" that had been inserted between Pretoria and the West. As the countries of the West sought to cement their political and economic relationships with the new states of Asia and Africa, and to check the spread of Soviet influence, their ties to white supremacist Pretoria increasingly constituted a potential liability. South Africa's governing elite was both aware of and concerned about this dynamic. In one of many speeches on this topic, Prime Minister Verwoerd told parliament in 1960 that the provision of Western economic assistance and diplomatic support to the newly independent states of black Africa constituted an "auction sale."

> In this auction between the Western nations and the East or Communism, the spirit is cultivated in Africa of standing . . . by one who offers most, or to take from both sides everything these African states can get, always to ask for more and to make bigger demands. . . . In this struggle between East and the West, the Western nations are evidently prepared to abandon all the White people in Africa . . . .[24]

Verwoerd's view of the implications of this global trend was clear and apocalyptic:

> It appears that a world psychosis has arisen of thinking only of the rights and privileges and freedoms of the non-Whites. . . . Do not let anybody suffer from the psychosis that the White man in Africa can just be swept aside in order to satisfy world opinion. . . . Therefore I say that I would like Britain, the U.S.A. and the other Western nations seriously to ponder that they will lose the only staunch friends they have—the Whites in Africa—if the White man in Africa is swamped by the Black masses, and in exchange they will not be rewarded by what they hope to receive: the gratitude and the alliance of all the African states. . . .[25]

The strains between Pretoria and the community of Western nations were, moreover, likely to increase as the government adopted repressive measures to deal with the drive for equality and political power that was being launched by South Africa's black majority during the 1950s.

Put simply, from the vantage point of the Afrikaner leadership seeking to maintain white supremacy in South Africa, the postwar situation posed this basic dilemma: how to suppress the emerging challenge of black political and economic power and at the same time gain legitimacy internationally. Apartheid in its instrumental aspects was an attempted solution to this dilemma. It was a strategy for maintaining white supremacy under the historical circumstances that characterized the decades immediately after the war. However much the Afrikaner leadership held to the ideological or consummatory justification for apartheid, there can be little doubt that the political elite was fully conscious of apartheid's significance in respect to the global and domestic currents of the postwar era. No less an authority on the subject than Dr. Verwoerd, chief architect of apartheid and prime minister from 1958 to 1966, justified apartheid policy to his followers by explaining that "we cannot govern without taking into account the tendencies in the world and in Africa. . . . We must have regard to them. . . . Our policy must take them into account."[26]

Numerous detailed analyses of the apartheid laws and their consequences are available, and it is not my intention to provide yet another one here. Suffice it to say that in seeking to secure white supremacy in South Africa the designers of apartheid did not create something completely new. Racial segregation, labor repression, and white minority political rule had characterized the South African system even before the creation of the modern state in 1910. Where apartheid differed from what already existed was in the completeness with which racial separation was sought, and in the locus within the state of racial control. Prior to 1948 the South African statute books contained a welter of segregationist and racially discriminatory laws, and these were administered with varying degrees of thoroughness by municipal, town, and village government bodies. Through apartheid the leadership of the National Party sought to elaborate, extend, and systematize the laws and regulations pertaining to racial segregation and to bring the administration of the resulting system under the direct control of a centralized state bureaucracy. The complete elaboration of racial separation and centralized control under state auspices were the twin hallmarks of the apartheid project.

The Instruments of Apartheid: Dealing with the "Black Threat"

As already discussed, the historical evolution of the South African economy and society had made the presence of millions of African people in South Africa's urban areas an unavoidable reality for South African whites. Soon after its electoral victory in 1948, the governing National Party extended and tightened up the administration of existing Group Areas Acts, which legally prescribed where different population groups could own property, reside, and work. As a means of reducing the perceived political liabilities imposed by the social realities of a maturing industrial economic order, the new governing group sought to consolidate the existing segregated neighborhoods so as to create a pattern of racially homogeneous and *physically separated* residential areas. In each city it established periurban townships for African, Indian, and "coloured" population groups that were several miles distant from the centers of white residence and business enterprise. By carefully linking the satellite black townships to their respective metropoles with only one or two transportation arteries, which could easily be cut, the government placed itself in a position to swiftly and effectively insulate the white cities from the townships and their numerous, potentially hostile, inhabitants. Mass uprisings and any other direct threats to the outnumbered white population could thus be fenced off and contained. The new periurban townships, planned with internal security considerations in mind, were also conceived as a means to facilitate the suppression of rebellion.[27] Thus apartheid's group areas policy offered the means to contain and defeat any uprising in the urban areas, while at the same time insulating the white minority from black political unrest.

For over two decades after 1948, the Group Areas Acts also played a role in a program designed by apartheid's architects to alter the racial demography of South Africa, so as to reduce the size of the African population in what was officially designated "white South Africa." Termed "influx control," this program had three basic components: (1) the Group Areas Act prohibition against Africans being present in South Africa's cities for more than seventy-two hours without official permission; (2) labor bureaus, which "canalized" labor by matching African workers with specific jobs and then granting them the required official permission to work for a specific employer and live in a designated urban township; and (3) strict enforcement of already existing "pass laws" so as to ensure compliance with the seventy-two-hour provision of the Group Areas Act. By this means the National Party government sought to remove from the South African heartland all but those Africans whose presence was economically necessary. The effort put into enforcement of influx control attests to the importance assigned to it by the governing group. In the 1966–75 decade prosecutions under laws restricting the movement of Africans numbered an extraordinary 5.8 million.[28]

Influx control was intended to meet the demand of mining and agriculture for a ready supply of cheap labor, and also to deal with the NP leadership's fears of being "overwhelmed" by an increasingly large urban African population. In addition, it undermined the existing black urban population's capacity for effective political organization. One consequence of the influx control system was to create a condition of permanent insecurity for the African population in the urban areas. For those who skirted the official system, entering the cities on their own in search of employment, there was the constant fear of arrest, prosecution, and rustication under the pass laws. For those who held officially designated jobs and concomitant permission for urban residence, there was the ever-present possibility that these would be withdrawn should officialdom deem their presence in the urban area "undesirable." Under such circumstance they would join the ranks of the "illegals," subject to immediate "endorsing out" of the urban area. The situation was only marginally better for the minority of urban Africans who, by virtue of long-term urban residence prior to the adoption of the seventy-two-hour law, had been granted permanent urban status under Section 10 of the Group Areas Act. "Section 10 rights" could be lost for a variety of legal infractions or because the government deemed their holder "undesirable." A loss of Section 10 rights brought with it the prospect of being "endorsed out" and forced to move to a rural area.

The threat of forced removal from the cities, which usually meant a calamitous disruption of family life and permanent loss of access to the main sources of livelihood, created powerful incentives for the individual to avoid calling himself to the attention of officialdom. The implication for political organization was profound. In the South African situation there was probably no better way to attract officialdom's attention than by political activity. Thus, since survival under the influx control system required maintaining a low profile, individuals were discouraged from joining political organizations.

In the history of apartheid, the decade of the 1950s was marked by the elaboration of policies to control the physical movement and social life of black South Africans, and with the creation of the centralized bureaucratic means for the implementation of these strictures. The 1960s saw the unfolding of apartheid's "grand political design," the policy of separate development. This evolution in the apartheid project represented the Afrikaner elite's response to the domestic and international security "threats" that characterized the postwar environment.

The mass movement of black opposition to white rule that had begun to take shape during the 1940s responded to the introduction of the apartheid system by organizing campaigns of defiance. Through mass civil disobedience and protest demonstrations, organizations within the black community, along with some white allies, sought to block the implementation apartheid. On March 28, 1960, in the black township of Sharpeville, a protest demonstration against the extension of the pass laws to women sparked an upheaval with broad ramifications. In this case the peaceful demonstrators, for the most part African women, were attacked by police, who shot and killed 69 and wounded another 178. The ANC responded to the carnage by calling a general strike that paralyzed the country for nearly three weeks, spurring a government crackdown in which a state of emergency was declared, ten thousand persons were detained, and the main African political organizations were outlawed.

Images of the Sharpeville massacre, carried abroad by the news media, galvanized international attention on the apartheid system, on the anti-apartheid campaign within South Africa, and on the state's efforts to suppress and silence opponents of racial separation. Pretoria found itself diplomatically isolated and faced with threats to its security and economic growth. International capital, which had played a considerable part in South Africa's economic development since the discovery of diamonds in 1867, took flight. The years 1960 to 1964 witnessed a huge capital outflow, creating a balance-of-payments crisis more severe than any experienced since the depths of the Great Depression in 1932. The United Nations, its ranks swelled by new African and Asian states that had just emerged on the world stage, sent Pretoria a clear message in 1960 when the General Assembly, by a vote of ninety-six to one, passed a resolution that requested all states "to consider taking such separate and collective action as is open to them . . . to bring about the abandonment of [apartheid] policies."[29] This resolution represented the first time that the UN called upon member states to take action against the apartheid state. During the next three years, repeated attempts were made to persuade member states to move against the white regime. In 1962 a resolution asking for economic and diplomatic sanctions as well as an arms embargo was passed by a vote of sixty-seven to sixteen, with twenty-three abstentions. Although not binding on member states, this resolution produced efforts that led in early 1964 to a partial embargo on weapons sales to Pretoria.

It was in this context of international isolation and hostility that Prime Minister Verwoerd introduced his plan for the eventual partition of South African territory into nine independent African states, and "white" South Africa. Called "separate development," this project was introduced in the late 1950s. As initially conceived, nine Bantustans would be created out of the 13 percent of South Africa's land area that had been "reserved" for African ownership by the Native Lands Act of 1913. Some economic development and limited powers of internal self-government were envisioned for these new entities, which were seen as both the future home of

Africans who would be removed from "white South Africa" by influx control and as the focus of political rights for Africans. From the outset, then, Verwoerd viewed separate development as a means of reducing South Africa's growing urban black population, and as a response to the international vulnerability created by the disenfranchisement of the black majority within the South African political system. This latter aspect of separate development was what Verwoerd described in January of 1959 as "taking into account the tendencies in the world and in Africa."

Six months later Verwoerd's point was reinforced for the Afrikaner leadership by the diplomatic isolation and international economic pressures experienced in the wake of Sharpeville. As a result the National Party was led to expand the notion of separate development, from the creation of Bantustan institutions operating within a South African state to the goal of actual partition of South Africa's territory. Verwoerd explained this new conception of separate development by direct reference to the Sharpeville-related international pressures to which Pretoria was being subjected.

> The Bantu will be able to develop into separate states. That is not what we would have liked to see. It is a form of fragmentation that we would not have liked if we were able to avoid it. In the light of the pressure being exerted on South Africa, there is however no doubt that eventually this will have to be done, thereby buying for the White Man his freedom and the right to retain his domination in what is his country.[30]

In this revised separate development vision, all persons of African descent would become citizens of one or another of ten independent states that had been metamorphosized from native reserves to Bantustans, then to homelands, and finally to independent "national states." Africans would have political rights only within these new independent entities to which they had been assigned by the government. Those Africans continuing to reside within South Africa proper would then be considered temporary sojourners in search of employment.

Separate development policy had the effect of legally transforming the African majority into citizens of other states. As such, they would have no more legitimate claim to participate in the governance of South Africa than Turkish guest workers have to participate in the governance of West Germany. By this means the South African system could be brought into line with international norms. Moreover, the entire exercise could be explained, justified, and defended—that is, sold to the world—in terms of the two values that were at the core of postwar liberalism: equality and self-determination. Thus the cabinet minister in charge of Bantu affairs defended separate development in this manner:

> Every people in the world finds its highest expression and fulfillment in managing its own affairs. . . . We want to give the Bantu that right also. The demand for self-determination on the part of the non-white nations is one of the outstanding features of the past decade. . . . If the white man is entitled to separate national existence, what right have we to deny that these People have a right to it also? Should the Bantu not have it? It will always be my task not only to respect these things of the Bantu, but to assist them to develop it as something beautiful.[31]

Apartheid: Dealing with the English-Speaking Community

While apartheid was the instrumental means adopted by the Afrikaner elite to deal with what they perceived as a political threat to whites from the black majority, it served simultaneously as a means for ensuring specifically *Afrikaner* political and material security. For the first half of the twentieth century, Afrikaners were for the most part small farmers or urban proletarians, many of whom were extremely poor. The reality of economic deprivation and the concomitant sense of cultural degradation were the ingredients upon which the National Party built its ethnonationalist movement in the 1920s and 1930s. To the NP, ethnic unity was important both as an ultimate value and as a means to break the grip of English-speaking politicians and industrialists, whom the party and its followers perceived as the architects of the Afrikaner's travail. Through unity, Afrikaners could translate their superior numbers (roughly 60 percent of the white population) into political power. With political power they had the means to control the economy and society, to break the perceived grip of English domination, and thus the potential to engineer their own economic, social, and cultural upliftment. Ironically, black people, who figured so prominently in the National Party's fears, were not seen as the prime source of the Afrikaner's oppression. Yet apartheid, directed at black people, would be used, as will be seen later in this chapter, as a vehicle for the Afrikaner's deliverance.

In summary, through the introduction of apartheid the National Party leadership sought three basic objectives: (1) to create a completely segregated society, in keeping with the precepts of Afrikaner politicoreligious doctrine, and in so doing preserve Afrikaner identity; (2) to secure white political supremacy and its resulting economic privileges from potential internal and external threats (the former represented primarily by the black majority and the latter by an international community increasingly inhospitable to notions of racial rule); and (3) to move the Afrikaner community into a position of social and economic parity with the English-speaking community, which had dominated the modern economy and urban sector since the dawn of capitalist economic development in South Africa. The first objective provided the "moral force," and ideological rationale, for the policies designed to pursue the last two more instrumental, and mundane, purposes.

Apartheid: The Achievement

At the beginning of the 1970s, some thirty years after the National Party had attained power, it certainly must have looked to the NP leadership as though they had accomplished through apartheid what they had set out to achieve. The black majority, after a decade of mass resistance to the introduction of apartheid laws, was quiescent by the mid-1960s. A combination of ruthless repression and apartheid measures had served to crush all organized manifestations of black political and economic power. While in the 1950s tens of thousands challenged white authority through boycotts, strikes, and the defiance of apartheid laws, after 1961, and for a period of fifteen years, there was not a single instance of significant mass political resistance.

On the labor front, the state's "success" can be measured by the decline in strike activity. Whereas between 1955 and 1960 the South African economy experienced an average of seventy-six strikes annually, in 1962 there were only sixteen strikes and in 1963 only seventeen.[32] The ANC and the Pan Africanist Congress (PAC), the two political movements in the forefront of African opposition to white rule (the former since 1912), were decimated by police action. With most of their leadership and cadre imprisoned and harassed, the activists who escaped arrest were forced to operate from exile in Tanzania and Zambia, far from the borders of the republic. At the same time, those of African descent within the republic found themselves faced with a labyrinth of security laws and repressive state agencies, and enmeshed in an ever more elaborate set of laws and regulations covering nearly every aspect of their existence. The political function of these restrictions was not merely to deny the majority formal representation, but seemingly to choke off any social and legal "space" for it to organize in defense of its own interests.

South Africa's white rulers could also take satisfaction from developments in their international situation. True, the international community had remained unwilling to accept separate development policy as a genuine instance of self-determination. True, too, Pretoria's policy of "detente"—whereby South Africa sought to achieve normal diplomatic relations with African countries through offers of economic assistance—had failed to break the united hostility of independent Africa. Yet in its most important external relationships, namely, those with the Western powers, Pretoria's position seemed increasingly sound. The 1960s had begun with a historically unprecedented strain in South Africa's relations with the West, as the latter reacted to the Sharpeville massacre and to the political turmoil and state repression that followed. But the domestic "peace" that resulted from the quashing of black political protests had ironically paved the way for a return to "normal" economic and political relations with the West by mid-decade. Foreign capital, which had fled South Africa in the wake of Sharpeville, began to flow back in, and in ever increasing amounts. Between 1965 and 1970, some $2.4 billion of foreign capital entered the South African economy. In contrast, in each of the six preceding years the capital flow moved in the opposite direction with a total net loss of $576 million in foreign capital over the period.[33]

On the diplomatic front, relations with the United States, the country with the greatest strategic and political significance for Pretoria, underwent a dramatic improvement. With the election of President Richard M. Nixon in 1968 and the appointment of Henry Kissinger as National Security Advisor, the U.S. policy in Southern Africa shifted toward Pretoria. Reasoning that "the whites are here to stay and the only way that constructive change can come about is through them," Nixon and Kissinger opted to work with Pretoria rather than encourage its opponents.[34] The policy they followed was described in a National Security Study Memorandum: "We would maintain public opposition to racial repression, but relax political isolation and economic restrictions on the white state."[35] This policy of "selective relaxation" involved a variety of alterations in U.S. actions toward South Africa: the United States began to sell aircraft and other equipment to South Africa that had previously been prohibited under the terms of the UN arms embargo; it voted against UN resolutions that sought to increase international pressure on Pretoria; its intelligence agencies developed a working relationship with their South African counterparts; and U.S. businesses, following the government lead, increased their investments in and trade with South Africa.[36] American leadership continued, on occasion, to express abhorrence of South Africa's racialism, but the policies emanating from Washington and the actions of the U.S. business community reinforced the unspoken message that acceptance, if not approval, of South Africa's sociopolitical order was increasingly the reality in international affairs.

The National Party's success in securing white rule was matched by the rapid social and economic rise of the Afrikaner ethnic group. "It is not an overstatement to say," writes a South African historian, "that . . . perhaps not in history has there been a case in which an entire under-developed people became affluent so quickly."[37] Apartheid and "state capitalism" were the twin means used by the Nationalists to accomplish this transformation. The latter involved a major expansion of the state into the economy, which allowed government to use regulation, licensing, and investment to create a "level playing field" between Afrikaner and English businessmen. In this manner the previously deprived Afrikaner community was able to participate in and successfully compete with English-speaking business in all sectors of the South African economy. Thus in the first fifteen years of National Party rule, between 1949 and 1964, the Afrikaner share of the private sector (measured as a percentage of national turnover) rose from 11 to 26.3 percent.[38]

State capitalism not only increased Afrikaner opportunities in the business sector, but by requiring the expansion of state agencies of economic production and control it opened up channels of advancement through state employment as well. In this respect apartheid, too, had a profound role. Involving in its essence the imposition of direct government control over virtually every aspect of black life, apartheid required the elaboration and expansion of the state bureaucracy. In this way a policy designed to control and repress the black majority became a means for the socioeconomic deliverance of the Afrikaner minority. The implementation of apartheid, along with the introduction of state capitalism, meant the creation of tens of thousands of new jobs in the public sector; jobs that were filled by Afrikaners. Thus by 1970, approximately 50 percent of all economically active Afrikaners were employed by the public and semipublic sector (in contrast to 17 percent of English-speakers), and 80 percent of all such jobs were occupied by Afrikaners.[39] A community that had, in the first half of the century, been increasingly marginalized and proletarianized, was transformed in two decades into a bureaucratic middle class.

The implementation of apartheid and the transformation of the Afrikaner occurred against a backdrop of economic growth and white prosperity. During the 1950s, and at an accelerated rate during the 1960s, the South African economy grew and matured. The 1960s witnessed an average annual growth in the GNP of 6 percent, the emergence of manufacturing as the dominant sector of the economy, and a dramatic increase in white incomes. Given the National Party's record of "success"—the elimination of the black political challenge, the engineering of Afrikaner socioeconomic transformation, the dynamism of the economy, the increasing prosperity of whites, and the more secure international environment upon which that dynamism and prosperity ultimately depended—it is not surprising that in the two decades prior to 1970 the National Party was able to dramatically consolidate its grip on state power. At the end of 1948, its position as governing party rested on a slim parliamentary majority of merely eight seats. Seventeen years later, in the general election of 1966, the Nationalists achieved the largest parliamentary majority in South African history, outnumbering the combined opposition by eighty-two seats.*

The developments of the 1960s generated among South Africa's white population, and its Afrikaner segment in particular, a sense of purpose, achievement, and confidence. In white politics, the late 1960s were a period of ideological clarity and self-assurance. Writing on the period, one Stellenbosch professor of history observed: "[M]any intellectuals for a decade believed with both fervour and fanaticism that apartheid was more than mere white domination: it was the restructuring of South Africa according to a vision of justice, all with a view to lasting peace, progress and prosperity. . . . [T]here was indeed a sense of purpose, dedication and destiny."[40] For the political leadership, this mood manifested itself in an attitude of confidence and self-satisfaction. Reflective of this are the 1967 remarks of Prime Minister John Vorster on the occasion of the seventh anniversary of the Republic: "It seems as if it was only yesterday that supporters, as well as opponents . . . wondered what the future of the Republic would be. Now, after seven years, South Africans have the answer to most—if not all—of their questions. Doubts have gone and fears have vanished."[41]

Yet before the 1970s had ended, the doubts and fears had reappeared. The sense of purpose and destiny had seemingly vanished; the vision had been reversed. The political leader of the Afrikaners was describing apartheid not as the road to lasting peace and progress but rather as a "recipe for permanent conflict" and a path to revolution. What explains this extraordinary change in perspective?

Notes

1. C. Dunbar Moodie, *The Rise of Afrikanerdom: Power, Apartheid, and the Afrikaner Civil Religion* (Berkeley: University of California Press, 1975).

2. Ibid., p. 110.

3. Ibid., p. 164.

4. Ibid., pp. 110–11.

5. Ibid., p. 111.

6. Quoted in Moodie, *Rise of Afrikanerdm*, p. 111.

7. D. Hobart Houghton, "Economic Development 1865–1965," in *The Oxford History of South Africa*, 2 vols., ed. Monica Wilson and Leonard Thompson (Oxford: Oxford University Press, 1975), vol. 2, p. 36.

8. See Stanley B. Greenberg, *Race and State in Capitalist Development* (New Haven: Yale University Press, 1980), app. B, table D.2, p. 425.

9. Calculated from tables A and B in ibid., app. p. 422.

10. Ibid., app. B, table B, p. 422.

11. Quoted in Stanley B. Greenberg, *Legitimating the Illegitimate* (Berkeley: University of California Press, 1987), p. 39.

12. Ibid.

*Nationalist Party = 126 seats; United Party = 93; Coloured Representatives = 4; Progressive Party = 1.

13. Ibid., pp. 33–39; see also Martin Legassick, "Legislation, Ideology, and Economy in Post–1948 South Africa," *Journal of Southern African Studies,* vol. 1, no. 1 (1974), 5–35.

14. See Leonard Thompson, "Afrikaner Nationalism," in Wilson and Thompson, eds., *The Oxford History of South Africa,* vol. 2, p. 407.

15. Ibid.

16. Greenberg, *Legitimating the Illegitimate,* p. 39.

17. Ibid.

18. See Philip Bonner, "Black Trade Unions in South Africa Since World War II," in Robert Price and Carl Rosberg, Jr., eds., *The Apartheid Regime* (Berkeley: Institute of International Studies, 1980), p. 178.

19. Ibid.

20. See Bonner, "Black Trade Unions," p. 178; see also Tom Lodge, *Black Politics in South Africa Since 1945* (London: Longman, 1983), 1–32.

21. See Lodge, *Black Politics;* see also Roland Stanbridge, "Contemporary African Political Organizations and Movements," in Price and Rosberg, eds., pp. 66–98.

22. Lodge, p. 20.

23. *Verwoerd Speaks,* ed. A. N. Pelzer (Johannesburg: APB Publishers, 1966), p. 177.

24. Ibid., pp. 361–62.

25. Ibid., pp. 362–63.

26. Ibid., p. 243.

27. See Pierre L. van den Berghe, "Racial Segregation in South Africa: Degrees and Kinds," in Heribert Adam, ed., *South Africa: Sociological Perspectives* (Oxford: Oxford University Press, 1971), pp. 39–40.

28. See Michael Savage, "Costs of Enforcing Apartheid and Problems of Change," *African Affairs,* no. 76 (1977), 295.

29. See Jack Spence, "South Africa and the Modern World," in Monica Wilson and Leondard Thompson, eds., *The Oxford History of South Africa* (Oxford: Oxford University Press, 1975), p. 513.

30. Quoted in Andre du Toit, "Ideological Change, Afrikaner Nationalism and Pragmatic Racial Domination in South Africa," in L. Thompson and J. Butler, eds., *Change in Contemporary South Africa* (Berkeley: University of California Press, 1976), p. 41.

31. Quoted in Moodie, *Rise of Afrikanerdom,* p. 268.

32. Bonner, "Black Trade Unions," p. 186.

33. See D. Hobart Houghton, *The South African Economy* (Cape Town: Oxford University Press, 1973), p. 181.

34. National Security Study Memorandum 39, rept. in Barry Cohen and Mohammed El-Khawas, eds., *The Kissinger Study of Southern Africa* (Nottingham: Spokesman Books, 1975), p. 66.

35. Ibid., p. 67.

36. Donald Rothchild and John Ravenhill, "From Carter to Reagan," in *Eagle Defiant,* ed. Kenneth Oye, Robert Lieber, and Donald Rothchild (Boston: Little Brown, 1983), p. 340; Ann and Neva Seidman, *South Africa and U.S. Multinational Corporations* (Westport, Conn.: Lawrence Hill, 1978), pp. 72–83; Cohen and El-Khawas, eds., pp. 24–33.

37. Hermann Giliomee, "Afrikanerdom Today: Ideology and Interests," unpublished manuscript (1978), p. 17.

38. Hermann Giliomee, "The Afrikaner Economic Advance," in H. Adam and H. Giliomee, *Ethnic Power Mobilized* (New Haven: Yale University Press, 1979), p. 171.

39. Giliomee, "Afrikanerdom Today," p. 25.

40. Giliomee, "Afrikanerdom Today," p. 6.

41. Quoted in J. Barber, *South Africa's Foreign Policy, 1945–1970* (Oxford: Oxford University Press, 1973), p. 213.

2

Cracks in the Monolith

In August 1979, South Africa's prime minister P. W. Botha warned his ruling National Party that apartheid was "the recipe for permanent conflict," and that for South Africa "the only alternative to revolution" was change.[1] They must "adapt or die," the prime minister told white South Africans. At the same time, prominent members of his cabinet were telling audiences abroad that "Apartheid as you have come to know it is dying and dead."[2] "Apartheid is dead," "Adapt or die"—these were startling utterances coming as they did from the chief spokesman for the South African government. Startling not only because they were being articulated by men who were among apartheid's foremost architects, or because for the previous thirty years the essential "rightness" of apartheid had been a sacred truth within Afrikanerdom, or because during that period Afrikaner political leaders had stressed that apartheid was the *only* way for South Africa to avoid racial friction. Startling, also, because they reveal a dramatic shift in perspective on the part of Pretoria's ruling group; a shift that can be understood as the surface manifestation of a fundamental crisis in the apartheid state.

As was shown in Chapter 1, at the outset of the 1970s the ruling group in Pretoria could and did view its situation with a good deal of confidence and satisfaction. While the apartheid strategy that they had been implementing since the National Party's electoral victory in 1948 was not without its disappointments, on the whole they found it to be an extraordinarily effective means of achieving Afrikaner goals. Yet, by decade's end leading Afrikaners were writing unfavorable obituaries for the system they had created.

I have argued that apartheid was developed as a strategy for the preservation of white supremacy under the particular historical circumstances existing at the end of World War II. During the 1970s, alterations in South Africa's domestic, regional, and global political situations, as well as basic structural strains in its economy, served to transform the country's domestic and international environment once again. These new developments, exacerbated by the manner in which economic strains and regional, domestic, and international political challenges interacted and reinforced one another, raised the fundamental question: *Did apartheid, in the historical circumstances that pertained thirty years after its inception, constitute a viable means to maintain white supremacy?*

28

TABLE 2.1.   Contributions of Sectors to National Economy
(percent)

Year	Agriculture	Mining	Manufacturing	Commerce	Other
1940	11.8	22.8	17.5	14.3	33.6
1945	12.3	14.4	19.9	14.1	39.3
1950	17.8	13.3	18.3	14.7	35.9
1955	15.1	12.3	20.4	15.3	36.9
1960	12.1	13.8	20.7	14.1	39.3
1965	10.2	12.7	23.5	14.2	39.4
1970	8.3	10.3	24.2	15.1	42.1

Source: Stanley B. Greenberg, *Race and State in Capitalist Development* (New Haven: Yale University Press, 1980), p. 426.

Economic Change and Apartheid

In the first two decades of apartheid the South African economy grew and matured rapidly. The manufacturing sector, given a boost by the wartime conditions of the 1940s, had by the mid-1960s overtaken mining and agriculture as the dominant sector of the economy. As can be seen in Table 2.1, by 1965 the contribution of manufacturing to gross domestic product (GDP) exceeded that of mining and agriculture combined. By 1970, manufacturing employed more people than any other sector, and in respect to employment generation had clearly become the most dynamic part of the economy. As can be seen in Table 2.2, during the 1960s the number of persons employed in manufacturing increased by nearly 70 percent. In comparison, mining generated employment growth during the same period of only 10.6 percent, and agriculture as an employer of labor showed a decline. From the mid-1960s it became clear to observers of the South African economy that "the importance of manufacturing in the future economic development of South Africa cannot be too greatly stressed. . . . [I]t must be the cornerstone of future expansion."[3]

The emergence of manufacturing as the leading sector of the South African economy had profound sociological and economic implications for the apartheid system. Sociologically, the rapid growth of manufacturing undermined the apartheid goal of preventing the development of a large and permanent population of African city dwellers. The pull of jobs in the urban manufacturing sector and the push of poverty in the rural "homelands" combined to vitiate the elaborate government effort at "influx control into the white areas." Rather than having been reduced, the size of the black population living in the white urban areas tripled in the first two decades of apartheid, from 1.6 million to over 5 million.[4] By 1970, persons of African descent exceeded those of European background in all but a few metropolitan areas.[5]

The existence of a large and growing African urban presence not only con-

TABLE 2.2.   Employment Generation, by Economic Sector

Year	Agriculture	Mining	Manufacturing	Commerce
1950	882,371	492,615	553,233	290,903
1960	913,345	593,048	692,400	363,057
1970	888,104	656,815	1,164,100	451,600
% increase 1950–60	3.5	20.4	25.2	25.2
% increase 1960–70	−2.8	10.6	68.1	24.2

Source: Stanley B. Greenberg, Race and State in Capitalist Development (New Haven: Yale University Press,1980), tables D.1, D.2, D.3, Statistical Appendix, pp. 425–26.

stituted apartheid's failure in respect to one of its core goals,* but an expensive failure as well. The state apparatus of influx control—the labor bureaus, administration boards, "aid centers," pass courts, and police—was manned by a veritable army of salaried public-sector employees. The consequent drain on the state treasury served, at the very least, as a painful reminder that the apartheid dream of creating a "white South Africa" would remain, despite the best efforts of the apartheid bureaucracy, little more than a legal fiction.

Economically, the growth of the manufacturing sector brought to a head contradictions between the needs of manufacturing and certain aspects of the apartheid system of labor control and repression. These elements of contradiction can be understood if the imperatives of manufacturing are compared with the needs of mining and agriculture, the mainstays of the South African economy for more than a century. The success of South Africa's mining industry and of its commercial agriculture rested on the ability of the white-dominated polity to guarantee an abundant supply of cheap, unskilled labor. This was especially the case for mining, where profitability and international competitiveness could be maintained, despite relatively low-grade ore bodies and the high engineering costs of deep level mining, through the comparative advantage of low-paid, "super-exploitable" labor. As already noted, one aspect of apartheid's influx-control system was an effort to ensure the continuation of this situation.

In contrast to mining and agriculture, manufacturing requires a work force that is literate, technically capable, and trained. In the early phase of its growth South African manufacturing could rely on the white segment of the population as its source of skilled labor. But by the late 1960s, as the industrial sector matured and expanded, the white population could not fill all the new manufacturing jobs that had been created. The large black population offered the obvious, indeed the only, answer to the labor needs of manufacturing. Thus, according to a government commission appointed in 1977 to investigate existing labor legislation, "There were

*Influx control probably did slow the pace of African urbanization, but that was a different matter from achieving the goal of holding constant, or even reversing, the number of Africans in the cities.

simply not enough skilled workers available to fill all the vacancies . . . with the result that increasing numbers of unskilled and semi-skilled workers, particularly Blacks, had to be trained and utilised to perform higher-level skilled jobs."[6] But the apartheid system contained core elements that prevented the acquisition of requisite skills and training by the majority population.

In pursuing its aims in respect to the maintenance of white supremacy, the National Party government had made comprehensive revisions in the system of education for Africans. Dr. H. F. Verwoerd, minister of native affairs in the mid-1950s, explained the political problems inherent in the existing system of black education: "By simply blindly producing pupils who were trained in European ideas the idle hope was created that they could occupy positions in the European community in spite of the country's policy."[7] This, Verwoerd explained, resulted in a "frustrated and rebellious [educated Bantu] who tries to make his community dissatisfied because of such misdirected and alien ambitions."[8] As a remedy, in 1953 the government introduced the Bantu Education Act. Its purpose was to create a completely separate and *different* school system for South Africa's population of African descent; one with a curriculum that would be directed away from the acquisition of skills and orientations associated with a modern society. The government's purpose and intent was made clear by Dr. Verwoerd when he presented the Bantu Education Act to parliament:

> It is the policy of my department that education should have its roots entirely in the Native areas and in the Native environment and Native community. . . . The Bantu must be guided to serve his own community in all respects. There is no place for him in the European community above certain forms of labour. . . . For that reason it is of no avail to him to receive a training which has as its aim absorption in the European community while he cannot and will not be absorbed there. Up till now he has been subjected to a school system which drew him away from his own community and . . . misled him by showing him the green pastures of the European but still did not allow him to graze there. . . . It is abundantly clear that unplanned education . . . disrupts the communal life of the Bantu and endangers the communal life of the European. For that reason it must be replaced by planned Bantu education.[9]

The introduction of Bantu education policy meant not only a decline in academic quality, but also a reduction in the opportunities for school attendance, especially for the urban African. In 1964 there were only six technical schools for Africans in the urban areas, with a total enrollment of just 385 students.[10] This dearth of post-primary opportunities was applauded by the Department of Bantu Education in 1966: "Our people in the cities are already complaining that they do not have a sufficient number of high schools. They will have a few high schools, but never enough, because according to Government policy, most of these schools should be situated in the homelands. . . . They will never get a trade school in the White cities again."[11]

Thus while the social demography of South Africa was changing toward a large, growing, and permanent population of urban Africans, and while the forces of economic development were shifting the nature of labor requirements toward a more technically skilled African work force, the apartheid education bureaucracy was working relentlessly to prevent Africans from acquiring the very skills and technical orientation needed by the most dynamic sector of the economy. As a result, when a manufacturer looked to the urban African population for workers to do the type of skilled jobs for which there were no longer sufficient white job-seekers, he found that 40 percent of the black male work force had no educational qualifications and 82 percent had less than six years of primary school.[12] This situation led a government-appointed commission to conclude in 1978 that "The low formal educational level of the largest segment of the South African labour force undoubtedly contributes to low productivity and increased training costs for employers. . . ."[13]

It was not just the poor quality of black education that raised production costs to the manufacturing sector; the system of influx control and the oscillating labor pool it created was also a costly burden. One way skilled labor differs from unskilled labor is in respect to replaceability. A worker performing a job that requires little or no skill can be removed and replaced by any other worker without loss of productivity. Conversely, in jobs such as those that dominate the production process in manufacturing, replacement is neither easy nor cost-free. First, the replacement worker must possess the requisite technical skills to carry out assigned tasks. And, even more significantly, mastering a production task requires learning specific skills and routines on the job. When an experienced worker is replaced by an inexperienced one, the new worker can be expected to be less productive until he achieves the same proficiency as the worker he replaced. This reduction in productivity can be considered the cost of training, and it is here that influx control imposed itself on the manufacturing sector.

As has already been noted, the system of influx control was intended to limit, indeed to eliminate, all African workers with a permanent residential base in the urban areas. Under this system, employers in cities were supposed to rely on a stream of short-term migrant workers, oscillating between rural and urban areas, and channeled to employers through government labor bureaus located in the rural homelands. Government statistics indicate that by 1970 this oscillating stream had grown to include more than 1.25 million people, and accounted for 40 percent of the black male work force employed in "white" areas.[14] In order to prevent Africans from moving into the cities outside the official labor-bureau channel, the influx-control system erected a permanent dragnet centered on the pass laws. Legal statutes made unapproved presence in cities a criminal offense, and administration boards, police, and courts, searched out, arrested, tried, fined, imprisoned, and rusticated the "illegals." All evidence indicates that both aspects of this system—the canalization of labor through labor bureaus and the discouraging of illegal migration through the application of pass laws—failed to achieve their influx-control purposes. A recent study of the labor bureau system reveals that by the mid-1970s most bureaus had effectively ceased to function as canalizers of labor, and the system was swamped by "illegals" moving to secure jobs in the cities outside of official channels.[15] This practice continued unabated despite the arrest of hundreds of thousands of Africans year after year for violations of the pass laws. The consequence of this situation was to render the urban-African work force highly unstable by adding a large "criminalized" segment of oscillating workers to the official stream of migrants. Workers in the urban areas were arrested, imprisoned, tried, and removed to the rural homelands only to return again to the cities illegally, renewing the cycle of work-arrest-rustication.

For manufacturers employing African labor the influx-control system proved costly. When their workers were caught in its pass-law dragnet the investment employers had sunk into training was lost, productivity declined and the hiring of new, inexperienced workers necessitated additional training expenses. And, of course, it was possible that the replacement worker, too, would run afoul of the pass laws. To make matters worse, employers were required to help pay the administrative costs of this system through a government service levy.* Thus influx control increased the cost of production both directly and indirectly.

A third contradiction between the growth of manufacturing and the apartheid system involves market size. Unlike South Africa's mining industry, which is export-oriented (virtually all of its mineral production goes to satisfy demand generated abroad), South Africa's manufacturing industry is geared to provide consumer goods to a domestic market, and that market has been held artificially small by the repressive labor policies of the South African state. By maintaining the black population as a reserve corps of cheap labor, living at little above bare subsistence, apartheid kept nearly the entire majority population outside the effective market for manufactured consumer goods. Thus a cheap labor policy, which was a boon to mining and agriculture, became an obstacle to expansion of manufacturing, once the market represented by the white minority became saturated. This was the contradiction that emerged during the 1970s. Its concrete manifestation is dramatically revealed by the plight of South Africa's automobile industry.

The manufacture of automobiles and related component parts expanded rapidly during the 1960s. By the end of the 1970s the industry stagnated, as it was plagued by problems of underutilization. With a capacity to produce some 400,000 cars, it faced a market able to absorb less than 200,000. The "white market," for which the industry had been geared, had become saturated, with 450 cars per thousand of population, while the "black market," with 40 cars per thousand, had barely been penetrated.[16] Indeed, given the subsistence incomes of all but a tiny fraction of the 20 million black South Africans, it is more correct to say that the black population has not entered into the market. Were the average consumption level of the black majority to be raised until it equals the level of whites, the size of the South African domestic market would triple.[17] For the automobile industry, as well as many other segments of manufacturing, the black majority represents a huge untapped reservoir of potential consumer demand. But realizing this potential and in so doing laying the foundation for future economic growth requires a substantial increase in black incomes. Consequently for manufacturing, in contrast to mining, low wages are not the *sine qua non* of profitability. A single manufacturer might well prefer low wages for his firm, but the interests of the manufacturing sector overall rest with rising

*The Services Levy Act (1952) required employers of black labor in urban areas to pay to the municipalities a monthly levy for each employee. When the administration of influx control was passed to newly formed administration boards, the Black Labour Act (1972) required employers to pay registration and labor bureau fees and a service levy to the boards. See Simon Bekker and Richard Humphries, *From Control to Confusion* (Pietermaritzburg: Shuter and Shooter, 1985), pp. 122 and 130.

black wage rates. "Economic growth," the Federated Chamber of Industries (FCI) told a government commission in 1971, "requires . . . an expansion of the purchasing power of the indigenous population of South Africa."[18]

The smallness of South Africa's market has also had a detrimental effect on the country's balance of payments. As with many other countries that were late to industrialize, the manufacturing sector in South Africa grew by following the path of import substitution, satisfying local demand for consumer goods that had previously been purchased from abroad. This did not, however, reduce overall import dependence, since the machinery and components that were used to produce the final consumer products were largely imported. Between 1957 and 1969, the value of South Africa's imports almost doubled, and the proportion accounted for by capital goods imports rose from 32 to 42 percent.[19] By the early 1970s producer goods—i.e., capital goods plus intermediate inputs—accounted for fully 83 percent of the value of South Africa's annual imports.*[20] The natural next stage in the evolution of an import substitution strategy is "industrial deepening," the substitution of locally produced capital goods and intermediate components for foreign purchases. But during the 1960s, when South Africa's manufacturing sector was growing rapidly, it could not make this transition. In order to be viable, capital and intermediate goods industries require economies of scale, and thus large markets. They could not be supported by the small South African domestic market. Thus producer goods had to be imported in larger and larger amounts.

By 1964, South Africa's foreign earnings from mineral exports could not cover the cost of a mounting import bill, and the economy experienced increasing deficits in its balance of payments from that year on into the 1970s. Unable to reduce the import bill through industrial deepening, the capacity of the economy to sustain the required level of imports was at risk. The small domestic market, maintained by apartheid, had thus become a structural impediment to industrial maturation and economic growth.

The multiple obstacles that apartheid placed in the path of South Africa's maturing industrial economy were manifested in a deceleration in the rate of economic growth during the 1970s. The average annual increase in gross domestic product of 3.6 percent for the period was down significantly from the growth rates of the previous two decades, 4.8 percent in the 1950s and 5.6 percent in the 1960s. The growth rates for 1975 and 1976 of 2.1 and 1.4 percent represented the smallest two-year increase in over thirty years. The economy's performance was barely keeping pace with growth in population, and in 1975 and 1976 GDP growth in per capita terms was actually negative.[21] The depth of the post-1975 recession was in part a function of the global economic slowdown that followed the 1973 OPEC-orchestrated oil price increases. But the extent of vulnerability of the South African economy to the global "oil shock," and the absence of a sustained recovery over the medium term can in part be attributed to structural flaws in the apartheid-constrained industrial economy. In any case, the economic slowdown had already made

---

*In 1987 the director of the South African Reserve Bank indicated that capital and intermediate goods still accounted for over 80 percent of his country's imports. See, *S.A. Barometer*, vol. 1, no. 2 (March 27, 1987), p. 20.

its appearance during the three years prior to 1973, when the average annual rate of growth in GDP of 4 percent was a third lower than it had been between 1964 and 1969.

Apartheid and Capitalist Industrialization

It is often and powerfully argued in the literature that the contradiction between a maturing capitalist order and the system of apartheid is little more than a chimera. Rather, the argument goes, apartheid represents the modernization of a system of racial domination, entirely consistent with the requirements of capitalist develop-ment. In this view, apartheid is a response to the needs of monopoly capital orga-nized on a global scale. Central to this thesis is the observation that the period of most rapid growth in South Africa's manufacturing sector and of its overall indus-trial maturation coincided with the introduction of apartheid, the 1950s and 1960s. Moreover, this transformation, it is often pointed out, was driven by historically unprecedented levels of foreign investment. It was the abundance of cheap labor provided by apartheid that allowed the highest profits available globally, and at-tracted the multinational corporations.

This argument may well be accurate for the first two decades of apartheid, but it is a static view. It does not take into account the medium-term implications for an expanding manufacturing sector of a small and fixed skilled-labor pool and con-sumer goods market. During the 1950s and 1960s, the rapidly growing manufactur-ing sector was able to utilize the skilled labor available in the white community, and to satisfy the consumer appetites of an increasingly affluent white minority. The constraints on productivity created by apartheid-imposed shortages of skilled and semiskilled labor were not evident until the early 1970s, and the growth constraints associated with the saturation of a small domestic market did not become obvious until later in the decade. The situation is a dynamic one. Apartheid, which in its first two decades served the growth interests of a fledgling manufacturing sector, became a fetter on growth as the sector expanded, matured, and developed new imperatives that could not be met within the existing apartheid structures.

It does not follow, as many proponents of capitalist development in South Africa have argued, that apartheid would disappear simply because it did not adequately serve the interests of the manufacturing sector. For one thing, the apartheid system represents more than just a means of labor repression and control, and thus these aspects could be altered and much of apartheid still remain. For another, the notion that the interests of a maturing capitalism would dictate the shape of South African government policy constitutes a rather crude form of economic determinism. In fact, in the first two decades of apartheid's implementation there is much evidence of the National Party government's defiance of the expressed interests of manufac-turing and of the economic and social "laws" of capitalist development, in favor of its own vision of South African society.

In 1948, shortly before the National Party's electoral victory, the government-appointed Fagan Commission (the Native Laws Commission of Inquiry) noted, and accepted as permanent, the sociological transformation that had accompanied war-time economic development. "We cannot get away from the fact," the commis-

sion's report stated, "that there is indeed a considerable Native population perma-
nently settled in the urban areas. . . . [A]rgument about the desirability or un-
desirability of that state of affairs is purely academic—it is a state of affairs that is
going to remain and that simply cannot be altered."[22] The Fagan Commission was
as accepting of the process of African proletarianization as it was of African urbanization: "[L]egal provision or an administrative policy calculated to perpetuate
migratory labour and to put obstacles in the way of stabilisation of labour, are wrong
and have a detrimental effect."[23] The Fagan Commission's view of South Africa's
socioeconomic realities was vehemently opposed by organizations representing agricultural and mining interests.[24] According to the Chamber of Mines, the "evils
that exist [in 1947] have arisen as a result of rapid urbanisation of Natives employed
in Commerce and Industry." Along with the South African Agricultural Union, it
called for increased state control of the African labor market and for the removal of
Africans from the cities.[25]

The National Party's perspective was consistent with, although not necessarily
dictated by, the alliance of maize and gold. The Sauer Report to the party took note
of "the danger of the flood of Africans moving to the cities,"[26] and asserted that
"influx to the cities must be subject to every possible restriction."[27] It recommended a "national system of labour regulation and labour control" that would
retard rural to urban migration, and which would allocate African labor "between
agriculture, mines and towns."[28]

Stanley Greenberg, in his seminal *Race and State in Capitalist Development*,
shows that this pattern of conflicting interests and National Party preferences continued through the 1950s and 1960s.[29] On the one hand, South African manufacturing and commercial interest groups periodically called for less state manipulation of
the labor market and for policies that would allow the stabilization of the urban
African work force. On the other hand, the National Party government, with support
from mining and agricultural interests, sought to continually strengthen the state's
control of labor markets and to undermine the stability and permanence of urban
African society. In 1967, the Government's Van Rensburg Committee inquired into
the implementation of the pass laws and concluded that influx policy had not
effectively controlled the labor market. It reported that the "flood of Bantu into the
cities" continues. But rather than accept the inevitability of this socioeconomic
trend, the committee called for a redoubled effort at influx control in order to keep
the numbers of urban blacks at "an absolute minimum."[30]

The government was also aware of the impediments to productivity and economic growth created by the small size of South Africa's domestic market. The
Viljoen Commission of 1958 recognized the problem, but rather than recommend
an end to labor repression as a solution, it urged that every effort be made to expand
exports so that the total market, domestic and foreign, would be sufficiently large to
sustain a growing South African economy.[31] This position was reiterated and reinforced by a government commission on export trade, appointed in 1971. It focused
on the balance of payments problems created by a manufacturing sector serving a
small domestic market and heavily reliant on the import of intermediate and capital
goods. Its proffered solution was the promotion of exports, so that foreign markets
might provide both the basis for large-scale production and the foreign exchange

necessary to sustain the importation of essential capital and consumer goods.[32] It emphasized that South Africa's traditional export leader, the mining sector, "will not adequately provide for the foreign exchange needs of the country, so that the export of manufactured goods will have to be increased as rapidly as possible."[33]

In summary, the nature of the contradiction between apartheid and economic modernization was well known to the National Party government throughout the period of its rule. For the first two decades this awareness did not affect policy, except insofar as the government sought to retard the social forces set loose by economic transformation. The implementation of apartheid, as envisioned in 1947 by the Sauer Committee, was zealously pursued. During the 1970s, however, the South African environment was altered in a manner that intensified and qualitatively transformed the contradictions, with new implications for apartheid, for the National Party, and for the maintenance of white supremacy.

First, by the beginning of the 1970s economic performance began to reflect contradictions that, in the previous decades, had remained largely hypothetical. Indeed, in the earlier period, performance largely belied theory, because during the 1960s the South African economy grew at a rate rivaled only by Japan among the industrial countries. With the economy growing, the manufacturing sector expanding, and white living standards rising, policymakers could avoid having to choose between apartheid structures and economic benefits. But in the third decade of apartheid, economic reality caught up to economic theory. A variety of problems— shortages of skilled and semiskilled labor, low levels of productivity, balance of payments deficits, market saturation, and plant underutilization—manifested themselves and impinged on prospects for future economic growth. Each of these difficulties was caused, in significant measure, by apartheid policies. As the 1970s passed, the leaders of the National Party increasingly faced a hard choice between key aspects of apartheid and future economic development and growth.

A second factor that made apartheid's economic constraints more politically pressing in the 1970s than they had been earlier involves the changing nature of the National Party's Afrikaner constituency. In 1948 when the government rejected the policy preferences of the manufacturing sector, as set forth by the Fagan Commission, and instead adopted policies favored by the alliance of maize and gold, the economic interests of the National Party's political base, the Afrikaner community, were almost entirely agricultural. Nearly all of its parliamentary members were elected from rural constituencies, and half of its MPs were themselves farmers.[34] Although they constituted a majority of the European population, Afrikaners in the late 1940s controlled only 11 percent of the private-sector economy outside of agriculture* (6 percent of manufacturing, 6 percent of finance, 1 percent of mining, and 25 percent of commerce).[35] But as a result of National Party rule and as a by-product of apartheid policy, the Afrikaner community underwent a socioeconomic transformation; its economic base shifted into all sectors of the modern non-agricultural economy as well as the state bureaucracy. By the mid-1960s over one-

---

*Approximately 80 percent of Afrikaner commerce was located in rural areas and consisted of small enterprise. Only about 10 percent of urban-based traders were Afrikaners. See Stanley Trapido, "Political Institutions and Afrikaner Social Structures in the Republic of South Africa," *American Political Science Review*, vol. 57, no. 1 (1963), pp. 80–81.

quarter of the private sector outside of agriculture was controlled by Afrikaners, and the proportion of Afrikaners in agricultural occupations dropped below 16 percent, from over 30 percent in the 1940s.[36] Looked at from another angle, between 1960 and 1980, as a consequence of a process of capital consolidation in agriculture, the number of white farmers fell from 106,000 to 70,000.[37] Hence, in the 1970s, in contrast to earlier decades, when business complained to government about the economic costs of apartheid it included the voices of prominent and financially powerful Afrikaners. Concomitantly, the small-farmer constituency that had traditionally stood opposed to the policy preferences of manufacturers, had dwindled, as well.

Not only had socioeconomic transformation increased the significance of non-agricultural economic interests within the National Party's constituency, but by the mid-1960s agriculture itself had begun to shift its position on the importance of labor control and repression. Along with the rest of the South African economy, white-controlled agriculture underwent modernization during the 1950s and 1960s. Among other things, this involved a move toward extensive mechanization and a simultaneous reduction in reliance on large numbers of African tenant farmers. As the agricultural economy moved away from dependence on huge numbers of un-skilled African workers the main agricultural lobby, the South African Agricultural Union (SAAU), dropped its traditional insistence that the state exercise ever more elaborate control over the market for African labor.[38] In sum, the social and economic transformations experienced in the first two decades of apartheid altered the nature of economic interests within the National Party's ethnic stronghold. In the 1970s, the forces pushing for an extension of apartheid were reduced, while the forces advocating an alteration in apartheid in light of its economic constraints were not only more numerous but now existed within the governing party's Afrikaner constituency.

Thus, a combination of economic stagnation, a change in the policy preferences of organized agricultural interests, and the transformed socioeconomic makeup of the Afrikaner community served to make the economic constraints of apartheid a far more serious problem for the government in the 1970s than had been true in previous decades. An additional factor that increased the salience of apartheid's economic costs involved changes in South Africa's regional, domestic, and global political situation. These elements of change, in their own way and in relationship to each other, made the economic costs of apartheid and its threat to continued economic growth more pressing. They, among other things, transformed apartheid's economic constraints from simply a matter of economic interest into a vital security concern. The preservation of white rule, not narrowly defined material interest, became the issue at stake.

A Transformed Regional Political Landscape

No single event had a more powerful impact on South Africa during the 1970s than did a change in political regime in a small and backward country in southern Europe. The coup in Portugal on April 25, 1974, precipitated a series of developments that would profoundly alter the political landscape of southern Africa, with implications for South Africa's national security and domestic peace.

Security in the Era of Decolonization

Since the mid-1950s Pretoria had been concerned that the era of African independence had implications for its own situation. This involved not only a foreboding that the rising tide of African nationalism might sweep southward from Ghana and Nigeria, eventually engulfing the African majority within South Africa. It encompassed also a concern with the security implications of isolation on a continent of independent African-ruled countries; countries whose racial makeup and contemporary history seemed to preordain their hostility toward the continuation of white rule on the Southern tip of Africa.

These concerns had abated dramatically by the mid-1960s, when it appeared that the tide of nationalist advance had been checked at the Zambezi River. In Pretoria's own southern African regional environs white power appeared secure. Angola and Mozambique remained Portuguese colonies, and Portugal had shown itself willing to expend considerable military resources to keep them so. Rhodesia was a de facto independent state, under white minority rule. The European settlers of that colonial territory had, in 1965, declared themselves free of Great Britain, so as to block the pattern of decolonization and majority rule followed by the British elsewhere in Africa. England showed little indication that it was willing to expend the resources necessary to reverse the action of its erstwhile colony, and the new white minority rulers gave every sign that they were committed to maintaining their positions of power. On South Africa's western flank, the territory of South West Africa/Namibia had been administered by South Africa under UN mandate since the end of World War I. Although the United Nations in 1965 had withdrawn Pretoria's legal mandate and announced that the territory was henceforth a UN responsibility, the means to force South Africa's withdrawal were lacking and its control remained secure.

The four territories—Angola, Mozambique, Rhodesia, and Namibia—each ruled by a white minority government, and each with a long-established working relationship with Pretoria, constituted a buffer zone between South Africa and the forces of African nationalism and black political power to the north. In the 1960s, this *cordon sanitaire,* as it was generally termed, afforded Pretoria significant protection against any threat that might come from the militaries of the newly formed African countries, or from their extraregional allies, particularly those of the "Eastern bloc." Likewise, after the early 1960s, the African National Congress, its organization within South Africa decimated by police action, was pushed into exile beyond the *cordon,* far from the borders of its home country. This provided an extra measure of security against externally launched ANC political mobilization and sabotage campaigns inside South Africa. Secure behind its *cordon,* Pretoria was able to decelerate the military build-up that had marked its security response to the initial period of decolonization and African independence. In 1960, the South African general staff had concluded, on the basis of a "military appreciation of the world situation," that it was vital for South Africa "to enhance its military capability and state of readiness. . . ."[39] There followed a rapid build-up of naval, air, and ground forces. Between 1960 and 1965, the regular troops in the South African Defence Force increased from 2,000 to 19,500;[40] the annual budget allocation for defense soared from 44 million to 230 million rand.[41] In these six years the military's share of the annual budget went from 6.6 to 21 percent.[42]

By mid-decade, as the forces of nationalism stalled at the Zambezi, Pretoria's sense of vulnerability diminished and so did the emphasis on military preparedness. "It is clear," writes one student of the period, "that the Minister of Defense was under pressure to reduce his spending in line with the generally perceived fading of the immediate threat."[43] The result of this shift in perception can be seen in the statistics on resource allocation. The numbers of regular recruits in the SADF remained roughly constant for nearly a decade, from 1966 through the mid-1970s,[44] and annual expenditures remained level, at between R250 and R300 million over a seven-year period (1966–73).[45] The portion of annual budgets devoted to the military actually diminished significantly; from the high of 21 percent of 1964–65 to 12 percent in 1972–73.[46]

Security in a Changed Regional Environment

When the Armed Forces Movement overthrew the Portuguese dictatorship in April 1974, the South African regional security framework crumbled. One of the earliest decisions made by the new Lisbon government was to dismantle its African empire. By the end of 1975 Mozambique and Angola had been granted independence. In both cases the new African governments were controlled by political parties that (1) professed a commitment to Marxism-Leninism; (2) had a history of opposition to apartheid; (3) had close fraternal ties with the ANC; and (4) had received substantial diplomatic, economic, and military assistance from the Soviet Union and its allies.

In the case of Angola, in the waning months of Portuguese rule Pretoria had intervened militarily in the conflict between three rival Angolan political movements, seeking to prevent the Popular Movement for the Liberation of Angola (MPLA), which the South African government viewed as Marxist and implacably hostile to its interests, from establishing military and political dominance.[47] By mid-1975 Pretoria was providing arms and military advisers to two factions, the National Front for the Liberation of Angola (FNLA) and the National Union for the Total Independence of Angola (UNITA), that opposed the MPLA. Then in October its military forces intervened directly in support of these movements, invading Angola from Namibia. Moving northward in what it called "Operation Zulu," the South African forces drove deep into Angolan territory. Within a month they were situated 100 miles south of Luanda, in an excellent position to seize the Angolan capital in coordination with the FNLA, which was attacking from the north. The MPLA, in contrast, was in serious danger of annihilation by early November, having lost nearly all of the territory it had gained in the military jockeying between July and September. It controlled, insecurely, only a narrow strip of territory in north-central Angola, the capital, and the small enclave of Cabinda.

In mid-November, however, several new factors radically altered the political/military balance within Angola and undermined the South African military intervention. First, the MPLA appealed to Cuba and the Soviet Union for military assistance. Cuba, which had provided only modest help, up until this point, now launched a large airlift of combat troops, heavy armor, and artillery to the Angolan battlefield.*[48] The Soviet Union provided logistical support, flew in thousands of Cuban troops in cargo planes, and supplied T-54 and T-34 tanks and 122mm mobile rocket launchers. Second, South African backing for the FNLA and UNITA discredited these movements within independent Africa, and the Soviet-assisted Cuban military efforts were applauded by most African states as an effort to protect Angola from conquest by a white supremacist South Africa. And, third, in mid-December, the United States Congress prohibited the Central Intelligence Agency from continuing to provide military and other forms of assistance to the FNLA and UNITA, something the agency had been doing covertly since January 1975. This last development was a major blow to the South African military intervention, since Pretoria believed that its efforts in Angola would be supported by Washington diplomatically and materially.† With its logistical lines stretched thin, facing approximately 12,000 Cuban combat troops backed by the Soviets, and believing that it had been abandoned by the United States, Pretoria withdrew from the fight. According to the South African minister of defense, South Africa was not prepared to stand alone for the "free world."[49] By the end of January 1976 its troops had been pulled back to the Namibia/Angola border area. A month later the military resistance to the MPLA collapsed.

On February 11, 1976, the African states recognized the MPLA as the legitimate government of the People's Republic of Angola by according it membership in the Organization of African Unity (OAU). The government of independent Angola was now controlled by a radical political movement that was openly hostile to Pretoria. To make matters worse from the South African vantage point, its unsuccessful intervention in the Angolan civil war had left a "residue" within Angola of some 20,000 Cuban combat troops, and had served to introduce the Soviet Union as a major diplomatic, if not military, factor in the affairs of southern Africa. "The impact of events in Angola on the RSA's security interests . . . will probably have far-reaching consequences in the long run," stated Pretoria's 1977 White Paper on Defense. ". . . [T]here is a Soviet shadow over parts of Africa."[50]

The independence of Angola and Mozambique, under radical governments, had significant implications for the stability of white rule in Rhodesia and Namibia, as well. Rhodesia's eastern border is contiguous with Mozambique. After independence this huge border area was made available to the military forces of the Zimbabwe African National Union (ZANU) as a sanctuary from which incursions into

---

*Prior to the South African advance on Luanda the Cuban presence in Angola involved approximately 1,000 "advisers" to the MPLA. In the first week of November 1975, with the South African column moving rapidly northward, the MPLA called on Cuba to help defend the Angolan capital. Cuba responded and on November 7 began airlifting combat troops from Havana to Luanda. The Portuguese declared Angola independent on November 11, and in the midst of an escalating civil war relinquished the government to the MPLA.

†Secretary of State Kissinger denied any U.S. "collusion" with the South African invasion, but Pretoria has insisted that its intervention in Angola was based on an understanding with Washington that the United States would back it with supplies of weaponry.

Rhodesia were launched. As a result, the Rhodesian civil war, which had been simmering since the mid-1960s, escalated rapidly and the military balance shifted decisively away from the government. The military advantages provided to the African nationalist forces by an independent and radical Mozambique created the conditions for the transition, in 1979, to majority rule in Rhodesia, which was renamed Zimbabwe in 1980. Now South Africa shared its northern border with an African government claiming to be Marxist, with a history of armed struggle against white rule, and with close ties to the ANC. South Africa's northern security border had become its own Limpopo River, rather than the Zambezi. The security of Namibia was also undermined by these regional changes. As Mozambique had done with ZANU, so the new African government in Angola did with the South West Africa People's Organization (SWAPO), the African nationalist movement which, with assistance from the Soviet Union, had been fighting a low-level war for control of South African–administered Namibia. After Angola's independence in late 1975, SWAPO units began operating from southern Angola, from where they could launch attacks into neighboring Namibia.

In sum, the last half of the 1970s witnessed the collapse of white rule in most of southern Africa, and with it the basis upon which Pretoria had rested its national security policy during the previous decade. The *cordon sanitaire* was now gone. Three white conservative governments, which were allies of Pretoria, had been replaced by radical-left African governments that were declared opponents of Pretoria; the Soviet Union and Cuba had become deeply involved in the southern African region; over 20,000 Cuban troops had engaged the South African military on Angolan soil, and Pretoria's forces had retreated and withdrawn, leaving a sizable extraregional Communist military presence directly north of Namibia; the ANC, with its close ties to the governing parties of Mozambique and Zimbabwe was now in position to place its cadre at the very borders of the South African republic, and SWAPO, with bases in Angola, could do the same in respect to Namibia.

Not surprisingly, these changes in the southern African political landscape increased Pretoria's perception of threat. "Undesirable influences and tendencies" in Mozambique, Angola, and Rhodesia, warned a 1975 government white paper on defense, "will undoubtedly encourage the radical elements in revolutionary organizations inside and outside [South Africa] and incite them to greater efforts."[51] A year later, after the SADF's costly involvement in the Angolan civil war, the South African defense minister said that the presence of Cuban troops and sophisticated Soviet weaponry in Angola had "introduced a completely new factor . . . virtually overnight."[52] Summarizing the republic's security situation under the heading "Threat to the RSA," the defense white paper for 1977 concluded: "The occurrences in Africa . . . led to an increase in the tempo of developments and this has brought the threats nearer in time."[53] Especially troubling to Pretoria was the clear realization, after their Angolan debacle, that in the event of external attack they could not count on assistance from the Western alliance, even if that attack involved the Soviet Union or its allies. The Angolan experience had shown, according to Prime Minister Vorster, that the West "had lost the will to take a firm stand against the increasing [Communist] menace." In his 1977 New Year's message he explained, "If therefore a Communist onslaught should be made against South Africa, directly or under camouflage, South Africa will have to face it alone, and certain countries which profess to be anti-Communist will even refuse to sell [us] arms. . . . This is the reality of our situation."[54]

As it had done in the initial period of African independence in the early 1960s, Pretoria sought an enhanced military capability in keeping with its understanding of the new political/strategic realities in southern Africa.[55] The commitment to military expansion and modernization, including a major program for the procurement and development of sophisticated new weapons systems, was reflected in soaring budget allocations for the military. Figure 2.1 reveals the dramatic rise in military expenditure that followed the collapse of the Portuguese empire in Africa. Defense spending nearly doubled in 1974 and then again in the following year. In each of the next two years the budget for the military increased by nearly a third. Over the period 1973 through 1980, defense expenditures recorded a jump of 454 percent; the share of defense in total government spending expanded from 12 to 20 percent; and, as a proportion of GNP, military expenditures rose from 2.3 percent to 5.2 percent.[56]

Security Threats, Economic Growth, and Apartheid

The heavy financial burden imposed by Pretoria's new security policy placed a high premium on a growing economy. The military modernization and expansion of the late 1970s could be accomplished and sustained, without cutting deeply into government commitments in nonmilitary areas, only under conditions of prosperity. That was how the military modernization program of the early 1960s had been financed, although even then the military was under political pressure to curtail its expansion plans.[57] A student of the period concluded: "It seems very likely, . . . in the absence of an economic boom and the associated heavy influx of foreign funds, that such a rapid growth in defense capabilities could not have been achieved without severe strains on the economy and a decline in the living standards of the white population."[58]

In the mid-1970s, in contrast to the previous decade, the prognosis in respect to economic growth had become increasingly problematic. The years 1975 and 1976 registered the worst GDP figures in over thirty years. Within government circles, this sluggish economic performance increased the salience of apartheid-related constraints on growth. This would have been especially so for the military, perceiving as it did the need for a major build-up in order to meet new challenges to national security, and requiring economic growth to pay its costs. Therefore, unreconstructed apartheid, to the extent that it constituted an obstacle to economic growth, represented a threat to national security.

Apartheid in the mid-70s represented a problem for the military in another respect as well. It placed constraints on manpower that undermined the military's ability to accomplish its assigned missions. According to one expert on defense matters, "As South Africa has moved towards a war footing [in the mid-1970s] the problem of manpower has continued to be the greatest constraint on Government

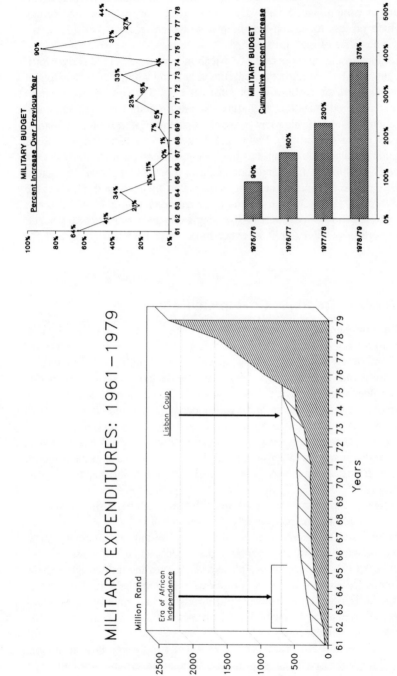

Fig. 2.1. Regional transformation and growth in military expenditures (*Source*: "Military Balance," Institute for Strategic Studies: rept. in *Facts and Reports*, 18:a, p. 2)

actions."[59] Under apartheid, only whites could be drafted, and the pool of approximately 750,000 white males between ages 18 and 35, from which the military had to draw its main combat personnel, also consisted of some 40 percent of the country's economically active whites.[60] Thus the availability of recruits was limited both by the size of South Africa's white population, and by the manpower requirements of its economy. As the military sought to adapt to new regional realities, adding new missions to its security role, it found itself at the limits of white manpower. "Our defense force cannot be large enough, strong enough, without the full participation of all our people," acknowledged a high-ranking officer. "We have need for military men of all colors."[61] Consequently, in the mid-1970s the SADF began to incorporate population groups other than whites in military service. In 1975 an Indian Training Battalion was created, and Indians were admitted into the SADF. In 1977 the government accepted the idea that there should be a national service and a cadet corps for "coloureds." The inclusion of Africans was approached more cautiously, but gradual moves in that direction were also made in the late 1970s.[62]

In beginning to recruit from population groups outside the white minority, the military was acting in accord with the imperatives of its own security-driven agenda. But apartheid was a clear obstacle to the creation of a sizable and dedicated fighting force. Not only did the inclusion of blacks run contrary to basic ideological principle, the recruitment of personnel to defend a system in which they were the subject of extensive discrimination and in which they were denied rights of citizenship and political participation, posed daunting problems in respect to motivation and loyalty.

Observers of South African affairs have often remarked on what they considered a paradox in the policy orientation of the SADF's senior officer corps: a preference for a tough stance toward external and internal "enemies," combined with support for a *verligte* ("flexible," "liberal," "enlightened") position on the question of apartheid reform. While the first aspect of this policy preference is expected, the second has been considered anomalous—the military generally being thought of as "hard-line" or "hawkish" across-the-board. One explanation offered for this apparent paradox is the nature of the technical training of the military elite. This training is thought to have a modern, cosmopolitan, and secular effect that makes military officers uncomfortable with apartheid ideology and practice. A more persuasive reason for the existence of the paradox I believe, is found in the situational constraints facing the SADF in the 1970s. The military's own definition of its defense mission, in what it perceived as a regional situation containing new and more serious threats, required vastly increased expenditures and access to more manpower than white South Africans could supply. The defense establishment needed a healthy economy to make heavy military expenditures politically feasible, and it needed access to a manpower pool of motivated and loyal citizens. Apartheid posed obstacles to the satisfaction of both requirements. The military, with its special interest in security matters, was therefore especially sensitive to the "counterproductive" elements in apartheid, and thus became a significant lobby for its alteration.

The Revival of Black Militancy

The mid-1970s were marked by a transformation in South Africa's domestic, as well as its regional political landscape. After fifteen years in which a combination of repression and newly fashioned apartheid structures had seemingly broken the spirit and the organizational backbone of black liberation, South Africa was swept by a mass rebellion more widespread, intense, and enduring than any in its history.

Trade Unionism Revived

The first major sign that the passivity imposed after Sharpeville was not as permanent as the architects of apartheid had hoped appeared in the early months of 1973, when a wave of strikes by black workers swept across Natal, the Eastern Cape, and the Rand.[63] Although blacks were legally constrained from forming trade unions and organizing strikes, tens of thousands of black workers put down their tools in a disciplined and ultimately successful effort to improve their wages. A total of 161 strikes involving over 60,000 workers occurred between January and April 1973. In contrast, in all of 1972 there had been only six strikes in which approximately 5,000 workers took part.[64]

The full significance of this renewed labor militancy will emerge later in this book. At this point, suffice it to say that the existence of a burgeoning black trade-union movement with a demonstrated capability for collective action, in spite of the apartheid system, served as yet another factor challenging the viability of apartheid as a long-term protector of white interests. The economic growth of the 1960s, and the foreign investment that was its engine, had rested on a foundation of extraordinary labor peace. Thus, the eruption of widespread labor unrest in the mid-1970s, at a time when a revitalized economy was viewed as a matter of national security, could not be viewed with equanimity within government circles.

At a broader political level, the emergence of effective worker organizations raised once again the specter of black power. For what is involved in black trade-union organization is an enhanced capacity for blacks to exercise the leverage created by white dependence on black labor. The salience of this "threat" was greatly elevated by the political upheavals that began to rock South Africa in June 1976.

The Soweto Uprising

On the morning of June 16 in the Johannesburg township of Soweto some 15,000 African schoolchildren gathered at Orlando West Junior Secondary School. They intended to protest the introduction of Afrikaans as the medium of instruction in secondary school courses.* The students were met by a detachment of police that tear-gassed the crowd and opened fire, killing two and injuring several others. This series of events touched off a rebellion against the apartheid system that was un-

---

*Afrikaans, which has evolved from the Dutch, is the language of the Afrikaners. English had been the language of instruction in African secondary schools, although plans to switch to Afrikaans had existed, unimplemented, since the introduction of Bantu education in the mid-1950s.

precedented in its scope and endurance.[65] The Soweto students fanned out into the sprawling township, erecting barricades, hurling stones and bricks at contingents of police, and smashing and burning government property. The police responded with pistol and automatic-rifle fire. The next day the rebellion grew and intensified. Fifteen hundred police reinforcements moved into Soweto, armed with sten guns, automatic rifles, and hand-machine guns. The morning began with youths burning school buildings and attacking offices of the West Rand Administration Board, the hated government agency that ran the townships. As police were dispatched to each new trouble spot they encountered large groups of youths manning barricades who stood their ground, battling the well-armed security forces with stones, bottles, bricks, and whatever sort of weapon or projectile they could muster. By noon of the second day of what was to become known as the "Soweto uprising," fighting was raging through the township. The ghetto of over 1.5 million black South Africans had turned, virtually overnight, into a war zone. A journalist described the scene as witnessed from Orlando police station that second evening:

> The only way in or out for whites was in an armoured convoy. Floodlights above the building peered through Soweto's perpetual night-time smog [showing] scores of armoured vehicles and hundreds of police. Every hour or so an armed patrol would set off into the darkness with a roar of diesel engines. The police used reinforced police vans or the high ungainly hippo personnel carriers for all patrols. The battered police vans with shattered windows outside the police station were a proof of the fate of unarmed vehicles in Soweto's dirty streets. Across the road from the police station is a sports field which is now a helicopter launching pad. Darkness grounds the choppers at night and the roar of their engines no longer disturb the policemen snatching sleep on the ground. Only the rattle of gunfire from the darkness or an officer's shouted command brings the men to their feet.[66]

By day three the uprising had spread from Soweto to other townships in the Transvaal, as well as to the University of Zululand in Natal and the University of the North, at Turfloop in the Northern Transvaal. In each place demonstrations were held in support of the Soweto students and residents. These were attacked by police, setting off the pattern of hit-and-run battles and burning of government property that had characterized the uprising in Soweto. Press reports of casualties during the first three days of the rebellion put the number of dead at 97 (two of whom were white), with 1,118 persons injured. Twenty-two policemen were reported injured. Other figures, based upon eyewitness, hospital, and mortuary staff reports, place the number of persons killed by police in the first three days at over 500.[67] In the ensuing weeks the uprising spread to most large African and "coloured" townships and to the black universities in the homelands.* It alternately flared up in one area and smoldered in another, in a sort of rolling rebellion. In the process the object of attack went from Bantu education and Afrikaans instruction to the entire edifice of apartheid and white supremacy. In the townships, the symbols and physical manifestations of apartheid and white authority were singled out and demolished. "Everywhere," reported the Government Commission of Enquiry into the re-

---

*The townships of Natal were relatively quiet throughout the period of the Soweto uprising.

bellion, "the property of Administration Boards was the target of the vandals."[68] One-hundred-and-eighty-four government beer halls and bottle shops, which help pay the costs of township administration, were demolished, as were 124 administration board buildings and 222 board vehicles.[69] Over 430 schools were burned down as was the administration building on the University of Zululand campus.[70]

As the uprising spread geographically, it deepened sociologically and diversified tactically. Adults, as parents and workers, joined the youths and students in the ranks of the rebels. Consumer and transport boycotts were introduced as weapons to bring economic pressure on the state, as was the political "stayaway," or general strike. The introduction of the political strike, given the critical role of the black working class in the South African economy, was an especially significant development. This weapon had been used in the resistance campaigns of the 1950s, and had last been attempted in 1961. Now three stayaways were launched in the Johannesburg area during the period of August through September 1976.[71] Each represented the most successful use of the political strike in South African history. When another stayaway was called for November 1–5 it was largely unsuccessful,[72] indicating a petering out of an uprising that had continued without letup for five months. Although a student boycott of the educational system would continue throughout 1977, the generalized uprising had subsided by the new year.

In defying the state and attacking its manifestations within the township communities, the black population, and particularly its youth, paid dearly. The repressive apparatus of a state dedicated to retaining its power was unleashed upon the demonstrators. According to official estimates, 570 were killed and 2,389 wounded;[73] unofficial estimates place the toll of dead and wounded much higher. The widely respected Institute of Race Relations calculated that 618 people had been killed by the police, and the most exhaustive nonofficial study of the rebellion concluded that the death toll from June to December 1976 was likely to have been over 1,000, with the number of injured exceeding 5,000.[74] Between July 1976 and June 1977 an extraordinary 21,534 people were prosecuted for offenses related to creating public disturbances—public violence, unlawful or riotous assembly, arson, and the like. Hundreds of others were detained during the uprising without being charged or brought to trial.[75]

Background to Political Revival

The apartheid system, and the welter of security laws that had accompanied its introduction, had been introduced by the National Party government, at least in part, to prevent the very type of onslaught that rocked South Africa during the last six months of 1976. Ironically, however, an examination of the background to the Soweto uprising reveals that the dynamics of the apartheid system itself played a major role in creating the conditions that produced a revival of black militancy in the mid-1970s.

For sustained collective actions against an existing sociopolitical order to occur certain ideological, organizational, and situational conditions must be met. Ideological conditions involve the existence of certain widely held beliefs: (1) the sense that individual grievances are in reality shared with many others, that they are in fact common grievances; (2) an understanding that commonly felt grievances are a product of the existing social, political, and/or economic order; and (3) the view that direct action by oppressed peoples can alter the system producing the common grievances. Organizational conditions involve the ability to plan collective action and to communicate a common message to large numbers of physically dispersed people. Situational conditions involve an increased sense of deprivation, as a result of either an absolute decline in material or status rewards, or an increased gap between what is expected in respect to material or status standards and what is actually attained. In South Africa of the mid-1970s, these three conditions came together, producing mass political militancy after a lull of over fifteen years.

Ideological and Organizational Developments

The black population's ideological predisposition and organizational capability for militant collective opposition to apartheid was enhanced during the first half of the 1970s by four developments.

1. *Generational Change.* The quiescence that characterized black opposition following the Sharpeville killings of 1960 can in part be understood as the consequence of political trauma. The political generation of the 1950s, oriented to non-violent protest demonstrations and to moral appeals to the liberal strand in South African politics, absorbed the full repressive brunt of the apartheid state: killings, mass arrests, torture, treason trials, life imprisonment, banned organizations, exile and the like. The effect was to stun an entire generation of black South Africans into political passivity. "The Port Elizabeth I grew up in in the late sixties and early seventies was very apathetic politically," writes Saki Macozoma. "People would refer to the struggles and repression of the early sixties as *lant' inkulu* (the big thing). . . . We [children] were not supposed to talk about the 'big thing.' "[76]

The political trauma produced by the Sharpeville-era repression was reinforced by the unfolding of apartheid's social reality. Because the National Party's program of forced removals, influx control, and separate development bred fear and insecurity, the 1960s were an extremely unsettled and precarious period for the urban black population. But by the mid-1970s an entirely new political generation had arrived on the urban scene—the cohort of 15- to 20-year-olds that spearheaded the Soweto uprising. Toddlers at the time of Sharpeville, they had not directly experienced the political trauma of the post-Sharpeville repression. Moreover, they were the first full "apartheid generation," having grown up in the world of pass raids, removals, and "endorsing out," leaving them without the pre-apartheid generations's illusions about South African liberalism. Thus, compared to their elders, they could be expected to be less unsettled by apartheid's impositions, more streetwise and hardened in respect to dealing with the police, and less sanguine in their expectations of white authority.

2. *Black Consciousness.* In 1959 the government officially segregated higher education in South Africa. It created universities with entirely black student bodies and located them in the rural Bantustans. Ironically, it was within this apartheid environment that Black Consciousness, a new ideological and organizational form of black opposition, was born in the late 1960s. A doctrine of cultural and psychological autonomy more than it is an explicitly political ideology, Black Consciousness, as its

name suggests, was directed more to the process of "conscientization" within the black community—to developing a sense of cultural pride, self-reliance, and solidarity—than to elaborating a political strategy for attacking the white-ruled state. In the words of Steve Biko, its leading exponent, "Black Consciousness is an attitude of mind and a way of life":

> Its essence is the realisation by the black man of the need to rally together with his brothers around the cause of their oppression—the blackness of their skin—and to operate as a group to rid themselves of shackles that bind them to perpetual servitude . . .[77]

Because Black Consciousness lacked an explicitly political program, the organizations that propagated it—the South African Students Organization (SASO) and the Black People's Convention (BPC)—were able to survive and operate, for a time, under the watchful eye of the state's security apparatus. SASO, formed in 1969, linked together students at the black universities, and the BPC, formed in 1972 by SASO leaders, sought to bring Black Consciousness to the wider community. The BPC eventually organized forty-one branches through which it not only spread its ideology, but also operationalized its philosophic commitment to self-reliance through a variety of action programs: health projects, literacy campaigns, and cultural activities.

In terms of its organizational expression, the Black Consciousness movement never significantly transcended its urban middle-class origins. Nevertheless, because the university students who were its early adherents became teachers, priests, ministers, and journalists, the basic theme of Black Consciousness ideology—liberation from both psychological and physical oppression through black solidarity and self-reliance—influenced a broad spectrum of the urban township population.[78] Neither SASO or the BPC were directly involved in the events of the Soweto uprising. But the secondary school students who initiated the protests against Afrikaans instruction and provided the rebellion with a loosely organized leadership, were heavily influenced by the intellectual tradition of Black Consciousness and by the spirit of defiance of white authority that it rekindled during the first half of the 1970s.

3. *Changes in System of Bantu Education.* For reasons both psychological and sociological, adolescence is a time of life that lends itself to radical beliefs and behavior. Youth, writes Erik Erikson, "in its search for the combination of freedom and discipline, of adventure and tradition, which suits its state . . . is ready to provide the physical power and the vociferous noise of rebellions, riots, and lynchings. . . ."[79] The adolescent's position in society compliments his psychological state, making it relatively easy for him to act upon psychologically driven radical impulses. Without the constraints imposed by marriage, family, and job, those in the adolescent stage are free to pursue their "deviant" intellectual, cultural, or political goals, with less risk of loss than their elders.

The likelihood that the propensities for radical behavior inherent in adolescence will find collective expression is enhanced by the institution of formal education. For the school provides a context for the emergence of group identity and organization by bringing together large numbers of like-minded and similarly predisposed young people. Thus, in understanding the leading role of black secondary school students in the Soweto uprising, we can add the universal aspects of the adolescent stage to the life experience of the post-Sharpeville generation. What is especially interesting about the early 1970s, in this respect, were changes in government policy that had the unintended effect of facilitating collective action by this new township generation.

As has already been discussed, during the 1960s it was a cardinal rule of government education policy to locate whatever secondary schools existed for Africans outside the urban areas. Consequently, the natural setting for the emergence of an organized expression of youth's radical impulses was largely removed from the black townships. In this manner, the South African government's policies of separate development and Bantu education indirectly worked to undermine the capacity of urban youth to act as a self-conscious group.

In the early 1970s, in response to the skilled manpower shortage facing the South African economy, Pretoria altered its policy regarding the placement of secondary schools in the black townships. The number of secondary schools for Africans was rapidly expanded, and many of these were located in urban areas.[80] This change was particularly evident in Soweto, the largest black urban township. Between 1972 and 1976 the number of secondary schools there doubled, while the number of pupils in attendance almost trebled, from 12,656 to 34,656.[81] Countrywide, secondary school attendance also multiplied, from 179,000 in 1974 to 390,000 in 1976,[82] a jump of 118 percent in merely two years.

The rapid expansion of secondary schools for blacks was accompanied almost simultaneously by the establishment of student organizations, and these quickly adopted an oppositional stance toward the authorities and the system of apartheid. In April 1971, student groups at three high schools in Soweto came together to form the African Students Movement. By 1972 branches of this organization were being formed at secondary schools outside Soweto and outside the Transvaal. In recognition of its national potential, the organization's name was changed to the South African Students Movement (SASM). A first annual congress of the movement was held in March 1972.[83] It was SASM that led the attack on the introduction of Afrikaans in high schools. Its Transvaal regional branch, the Action Committee, planned the fateful demonstration against Afrikaans instruction in Soweto on June 16, 1976. As the uprising in Soweto flared, the Action Committee was transformed into the Soweto Student Representative Council (SSRC), drawing delegates from student councils in most of the township's secondary schools. It was the SSRC that would provide rudimentary leadership and coordination for the uprising that continued for more than six months. In 1978, at the trial of eleven SASM leaders, the state provided some insight into the extent of political organization and coordination that existed among high school youth. In presenting its evidence it listed 55 schools that were connected to the SSRC, and named more than 80 students drawn from 22 schools who had been SSRC delegates.[84]

4. *Regional Transformations*. The Soweto uprising erupted in the context of a rapidly changing political order in the southern African region. The withdrawal of Portugal from Angola and Mozambique, after years of armed insurgency by African

nationalist movements; the retreat of the South African military from Angola in the face of attack by African and Cuban troops; the intensifying guerrilla struggle against white minority rule in Rhodesia, accompanied by increasing international support for the African insurgents—these events had a galvanizing and radicalizing impact on the politically conscious strata of South Africa's black population. Developments in the region revealed that white rule was not invincible, and created among South Africa's black youth an atmosphere of hope and expectation regarding the prospects for their own liberation from the deprivations associated with white supremacy. The manner in which these developments took place, moreover, validated the efficacy of militant collective action. "Parents now find themselves in the process of being brushed aside by the far more militant younger generation," Helen Suzman told the Cillie Commission. "The days of patient submission are over for them. . . . The occurrences beyond our borders in Mozambique and Angola and Rhodesia have not escaped their notice."[85]

It is impossible to measure the precise extent to which regional events had a radicalizing effect on South Africa's black youth. But there exists ample evidence that the younger generation was aware of what was happening in the region, and that young people drew from these events a radical lesson regarding what had to be done to alter their own situation. The collapse of Portuguese colonialism in Mozambique and the imminent introduction there of majority rule, led the BPC and SASO to call for "Viva Frelimo" rallies to be held nationwide.[86] Twelve hundred students attended one such rally at the "Bantustan university" at Turfloop in the northern Transvaal, in defiance of government efforts to ban the meeting and despite the presence of eighty-two policemen equipped with guns, tear gas, and police dogs.[87] A poster, plastered on the walls of university buildings announcing the Viva Frelimo rally, dramatically demonstrates the relevance to their own situation that black students saw in the transformations occurring outside their country.

> Frelimo fought and regained our soil, our dignity. It is a story. Change the name and the story applies to you. The dignity of the Black Man has been restored in Mozambique and so shall it be here. Black must rule. We shall drive them to the sea. Long live Azania. Revolution!! Machel will help! Away with Vorster Ban! We are for Afro black Power!!! Viva Frelimo. Power!!! We shall overcome.[88]

A year and a half later, a placard with essentially the same message, although focused on Angola and expressed more tersely, was displayed at the fateful student demonstration in Soweto on June 16, 1976: "*It happened in Angola. Why not here??*"[89]

The manner in which regional transformations had altered South Africa's domestic political situation, especially with respect to the black population, was not lost on the South African government. Its official report on what it termed "the riots at Soweto and elsewhere" concluded, in part: "The political and military events in Southern Africa . . . helped to create a state of mind in which rebelliousness could easily be stirred up."[90]

Situational Conditions
On the surface the early 1970s were characterized by increasing apartheid control and continuing political passivity on the part of South Africa's black population.

But on a deeper level, developments were occurring that would provide the ideological orientation and organizational capability necessary for a mass uprising against the apartheid state. A new generation had come of age, and was now available for recruitment and commitment to a struggle for liberation. Black Consciousness provided an ideological orientation for this generation—keeping alive and amplifying ideas about oppression and the inherent human right to liberation, providing an intellectual and psychological basis for solidarity among the dispossessed, and focusing on the common enemy. The political upheavals in neighboring states served to reinforce and extend the Black Consciousness message—exposing the vulnerability of white minority rule, demonstrating that it was not invincible, and providing a lesson in the efficacy of militant and armed collective action. Black Consciousness also spawned new forms of organization, as did the alterations in government education policy. Organizations such as the Black People's Convention, South African Students Organization, and student councils in the high schools, provided forums for the emergence of new political and community leaders and for the development of their skills in planning, communication, and coordination. They also provided a training experience in surviving and operating in the highly repressive environment of the apartheid state. As these ideological and organizational conditions were germinating, the material situation of South Africa's black urban population, always harsh, and for most offering little more than biological subsistence, had begun to deteriorate even further.

As we have already discussed in some detail, the first half of the 1970s was a period of sluggish economic performance, with various aspects of apartheid acting as a drag on an increasingly mature industrial economy. In 1975 and 1976 sluggishness was transformed into recession; in per capita terms the economy's output could be said to have actually shrunk,[91] resulting in diminished employment opportunities for the black population. The rapid expansion in the labor force that had characterized the South African economy in the 1960s began to slow in the 1970s, and in 1975 and 1976 the decrease in available new jobs was dramatic. In certain sectors large numbers of Africans were laid off. In construction, for example, 60,000 semi- and unskilled African workers lost their jobs in the first three quarters of 1976.[92] The overall level of unemployment among urban black workers is difficult to determine since under apartheid the unemployed are supposed to leave the urban townships and "return" to the homelands. Consequently, official statistics are unlikely to report unemployment among the black population in the urban areas. It is thus interesting that these statistics reveal a growth in unemployment and underemployment in the homelands of 252 percent between 1972–73 and 1975–76 (from 329,000 to over 1 million persons unemployed).[93] The willingness of huge numbers of black workers to join political stayaways in the summer of 1976 may be understood, in part, as a reflection of the increasingly precarious position into which the economic recession had cast the black working class.

At the same time that economic recession threatened black jobs, the South African economy was hit with unusually high rates of inflation. While the consumer price index increased less than 4 percent per annum during most of the 1960s, the rate of increase for the period 1969 to 1976 averaged 9.1 percent. The increases in the cost-of-living index for the last three years of this period were 12 percent, 14 percent, and 11 percent respectively.[94] The cost of food and transportation, two of the most significant items in urban black expenditure, led the inflationary push.[95] One study estimates that the cost of essential commodities for African urban families rose by 40 percent between 1971 and 1973.[96]

A third element in the deteriorating situation of the urban black population was a massive shortage in available housing. This housing crisis was a direct consequence of apartheid policies that were adopted at the end of the 1960s, replacing principles spelled out in 1922 by the Stallard Commission.[97] After World War I, permanent residence in the towns was declared the exclusive right of whites. Black city-dwellers were considered temporary residents and were accommodated in state-built houses that they could rent for the period of their stay. Verwoerdian apartheid doctrine added to the Stallard principles the notion that the size of the "temporary" black urban population should be frozen, or even reduced. Black housing, under this apartheid vision, was to be provided in the so-called homelands, not in the "white" urban areas. In 1968, official housing policies were adopted so as to give practical effect to these apartheid ideas. The government's Riekert Commission, reflecting on this new development, wrote: "The official [housing] policy from 1968 was, in regard to Black workers in White areas, to provide family housing in the Black states [homelands] as far as possible rather than in the Black residential areas surrounding the White cities and towns where they worked."[98] This change in policy is very clearly reflected in the allocation of funds and in related housing construction. After 1968 both declined steadily in the "white" urban areas, as official policy emphasized residential development within homeland jurisdictions.[99] Between 1972 and 1975 the government spent R138 million for housing in the homelands, compared to only R27 million in the urban areas of the republic.[100] The impact of this expenditure pattern on housing for the urban black population can be gleaned from Table 2.3, which lists new housing built in Soweto between 1970 and 1975. The city of Pretoria represents an even more dramatic case of the policy of "freezing" family housing in urban areas. Between 1967 and 1976, not a single house for an African family was constructed.[101] In the entire republic, only 9,808 family houses were built for Africans during 1975. In comparison, in 1957–58 in Johannesburg alone, 11,704 such houses were constructed.[102] At the time that the government was cutting back on the provision of new accommodations for Africans in the cities, many older townships deemed to be located "too close" to white residential areas were being demolished, reducing the existing housing stock available to Africans.[103]

The period during which Pretoria implemented its policy of freezing urban African accommodation was also a period of rapid urbanization. Testimony before the Cillie Commission investigating the Soweto uprising indicated that in ten major

TABLE 2.3. New Houses in Soweto,
1970–75

1970	1971	1972	1973/1974	1975
3,703	1.089	954	—	575

Source: South African Institute of Race Relations, General Survey 1975, (Johannesburg, 1976) p. 84.

urban areas the total African population had doubled between 1971 and 1975 while new housing stock had increased by only 15 percent.[104] The result was a housing crisis of mammoth proportions. The Riekert Commission estimated that at the time of the Soweto uprising there existed a housing backlog of some 141,000 units. This conservative estimate was an amount equal to over 30 percent of existing housing units for Africans. At the same time, there existed an estimated shortage of 126,000 beds in workers' hostels, an amount equal to 40 percent of existing hostel accommodation.[105] Because of the shortage of housing, many individuals and families became lodgers with housed families, creating problems of overcrowding.[106] In Soweto the average number of people living in the standard small four-room house had by 1976 reached fourteen.[107] Those new urban arrivals who were unable to find lodging in one of the already crowded family houses or single-sex dormitories, erected makeshift squatter dwellings, or they slept in the streets. Thus to the problem of overcrowding were added squatting and homelessness. In sum, in the first half of the 1970s government efforts to implement the social-engineering goals of apartheid had created a gigantic housing crisis in the African townships and had produced a consequent deterioration in the living conditions of urban Africans.

Not only was housing scarce and the living situation worsening, but in the early 1970s urban Africans found themselves forced to pay more for the inadequate housing that was available. This change, too, was a consequence of government efforts to bring apartheid practice into line with apartheid doctrine. During the first twenty years of apartheid, African urban townships were administered by the white municipal authorities in whose jurisdictions the townships were located. This was the same arrangement that pertained prior to the apartheid era. By the late 1960s, disquiet within the National Party about the increasing size of the urban African population led to criticism of municipal authorities, who were alleged to be undermining apartheid by the laxness with which they enforced influx-control regulations.[108] In order to make influx control more effective the government, in 1971, removed administrative authority of the townships from the local municipal authorities, and created twenty-two regional Black Affairs Administration Boards. Directly responsible to the central government executive, administration boards were vested with responsibility for the administration and control of all affairs (with the exception of education) in the black townships.[109] So as not to represent a new burden on the state treasury, the administration boards were expected to be financially self-supporting, utilizing revenues extracted from the township inhabitants themselves.

The boards had the same sources of finance for running the townships as had the municipalities—a monopoly on sorghum beer production and sale, a monopoly on the retailing of liquor in the townships, services levies on white employers of black labor, and rent payments by black residents of the townships. Rent charges include two components, the major one being the service charge paid by residents to the board for things such as water, refuse collection, welfare, recreation, and road maintenance. The smaller component of "rent" covers interest on and redemption of loans incurred by the government for house construction, fire insurance, and the costs of house maintenance.[110] Immediately prior to the introduction of the administration boards, a senior government official characterized these revenue sources as "sufficient for Administration Boards to perform their duties adequately without recourse to the state for additional assistance."[111]

The financial effects of ending municipal control over the townships proved to be far more consequential than the government had anticipated. What had not been foreseen was that the municipalities had been subsidizing the administration of the townships both directly, by transferring funds from accounts not supported by township extractions,* and indirectly, by charging fees pegged at below-market value for services such as water, refuse removal, road repair, and the like.† When municipal authority over the townships was ended and responsibility passed onto the administration boards, municipal governments ended their direct subsidies and began to charge the boards market prices for the services they continued to supply to the townships. This meant that the boards needed to generate major new revenues in order to cover their operating expenses. Although the situation achieved crisis proportions by the late 1970s, the problem was evident at the very inception of the boards.[112]

Unable to draw on either the state treasury or the resources of the white municipalities, the administration boards increased township rents and service charges. The West Rand Administration Board, whose jurisdiction included Soweto, raised rents 25 percent within a year of its creation. A year later it again faced a deficit (of R3.4 million) and introduced a second round of rent increases. Many of the other boards followed a similar approach. The Central Transvaal Board, with responsibility for Pretoria's townships, imposed a 50 percent rent increase in 1975 in order to cover a deficit of R3 million. In January 1976, the Cape Peninsula and East Rand boards introduced rent increases of up to 100 percent.[113]

Thus, at the very moment when recession and inflation were threatening living standards, and when state policy had precipitated a housing crisis, the government's efforts to tighten the influx-control system had the unforeseen consequence of putting further pressure on urban African living standards by increasing the cost of housing. The political implications of this situation were magnified by the fact that the deterioration in material conditions followed almost a decade of steady increases in black working-class incomes.[114] Both relative deprivation theory and empirical research on revolution indicate that this sort of situation, in which standards of living worsen after a period of improvement, creates the ideal conditions for mass rebellion. In mid-1976, then, South Africa's black townships were primed for a renewal of militant mass resistance to the apartheid regime. Figure 2.2 represents, in schematic form, the interaction of elements that produced the urban uprising of June through December 1976. The ideological and organizational requisites for mass political opposition germinated in the first half of the decade, and combined within an urban socioeconomic milieu that, after 1973, grew increasingly harsh and

*For Soweto the subsidy from the Johannesburg City Council was R2 million per annum. In Port Elizabeth the direct subsidy was usually not less than a quarter of a million Rand. See, Tom Lodge, *Black Politics in South Africa Since 1945* (London: Longman, 1983), p. 330; and Simon Bekker and Richard Humphries, *From Control to Confusion* (Pietermaritzburg: Shuter & Shooter, 1985), p. 145.

†There are reports of municipalities subsidizing as much as 90 percent of the actual cost of services provided to the townships. In one case only a nominal amount of R600 per year was debited for sanitary services the actual cost of which amounted to R6,000 per year. See Bekker and Humphries, p. 144.

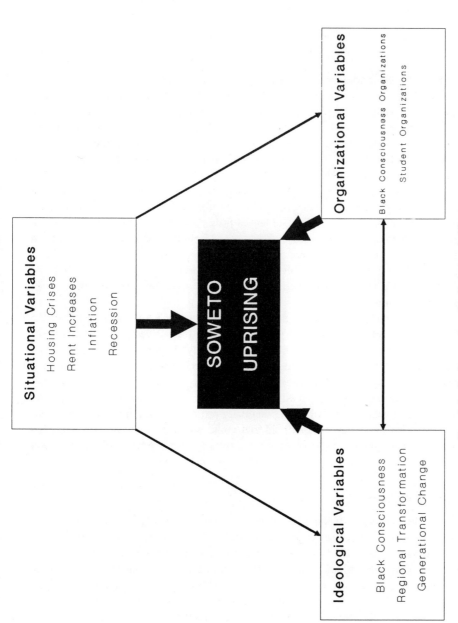

FIG. 2.2. Background to the Soweto rebellion

precarious. When on June 16 police fired on Soweto schoolchildren demonstrating against Afrikaans language instruction, a spark was struck that ignited this volatile mixture.

Rebellion Against the State

Although the Soweto uprising represented a significant advance in black opposition to white rule—it broke through the political passivity that had reigned since Sharpeville and it was the most sustained episode of militant mass resistance in South Africa's modern history—it also starkly revealed the limits of that opposition in the mid-1970s. The mass movement that sprang into existence after June 16 lacked clearly articulated goals in respect to overthrowing the apartheid system, and its organization and leadership was rudimentary and inchoate at best. Due to the essentially spontaneous form of the rebellion, no clear program, strategy, or central insurrectionary organization emerged. At the same time the ferocious attack on all manifestations of the apartheid state leaves little doubt that the politically engaged urban youth sought to remove the state presence from the townships. Soweto was a rebellion *against* established authority, rather than an insurrection, which seeks to *replace* established authority with an alternative form of governance. It would be another eight years before the latter form of mass opposition would make its appearance in South Africa.

The immediate threat of the Soweto uprising in respect to the survival of the existing white-ruled state was not great. The state's repressive capability was never fully taxed, its security forces were not significantly challenged, and the financial cost of property lost and damaged, although substantial, was not vital to either the survival of the state or the well-being of South Africa's white minority. Nevertheless, the rebellion and its repressive aftermath introduced new dynamics into the South African situation. These had potentially profound medium-to-long-term consequences for the future of apartheid and white minority rule; consequences that involved the ideological cohesiveness of the ruling group, the future of domestic and regional security, and the possibilities for economic growth.

Ideological Cohesion

One of the hallmarks of the Afrikaner community in the 1960s, and especially of its political and intellectual elite, was its ideological cohesion and self-confidence. The ideology of apartheid, to which the Afrikaner adhered with such fervor, rested on twin normative pillars. One was the notion that the maintenance of "group identity," the goal toward which Afrikaner nationalism was single-mindedly directed, could be achieved only under conditions of social and cultural separation. The other was the belief that apartheid was a superior social arrangement for avoiding conflict in a racially and ethnically heterogeneous society. Whereas social integration, what National Party thinkers termed "forced integrationism," produced intergroup friction, separation was a means, perhaps the only means, to intergroup peace.

As political power and socioeconomic advance transformed the Afrikaner community, its orientation became increasingly secular and secure; the obsession with threats to ethnic group identity that had characterized the 1930s and 1940s was gradually eroded.[115] Consequently, by the early 1970s apartheid's alleged contribution to social and political harmony had emerged as the primary moral basis for the apartheid order. The outbursts of ethnic conflict in independent sub-Saharan Africa, Europe, and the United States in the late 1960s reinforced the Afrikaner intellectuals in their view of the correct way to order social relations. In particular, the racial rioting that convulsed most large cities in the United States during 1967 and 1968 was taken as a comparative indication of apartheid's superiority over "forced integrationism." In contrast to the *disintegration* that America was experiencing, the designers of apartheid, and white South Africans in general, could note that their country was experiencing over a decade of political peace.

The Soweto uprising, which took the Afrikaner elite by surprise, demolished the remaining normative underpinning of apartheid ideology. Given the ferocity of the attack on the manifestations of white supremacy, the depth and breadth of sympathy for the rebellion within the black community, and the sustained nature of the revolt, the claim of apartheid's superiority as a moral and practical basis for social harmony simply disintegrated. The Afrikaner governing elite and its followers thus lost the ideological foundation for their self-confidence and along with it the sense that they had a correct and superior guide to ordering political and social relations. A comment appearing in an Afrikaans-language newspaper in January 1977 illustrates the ideological trauma and confusion that Soweto produced in the ruling group:

> It is in times like these that a nation needs a vision, such as the one we had when we seized upon the idea of separate freedoms. Then, too, we were aware of the dark times that lay ahead, but somewhere in the tunnel we saw a glimmer of light and we made our way in that direction. Now we find ourselves once more in such a tunnel.[116]

The ideological dislocation within Afrikanerdom was such that leading figures came to view apartheid as a cause of South Africa's intergroup conflict rather than a solution for it. The most dramatic evidence for this can be found in the Cillie Commission report on the Soweto disturbances. In July 1976 the government appointed Supreme Court Justice Petrus Malan Cillie to undertake an inquiry into "the riots at Soweto and other Places . . . and the causes which gave rise thereto."[117] Advised by P. N. Hansmeyer, a senior officer of the Department of Bantu Administration, Justice Cillie traveled throughout South Africa in pursuing his inquiry, taking testimony from 563 witnesses.[118] The commission's activities, the testimony before it as well as its report, were given extensive coverage in the South African media. Although the commission adhered to the "official" theme that the Soweto "rioting" was the work of "outside agitators" and could be traced to Moscow, there is in the commission's report a second and contradictory theme: in seeking an explanation for the Soweto disturbances, primary emphasis is placed on a variety of apartheid's central features, which, the report suggests, created the social and attitudinal conditions that produced the uprising. Below are presented some of the findings and conclusions of the Cillie Commission as these pertain to aspects of apartheid:

INFLUX CONTROL

. . . influx control and related matters were . . . contributory factors [in the rioting]. There can surely not be many residents who have never come into conflict with these provisions or the persons who apply them, or who have never discussed these matters which, without doubt, caused dissatisfaction among them. An attitude of mind has been created that could make many of them resort to rioting.[119]

ADMINISTRATION BOARDS

There was so much dissatisfaction with administration boards that many black residents were worked up to the point where they could easily resort to rioting.[120]

DISCRIMINATION

Discrimination . . . has engendered not only dissatisfaction but also a great hatred in many. This dissatisfaction and hatred were some of the main factors that created the milieu and the spirit of revolt.[121]

ECONOMIC HARDSHIP AND DISCRIMINATION

Since salaries are such an important factor in one's existence, and these facts concerning low and differentiated salaries are so well known, they were undoubtedly a factor that engendered discontent. . . . [T]his was a contributory factor in the rioting.[122]

[T]he inadequacy of housing facilities and the attendant discomforts had contributed to a certain extent to the state of frustration, discontent, and rebelliousness . . . which could so easily lead to revolt and rioting.[123]

That a government-appointed commission, especially one closely advised by the Department of Bantu Administration, could present apartheid as part of the South African problem rather than the solution, and that this was deemed acceptable by officialdom, is a dramatic indicator of the extent to which Soweto helped force a disintegration of the ideological unity and coherence that had characterized the apartheid state during the first two-and-a-half decades of National Party rule.

A Resurgent African National Congress

Although the African National Congress did not initiate or play a significant role in planning or organizing the Soweto uprising, the political environment in South Africa's townships during the second half of 1976 provided the context for a re-emergence of the ANC out of the limbo of exile. By the mid-1980s the process begun in 1976 had led to a situation in which the ANC could justifiably claim more support than any rival political group within black politics,[124] and in which it was widely recognized inside and outside of South Africa that an ANC role was central to any South African future. By temporarily disrupting the state's control over the black townships, the 1976 uprising had the effect of creating political space for the ANC. Through the frequent distribution of political leaflets and pamphlets supporting the rebellion,[125] the ANC was able to emerge from underground and reestablish a public presence within the township communities. The political ferment that characterized these communities, moreover, substantially increased the audience receptive to the ANC's message, transmitted through radio broadcasts from neighboring countries and literature distributed within South Africa. Through these means a new generation of recently politicized and radicalized black South Africans were simultaneously introduced to the liberation organization that had been banned and largely driven out of South Africa sixteen years earlier. In short, the milieu of revolt that characterized the townships in 1976 offered the ANC a receptive environment for fashioning political perceptions and loyalties, and the ANC took advantage of it.

The harsh repression of the Soweto uprising provided a second, if unintended, benefit for the ANC. By the end of 1976 thousands of young people were fleeing the townships and South Africa, crossing the border into Mozambique, Lesotho, Botswana, or Swaziland. Many of them were seeking to continue the struggle for liberation through armed resistance. The ANC, because of its international support and because it had a military wing, Umkhonto we Sizwe, was in an ideological, financial, and organizational position to offer them such an opportunity. Thus the repression of the Soweto uprising had the paradoxical effect of supplying the ANC with a new army of young, committed, and relatively well-educated recruits. The South African police estimate that by 1978 the ANC was providing insurgent training to approximately 4,000 recent refugees.[126]

This development was facilitated and its significance amplified by the regional changes that had occurred during 1975—the independence under radical governments of Mozambique and Angola. The ANC was in a position by 1977 to move its operations closer to South Africa, and in the case of Mozambique, to the eastern border of the republic. Now, the ANC could more easily receive political refugees and infiltrate its military cadre into South Africa. Capacity for providing military training to the flood of new political refugees also increased as newly independent Angola made facilities available to the ANC. These enhanced capabilities are reflected in the increased frequency of Umkhonto sabotage attacks that followed in the wake of Soweto. In the five-month period, November through March 1978, the explosion of a sabotage device occurred on the average of one per week.[127] There were 119 such attacks and explosions between 1977 and 1981.[128] The frequency of sabotage attacks then tripled—averaging 48.5 per year during the period 1981–84, compared to 16 per year for the 1977–80 period.[129] The three years between the Soweto repression and the jump in incidents of sabotage indicates, perhaps, a time-lag during which the new "Soweto exiles" were recruited and trained by the ANC. In any case, the attacks on railway lines, government and other public buildings, power installations, bus and train depots, and the like, which began during the

Soweto uprising and accelerated throughout the 1980s, represented the most significant sabotage campaign in modern South African history.

This intermeshing of domestic rebellion, a politically and militarily resurgent ANC, and the radicalization of the southern African political environment served to heighten the South African government's perception that a new order of threat was emerging. Any one element by itself would have been troubling, but the existence and interaction of all three suggested to Pretoria that its strategic situation had been fundamentally altered and that a major state response was required.

International Reverberations

While the direct threat to the apartheid state posed by Soweto was not particularly grave, the rebellion and the repression with which it was met produced international reactions that posed ominous short- and long-term problems for the apartheid regime. The harsh treatment meted out by the state in order to reestablish "law and order"—including not only the police repression of township "unrest" but also the banning of Black Consciousness organizations in 1977, the detention of prominent black citizens, and the death in police custody of Steve Biko, founder and leader of the Black Consciousness movement—were communicated to the world community via the print and electronic media. The reactions of foreign governments and private organizations to events in South Africa created a fundamental restructuring of South Africa's international situation. This changed global environment and the problems it posed for the maintenance of the South African sociopolitical order constitutes the fourth crack in the apartheid monolith that developed in the mid-1970s.

The Post-Soweto International Environment

The Soweto uprising, and its brutal suppression, galvanized the attention of the international public, and emphasized anew the pariah status that South Africa's domestic arrangements conferred upon it within the international community. It revived the whole issue of the international acceptability of racial rule, something that Prime Minister Verwoerd had sought to lay to rest through the policy of separate development, and it subjected South Africa to the type of worldwide pressure that Verwoerd's program was designed to avoid. Moreover, it did so at a moment when Pretoria was becomingly increasingly vulnerable both domestically and internationally. Her regional environment had just turned intensely hostile, and threatened to become even more so, as the military fortunes of the insurgents in neighboring Rhodesia improved. Her defense force was in direct confrontation with an expeditionary Cuban army, backed by the Soviet Union. In order to pay for the enhanced military security dictated by an altered regional political environment, Pretoria needed economic growth, and that required ready access to foreign capital and technology, as well as to global markets for South African–produced goods.

The international repercussions that followed Soweto struck directly at Pretoria's strategic and economic vulnerabilities. Since the mid-1960s the South African government had worked carefully, and with considerable success, to create a cooperative diplomatic and strategic relationship between itself and the Western powers—in particular the United States. Soweto and its repressive aftermath sharply reversed this process, producing the greatest diplomatic estrangement of South Africa from the West in that country's modern history. This was most clearly manifest at the United Nations. Within three days of the start of the Soweto uprising, the Security Council passed a resolution "strongly condemning the South African Government for its resort to massive violence against and killing of the African people," and calling on the government to "eliminate apartheid."[130] More significantly, in November 1977 the Security Council unanimously adopted a *mandatory* arms embargo against the Republic of South Africa. African members of the UN had campaigned for such an action since 1961, but because of the objection of the Western powers the best they could obtain was a resolution calling upon member states to voluntarily refrain from selling arms to the apartheid state. Now, in the aftermath of Soweto, the Security Council, with the approval of the key Western members, required all States to "cease forthwith any provision to South Africa of arms and related material of all types. . . ." and "all types of equipment and supplies and grants of licensing arrangements for the manufacture or maintenance" of military equipment.[131] In the United States, the Carter administration went beyond the UN-mandated arms embargo by barring the export or re-export of any US-origin products and technical data to the South African military or police forces.[132] Concretely, the multilateral and bilateral actions taken against Pretoria meant that South Africa would find it increasingly difficult to purchase sophisticated military equipment and so-called "gray-area" technology—i.e., civilian equipment with a potential military use, such as certain computers, light aircraft, and helicopters.

Perhaps more significant than the strategic costs of the global isolation that followed Soweto was its psychological impact. For Pretoria, and white South Africans in general, the events of 1977 called into question the validity of their sense of identity as an "outpost" of the West, and created a sense of extreme exposure. First, there was the involvement of large numbers of Cuban combat troops in Angola and later (in 1978) in the Ethiopian/Somali war over the Ogaden region. This raised the specter, in Pretoria, of future intervention by Communist powers in support of attacks on South Africa by neighboring African states or by domestic revolutionaries. Second, there was the belief in South African policy circles that Washington had abandoned Pretoria in Angola, and in so doing reneged on an agreement to jointly oppose Soviet expansion. In addition to these events, the U.S. reaction to Soweto, projected in statements by top officials in the new Carter administration—including the president, vice president, secretary of state, and UN ambassador—strongly indicated to the South Africans that they could no longer count on the world's most powerful anti-Soviet nation, even in the event of a direct communist assault.*

*The Carter administration's policy toward South Africa was not entirely consistent with the condemnatory statements that characterized its first months in office. Concrete policy in respect to pressure on the apartheid regime never matched public rhetoric. Indeed, members of the administration, especially Andrew Young, maintained that economic growth would facilitate sociopolitical change, and thus Carter

Especially disturbing to the South African government was a statement by Vice President Walter Mondale calling for a political system in South Africa based upon "one man, one vote." The idea that the introduction of a system of majority rule was being made a required condition for good relations with the United States was greeted in Pretoria, and in the South African white community generally, with a mixture of shock, resentment, and protest. The manner in which Pretoria perceived its altered global environment and the implications it drew for the future can be gleaned from comments by South African Prime Minister John Vorster, made in August 1977 in an address to his Ministry of Foreign Affairs:

> The US Government is now set on a course, [which] can lead only to one thing as I see it—namely, to chaos and anarchy in Southern Africa. In other words, if they persist with this pressure, the end result for Southern Africa will be exactly the same as if it were subverted by the Marxists. In the one case it will come about as a result of brute force; in the other case it will be strangulation with finesse.
>
> I say to the free world: Do not make it impossible for South Africa to play its role in the free world. I would put the question: If, as a result of your actions, South Africa is destroyed, what will come in its place? . . . On behalf of my country and my people, I say to the free world: Why make an enemy of the one country in Africa which can be relied on if the crisis eventually comes?[133]

The strategic problems that followed upon Pretoria's post-Soweto diplomatic debacle should not be exaggerated. There was no immediate and dire threat to the security of the state. For one thing, at the time that the 1977 international arms embargo was imposed, ARMSCOR, South Africa's state-owned armaments industry, was already meeting about three-quarters of the country's weapons needs.[134] For another, the countries to the north of South Africa may have been hostile toward the apartheid state, but they lacked the military capability to launch a sizable attack, as did the revolutionary organizations inside South Africa. Nevertheless, international isolation and the willingness of the Western powers to cooperate in a global arms embargo threatened Pretoria's medium- to long-term future.

Although ARMSCOR had managed to achieve an impressive record of arms self-sufficiency, it was unable to produce the types of weapons systems (jet fighters, naval craft, guided missile systems) required by the strategic demands of the changed southern African political environment. The manufacture of these high-technology systems requires a very large outlay of resources for investment and for the development of engineering knowledge. Without access to external sources of capital and technology, an economy the size of South Africa's could undertake such an investment burden only with great difficulty. The economic strain of producing

---

generally opposed the imposition of economic sanctions and even sought to encourage additional U.S. investment in South Africa. By the second half of the administration's term in office, it sought to enlist Pretoria's assistance in ending minority rule in Rhodesia and consequently relaxed its public stance against the apartheid regime. Nevertheless, the early statements by senior officials and the policy of limiting sales of high-technology goods set a general tone of hostility between Washington and Pretoria that lasted throughout Carter's presidency.

advanced weapons systems with internally generated resources was amplified in the South Africa of the late 1970s by a half decade of economic stagnation.*

The lack of self-sufficiency in high-tech weapons production was not an immediate threat to Pretoria, since South Africa's radical neighboring states had very limited military capability in 1977. But it could hardly look with equanimity to a long-term future in which it stood alone against increasingly capable African countries that were closely supported by the military might of the Soviet Union.

Once again the simultaneity of the challenges experienced by the apartheid regime is significant. International isolation would not have been nearly as serious a problem had it not coincided with a fundamentally altered and more threatening regional environment. Likewise the changes in regional political orientation would not have been nearly as threatening without the dark clouds of uncertainty created by the global reactions to Soweto.

While the strategic implications of the international reaction to the Soweto uprising were not expected to affect South Africa until some time in the medium-term future, the economic reverberations were felt almost immediately. Like the impact in the strategic sphere, these were not of such magnitude as to threaten the collapse of the existing politico-economic system, but they involved significant short- and long-term constraints on the growth of the South African industrial economy. These repercussions can be classified in three categories: constraints on access to foreign capital and technology; constraints on foreign trade; and "directed investment."

Constraints on Access to Foreign Capital and Technology

From about 1961 to 1976, foreign-owned multinational corporations had invested heavily in the South African economy, and their capital and technology played a central role in the modernization and maturation of the South African industrial system. Following Soweto, the flow of direct foreign investment, which had amounted to over $6 billion between 1974 and 1976, slowed to a trickle.[135] The capital flow via long-term lending from the international banking system also dried up. In 1977, South Africa was able to raise only $33.2 million on the international bond and Eurocurrency markets, an amount equal to just 3 percent of the 1976 total.[136]

Several factors combined to produce this reversal of fortunes in respect to access to foreign capital markets. The Soweto unrest—the violence, political strikes, boycotts, detentions, and deaths—undermined South Africa's investment climate, raising fears about work-force volatility and doubts about long-term political stability. In other words, Soweto raised danger signals in respect to future business prospects, and this was reflected in the risk assessments that international firms use in the selection of investment sites. On one "risk index" used by businesses in the

---

*Already by mid-1977, Pretoria was fending off internal complaints that too much money was being spent on defense—to which Prime Minister Vorster responded: "That is precisely what the communists want and all those who seek our downfall." See, *Africa Confidential*, vol. 28, no. 11 (May 1987), p. 3.

United States, South Africa was moved from the "acceptable risk" category to the "moderate risk" category in 1977. Projecting future trends, the index predicted that by 1980 South Africa would be categorized as a "prohibitive risk"[137] In early 1978, the chairman of Manufacturers Hanover Corporation, explaining his bank's reluctance to undertake new loans to South Africa, explained that "apartheid was having a direct and growing negative impact on the risks involved in making loans to South Africa."[138]

Probably more important than the "risk assessment factor" in affecting corporate investment behavior were the campaigns launched by dissident stockholders in Europe and, especially, in the United States. News of events in South Africa stimulated an anti-apartheid movement on both sides of the Atlantic. This movement sought to get churches and universities, with their large blocs of stock, to pressure international businesses into cutting back their investments in and loans to the Republic of South Africa. Thus in 1977, five major U.S. companies—Texaco, Standard Oil of California, Goodyear, General Electric, and Ford—faced shareholder resolutions filed by church groups calling for a termination of South African operations. Another four—Mobil, Newmont, Phelps-Dodge, and General Motors—faced resolutions opposing any expansion of operations. At the same time fifteen churches with stock in five major U.S. banks—Citibank, Manufacturers Hanover Trust, Morgan Guaranty Trust, Continental Illinois, and First Chicago—filed resolutions asking for a policy prohibiting loans to the South African government.[139] In Great Britain, the Midland Bank was subject to a similar resolution, sponsored by church shareholders and the Greater London Council.[140] In no instance were the anti-apartheid shareholders able to muster sufficient votes to pass their resolutions, but they had an impact on corporate policy nevertheless. They forced corporate staffs to spend time and money mobilizing proxies against the "dissident" resolutions; they staged protests at meetings of the boards of directors, disrupting normal business agendas; and their campaigns drew unfavorable and unwanted publicity to corporations with ties to South Africa. The result was that the anti-apartheid movement in the United States and Europe created a "hassle factor" that increased the opportunity costs of corporate investment in South Africa.

Governments also played a role in reducing South Africa's access to capital and technology. "At some point we've got to come to the conclusion we no longer are going to finance apartheid," stated U.S. Ambassador to the United Nations Andrew Young in 1977.[141] A few months later, in January 1978, a Senate committee recommended that "U.S. policy should be changed to actively discourage American foreign investment in South Africa." Specifically, the committee recommended that the United States "withdraw facilities of the U.S. Government which promote the flow of capital or credit to South Africa," and "deny tax credits to those U.S. corporations paying taxes to the South African Government."[142] Even without the actual implementation of restrictive policies, the hints of future restrictions and prohibitions, combined with public and private pronouncements by senior officials, added to an atmosphere in which doing business in South Africa was fraught with uncertainties. A Nigerian government action, withdrawing all of its deposits from Barclays Bank and expelling one-third of the expatriates in Barclays' Nigerian subsidiary, in retaliation for the purchase of $14 million in South African defense bonds by Barclays Bank of London, served to underscore the risks of post-Soweto involvement in South Africa.[143]

In sum, the multinational corporations, either because they had doubts about the stability of the republic, or because they were under pressure from their share-holders or their home governments, or for a combination of these reasons, no longer considered South Africa a particularly attractive place for investment purposes. Some of the largest multinational firms, in an effort to counter the negative publicity that their South African operations had engendered, publicly announced that they would not expand their South African holdings, and explicitly linked this decision to the country's domestic political and social arrangements.* The General Motors Corporation issued a statement that read in part:

> The corporation has no present need for, and has no intention of, further expanding its productive capacity in South Africa. The single most important factor in the creation of a more promising investment climate in South Africa is a positive resolution of the country's pressing social problems, which have their origin in the apartheid system.[144]

The international banking system, whose loans were an alternative source of capital to direct investment by multinational corporations, acted similarly. Major banks in the United States, Great Britain, and the Netherlands adopted policies that either ended new lending to South Africa altogether, or limited the types of situations in which loans could be made.[145] David Rockefeller, head of Chase Manhattan, the U.S. bank with the largest South African loan portfolio, announced that Chase was ending "loans that in our judgment tend to support the apartheid policies of the South African government."[146] South Africa's rapidly deteriorating situation in respect to international capital markets was underscored by the managing director of Barclay Bank's South African subsidiary. Returning to Johannesburg from London, where he had failed to raise two small loans, he explained: "Most British and some American banks were of the opinion that their exposure to South Africa at the present time was as far as they were prepared to go, bearing in mind the recent disturbances [in] our black townships."[147]

By 1978, South Africa had been cut off from new long-term loans and was forced to pay premium interest rates for the short-term lending it was able to arrange. The gravity of the situation was revealed by the government's proposed budget for 1977–78. The budget projected no new foreign loans to the South African government and imposed a 15 percent surcharge on all imports.[148] Unable to cover the foreign exchange costs of its import bill with infusions of capital from abroad, the government sought to alleviate its balance-of-payment problem by cutting back on imports. In his budget message to parliament, Finance Minister Owen Horwood acknowledged that a decline in the level of foreign bank loans had been caused by the domestic political situation, which had received "biased and exaggerated reports in overseas news media."[149]

---

*Among the multinational corporations to make such statements were General Motors, Ford, Eastman Kodak, and Gulf and Western. See Tom Wicker, "Should American Business Pull Out of South Africa?" *New York Times Magazine,* June 3, 1979, p. 31.

Not only was the flow of new capital into South Africa woefully inadequate, but in the aftermath of Soweto foreign firms began to repatriate an unusually large proportion of their local earnings. Traditionally, foreign firms reinvested about 60 percent of their local profits within South Africa, but during 1976 and 1977, in a pronounced shift, American companies withdrew nearly two-thirds of their earnings from South Africa.[150] The combined effect of increased profit repatriation, constraints on foreign borrowing, and lack of new direct foreign investment, was a dramatic turnabout in South Africa's net capital flow. Within six months of Soweto, the amount of capital leaving the country greatly exceeded that which was coming in. The capital account swung from a net inflow of $660 million in 1976 to a net outflow of $677 million in 1977, and an even more massive outflow of $1,073 million in 1978.[151] Heavily dependent as it is on money from abroad for investment and for the foreign exchange required to import machinery, the overall performance of the South African economy reflected the foreign capital squeeze. From the Soweto uprising until the end of the decade the average annual growth in gross domestic product was only 2.8 percent, a rate barely keeping pace with the increase in population.

Constraints on Foreign Trade

The foreign trade sector loomed large in Pretoria's hopes for an economic resurgence in the 1970s. The export of manufactured goods was viewed as a means of (1) curing a balance-of-payments problem that was becoming chronic; and (2) resolving the contradiction between the apartheid-created small domestic market and the prospects for continued economic growth. Since the late 1950s, when the Viljoen Commission had proposed export promotion as a way to service a market large enough to sustain the expansion of South Africa's manufacturing sector, foreign markets represented the means to combine economic modernization with apartheid practices. But the international repercussions of Soweto threatened to close off this option. Soweto gave significant new impetus to a long-standing effort by sub-Saharan African countries to have the United Nations launch a campaign of economic sanctions, particularly trade sanctions, against South Africa. Although an immediate embargo on South African products was unlikely, given the opposition of the Western member-states in the Security Council, the willingness of the Western powers in 1977 to approve a resolution barring the sale of arms to South Africa was a pointed indicator to Pretoria that the West's veto of economic sanctions could not be counted on as permanent.

At the same time that international diplomatic activity threatened Pretoria's future trade prospects, short-term commercial credits for trading with South Africa were proving more difficult to obtain. During 1977 the domestic political pressures on private Western banks and on government agencies that provide and/or insure such credit threatened to sharply curtail trade-financing loans.

Perhaps most troubling from Pretoria's vantage point was that South Africa's negative image could make its products a hard sell on the international market. For a manufacturing sector that faced competition not only from established producers in Europe and America, but from low-cost manufacturers in the Far East, the political baggage that was attached to a "made in South Africa" label might well add enough opportunity costs to discourage the importation of South African goods. Why should an importing firm serving a European or American market risk a politically hostile reaction from even a small portion of its potential customers, if the same product is available from a source that carries no equivalent risk? This was the dilemma that apartheid posed to South Africa's manufacturers. Because manufacturing was the country's most dynamic economic sector and the key to its economic future, the constraints imposed by apartheid on the export of manufactured goods also threatened South Africa's long-term economic well-being.

"Directed Investment"

In the world of international business it is customary for subsidiaries of multinational firms to adapt their practices to the laws and customs of the country in which they are located. Accordingly, in the Republic of South Africa foreign companies adhered to apartheid laws and practices in labor matters and in organizing workplace social relations. In the wake of Soweto, however, several efforts were launched that sought to persuade foreign-owned businesses to organize the workplace and treat their employees in a nondiscriminatory manner regardless of what was mandated by South African law or custom.

In early 1977, in reaction to the events of Soweto, Dr. Leon Sullivan, an American, a black Baptist minister, and a member of the General Motors board of directors, initiated an effort to have U.S.-owned companies adhere to a "code of conduct" for their South African operations.[152] In March, twelve American firms released a statement pledging that their future operations would reflect adherence to the six principles of the "Sullivan Code."[153]

1. Nonsegregation of the races in all eating, comfort, locker rooms, and work facilities.
2. Equal and fair employment practices for all employees.
3. Equal pay for all employees doing equal or comparable work for the same period of time.
4. Initiation and development of training programs that will prepare blacks, coloureds, and Asians in substantial numbers for supervisory, administrative, clerical and technical jobs.
5. Increasing the number of blacks, coloureds, and Asians in management and supervisory positions.
6. Improving the quality of employees' lives outside the work environment in such areas as housing, transportation, and schooling, recreating, and health facilities.

Within six months the number of U.S. firms signing the Sullivan Code had increased from the initial twelve to fifty-four.[154] By November 1979 the signatories numbered 135 (out of approximately 300) U.S. firms doing business in South Africa.[155] Shortly after the introduction of the Sullivan Code, the Canadian government followed suit, and the European Economic Community introduced its own code of conduct for companies from EEC member states.[156] Similar to the Sullivan

Code, the EEC effort went further in one very significant respect. It required companies to recognize black trade unions and to engage them in collective bargaining, something that was discouraged by apartheid law and South African government policy.

Opponents of apartheid both inside and outside of South Africa were highly critical of the Sullivan Code, the EEC measure, and similar efforts.[157] They reasoned that by emphasizing workplace apartheid, these stipulations did little to spur fundamental change in the larger system of social and political apartheid. One critic of the Sullivan Code captured the essence of this position by quoting a black South African church leader: "These principles attempt to polish my chains and make them more comfortable. I want to cut my chains and cast them away."[158] Critics of Sullivan's axioms also argued that codes of corporate conduct served as a legitimating "fig leaf" to cover a continued corporate presence in South Africa when what was needed was a withdrawal of foreign companies.

Nonetheless, the South African government was disturbed by the movement toward directed investment. For Pretoria perceived, correctly, that through such schemes multinational corporations, upon whom the South African economy was critically dependent, could be made a conduit for foreign political groups to change social practices within South Africa. The report of the Wiehahn Commission, appointed by Prime Minister John Vorster in 1977 and charged with examining the existing apartheid system of industrial relations, reveals the concern with which officialdom viewed the introduction by foreign organizations of corporate codes of conduct. According to the commission, the codes were a matter of serious concern that called for government action:

> [I]t would be naive to deny the fact or ignore the effect of international attempts to influence labour and other policies in South Africa. The presence of subsidiaries of multinational enterprises . . . creates a conduit through which strong influences and pressure can be exerted on [the] country's policies and practices. . . . [T]he persistent growth of multinational influence, particularly in the field of labour, is bound to lead to a peculiar proliferation in our labour system—alien labour practices of multinational enterprises (developing from the different foreign labour codes of conduct) being pursued alongside local practices. [This] could create extreme stress, . . . a development which is indeed already taking place.[159]

The immediate effects of the Sullivan and EEC codes of conduct were probably of less significance to Pretoria than the principle and precedent that their existence embodied, namely, that foreign entities could define appropriate conduct and require conforming behavior from actors within the territory over which the South African state was supposedly sovereign. For Pretoria, directed investment as represented by codes of corporate conduct raised the disturbing prospect that it might have to choose between violations of apartheid custom and law, on the one hand, or a reduction in the involvement of multinational corporations, with their vital capital and technology, on the other. Thus, in the aftermath of Soweto, the phenomenon of international strategies of directed investment, while not threatening to either dismantle apartheid or bring down the white-ruled state, did increase the risks and raise the potential costs of a continuing commitment to apartheid.

Apartheid: The Crumbling Foundation

In the mid-1970s South Africa was subjected to four nearly simultaneous shocks, each of which was either produced by, or contained implications for, the apartheid system. First, the economy experienced the effects of several structural strains that were a function of apartheid's impact on labor and consumer markets—a lack of sufficient skilled labor, an unstable work force, a small domestic market for consumer manufactures, and a consequent underutilization of installed plant capacity. Second, the state's regional security framework was torn asunder by changes in the political makeup of neighboring territories, as Portuguese colonial authorities were replaced by radical African governments backed by the Soviet Union and its allies. Third, black political opposition within South Africa, dormant since the early 1960s, exploded throughout the urban townships and revealed a willingness to resist the imposition of apartheid "law and order." Fourth, efforts to restore "peace" through forceful means produced an international reaction that isolated South Africa diplomatically and pressured it economically.

Each of these "shocks" can be thought of as producing fissures in the apartheid edifice, much as a building's foundation might develop cracks from the shock waves of an earthquake. Faced individually, these fissures would not have posed a very significant challenge to the South African governing elite, or threatened the viability of the apartheid edifice they had been constructing for three decades. But the central feature of Pretoria's mid-1970s reality was that the apartheid shocks and the fissures that they opened did not impact separately but rather in combination. Moreover, the interaction of events had a synergistic effect—the shocks and their consequences affecting and reinforcing each other. Figure 2.3 offers a schematic representation of this synergistic interaction.

The transformation of the southern African region from a buffer zone of white rule into a frontline of radical anti-apartheid states increased Pretoria's sense of external danger, leading it to drastically increase its military expenditures. The state's ability to comfortably finance these new expenses was rendered problematic, however, by apartheid's threat to economic growth. Economic stagnation induced by apartheid, which, taken in isolation, raised concerns about material well being, became a national security problem as well when combined with regional political transformation. Regional change also had an impact on the apartheid state's internal security, for it provided a psychological stimulus for the reemergence within South Africa of black opposition to white rule. The resultant local turmoil in turn heightened the threat posed by the regional frontline states, for they constituted actual or potential sanctuaries for an ANC revitalized by the Soweto uprising.

The revival of militant black opposition inside South Africa not only dissolved Pretoria's faith that apartheid was a means to lasting domestic peace—it compounded the cost of apartheid's threat to economic expansion. Establishing long-term internal tranquility and at the same time maintaining the racial status-quo meant not just expanded expenditures on the police, but also an improvement in material conditions within the townships and the availability of jobs for urban residents. Only in an expanding economy could these costs of domestic "law and order" be met without sacrificing white living standards and privileges. But the

The Decade of the 70's Four "Shocks" to Apartheid

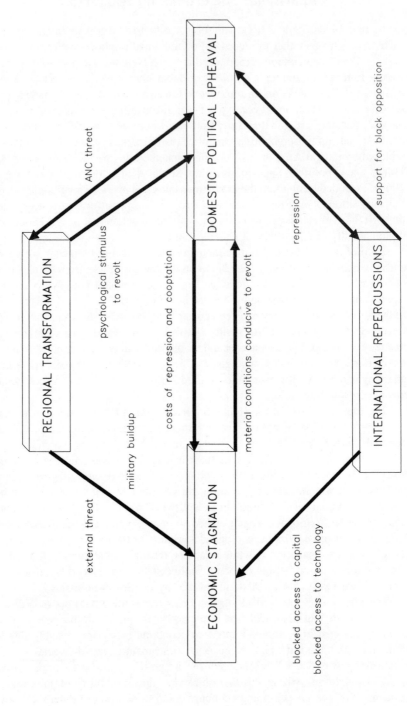

FIG. 2.3. Apartheid's altered environment

internal political upheaval and the state's repressive response to it generated international reverberations that increased the obstacles to economic expansion. Moreover, the international reaction involved the provision of moral and financial support to black political and labor organizations, strengthening them in their ability to resist the apartheid state and thus reinforcing the domestic security "threat," as seen from Pretoria. And resorting to traditional repressive means to protect apartheid would simply intensify the international threat to economic growth.

In physics the concept of resonance involves an amplification in the vibrations of one body when it experiences reinforcing vibrations at the same frequency from another body. This notion of resonance captures the special quality of the situation faced by Pretoria. The four shocks experienced in mid-decade interacted so as to have a "resonance effect," widening the cracks in the apartheid monolith. The situation facing the leaders of the National Party in the late 1970s was this: apartheid had been introduced by them in large measure to ensure the maintenance of white supremacy in the historical circumstances that pertained at the close of World War II. By the end of the 1970s circumstances changed dramatically; apartheid, which had been a means to maintain white supremacy, had come to represent a threat to it. Faced with the combined and interactive effect of the four "apartheid shocks" of mid-decade, apartheid came to appear more like the problem than the solution. It is in this context that we can comprehend P. W. Botha's political transformation from a chief implementer of apartheid into the Afrikaner leader who would tell white South Africans that apartheid was a recipe for revolution and disaster and that they must "adapt or die."

Notes

1. See P. W. Botha, speech to the Natal Congress of the National Party, *South African Digest,* August 24, 1979, p. 1.

2. See report of speech by Minister of Cooperation and Development Piet Koornhof, in *Africa Index,* vol. 2, no. 12, June 16–30, 1979, p. 44.

3. D. Hobart Houghton, *The South African Economy* (Cape Town: Oxford University Press, 1973), p. 133.

4. See S. P. Cilliers and C. J. Groenwald, "Urban Growth in South Africa 1936–2000" (University of Stellenbosch, Department of Sociology, Occasional Paper No. 5, July 1982), calculated from Tables 1 and 4 of statistical appendix.

5. Ibid., Table 7, statistical appendix.

6. South Africa, *The Commission of Inquiry into Labour Legislation* (Wiehahn Commission Report) (Johannesburg: Lex Patria Publishers, 1982), p. 1; see also, South Africa, *Report of the Commission of Inquiry into Legislation Affecting the Utilization of Manpower* (Riekert Commission Report) (Pretoria: Government Printer, 1979), pp. 27 and 245.

7. *Verwoerd Speaks,* edited by A. N. Pelzer (Johannesburg: APB Publishers, 1966), p. 67.

8. Ibid., p. 74.

9. Ibid., pp. 83–84.

10. See David Welch, "The Growth of Towns," in Monica Wilson and Leonard Thompson, eds., *Oxford History of South Africa,* vol. 2 (London: Oxford University Press, 1975), p. 227.

11. *Bantu Educational Journal*, November 1966, editorial, quoted in Welch, "Growth of Towns," p. 227.

12. Data from 1970 census. See Wiehahn Commission Report, p. 165.

13. Ibid., p. 167.

14. See Jill Nattrass, *The South African Economy: Its Growth and Change*, (Oxford: Oxford University Press, 1981), p. 115.

15. Stanley Greenberg, *Legitimating the Illegitimate* (Berkeley: University of California Press, 1987), pp. 29–55.

16. See, Auret Von Heerdan, "Running on Empty: How the Motor Industry Fizzled to a Halt," Johannesburg *Weekly Mail*, January 23–28, 1987.

17. Houghton, *South African Economy*, p. 134.

18. See South Africa, *Report of the Commission of Inquiry into the Export Trade of the Republic of South Africa* (Pretoria: Government Printer, 1972), p. 30.

19. Ibid., pp. 40–41.

20. Department of Statistics, *South African Statistics*, various years, table entitled "Imports by Use and Stage of Processing," data aggregated in Richard C. Porter, "International Trade and Investment Sanctions," *Journal of Conflict Resolution*, vol. 23, no. 4 (December 1979), p. 589.

21. Growth rates calculated on basis of data from the Nedbank Group, *South Africa: An Appraisal* (Johannesburg: Nedbank Group Economic Unit, 1977), pp. 45–46; and Houghton, p. 260.

22. Quoted in Greenberg, *Legitimating the Illegitimate*, pp. 36–37.

23. Ibid., p. 37.

24. See Stanley Trapido, "South Africa in a Comparative Study of Industrialization," *Journal of Development Studies*, vol. 7, no. 3 (April 1971), p. 309.

25. See Greenberg, *Legitimating the Illegitimate*, p. 38.

26. Quoted in Rene De Villiers, "Afrikaner Nationalism," in Wilson and Thompson, *Oxford History of South Africa*, p. 407.

27. Quoted in Greenberg, *Legitimating the Illegitimate*, p. 38.

28. Ibid.

29. Stanley B. Greenberg, *Race and State in Capitalist Development* (New Haven: Yale University Press, 1980), pp. 176–208, passim.

30. Greenberg, *Legitimating the Illegitimate*, p. 47.

31. See Houghton, *South African Economy*, pp. 132–33.

32. South Africa, *Report of the Commission of Inquiry into the Export Trade of the Republic of South Africa*, pars. 47 and 48, pp. 18–19.

33. Ibid., par. 48.

34. Greenberg, *Race and State*, p. 88.

35. Hermann Giliomee, "The Afrikaner Economic Advance," in Hermann Giliomee and Heribert Adam, *Ethnic Power Mobilized* (New Haven: Yale University Press, 1979), p. 171.

36. Hermann Giliomee, "Afrikanerdom Today: Ideology and Interests," unpublished manuscript, 1979, p. 18.

37. See Robert Davies, "Nationalisation, Socialization and the Freedom Charter," *South African Labour Bulletin*, vol. 12, no. 2 (January/February 1987), p. 87.

38. Greenberg, *Race and State*, pp. 91–100.

39. See *Review of Defence and Armaments Production, 1960–1970* (Pretoria: Defence Headquarters, April 1971), pp. 5–6, quoted in, Robert S. Jaster, "South Africa's Narrowing Security Options," *Adelphi Papers*, no. 159 (London: International Institute for Strategic Studies, 1980), p. 10.

40. See Jaster, p. 13.

41. Ibid., p. 16.

42. Ibid.

43. Ibid.

44. Ibid., p. 13.

45. Ibid., p. 16.

46. Ibid.

47. For a discussion of the South African military intervention, see John Marcum, *The Angolan Revolution: Exile Politics and Guerrilla Warfare (1962–1976)* (Cambridge: MIT Press, 1978), pp. 266–72.

48. See Charles Ebinger, "Cuban Intervention in Angola: A Dissenting Opinion," African Studies Association Meeting, November 1979. See also Jiri Valenta, "The Soviet–Cuban Intervention in Angola, 1975," *Studies in Comparative Communism,* v. 11, Nos. 1 and 2, Spring/Summer 1978, pp. 3–33; Marcum, *The Angolan Revolution,* pp. 269–75; and William LeoGrande, "Cuba's Policy in Africa, 1959–1980," *Policy Papers in International Affairs* (Berkeley: Institute of International Studies, 1980).

49. See "Angola and the United States: A Chronology," *Africa Index,* August 5, 1981, p. 11.

50. Department of Defence, Republic of South Africa, *White Paper on Defence and Armament Production, 1977,* (Pretoria, 1977), p. 6, par. 14.

51. *White Paper on Defence, 1975* (Pretoria: Government Printer, 1975), pars. 15 and 17, pp. 6–7.

52. Quoted in Jaster, "South Africa's Narrowing Security Options," p. 28.

53. *White Paper on Defence 1977,* p. 7, par. 141.

54. Quoted in Jaster, "South Africa's Narrowing Security Options," p. 31.

55. See *Hansard,* April 22, 1975, col. 4551; *Hansard,* May 6, 1976, col. 6218. See also Jaster, pp. 27–30.

56. See Jaster, "South Africa's Narrowing Security Options," p. 16; and P. S. Botes: "The Administrative Aspects of a National Defence Programme," *ISSUP Strategic Review,* September 1979, reprinted in *South Africa Foundation News,* vol. 5, no. 11 (November 1979). See also Colonel Norman L. Dodd, "The South African Defence Force," *RUSI Journal,* March 1980, p. 5.

57. Jaster, "South Africa's Narrowing Security Options," p. 17.

58. Ibid.

59. Ibid., p. 29.

60. Ibid.

61. Quoted in Jack Foisie, "Races Mix in S. Africa Armed Forces," *Los Angeles Times,* September 12, 1980, p. 10.

62. See *South African Digest,* May 30, 1980, p. 1; see also, Jaster, "South Africa's Narrowing Security Options," p. 30.

63. See Philip Bonner, "Black Trade Unions in South Africa Since World War II," in Robert Price and Carl Rosberg, eds., *The Apartheid Regime* (Berkeley: Institute of International Studies, 1980), pp. 186–87. See also, Tom Lodge, *Black Politics in South Africa Since 1945* (London: Longman, 1983), pp. 326–27.

64. Lodge, *Black Politics,* p. 327.

65. This discussion of the rebellion that began in Soweto relies heavily on a number of sources, especially Alan Brooks and Jeremy Brickhill, *Whirlwind Before the Storm* (London: International Defence and Aid Fund for Southern Africa, 1980); Lodge, pp. 321–356; and Republic of South Africa, *Report of the Commission of Inquiry Into the Riots at Soweto and Elsewhere* (Cillie Commission Report), (Pretoria: Government Printer, 1980).

66. Brooks and Brickhill, *Whirlwind Before the Storm*, pp. 16–17.

67. Ibid., p. 250.

68. Cillie Commission Report, p. 526.

69. Ibid.

70. Ibid., p. 530.

71. *S.A. Barometer*, vol. 1, no. 5 (May 8, 1987), p. 70.

72. Ibid.

73. Cillie Commission Report, pp. 522 and 525.

74. Brooks and Brickhill, *Whirlwind Before the Storm*, pp. 255–56.

75. Ibid., p. 260.

76. Saki Macozoma, "Notes of a Native Son, *Monitor* (The Journal of the Human Rights Trust, Port Elizabeth), special issue, 1988, p. 56.

77. Steve Biko, *I Write What I Like* (San Francisco: Harper & Row, 1986), pp. 91–92.

78. See Lodge, *Black Politics*, pp. 323–24.

79. Erik Erikson, *Young Man Luther* (New York: Norton, 1958), p. 42; see also, Kenneth Keniston, *Young Radicals: Notes on Committed Youth* (New York: Harcourt, Brace & World, 1968), p. 103.

80. See Brooks and Brickhill, pp. 40–44; see also Cillie Commission Report, p. 72.

81. Brooks and Brickhill, *Whirlwind Before the Storm*, p. 42.

82. Cillie Commission Report, p. 72.

83. See Brooks and Brickhill, *Whirlwind Before the Storm*, pp. 85–89.

84. Ibid.

85. Quoted in Cillie Commission Report, p. 580.

86. See Baruch Hirson, *Year of Fire, Year of Ash, The Soweto Revolt: Roots of a Revolution?* (London: Zed Press, 1979), p. 89.

87. Ibid., p. 90.

88. Ibid.

89. Quoted in Cillie Commission Report, p. 580.

90. Ibid.

91. The Nedbank Group, *South Africa: An Appraisal* (Johannesburg: Nedbank Group Economic Unit, 1977), pp. 45–46.

92. See Books and Brickhill, *Whirlwind Before the Storm*, p. 201.

93. The Nedbank Group, pp. 119–20.

94. Ibid., p. 258.

95. Ibid., p. 259.

96. See David Hemson, "Trade Unionism and the Struggle for Liberation in South Africa," *Capital and Class*, no. 6 (1978), p. 19, referred to in Lodge, p. 357, n. 17.

97. See David Welsh, "The Growth of Towns," in Wilson and Thompson, vol. 2, p. 191.

98. Riekert Commission Report, p. 200, par. 4.387.

99. Ibid.

100. Simon Bekker and Richard Humphries, *From Control to Confusion* (Pietermaritzburg: Shuter & Shooter, 1985), p. 84.

101. Brooks and Brickhill, *Whirlwind Before the Storm*, p. 179.

102. Ibid., pp. 178–79.

103. Ibid.

104. *Rand Daily Mail*, February 2, 1977.

105. Riekert Commission Report, table 3.40, p. 112.

106. South African Institute of Race Relations, *Survey of Race Relations in South Africa, 1976* (Johannesburg: Institute of Race Relations, 1977), p. 190.

107. Ibid.

108. See Bekker and Humphries, *Control to Confusion*, pp. 6–8.

109. Ibid., p. 11.

110. Ibid., pp. 119 and 131.

111. P. G. J. Koornhof, quoted in ibid., p. 130.

112. Bekker and Humphries, *Control to Confusion*, pp. 143–50.

113. See Brooks and Brickhill, *Whirlwind Before the Storm*, pp. 175–76.

114. See Merle Lipton, "British Investment in South Africa: Is Constructive Engagement Possible?" *South African Labour Bulletin*, vol. 3, no. 11 (October 1976) pp. 10–48; see also Merle Lipton, "The Debate About South Africa: Neo-Marxists and Neo-Liberals," *African Affairs*, vol. 78, no. 310 (January 1979), pp. 57–80.

115. See Hermann Giliomee, "The Growth of Afrikaner Identity," in Giliomee and Adam, pp. 118–19.

116. *Rapport*, January 2, 1977; quoted in ibid., p. 130.

117. Cillie Commission Report, p. 2.

118. Ibid., p. 18.

119. Ibid., p. 593.

120. Ibid., p. 600.

121. Ibid., p. 604.

122. Ibid., p. 608.

123. Ibid., p. 606.

124. See Mark Orkin, *The Struggle and the Future: What Black Africans Really Think* (Johannesburg: Raven Press, 1986), pp. 34–39.

125. See Brooks and Brickhill, *Whirlwind Before the Storm*, p. 69; also pp. 94, 206, 213, and 236.

126. *Rand Daily Mail*, June 2, 1978, quoted in Lodge, p. 339.

127. Ibid., p. 340.

128. Data collated from press reports by the Institute for Strategic Studies at the University of Pretoria, reported in *S.A. Barometer*, vol. 1, no. 7 (June 7, 1987), p. 101.

129. Ibid.

130. United Nations, Security Council, Resolution 392 (1976), June 19, 1976.

131. United Nations, Security Council, Resolution 418 (1977), November 4, 1977.

132. See Committee on Foreign Affairs, U.S. House of Representatives, Hearings on Controls on Exports to South Africa, December 2, 1982, p. 185.

133. See *South African Digest*, August 12, 1977, pp. 1–2.

134. See *South African Digest*, July 1, 1977, p. 2.

135. See Desaix Myers III, Kenneth Propp, David Hauck, and David Liff, *U.S. Business in South Africa* (Bloomington: Indiana University Press, 1980), pp. 39–44. See also *Africa Research Bulletin*, August 15–September 14, 1977, p. 4402; and, Barclay's, *Country Reports: South Africa*, May 3, 1979 (London: Barclays Bank Group), p. 2.

136. See Myers et al., *U.S. Business in South Africa*, p. 42.

137. Ibid.

138. Quoted in "Apartheid: South African Credit Bar," *New York Times*, April 22, 1978, p. 25.

139. See Timothy Smith, "U.S. Firms and Apartheid: Belated Steps Analyzed," *Africa Today*, vol. 24, no. 2 (1977), p. 31.

140. See Martin Bailey, "Foreign Loans Are Drying Up for White South Africa," *New African*, June 1977, p. 575.

141. Quoted in ibid.

142. U.S. Congress, Senate, Committee on Foreign Relations, Subcommittee on Africa, *U.S. Corporate Interests in South Africa*, January 1978, pp. 13–14.

143. See David Ottaway, "Nigeria Flexes its Economic Muscle at Barclays Bank," *Washington Post*, April 10, 1978, p. 1.

144. Quoted in Smith, "U.S. Firms and Apartheid," p. 32.

145. See Bailey, "Foreign Loans," p. 575.

146. Quoted in Smith, "U.S. Firms and Apartheid," p. 33.

147. Quoted in Bailey, "Foreign Loans," p. 575.

148. Ibid.

149. Quoted in ibid.

150. See Myers et al., *U.S. Business in South Africa,* p. 42.

151. Ibid., p. 43.

152. See Myers et al., *U.S. Business in South Africa,* pp. 93–95.

153. "The (Sullivan) Statement of Principles," (Philadelphia: International Council for Equality of Opportunity Principles, Inc., November 8, 1984).

154. See "South Africa: Multinationals Are Caught in the Middle Again," *Business Week,* October 24, 1977, p. 4.

155. See Myers et al., *U.S. Business in South Africa,* p. 93.

156. Ibid., p. 95.

157. See, for example, Smith, "U.S. Firms and Apartheid." See also Elizabeth Schmidt, *One Step in the Wrong Direction: An Analysis of the Sullivan Principles as a Strategy for Opposing Apartheid* (New York: Episcopal Church People for a Free Southern Africa, 1983, revised January 1985).

158. Quoted in Smith, "U.S. Firms and Apartheid," p. 30.

159. *The Complete Wiehahn Report* (Johannesburg: Lex Patria Publishers, 1982), p. 4, par. 1.16.4.

3

Confronting Contradictions

Officialdom's Response to Crises

The simultaneous crises that confronted the Afrikaner political elite in the mid-1970s revealed that the apartheid edifice contained two interrelated structural contradictions: one economic, the other political/strategic. First, labor-repressive aspects of apartheid had become a fetter on a maturing industrial economy. Second, the political, economic, and social deprivations that apartheid imposed on South Africa's black majority created such intense alienation as to periodically threaten internal peace. The efforts of the state to reimpose order by use of its security forces touched off an international reaction that undermined South Africa's access to global markets for vital economic resources. Thus apartheid's political/strategic contradiction deepened its economic contradiction. It both increased the threat to future economic growth, and rendered infeasible an otherwise attractive method for ameliorating the conflict between apartheid and a maturing industrial order—i.e., the substitution of an international for a domestic market to serve an expanding manufacturing sector.

The two contradictions were linked the other way around, as well. Apartheid's threat to a healthy and growing economy increased the likelihood that the social and economic deprivations experienced by the black majority would worsen, with the result that alienation would deepen and disruptions become more widespread. In addition, the apartheid-constrained economy would be hard-pressed to finance the larger outlays on security made necessary by the increased threat to internal peace. This synergistic relationship between economic and political/strategic contradictions is displayed schematically in Figure 3.1.

Contradictions and Elite-Sponsored Change

Contradictions are intellectual constructs that are elaborated by analytic observers. Policymakers do not necessarily experience or understand their world in exactly the same way as does the analyst. But if analytically constructed contradictions are accurate reflections of the antithetical dynamics within a social system, then they

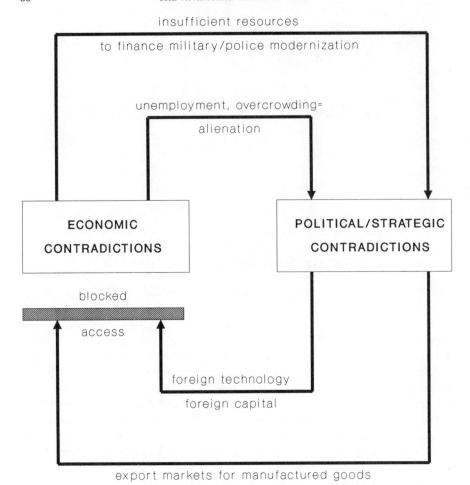

FIG. 3.1. Links between economic and political contradictions

will be experienced by policymakers as serious and recurring crises that are seemingly unresolvable within the parameters of the existing system. Solutions are unavailable because conventional practices and the principles that underlay them are the root causes of the crises. At a certain point some policymakers may come to understand that the crises can be resolved and threats effectively contained only if policy moves outside the system's parameters; that is, violates accepted practice and cherished principles. This is likely to happen when elements of a political elite view the crises being confronted as a threat to some goal that transcends in its value the contradicted system in which the crises are generated. For example, military officers may seize power in a democratically organized polity in order to preserve their conception of national interest or national honor. The system-values of civilian control and of the electoral basis for office-holding are violated in the service of what the military officers conceive of as a more transcendent value. Democratic order is sacrificed on the altar of national preservation.

In the mid- and late 1970s a specific variant of the above process occurred within the South African governing group. Apartheid's contradictions had become manifest in the set of interrelated crises that were described in Chapter 2. As we have seen, the apartheid system not only created these crises but blocked their resolution, since policies that might have overcome one or another problem implied violations of apartheid theory or practice. This led important segments of the Afrikaner political elite to conclude that significant aspects of apartheid needed to be altered or even jettisoned.

This inclination toward change was initially signaled in the summer of 1977 by the report of a Parliamentary Committee on the Constitution, and the appointment of two government commissions. One commission, the Wiehahn Commission, was charged with investigating industrial relations and trade-union rights; the other, the Riekert Commission, was instructed to study the system whereby the state controlled the movement of Africans from rural "homelands" to industrial cities. The mandates of both commissions indicated that officialdom was concerned about the inefficiencies associated with apartheid's economic contradictions, and that the government expected reports that would focus on altering apartheid practice. The Wiehahn Commission was instructed to make recommendations regarding "the adjustment of the existing system" so that it will "provide more effectively for the needs of our changing times."[1] The Riekert Commission was told to make recommendations "with a view to the elimination of bottlenecks and other problems experienced by both employees and employers in the utilization of labour."[2]

The report of the Parliamentary Committee of the National Party, which was issued at almost the same time as the Wiehahn and Riekert commissions were appointed, signaled an inclination to reform the political system as well. The report introduced a set of constitutional recommendations involving the extension of parliamentary representation to Indian and so-called "coloured" population groups.[3] Although continuing to exclude the African majority, and placing strict limits on the actual power that Indian and "coloured" representation could entail, these recommendations constituted a sharp reversal of the National Party's policy of completely barring Indian and Coloured participation in central government.*

These initial indications of a reformist tendency within the governing elite occurred during the prime ministership of John Vorster. A certain pragmatism had always characterized Vorster's administration, as adjustments in apartheid were made to accommodate real-world constraints on the implementation of doctrine. But the Vorster government had nevertheless always been steadfast in its claim to be adhering to the principle of apartheid even when pragmatically violating it. A significant strengthening of the reformist thrust was thus marked by the appointment of P. W. Botha as prime minister, after Vorster resigned in 1978. It was Botha who made domestic reform the centerpiece of government rhetoric, and who defined the government's purpose as adaptation and change. In contrast to his predecessor, he proclaimed that his government intended to move away from apartheid. His state-

---

*At the same time, the creation of *separate* parliamentary chambers for Indians, coloureds, and whites, which was the core of the parliamentary committee's proposals, can be viewed as consistent with apartheid principle.

ment, in 1979, that "apartheid is a recipe for permanent conflict," and his warning that South Africa's whites must "adapt or die," are dramatic indicators of the extent to which the multiple crises of the 1970s altered the perspective of the dominant faction within the ruling National Party.

But what was the transcendent goal that the Afrikaner governing elite sought to serve through dismantling major aspects of apartheid? Simply put, it sought the very same thing that its predecessors had when they introduced apartheid, namely, the maintenance of white political supremacy in South Africa. In one of his earliest statements about the need for change, Botha enunciated a principle that he would reiterate time and again: "The right of self-determination of the White nation must not be regarded as being negotiable."[4] In other words, the proclaimed intent to eliminate apartheid was not conceived as involving a loss of control over the political system by the white minority. "We are prepared to have a devolution of power," reiterated Botha, some ten years after the above statement of principle, "but not to relinquish it."[5]

White Supremacy Versus Apartheid

The principle enunciated by P. W. Botha quoted above contains an important and frequently overlooked key to an understanding of Pretoria's efforts to deal with the post-1970s crisis of the South African state. In order to comprehend the implications of Botha's reformist orientation it is essential to draw an analytic distinction between apartheid and white supremacy. Unfortunately, it has become commonplace to treat the two as synonymous. Thus the phrase "the apartheid regime" is commonly used as a referent for the entire South African political, economic, and social system. Those seeking fundamental change demand an "end to apartheid," and refer to themselves as part of an anti-apartheid movement. The merging of the concept of white supremacy with that of apartheid has created a good deal of confusion in discussions of the meaning and significance of the South African government's reform effort. For the two are not the same thing. White political supremacy and the socioeconomic privilege that flows from it characterized South Africa long before the concept of apartheid was developed and instituted by the National Party.

At the beginning of Chapter 1, I showed how a good deal of apartheid was fashioned to maintain an already existing white supremacy against the social, economic, and political forces unleashed by World War II. Much of apartheid was introduced in an attempt to secure white power domestically and legitimate it internationally under the changing postwar circumstances. Apartheid was a means; the maintenance of white supremacy was the end. Thus it is possible, under yet another set of historical circumstances, to plan to end apartheid while seeking to preserve white supremacy; i.e., to find a new means to serve the same end. This logic is the essential key to understanding government policy under P. W. Botha. Apartheid came to be viewed by the dominant faction within the National Party elite as no longer serving the instrumental purposes for which it was fashioned. Under the changed circumstances in which South Africa found itself in the 1970s apartheid had become both a costly and ineffective way to preserve white control. From the vantage point of maintaining white supremacy, an evolving domestic socioeconomic system and an altered global environment had rendered apartheid a liability. The National Party elite consequently sought an alternative means of securing white control at home and legitimating it abroad. It adopted a new strategy, of which reform was a major component.

Change: Significant or "Cosmetic"?

Failure to distinguish apartheid from white supremacy has led many observers to characterize the reforms introduced during the 1980s as insignificant, or "merely cosmetic." These critics of Pretoria measure change in terms of the formal distribution of political power; i.e., according to the legal-institutional structures of white supremacy. By that measure the changes in law and policy introduced during the 1980s can certainly be considered insignificant. But the yardstick of formal racial power is not the only one by which to assess Pretoria's reform efforts, and using it exclusively blinds the observer to potentially significant developments in areas outside the formal institutional structure of power.

In this book I treat Pretoria's reform effort as significant in two basic respects. First, I view it as nothing less than an attempt to change the system, or mode—if not the fact—of racial domination. A fundamental alteration in the system of racial domination would profoundly affect how one analyzes the dynamics of South African politics, the behavior of actors within South Africa, the way external actors relate to it, and the strategies and tactics that the opposition to Pretoria utilizes to end minority racial rule.

Second, I view political and social action as having both manifest and latent consequences, with the latter potentially differing from and being as significant as the former. Although the manifest intent of South Africa's governing elite may have been to reinforce white rule, it cannot foresee or control all the consequences of its policy actions. Neither can it control the reactions and responses to those policies of all actors at home and abroad. Consequently the latent or unintended consequences of Pretoria's reformist program may in the end have a significant impact on the distribution of political power, the governments' overt intentions notwithstanding. The intent, as far as the distribution of power is concerned, may well be "cosmetic," but the political, social, and economic dynamics into which reforms are introduced may produce a significant erosion of white power, nonetheless.

Reform and Afrikaner Identity

Both the willingness of the National Party elite to contemplate a non-apartheid mode of white supremacy, and its ability to move state policy in such a direction, were facilitated by the socioeconomic changes experienced by Afrikanerdom under National Party rule. The doctrine of apartheid—the belief in the imperative of complete race separation—was originally rooted in the intense feelings of ethnic-group deprivation and insecurity that characterized the Afrikaner people in the first half of the twentieth century.[6] Race separation was a means to ensure ethnocultural survival in the face of perceived exogenous threats, as it was simultaneously a means to preserve the political control of a white racial minority. The Afrikaner community's sense of insecurity and obsession with ethnic identity can thus be seen as contributing to the National Party's preference for apartheid as a particular mode of white supremacy.

By the mid-1970s, the socioeconomic environment that had made ethnic identity the Afrikaner's primary concern no longer existed. Some twenty-five years of increasing National Party domination of every aspect of the state apparatus, the related transformation of the Afrikaner proletariat into a solid bureaucratic middle class, and the concomitant penetration of the industrial and commercial economy by the Afrikaner community, had served to reduce the sense of economic and cultural insecurity that gave rise to the obsession with identity. In an attitudinal survey conducted by South African sociologist Lawrence Schlemmer in 1977, Afrikaners were found no longer to be especially concerned about matters involving their cultural identity. Instead, their fears focused on perceived threats to *white* physical security and material interests posed by the specter of black power.[7] With this type of orientation among its Afrikaner constituency, the National Party elite was able to detach the goal of "white survival" from the more parochial concern for Afrikaner identity, and to give the former clear priority.[8] In sum, the effects of extended National Party rule had laid the sociocultural foundation for the NP leadership to, in effect, draw a distinction between apartheid and white supremacy and to attend to the latter by abandoning significant aspects of the former.

Despite their increased secularization and urbanization, Afrikaners could not be expected to end all commitment to race separation as the essential basis of the South African social order. For one thing, no less than thirty years of National Party propaganda and indoctrination had supported the consummatory view that separation of the races is divinely ordained as part of God's plan to maintain an Afrikaner nation. For another, that same thirty-year period was one in which apartheid coincided with, and was credited for, an impressive improvement in the standard of living and sense of safety enjoyed by most white South Africans. These constituted duel elements—ideological and material—of the National Party elite's political dilemma. NP leaders had made a strategic decision that, over the long term, continued material well being and physical security required jettisoning apartheid in order to save white supremacy. They now had to convince their Afrikaner constituency that the risks of abandoning the familiar and, until recently, apparently successful apartheid formula, were worth the promise of what were, after all, hypothetical long-term benefits.

The dominant faction of the National Party leadership had an impressive array of weapons at their disposal to carry their constituency along with them. Through the party they controlled an elaborate cultural and information network, and through the state they controlled a vast patronage machine. Yet the opponents of change were not without their assets. They could call upon the fears of whites that any deviation from race separation would erode the control that was believed essential for the maintenance of their privileged status. Or, in the political idiom of Afrikanerdom, they argued that movement away from apartheid threatened white "self-determination" and would destroy the white "way of life." And in making such an attack on the reformists the opponents of change could appeal to whatever affective commitments still existed to the Afrikaner's view of race separation as an essential part of a divinely ordained design for maintaining an Afrikaner nation.

This combination of concern with material interests and long-held ideological and normative beliefs was a powerful mix. It allowed that part of the Afrikaner political elite opposed to change to attract a sizable following among Afrikaner voters. By the early 1980s the clash between the *verkramptes,* that element of the elite that stood opposed to change, and the *verligtes,* those favoring a strategy of adaptation, would split Afrikanerdom politically. It would, by mid-decade, result in the formation of a new Afrikaner political party, the Conservative Party. By 1987 that new verkrampte party would be able to challenge the National Party's majority among Afrikaner voters.* The "threat from the right" complicated the task of the National Party leadership as it attempted to move away from apartheid.

A "Total Strategy" For Maintaining White Supremacy

Reform is the major but not the only component of Pretoria's effort to deal with the contradictions that faced the South African state after the mid-1970s. Government officials labeled their overall effort a "total strategy," indicating the comprehensiveness of the state's response in respect to both policy initiatives and the organizational support for policy implementation. The concept of total strategy was first introduced in 1975 by P. W. Botha, the then minister of defense. Noting the "sweeping changes [the end of Portuguese colonialism] in some of our neighbouring states," and highlighting the potential radicalizing effects these changes might have on domestic South African black politics, Botha asserted in his Defence White Paper that "survival" required more than mere military defense. It required the state to "muster all . . . activities—political, economic, diplomatic and military." This, he said, "is the meaning of 'total strategy.' "[9] Two years later, during which time Mozambique and Angola became independent states under Marxist governments, South Africa suffered its military/political debacle in Angola, a guerrilla insurgency in Rhodesia escalated, and the Soweto uprising burst forth, Botha made the notion of total strategy the centerpiece of his 1977 Defense White Paper. He called for "a total national strategy . . . applicable at all levels and to all functions of the state structure," and incorporating "political, economic, psychological, technological and military means."[10]

The white papers of 1975 and 1977 give increasing attention to "total national strategy" as a counter to a perceived revolutionary threat to white rule, or, to use the language of the 1977 Defence White Paper, to "the right of self determination of the white nation."[11] These documents say little about the actual content of total strategy, but provide progressively elaborate descriptions of proposed new government structures that were to undertake the task of "national strategic planning."[12] The actual policy content of total strategy would emerge from these structures once they were formed.

---

*In the 1987 parliamentary elections the Conservatives garnered nearly 45 percent of the Afrikaans-speaking vote.

The implications of P. W. Botha's concept of total strategy for South African governance first became apparent in the 1977 white paper. The defense minister indicated that the State Security Council (SSC), an obscure government agency that had been created in 1972, would be charged with formulating the "total national strategy for the RSA,"[13] and that defense services were only a relatively small aspect of his conception of a total strategy. Some fourteen functional aspects of national security that required attention from the SSC were listed; only three of them—intelligence services, security services, and military/paramilitary action— can be considered to be security-related in the usual sense.*

Within a year of the issuance of the 1977 Defence White Paper, Botha was named prime minister. Under his sponsorship the State Security Council was transformed from a relatively inactive advisory board on intelligence matters, into a policy-formulating body involved in virtually all matters domestic and foreign; a body that many informed observers consider to have by the mid-1980s supplanted the cabinet as the supreme source of power and policy during the Botha years.[14] Chaired by the state president,† the SSC met twice a week and recommended policy to the cabinet.[15] Its membership reflected the definition of "total national strategy" presented by Botha in the 1977 Defence White Paper. Regular members included the heads of each branch of the South African military, police, and intelligence services, the ministers holding the most important government portfolios (foreign affairs, defense, law and order, constitutional development and planning, finance), and senior bureaucrats from several key government departments. As the SSC was transformed, an organizational infrastructure, called the National Security Management System (NSMS), was developed to provide a policy-implementating capability to go along with the SSC's policy planning functions.‡ Within the NSMS, a work committee, drawing its members from various government agencies and departments, provided technical and expert backup to the SSC, and facilitated interdepartmental coordination in the formulation and implementation of the total strategy.[16] The work committee, itself, operated through thirteen interdepartmental subcommittees whose functional division of labor coincided closely with the tasks specified by Botha in his 1977 white paper.§ In addition, a sizable secretariat was formed to

*The other eleven areas requiring the attention of the SSC in the national strategic planning process were political action; economic action; psychological action; scientific and technological action; religious/cultural action; manpower services; national supplies, resources and production services; transport and distribution services; financial services; community services; and telecommunication services.

†In 1983 a new constitution was introduced that abolished the office of prime minister and created in its place the post of state president. In 1984 P. W. Botha became state president. He served in that capacity until September 1989.

‡The basic design for this infrastructure was contained in a 1975 report of the Public Service Commission, which under the instigation of Defense Minister Botha, had undertaken a study to improve the state machinery for combating threats to the national security. See statement to the press by Lieutenant General Andre J. Van Deventer, SADF, Chief of the Secretariat and Secretary to the State Security Council of the Republic of South Africa, September 21, 1983, p. 1, reprinted in James M. Roherty, "The Security Management System in South Africa's 'Total National Strategy,' " study for the Center for Naval Warfare Studies (Newport, Rhode Island: Naval War College, 1984), app. A.

§Subcommittees: manpower, transport, national economy, civil defence, government funding, science and technology, cultural affairs, community services, security forces, telecommunication and electrical power supply, national supplies and resources, political affairs, and security.

support the work of the SSC, the work committee, and the interdepartmental subcommittees.[17]

To provide the NSMS with a policy-implementing capability a special infrastructure of Joint Management Centres (JMC) was created. By 1986 there were nine regional JMCs operating in newly designated "economic development areas"; some 60 sub-JMCs operating in major metropolitan areas; and 448 mini-JMCs operating in local areas, such as townships.[18] At each level of operation, the JMC brought together military and police officers, government officials, state bureaucrats, and businessmen. At all three levels the work of the JMCs was conducted through three specialist committees: one to deal with security matters; another to handle political, economic, and social problems; and the third to manage communications and propaganda. These functional divisions reflect the essence of the "total strategy" concept, a multi-pronged response to the Republic's perceived security threats, combining socioeconomic policy and ideological or psychological warfare with more conventional police activities.

The establishment of the National Security Management System, with the SSC at its apex and the mini-JMCs at its base, represented nothing less than the achievement of what P. W. Botha in 1977 described as a primary "national objective required for the continued existence of the RSA and all its people":[19]

planning total national strategy . . . for coordinated action between all government departments, government institutions and other authorities to counter the multidimensional onslaught against the RSA in ideological, military, economic, social, psychological, cultural, political and diplomatic fields.[20]

The various defense white papers published during the 1970s are useful in providing a fairly clear sense that the National Party elite associated with P. W. Botha thought in strategic terms when confronting the multiple crises that faced the South African state. Some observers have characterized Pretoria's policies during the 1980s as "ad hoc," incoherent, and contradictory. The defense documents suggest otherwise. They reveal a National Party leadership seeking a conscious and coordinated design for preserving white rule under the changed historical circumstances of the last quarter of the twentieth century. The defense documents also provide a clear picture of the organizational "architecture" that Botha and his associates deemed necessary for developing and implementing a multidimensional approach to security. They are remarkably accurate predictors of the security apparatus that was in fact rapidly constructed once Botha acceded to the prime ministership. These documents are of little help, however, in revealing the substance of total strategy. They delineate neither concrete policies nor the underlying logic that transforms discrete policies into a strategy. The former are revealed in the government policies that emerged from the National Security Management System after 1978; the latter can be inferred from an examination of these as well as of government statements explaining their purpose.

The policy aspect of total strategy, as distinct from its organizational architecture, can be divided analytically into three components—reform, repression, and regional hegemony.

Domestic Reform

Through policies that substantially altered the apartheid edifice—what government referred to as its commitment to reform—Pretoria pursued four primary objectives: (1) to free the economy from the bottlenecks imposed by apartheid; (2) to create a black socioeconomic strata with material and status interests that would be threatened by radical transformation; (3) to coopt a significant segment of the black population into the existing framework of power by making available opportunities for black economic and social advancement and by ameliorating living conditions in the urban black townships; and (4) to "normalize" South Africa's status internationally by bringing its domestic sociopolitical arrangements into line with international standards.

Because the economic and political contradictions of apartheid are linked, these four objectives are likewise interconnected. The gains achieved in respect to any one objective enhance the prospects of the others. Figure 3.2, on the following page, summarizes the relationship between the objectives of reform and the overarching goals of total strategy, and illuminates their interactive qualities. Removing apartheid constraints on African labor mobility, urban residence, educational opportunities, and wages would open the future for economic growth and create the economic, educational, and legal opportunities for the emergence of a significant and stable urban-based black middle class. Such a socioeconomic strata among Africans would, in theory, provide both the technical skills and consumer dollars required for an expanding industrial economy, and a political buffer against the mass appeal of revolutionary change. Removing the most glaring aspects of official racism would facilitate the political cooptation of a newly emergent African middle-class, and simultaneously eliminate that which distinguishes South Africa from every other state in the world and earns it international opprobrium. By thus establishing a "normal" status for South Africa internationally, the South African economy could be protected from the threat posed by an ever ominous atmosphere of impending sanctions.

Reform and the Business Community

As its objectives indicate, Pretoria was addressing multiple audiences by adopting its program of domestic reform. This audience included those black South Africans in a position to achieve middle-class economic status; the international community; and big business, both foreign and domestic. The government needed to restore business confidence in South Africa's future if it was to induce industrialists to make the long-term investments necessary for renewed economic growth. Additionally, as will become clear in later chapters, Pretoria viewed the private business sector as a vital partner in its reform project. Making a middle-class life-style available to significant numbers of black South Africans requires massive expenditures in the areas of housing, education, health care, recreation, and the like. If the government were to pay for this upgrading of black living conditions, especially in a sluggish economic environment, it would have to raise taxes and redistribute resources away from the white population. In order to avoid this politically costly alternative Pre-

INTERACTIVE GOAL STRUCTURE

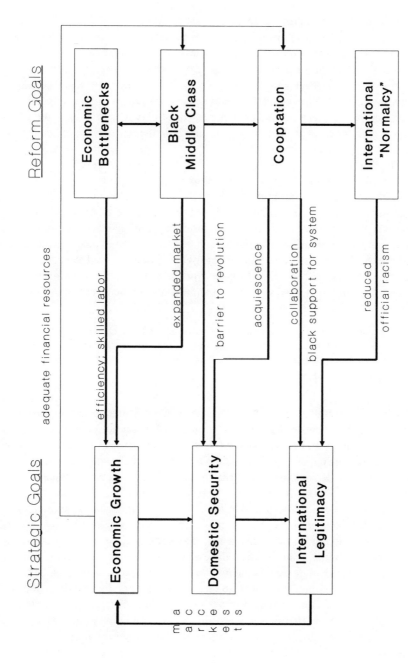

Fig. 3.2. Relationship of reform to "total strategy"

toria chose to rely heavily on private capital to finance the improvement in the physical conditions of black life. After Soweto, however, capital had made it clear to the state that change in the apartheid system would be the price of partnership.

In Chapter 2 we saw how in the wake of Soweto *foreign* capital had sent such a message to Pretoria. Domestic big business was at the same time also letting Pretoria know about the need for change. Sir Albert Robinson, chairman of a large Johannesburg industrial firm, in a move typical of the immediate post-Soweto period, issued the following call: "We are entering a decisive phase in the history of South Africa. . . . The business community must play its part in applying pressure to encourage peaceful change, more particularly in the field of race relations and the breaking down of discrimination."[21]

The dissatisfaction of capital with the state's response to the crises of the 1970s crystalized in the creation of the Urban Foundation. Organized in late 1976 by some of South Africa's most prominent industrialists and funded by some of its largest business firms, the Urban Foundation set out to lobby government for change and to undertake the amelioration of living conditions in the urban black townships, particularly in regard to housing. The initial response of Pretoria to the political activities of domestic business was extremely negative, driving the wedge between capital and the state even further. Prime Minister Vorster issued a warning to business at the national convention of the Associated Chambers of Commerce in late October 1976:

> Efforts to use business organizations to bring about basic change in government policy will fail and cause unnecessary and harmful friction between the Government and the private sector. You cannot ask me to implement policies rejected by the electorate and in which I do not believe.[22]

When P. W. Botha became prime minister in 1978, the posture of government toward business changed dramatically. At the 1979 Carlton Conference, organized by the government and attended by 300 leading businessmen, Botha urged business to participate, in cooperation with the government, in the economic development of southern Africa. He acknowledged that business had made valid criticism of state policies, and declared his government's receptivity to business input. "There has been much criticism in the past that the South African economy, and business in particular, labours under too many rules, regulations and restrictions. . . . The Government has not let these criticisms, inasmuch as they are constructive, pass unnoticed."[23] Botha promised to reduce state controls over economic affairs, to appoint businessmen to his Economic Advisory Council, and to initiate major reforms in the apartheid system. Capital was being wooed into partnership in the implementation of Botha's notion of a "total national strategy." The Carlton Conference would be the first of a series of high-level conferences, held every several years, at which the government would seek to assure a skeptical business audience of the sincerity of its reformist intentions. Yet, the "partnership" between state and capital in the reform of apartheid would remain uneasy, as the government sought to introduce change in order to reassure its vital business audience, and as business demanded more than the government was willing or able to give.

Reform and Repression

The notion of reform implies something about change—its direction, scope, and speed. A reform, writes Albert Hirschman, is a change in which "the power of hitherto privileged groups is curbed and the economic position and social status of underprivileged groups is correspondingly improved."[24] It is, in other words, a change that represents greater inclusion of previously excluded groups in the distribution of society's social, economic, and political goods. Revolutionary change is also of this type, but what distinguishes reform is its limited scope in respect to the extent and range of inclusion and the relative slowness at which it occurs.

Reform and repression are usually viewed as imcompatibles, but in most situations they are in fact reverse sides of the same coin. As Samuel Huntington has noted, "reform and repression may proceed hand-in-hand. . . . Effective repression," he explains, "may enhance the appeal of reform to radicals by increasing the costs and risks of revolution and to stand-patters by reassuring them of the government's ability to maintain order."[25] This proposition correctly implies that reform is not an alternative to repression but rather to revolution—i.e., to complete inclusion at a rapid pace. It also implies an important corollary: the more limited the intended reform in relation to the expectations of the underprivileged, the greater the repression required for successful reform. This follows because reform involves both a willingness on the part of the relatively privileged to relinquish some of their power, status, and wealth, and a corresponding willingness on the part of the excluded to acquiesce in a still unequal structure of power and privilege in return for partial amelioration of their deprivation. Such acquiescence is what is meant by cooptation. If the expectations and resultant political demands of the excluded are limited, then the cooptation process involves little problem for the ruling group, and reform can be "successfully" implemented without repression. If, however, the excluded demand rapid changes that imply fundamental alterations in political institutions, governmental elites, public policy, social structure, and the distribution of material goods—i.e., if they expect changes that amount to revolution—than cooptation of a politically significant segment of the underprivileged becomes much more difficult and the prospects for successful reform problematic. In such a situation repression becomes the basis for successful reform. It lowers the expectations of the underprivileged by (1) demonstrating the power of the status-quo forces; (2) revealing the high costs and risks that attend the commitment to rapid and fundamental change; and (3) rendering the prospects for a reordering of society along revolutionary lines dangerously utopian. If repression succeeds in lowering expectations, then the prospects for cooptation are enhanced and reform can move forward.

The above provides a general framework for understanding the importance of repression in Pretoria's total strategy. The events of the mid-1970s raised both the hope and the specter of revolution. For the black majority, the collapse of white rule in the face of African armed resistance in Mozambique, Angola, and Zimbabwe, in combination with the spirit of militant resistance born in the Soweto uprising, served to raise expectations not only for a reduction in racial discrimination but of an early end to white minority rule. For many whites the same events served to escalate fears about internal security and a loss of political control.

Within Pretoria's total strategy, repression was a means to deal with both black hopes and white fears. In regard to the black majority, the coercive arm of the state was deployed to destroy extraparliamentary organizations whose demands went beyond the government's own reform plans; and to deal a psychological blow to the black community. Pretoria hoped that by demonstrating the power of the state and the relative impotence of its opponents, the credibility of the revolutionary option would be undermined and its proponents rendered dangerous utopians in the eyes of their own community. With the revolutionary option seemingly foreclosed, the expectations of the majority community in regard to change would decline, and blacks would be willing to accept a more limited form of inclusion, i.e., cooptation. Thus, Pretoria used repression to make its reform program acceptable to its black audience.

Repression against blacks was also intended to bolster the white minority's confidence in the ability of the state to maintain control over the pace and direction of change. In this way, the National Party leadership under P. W. Botha hoped to enhance the white community's sense of security and thus maintain an electoral constituency for its efforts to alter apartheid. Looked at from a somewhat different angle, by demonstrating through repression the state's ability to maintain control, the government sought to avoid wholesale political defection to those leaders who objected to any move away from dogmatic adherence to apartheid doctrine.

If the only audience for South African reform was domestic, then the ability of Pretoria to act on the analytic symbiosis between reform and repression would have been relatively easy. But overt repression of the black majority has historically been the driving force in South Africa's international isolation. To the extent that one of the primary goals of total strategy was international acceptability, Pretoria needed to avoid reinforcing its repressive international image.

Reform is a means to coopt the black population into a program of limited change; it is also a way to achieve a "normal" status for South Africa internationally. Repression is a means to limit black expectations so as to provide a psychological orientation toward reform; it is also the surest means to international isolation and to reinforcing Pretoria's "pariah" status in the global community. This glitch in the symbiosis between reform and repression created by the international audience for South Africa's internal change process came to represent a crucial vulnerability in Pretoria's total strategy.

Regional Policy

The third component of total strategy was regional in scope. The multiple crises of the mid-1970s revealed that the new challenge to white supremacy involved an interactive combination of domestic and international elements.[26] The regional transformations of 1974–79 amplified both aspects of this threat. On the one hand, the anti-apartheid sentiments of Pretoria's new neighbors and their actual or potential collaboration with the African National Congress enhanced revolutionary orientations and prospects within the South African black community. On the other hand, the activities of southern African states in various international forums, such as the

TABLE 3.1. Imposition of Regional Hegemony

Country	Military Attack	Destabilization	Economic Pressure
Angola	Invasion, intermittent, 1980–89 Air attack, intermittent, 1979–89 Occupation of Cunene Province, 1979–85	Support for UNITA, 1976–89	
Botswana	Commando raid, 6/85 Commando raid, 5/86		Delayed Customs Union payments
Lesotho	Commando raid on ANC houses, 12/82 Commando raid on ANC houses, 12/85	Support for LLA* Support for coup, 12/86	Border closure, 1983, 1986 Delayed Customs Union payments
Mozambique	Commando raid on ANC houses, 12/81 Air strike against ANC houses, 5/83	Support for RENAMO, 1979– (reduced level of support after Nkomati)	Cut employment of mine workers, reduced use of railroad and ports
Zambia	Commando raid, 5/86		
Zimbabwe	Commando raid on airfield, 7/82 Commando raid, 8/82 Commando raid, 5/86	Support for ZAPU† and Ndebele dissidents, 1979–81	Petrol cutoff, rail delays

*Lesotho Liberation Army
†Zimbabwe African People's Union

OAU, the United Nations, and the Non-aligned Movement, encouraged a global atmosphere conducive to international pressure against the apartheid state.

Prior to the mid-1970s, South Africa's system of racial rule had been protected by the *cordon sanitaire* of white-ruled states to its north. After the collapse of the Portuguese African empire, Pretoria sought to *neutralize* the effects of the regional transformation by forcing its neighbors to recognize South Africa's hegemony in regional affairs.[27] Through the application of its military and economic superiority, South Africa sought to force its neighbors to accept a set of rules of regional inter-state behavior that were consistent with its definition of security. Specifically, during the 1980s regional hegemony was pursued through direct military attack, "de-stabilization" (support for insurgent movements), and economic pressure.* Pretoria's use of these policies is summarized in Table 3.1.

First, the South African military launched cross-border attacks. These have taken the form of large-scale air and ground assaults, as occurred regularly in Angola between 1979 and 1989, or commando raids, as were directed against Botswana, Lesotho, Mozambique, Zambia, and Zimbabwe, as well as Angola. Second, South Africa has provided extensive assistance to insurgent movements in Angola and Mozambique. The provision by Pretoria of military equipment, logis-

*In conventional usage the term "destabilization" refers to the entire South African strategy.

tical and communications assistance, training, and, in the case of Angola, direct air and ground support, have helped the Resistencia Nacional Moçambicana (RE-NAMO) in Mozambique and the National Union for the Total Independence of Angola (UNITA). The third component in Pretoria's effort to establish hegemony involved the use of South Africa's pivotal position in the regional economy. The landlocked countries of southern Africa depend on the South African transportation and port network for at least two-thirds of their imports and exports. South African mines employ several hundred thousand migrant workers from neighboring countries, who remit a portion of their earnings home in the form of foreign exchange. Pretoria has been able to take advantage of these and other dependencies to squeeze the economies of her neighbors. Mozambique, Lesotho, and Zimbabwe have been particular targets for South Africa's economic leverage.

The campaign of military, political, and economic pressure served a number of purposes for Pretoria. The most immediate goal had been to eliminate the ANC from southern Africa. What was sought, however, was not simply the expulsion of the ANC cadre and organizational infrastructure. Rather, Pretoria hoped to force regional states into signing formal treaties of nonaggression, the key provision of which was the establishment of a joint security commission. Such a treaty was signed by South Africa and Swaziland in 1982, but the first acknowledgement of a "nonaggression" treaty was the Nkomati Accord, signed with much public fanfare by South Africa and Mozambique in March 1984. Almost two years later, in January 1986, P. W. Botha proposed creating a regionally based "permanent joint mechanism for dealing with matters of security."[28] Should his proposal for a joint security mechanism "be ignored or rejected," Botha warned that Pretoria "would have no choice but to take effective measures in self-defence."[29] In other words, it would continue its regional policies of military attacks, support for insurgent movements, and economic pressure.

This emphasis on formal treaties and joint security mechanisms can be understood in terms of Pretoria's drive for international acceptability.[30] If African countries are seen to be engaged diplomatically with Pretoria, and, more significantly, if other African security forces are actively cooperating with their South African counterparts, a sharp break in the Africa-wide consensus on the need to ostracize South Africa would be achieved. With Africa divided on the issue of cooperative engagement with Pretoria, and some staunchly anti-apartheid African states actually actively engaged with it in repressing the ANC, the way would presumably be open for Western countries to reduce the pressure on, and improve their relations with, South Africa. As one South African newspaper put it, nonaggression pacts with regional neighbors "were a road back into the world."[31] Consequently, when Mozambique signed the Nkomati Accord the occasion was hailed in South Africa as a major breakthrough. "A completely new . . . game is under way," wrote one South African media commentator, "and with so many new teams in the league it should be clear to all but the most dense of overseas observers that there is just no place on the field for purveyors of sanctions, boycotts, and disinvestment."[32]

In summary, then, through the use of military and economic power, Pretoria sought to create a "neutral" cordon of African states to its north. Under a regime of South African regional hegemony southern African states would be expected to

(1) prevent their territory from being used in any manner by the ANC; (2) intensify their economic dependence on the South African economy and transportation network; (3) silence their calls for economic sanctions; and (4) facilitate Pretoria's return to international respectability through active cooperation with Pretoria on matters of "mutual security."

Pretoria's regional strategy of hegemony contained an inherent tension. On one hand, it desired to form cooperative relationships with African states as a means of achieving international acceptability; on the other hand, the methods it used to bludgeon its neighbors into such cooperation strained even further its global relationships. Moreover, should the policy of destabilization result in the overthrow of existing governments, Pretoria was not likely to reap any benefits: alliances with new governments that owed their existence to Pretoria could be expected to be relatively worthless internationally.

South African policymakers were divided in their response to the inherent tension between international goals and the means used to achieve regional hegemony. The military and security agencies, charged with carrying out destabilization policies and armed attacks, favored what I will call "regime reconstitution." They sought during the 1980s to destroy and dislodge the "Marxist" regimes in Angola and Mozambique, and to replace them with governments beholden to Pretoria. A second approach, what I term "cooptive domination," came to be associated with the South African policymakers responsible for foreign affairs and the economy. This approach seeks to use destabilization, military attack, and economic leverage to so weaken neighboring governments that out of desperation, and an instinct for political self-preservation, they will accept Pretoria's hegemonic rule and cooperate in its neutralization objectives. In contrast to regime reconstitution, this tactical orientation, while pursuing a weakening of neighboring governments, does not seek their replacement.

During the decade of the 1980s, the two tactical approaches of regime reconstitution and cooptive domination contended with each other within Pretoria's policy circles. Which line came to dominate depended on two related factors: the level of financial difficulty faced by the government, and the propitiousness of the international situation for a diplomatic breakthrough. Economic and financial difficulties increased the pressure to break out of international isolation, and raised the salience of the costs of destabilization and military campaigns. Thus, at such times the "security agreements" with existing neighboring governments seemed especially attractive; they provided the basis for a diplomatic initiative toward the West, and they promised to reduce financial burdens by ending destabilization and military actions. The Nkomati Accord of 1984 and the Angola/Namibia Accord of 1988 represent the most notable successes of the cooptive domination approach. However, if diplomatic initiatives do not produce the promised international benefits then the proponents of regime reconstitution can assert their tactical line in regional policy. Such was the case when, due to political developments within South Africa, the Nkomati Accord failed to produce the expected diplomatic breakthrough. There then ensued four years of escalating military involvement in Angola, and continued low-level destabilization in Mozambique, leading in late 1988 to a return to the tactic of cooptive domination with the signing of the Angola/Namibia Accord.

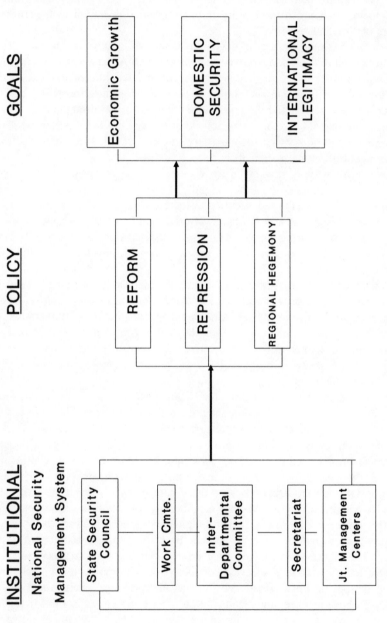

FIG. 3.3. Components of "total national strategy"

Summary

In the late 1970s, the governing elite in South Africa developed a set of institutions and policies to deal with the economic and political contradictions built into apartheid, the manifestations of which had rocked the apartheid state in mid-decade. It referred to this institutional and policy response as a total national strategy. Figure 3.3 provides a schematic overview of core elements of total strategy—the organizational innovations in South African governance, the key components of policy, and the basic goals toward which new structures and policies were directed.

Notes

1. *The Complete Wiehahn Report* (Johannesburg: Lex Patria Publishers, 1982), p. xxxii.

2. *Report of the Commission of Inquiry into Legislation Affecting the Utilization of Manpower* (Riekert Commission Report) (Pretoria: Government Printer, 1979), p. 1.

3. "South Africa's New Constitutional Plan," South African Embassy, Washington, D.C., *Backgrounder,* no. 10 (1977).

4. See Department of Defence, Republic of South Africa, *White Paper on Defence and Armament Production, 1977* (Pretoria, 1977), p. 3.

5. *The Citizen,* May 1, 1987.

6. See C. Dunbar Moodie, *The Rise of Afrikanerdom* (Berkeley: University of California Press, 1975), pp. 245–258.

7. See Lawrence Schlemmer, "Change in South Africa: Opportunities and Constraints," in Robert M. Price and Carl G. Rosberg, Jr., eds., *The Apartheid Regime* (Berkeley: Institute of International Studies, 1980), pp. 258 and 267.

8. See Heribert Adam, "Survival Politics: Afrikanerdom in Search of a New Ideology," *Journal of Modern African Studies,* vol. 16, no. 1 (December 1978), pp. 657–69.

9. Department of Defence, Republic of South Africa, *White Paper on Defence and Armament Production, 1975* (Cape Town, 1975), p. 3.

10. *White Paper on Defence, 1977,* p. 5.

11. Ibid., p. 3.

12. Department of Defence, Republic of South Africa, *White Paper on Defence and Armaments Supply, 1979* (Cape Town, 1979), p. 2.

13. *White Paper on Defence, 1977,* p. 5.

14. See, for example, "South Africa: The Government in the Shadows," *Africa Confidential,* vol. 28, no. 14 (July 8, 1987), pp. 1–4.

15. See "The Uniformed Web that Sprawls Across the Country," *Weekly Mail,* October 3–8, 1986, pp. 12–13; and ibid.

16. *Weekly Mail,* October 3–8, 1986, pp. 12–13; see also *White Paper on Defence, 1979,* p. 2, par. 6.

17. See *Africa Confidential,* vol. 28, no. 14 (July 8, 1987), p. 2.

18. See ibid., and *Weekly Mail,* October 3–8, 1986, p. 12.

19. *White Paper on Defence, 1977,* p. 8.

20. Ibid.

21. Albert Robinson, statement of the chairman to the annual meeting of the Johannesburg Consolidated Investments Co., Ltd. (Johannesburg, November 1977), p. 3.

22. Quoted in Merle Lipton, *Capitalism and Apartheid* (Towata, New Jersey: Rowman and Allenheld, 1985), p. 179.

23. *Towards a Constellation of States in Southern Africa,* "Meeting Between the Prime Minister and Business Leaders, Carlton Centre, Johannesburg, 22 November 1979" (Pretoria: Information Services of South Africa, 1980), p. 6.

24. Albert O. Hirschman, *Journeys Toward Progress* (New York: Twentieth Century Fund, 1963), p. 267.

25. Samuel P. Huntington, "Reform and Stability in South Africa," *International Security,* vol. 6, no. 4 (Spring 1982), p. 9.

26. See Robert M. Price, "Security and Growth: The International Factor in South African Policy," *Annals of the American Academy of Political and Social Sciences,* no. 489 (January 1987), pp. 103–22.

27. See Robert M. Price, "Creating New Political Realities: Pretoria's Drive for Regional Hegemony," in James Coleman, Richard Sklar, and Gerald Bendor, eds., *African Crises Areas and U.S. Foreign Policy* (Berkeley: University of California Press, 1985), pp. 64–88. See also Robert M. Price, "Southern African Regional Security: Pox or Pax Pretoria," *World Policy Journal,* vol. 2, no. 3 (Summer 1985), pp. 533–54; and Robert M. Price, "South Africa and Afro-Marxism: Pretoria's Relations with Mozambique and Angola in Regional Perspective," in E. Keller and D. Rothchild, eds., *Afro-Marxist Regimes* (Boulder: Lynne Rienner Publishers, 1987), pp. 257–80.

28. See "Text of State President's Speech upon Opening of 1986 Parliament," *South African Digest,* February 7, 1986, p. 100.

29. Ibid.

30. For a fuller discussion see Robert M. Price, "South Africa and Afro-Marxism," pp. 264–69.

31. *Sunday Times* (Johannesburg), March 18, 1984, repr. in *South African Digest,* March 23, 1984, p. 19.

32. *Natal Mercury,* May 5, 1984, repr. in *South African Digest,* May 11, 1984, p. 21.

4

Change and Continuity: Pretoria's Reform Program

Whether, in its efforts to reform apartheid, Pretoria was following a conscious strategy, or whether it was instead simply responding ad hoc and incoherently to immediate political pressures, has been a matter of considerable disagreement among observers. Upon examination, however, the "grand design" *vs.* "muddling through" interpretations of Pretoria's actions often involve differences that are more apparent than real. It should be clear from the discussion in the preceding chapter that I view Pretoria's reform program as one component of a "grand design," i.e., a consciously developed strategy to preserve white rule. Such a view of Pretoria's policies has been called into question by some of the most well-informed observers of the South African political scene. For example, Steven Friedman, a knowledge-able and insightful critic of Pretoria, writes in the left-liberal *Weekly Mail:*

> [G]overnment critics have seen a coherence to [Pretoria's] plans which weren't visible to most of us. . . . [T]he government "grand design" hadn't been visible because it wasn't there. . . . [G]overnment moves were more an ad hoc response to pressure than a well worked-out attempt to impose its will.[1]

The fallacy in the above line of analysis is that it equates a grand design with a blueprint. But the two are not the same thing. The former is a general strategy; a broad outline or conception for achieving some goal. The latter is a completely worked out, detailed, and specific plan for operationalizing a general conception. An architect when creating a building, for example, will usually have a set of general ideas about how he wishes to organize space—his grand design. The general conception, and the sketches that visually represent it, will exist prior to the architect's having drawn up a blueprint—a detailed construction plan incorporating everything from the exact size of each room to the precise location of every electric socket. An architect may well alter his blueprint several times in order to better execute the ideas that make up his grand design. He may also have to create new blueprints incorporating special engineering knowledge if he encounters unforeseen circumstances, such as unstable soil conditions. All of these changes in construction plans do not belie the fact that the architect has a grand design; rather, they represent his efforts to better execute his general ideas as his knowledge becomes more complete.

What holds for architects can also hold for government policymakers and strategists. The situation of the South African governing group in respect to its plans for change corresponds to the architectural metaphor. By the end of the 1970s P. W. Botha and other National Party leaders had a relatively clear idea of their goals— creating a situation conducive to permanent domestic political peace, ending South Africa's pariah status internationally, and returning the country to the path of sustained economic growth. They also had a clear sense that reform of apartheid was required to achieve these goals. And they had begun to elaborate a general set of ideas about the changes that would be needed to produce the desired results. In late August 1979 Botha presented these ideas to the South African public. He referred to them as "twelve principles," and announced that they were the basis for a "plan for the Republic's future."[2] These principles provide the first clear indication of the overall content of Pretoria's "total strategy."* By extrapolating from them, one can infer Pretoria's "grand design" for domestic reform, that is its general conception of the direction, parameters, and limits of the changes that would be introduced. The existence of a grand design does not, however, imply the existence of a blueprint for the introduction of specific laws and policies. These would be introduced, sometimes haltingly, over the next decade, as the governing group sought to both operationalize its general strategy and to effectively counter various domestic and international pressures, some expected and others unforeseen. Thus there is no necessary contradiction between those who see a conscious strategy and those who hold that Pretoria lacks a well worked out design. We can say that in respect to reform the South African government had a grand design but lacked a blueprint.

Although the government moved uncertainly and hesitantly, it was not introducing changes that were unconnected and incoherent, as observers like Steven Friedman suggest. On the contrary, virtually every policy change introduced in the 1980s is either specifically predictable on the basis of the 1979 "twelve principles," or consistent with the logic that they embody.[3] A major objective of this chapter will be to reveal that logic, and to demonstrate how the many discrete changes introduced by Pretoria fit into it.

Those who argue that the South African government lacked a clear sense of direction, a general design for change, often point to the existence of disagreement

---

*The twelve principles were: the acceptance of a multinational society and the existence of minority groups; the acceptance of the principles of "vertical differentiation" and self-determination in as many areas as possible; the greatest possible consolidation of the homelands; a division of power between whites, Indians, and "coloureds," with consultation and joint responsibility on matters of common concern; the acceptance of the principle of separate schools and amenities; the scrapping of "unnecessary" discrimination measures; economic independence; striving toward a constellation of southern African states with mutual respect for each other's points of view; the determination to defend South Africa from foreign intervention; a neutral position for South Africa in which its interests would be of paramount importance; effective decision-making on the basis of a strong defense force and a clean administration; the maintenance of the free enterprise system.

between members of the ruling group as evidence for their point of view.[4] That there were differences among members of the South African cabinet during the 1980s is clear, but one must distinguish tactical from strategic differences. Agreement on goals and on a strategic vision for attaining them does not preclude differences, even intense ones, over the details of implementing strategy. While members of the National Party leadership have disagreed over tactical emphasis within a general strategy, and on the timing of one or another reform, there is little evidence of lack of consensus on the general strategic design that I will elaborate below. Those Nationalist leaders who broke with this consensus exited the party, either on the right where they formed the Conservative Party, or on the left where they founded the National Democratic Movement, and later joined the Democratic Party.

The Reform Program

In the previous chapter I had indicated that the reform aspect of total strategy was directed at four primary objectives—the removal of economic bottlenecks associated with apartheid, the creation of an African middle class, the political cooptation of the black population, and the "normalization" of South Africa's international status. The reform program introduced to achieve these goals can be analytically divided into four basic components: (1) upgrading black urban living conditions; (2) deracializing official and public life; (3) controlling the black population through substituting decentralized and indirect means for the coercive arm of the central state; and, (4) redesigning the constitutional order so as to allow for black political participation in a form that does not threaten ultimate control by whites.

Township Upgrading

The multiple crises that confronted Pretoria during the 1970s drew attention to the townships in which Africans, so-called "coloureds," and Indians are required to live under apartheid laws. It was in these peri-urban racial ghettos that Pretoria's three basic problems—economic stagnation, domestic political unrest, and international isolation—came together. The Soweto uprising was essentially a township phenomenon, spearheaded by urban youth. The black worker, whose increasing militancy since the Durban strikes of 1973 threatened to undermine South Africa as a haven for multinational investors, and who during the Soweto uprising showed a growing willingness to support radical youth with political strikes, was a township resident. Townships represented both a source of skilled workers, and an enormous untapped domestic market for South Africa's manufactured goods. And the townships, easily accessible to journalists, offered the international media vivid material to reveal the reality of black deprivation in South Africa.

The Cillie Commission, appointed in June 1976 to investigate the causes of the Soweto uprising, concluded that the rebellion resulted at least in part from the poor living conditions in the black townships. As noted in the commission's report, an inadequate housing supply, the nearly complete absence of electrification, a lack of running water, insufficient social amenities, and poor transportation to adjacent urban centers had contributed to a state of mind among township residents that "could easily lead to revolt and rioting."[5] The Riekert Commission, appointed in August 1977 to investigate the economic and other problems created by the system of influx control, and reporting a year later, urged a major reorientation in government policy toward the townships and their residents.[6] With P. W. Botha's accession to the prime ministership in 1978, the Cillie Commission findings and the recommendations of the Riekert Commission became part of an evolving program of urban reform, incorporating both the physical upgrading of the townships and an alteration in the legal, economic, and social status of township residents, particularly those of African descent. The link between urban reform and political stability was both explicit and publicly stated. According to Deputy Minister of Law and Order Roelf Meyer, housing, education, and health had to be improved if the "revolutionary onslaught" was to be countered.[7]

In committing itself to upgrade the black townships, Pretoria faced three formidable barriers. First, there was an ideological impediment. The government's longtime refusal to allot adequate resources to the black townships represented much more than an effort to enrich whites at the expense of blacks. It was also a reflection of apartheid's basic ideological notion that people of African descent had no permanent place within "white" South Africa. Africans residing in the urban areas were conceived of as temporary sojourners who would return to their permanent residences in the homelands as soon as the "white economy" could dispense with their labor. With such a guiding vision, reducing investment in township physical infrastructure to an absolute minimum represented simple frugality, if not rationality. Why invest heavily in something that is only temporary? A policy of upgrading black townships thus required abandoning fundamental and long-cherished ideological notions. It meant accepting not only that black residential areas were a permanent part of South Africa, but also that the persons of African descent who resided in them were permanent members of South African society.

Second, township upgrading faced a policy constraint. From the mid-1950s, the National Party had sought to use government policy to make urban life unattractive for Africans and thus discourage their urban residence. By depriving the townships of adequate physical resources, and by directing whatever resources were made available for the black population to the homelands, the South African government hoped to first stem, and eventually reverse, the movement of Africans from rural areas into the "white" cities. Thus in the 1960s, Pretoria adopted a policy of freezing the construction of both family housing and secondary schools in urban areas. The few new houses and high schools that were built were located in the rural homelands. The consequence of this policy was a massive housing crunch, overcrowding, and the proliferation of shanties.

Third, there was a question of finding adequate resources. Depriving the townships of resources had been the obverse of making more government funds available to the white community. It was one aspect of the apartheid state's appropriation of economic surplus from the black majority. Did the commitment to spend more on the townships imply a redistribution of wealth the other way around, from white to black? If not, from where would the necessary resources come?

Of the three obstacles in the path of township upgrading, the ideological barrier was the easiest to overcome. By the late 1970s only the most unreconstructed dogmatists among the National Party elite continued to hold to the Verwoerdian vision of a completely "white" South Africa, in which blacks constituted a dwindling category of temporary workers. Demography and economy had combined to force most of the leadership to accept as reality what the Fagan Commission had asserted and the National Party rejected some thirty years earlier—that the black urban work force was a necessary and permanent feature of South Africa, and that government efforts do prevent black urbanization would be ineffectual and economically harmful. This much was probably widely understood by early in the decade. One of the effects of Soweto was to add the persuasive force of politics to that of demographics and economics. The uprising revealed to the National Party leadership that the pursuit of the utopian fantasy of a South Africa "cleansed" of African urbanites was politically as well as economically costly. Thus Soweto served as a catalyst. It forced Pretoria to publicly accept what it had for some time known privately: that contrary to apartheid doctrine, black urbanization was an increasing and permanent feature of South African society and economy.

This was very much the message of the Riekert Commission Report of 1978 and of the accompanying government white paper. The very first point made by Riekert was to note that "black labour represents by far the largest proportion of the total labour force . . . in the so-called 'White area,' " that it was growing significantly faster than the white component, and that it was concentrated in the cities.[8] In the white paper that accompanied the release of the Riekert Commission Report, Pretoria finally acknowledged what big business and the English-speaking political opposition had been asserting for decades:

> The Government accepts that there is a common economic system in South Africa, which means, among other things that the various population groups participate in the labour market and that their participation will be restructured in the work place. It follows that measures and regulations that hamper the effective functioning of the common economic system, without contributing towards the achievement of other objectives, cannot be justified.[9]

The report of the Riekert Commission represents a watershed in the ideological evolution of National Party rule. From that point on officialdom discarded the doctrinal apartheid conception of the urban black worker as a transient, and the black township as a short-term aberration. Instead Pretoria officially acknowledged, indeed proclaimed, what the English-language *Sunday Times* termed "the recognition . . . of the permanence of the urban black."[10]

Riekert's significance goes beyond the ideological change that it legitimated. Far more important were the major alterations in policy that it proposed. These are significant not only because they represented departures from existing apartheid practices, but even more because they reveal a vision of how African urbanization could be made to contribute to economic growth, social peace, and political stability. In other words, an examination of the Riekert report provides us with a window into the National Party leadership's strategic thinking at a very early point in the reform process. As such it deserves careful examination.

The Riekert Report

The Riekert Commission developed its recommendations in terms of a frame of reference—what it called "general points of departure and approach."[11] The explicit statement of this "approach" reveals both Pretoria's perceptions of the problems confronting South Africa, and the parameters within which it intended to deal with these challenges. The starting point for the commission's work was a recognition that the apartheid mechanism of influx control—the elaborate system of direct state control over the allocation and geographic mobility of African labor and, relatedly, of African urbanization—was simply not geared to South Africa's changing needs. Thus, Riekert wrote:

> The Commission was particularly struck by the extensive complicated and . . . overlapping measures, i.e., statutes, regulations, administrative rules and practices . . . [which] gave rise to all kinds of market failures, for example discrimination, labour shortages or surpluses, the rise of sub-markets, wage levels that were not related to productivity, imperfect mobility—vertical and horizontal—defective knowledge of the labour market, the sub-optimal allocation of labour, *the limitation of economic growth and development,* dissatisfaction and frustration among workers and employers at some measures and the *consequent disturbance of relations between population groups.*[12]

In this description of the consequences of influx control, the commission revealed that its attention was directed at two basic objectives: creating a situation in respect to labor mobility and African urbanization that would (1) increase economic efficiency and (2) reduce political opposition. As Riekert himself wrote in the next passage of his report: "The Commission set itself the goal of . . . identifying the various *market failures* and *points of friction** arising from the existing framework and of eliminating them."[13] Eliminating economic inefficiency and political "friction," however, was to be achieved within the basic South African political status quo;† or, as Riekert expressed it, "within certain political parameters which were taken as given."[14] To achieve its twin objectives, the commission called for major alterations in the system of influx control, and for new legislation that would "explicitly make provision for the social and economic development of urban . . . Black communities that live in the White area."[15] The latter recommendations are the ones that concern us at this point.

The Riekert proposals for the development of "established" black urban communities are especially interesting because they reveal a specific conception of urban-oriented reform; a conception with clear and important political implications. Since the Riekert recommendations were introduced by the government over a ten-

---

*In the political lexicon of modern Afrikanerdom, *"friction"* is a code word for conflict situations that may lead black persons to oppose the system of white domination.

†The government, in its white paper accompanying the release of the Riekert Commission Report, also indicated the political limits of reform. It stated that "measures and regulations that hamper the effective functioning of the economy . . . cannot be justified [unless they were] contributing towards the achievement of other objectives" (par. 5). Presumably political control was the primary "other objective."

year period, we can assume that the commission's conception of urban reform was shared by those in power.

Notably, the commission distinguished between what it termed "the *established* inhabitants of urban Black residential areas,"[16] and urban residents who were considered commuters, migrants, vagrants, squatters, etc.. This latter and larger category of individuals was not, in the commission's view, entitled to rights of permanent residence. The former category of "established residents," or what some have termed "urban insiders," were defined by Riekert as those who had acquired "residential rights" under Section 10 of the Group Areas Act,[17] i.e., individuals who through continuous residence and/or employment could establish a legal claim to reside in one of the townships.*[18] The Riekert recommendation, accepted and eventually implemented by the government, was to treat the two categories of urban dwellers very differently. New and what were alleged to be more efficient and effective means were recommended to keep "outsiders" out of the urban residential areas. For the Section 10 "insiders," the commission proposed that residential rights be secured, that other rights and privileges be extended, and that living conditions in general be improved. Specifically, Riekert proposed:

1. New legislation that would reflect the government's recognition of permanent "Black communities in the White area," and would thereby protect "the existing and future rights of the established inhabitants of urban Black residential areas;" (par. 6.14(p)).

2. The right of geographic mobility between black townships, and the "transferability of [the right of urban residence] between urban areas," for established Black residents (par. 6.14(d)(i), 4.158, 4.205).

3. Individuals with the legal right to urban residence should be allowed to have their families join them in the urban area (par. 4.205(c)).

4. "[G]ranting [established inhabitants] the right to buy their own houses," and "the active promotion of home-ownership" by the state (par. 6.14(p)(ii), and 6.14(n)(i)).

5. "[D]iversification of the housing pattern in urban Black residential areas by making provision for suburbs of a higher standard, . . . private hotels, flats, youth centers, etc" (6.14(n)(iii)).

6. "[R]emoval of certain restrictions in respect of Black traders;" and "positive promotion of Black enterprise in trade and light service industries" (par. 6.14(i)(iii), 6.14(i)(j), and 4.232).

7. Opening up "free trade areas" in the Central Business Districts (CBDs); that is, allowing black businessmen and professionals to operate in the downtown areas of the "white" cities (par. 6.14(i)(k)).

---

*At the time the Riekert report was issued, estimates put the number of "urban insiders" at 1.5 million out of at least 9 million African urban dwellers. Later statements from government officials suggest that Pretoria saw the category as including approximately 5 million persons. The difference is probably that the later estimates rely on a functional definition of the "insider" category rather than on a strictly legal (Section 10) determination. The more recent interpretation classifies as "urban insiders" black professionals and skilled and semi-skilled workers who are employed on continuous contracts by manufacturing and service firms. This category would be larger than those with "Section 10 rights" because while the economy was rapidly expanding during the 1960s, the government created administrative obstacles to the extension of Section 10 rights to newly employed Africans.

Viewed in combination, these proposals are a design for creating an environment conducive to the emergence within the townships of a black middle class—a social category made up of professionals, artisans, and skilled laborers characterized by permanent employment, stable family life, and property ownership. Such a social strata could be expected to support government efforts to limit the size of the black population in urban areas, for the "outsiders" would be a threat to the black bourgeoisie's newly found stature and life-style. The "outsiders," unemployed or only marginally employed, without proper housing accommodations, with little education, and often single men far from their families, would represent poverty, overcrowding, crime, rape, and the like; that is, they would threaten home and property, the twin pillars of the middle class. Just as the new black middle class could be expected to stand with the government against the "outsiders," it could be expected to view revolutionaries as a direct threat to its recently attained property interests. As one business organization put the matter in a memorandum to the prime minister, "materialistically minded" blacks will back the whites against the "irresponsible economic and political ambitions" of black agitators.[19]

Since each of the Riekert recommendations in regard to the "development" of black urban areas involved matters that had been prohibited by apartheid laws and administrative policies, it is not surprising that the transformation of recommendations into policy, and the implementation of that policy, caused confusion and conflict.[20] The ideologically unreconstructed *verkrampte* faction of the National Party opposed the Riekert changes on both principled and practical grounds. A significant portion of Afrikaner voters were naturally concerned that the proposed changes would erode their standard of living. State bureaucrats resisted change for fear that the elimination of apartheid controls would render their positions irrelevant. Pretoria itself presented an ambiguous and therefore confusing message to the public and to the state officials charged with implementing the Riekert changes.[21] It viewed all black persons in South Africa as nationals of apartheid-created homelands; yet some black persons were now apparently deemed worthy of enjoying some South African citizenship rights. Moreover, the government was far from certain about the risks attendant upon adopting some of the more far-reaching Riekert recommendations. Pretoria therefore delayed implementing several major suggestions until 1986, some seven years after they had been introduced.

Although these political, ideological, and bureaucratic obstacles delayed or undermined the transformation of some of Riekert's recommendations into policy, Pretoria did move nonetheless along the path Riekert had laid out. This was especially true in respect to upgrading townships into "established urban communities."

Post-Riekert Reforms: Home Ownership

One of the earliest government moves after the release of the Riekert Commission Report was to alter the apartheid legal system so as to permit home ownership for black persons living in "white" areas of South Africa. In 1978, the Black Urban Areas Consolidation Act was amended to make black persons holding "Section 10 rights" eligible to register a ninety-nine-year right of leasehold over property in black townships. While this statutory amendment recognized rights to urban permanency for some black South Africans, it should be noted that in 1978 the government was not yet ready to accept outright ownership of property for Africans within what had, since 1913, been considered *white* South Africa. The 1978 reform of the Black Urban Areas Act provided for leasehold, not ownership, and pertained to houses, not the land upon which they were built. In subsequent years, however, Pretoria further modified the statutory restrictions on black home ownership so that Africans with rights to permanent residence could purchase outright their own houses and the land upon which the houses stood. In 1986, legislation extended full freehold property rights to urban Africans that had been denied them by earlier apartheid laws.[22]

Although the reforms in the area of black home ownership represented a reversal of certain apartheid tenets, they did not involve deracialization in the domain of either residence or home ownership. While those of African descent could, after 1986, own property and houses in the so-called "white" area, they could do so only within the geographic zones prescribed for blacks under the Group Areas Act. Moreover, not just any black person could reside in or purchase a house outside of the homelands. Homeownership in "urban" areas was intended to be a prerogative of only "established residents"—those with claims to long-term employment contracts. Consequently, the purchase of a home was contingent upon compliance with elaborate bureaucratic procedures designed to ensure that the buyer was "the right type of African." Prospective buyers, if they were black, had to prove that they were married and that they possessed "legal competence" to purchase.[23] They also had to provide the names, addresses, nationalities, and identity numbers of would-be occupants of the house.[24] These procedures, intended to ensure that home ownership would remain a prerogative of "urban insiders," along with the racially based legalities of the Group Areas and Native Lands Act, combined with financial constraints to slow down and thus reduce the impact of home-ownership reform. The first two freehold title deeds were obtained by Africans in November 1987, more than a year after the restoration of freehold rights to persons of African descent.[25] At the end of March 1988, only 42 freehold sales of houses to Africans had occurred in the whole of "white" South Africa. By January 1989, the government announced a nineteen-fold increase in freehold sales, but even then the total represented only 817 houses.[26] In contrast, in the area of leasehold, where racial law was less encumbering, the number of long-term house leases sold to Africans stood at 101,243 at the beginning of 1989.[27]

Black Business

Business activity is a second area in which government has sought to modify the apartheid system so as to allow for the emergence of an urban African middle class. The need to facilitate the growth and development of black businesses has been a constant theme of Pretoria's in the era of reform, and government spokesmen have acknowledged that the apartheid system unfairly limits the opportunities available to black business. A primary such constraint is the Group Areas Act, which among its myriad features, segregates business areas racially by prohibiting black businesspeople from owning property, renting premises, or carrying on commerce in areas designated as "white." The Group Areas Act has been the apartheid system's legal mechanism for denying blacks access to the core economy in any role other than that of laborer. With the *verligte* emphasis on reform and the development of a black middle class, Pretoria moved, in the 1980s, to alter this situation of complete exclusion. A new section of the Group Areas Act was created to empower the state president to declare "free trade areas"—geographic zones that are open to businesspeople of all races. Under a new procedure, the Group Areas Board could advise the state president to open free trade areas, after considering applications from local authorities. This method of introducing change led to the gradual expansion of business opportunities for black businesspeople and professionals in the central business districts of South Africa's major cities and towns. As of mid-1987, forty-eight CBDs had been declared open for trading by businesspeople of any race;[28] by the end of 1988 the number of open CBDs had grown to ninety.[29]

The method chosen by Pretoria to create free-trade areas had an effect on both the timing and nature of reform. Although in the post-Riekert era government no longer *required* segregation of business areas, it did not commit itself to desegregate business activities nationwide. *The change was from mandatory segregation to permitting desegregation.* For a variety of reasons, some already discussed, Pretoria probably favored more rather than less desegregation in the area of business activity, but it was unwilling to impose such practices. Instead, it left the matter to local authorities to initiate. This has meant that the process of opening free-trade areas has been relatively slow, and that the extent to which the economy has actually been opened to black businesspeople and professionals has been limited. It is notable that free-trade areas have, with a single exception, all been declared in the downtown business districts and not in the "white" suburbs.[30] Even when the local authorities of a "white" suburban area requested that their entire municipality be declared an open business district, as did the town council of Johannesburg's Sandton suburb in October 1988, the government refused, stating that it was policy "to open only central business areas and regional centres which serve all the race groups."[31] But, significantly, it is the suburban shopping centers with their predominantly white clientele that offer the most lucrative trading opportunities for fledgling black businesses. Thus in the area of black business the method Pretoria has adopted to reform apartheid allows for change in those locations readily observable by the international community (the city centers), while at the same time limiting change where black competition with white interests would be most effective (in suburban shopping areas).

Education

Enhancing opportunities for education was another component of the effort to upgrade black urban life. Although educational reforms were targeted more broadly than on the urban areas alone, the "established" urban residents would be the predominate beneficiaries if significant improvement occurred. As already discussed, in pursuit of its apartheid vision the National Party had sought to retard rural–urban migration by making urban townships unattractive places of residence, and hence had deprived the black urban areas of educational resources, especially of high schools. By the early 1970s, as the governing elite began to acknowledge that the shortage of skilled labor had become a threat to economic growth, this policy began to change. New secondary schools were opened in townships like Soweto, and some black students were permitted to enroll in "white" universities. In the wake of the Soweto uprising and with the new orientation toward black urban areas that followed the Riekert Commission report, this policy change was reinforced and intensified. There occurred a dramatic increase in state expenditure on African education, and in black enrollment in high schools and universities (see Figure 4.1). The number of African high school graduates doubled between 1975 and 1978 (from 5,529 to 11,167), increased by a factor of almost eight by 1984 (to 83,000), and is projected by the government to reach 190,000 by the year 2000.[32] The number of African students attending the so-called white universities increased more than twofold between 1974, when only 309 African students had been granted government permission to attend, and 1980, when the number attending was 788.[33] By 1986, Africans enrolled at the English-speaking "white" universities numbered 3,428.[34] Government expenditure on black education mirrored these upswings in enrollments. Spending on African education, which stood at only R27 million in 1972–73, rose to R566 million by 1981–82.[35] By 1988–89 the state's expenditure on African education outside the homelands stood at over 1½ billion rand.[36]

These impressive quantitative gains were not matched by reforms that would improve the quality of education offered black South Africans. Indeed, since the number of students climbed much more rapidly than did the construction of class-rooms or the availability of qualified teachers, the quality of education probably declined. The educational deprivation produced by thirty years of Bantu education, limited resources, and Pretoria's vision of what it would and could reform, all combined to achieve this result.* The government acknowledged that, as of 1985, some 80 percent of the teachers in African schools were themselves educationally "underqualified."[37] Only 17 percent of African high schools offered mathematics to students in their final year.[38]

The problems stemming from resource scarcity, school overcrowding, and teacher underqualification have been exacerbated by Pretoria's refusal to dispense with two pillars of the apartheid system: the notion of separate educational systems for the different race groups and the Group Areas Act. Due to these strictures, thousands of students in overcrowded black schools could not be accommodated in underutilized white facilities.[39] In 1989, there were 278,526 vacant places in white state schools, which was estimated to represent R1.5 billion worth of idle classroom space.[40] The government has allowed some private schools to enroll a small number of black students† and thus develop a racially mixed student body.[41] While doing

---

*Only 20 percent of the teachers in African primary and high schools have completed secondary school. Only 2.6 percent hold university degrees. Of the high school teachers, only about one-quarter have themselves completed high school. On the average, each high school has only about one university graduate. See Department of Education and Training, *Annual Report for 1981,* (Pretoria: Government Printer, 1982); and Kenneth Hartshorne, "The Unfinished Business: Education for South Africa's Black People," *Optima,* July 30, 1981, pp. 30–31.

†In June 1987 there were approximately 7,500 black pupils attending some 330 "white" private schools in South Africa. See *Citizen,* June 17, 1987; and, SAIRR, *Social and Economic Update,* vol. 2, 1987.

African High School Graduates

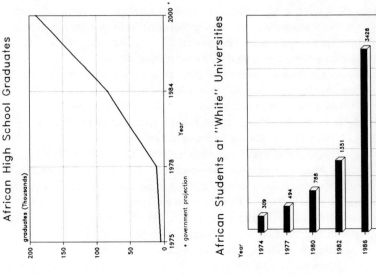

graduates (Thousands)

200

150

100

50

1975   1978   1984   2000 *

Year

* government projection

African Students at "White" Universities

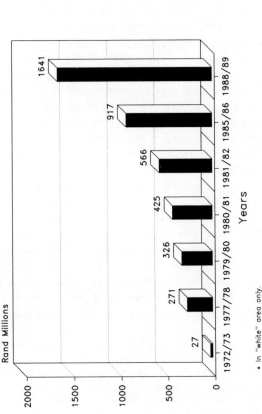

Year

1974   309
1977   494
1980   788
1982   1351
1986   3428

0   500   1000   1500   2000   2500   3000   3500   4000

University Students

Government Expenditure

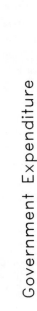

Rand Millions

2000

1500

1000

500

0

27   271   326   425   566   917   1641

1972/73 1977/78 1979/80 1980/81 1981/82 1985/86 1988/89

Years

* In "white" area only.

FIG. 4.1. Resources and opportunities for African education (*Source*: C. T. Verwey et al., eds., *Education and Manpower Production* (Bloemfontein University of the OFS, 1982), no. 2, p. 5; *SA Barometer*, August 14, 1987, pp. 184–85; John Marcum, *CSIS Africa Notes*, no. 41, p. 4; South African Institute of Race Relations, *Race Relations Survey, 1988/89*, p. 242)

little to alleviate overall educational disparities, this adjustment in the strict application of Bantu education and Group Areas Acts contributed to Pretoria's goal of creating an urban African middle class.

Physical Infrastructure

Expansion of educational opportunities, removal of legal barriers to business activity, and legal rights to permanent urban residence were all reforms directed at altering the social and economic status of individuals. Another aspect of the National Party's urban-oriented reform involved a commitment to upgrade the physical infrastructure of the townships. Indeed, the first item on the Botha reform agenda was the announcement of a program of housing construction, electrification, water and sewerage hookups, and the provision of better recreational amenities for the urban townships. "Black residential areas are to be upgraded by the Government to improve living standards . . . [and] to make these places more attractive and better able to meet people's needs," announced the deputy minister of cooperation and development, in a statement typical of the Botha era.[42] The Riekert Commission's report and its acceptance by the government eliminated the twin ideological impediments to physical upgrading: the idea that expenditure on townships was inherently wasteful because they were temporary, and the notion that townships should, in any case, be unpleasant places so as to discourage African migration to the cities. Clearing away the ideological impediments, however, merely left exposed a much more intractable obstacle to implementing the government's new design for urban living: making the townships reasonable environments for the middle-class lifestyle envisaged by Pretoria was, simply in monetary terms, a gigantic task. For example, supplying electricity to the approximately 2.5 million black urban households that lack it was estimated to have a capital cost of 10 billion rand (approximately $5 billion).[43] The enormity of this need rendered marginal even the expenditure of significant sums during the 1980s, such as the R206 million that was spent to electrify 105,000 Soweto houses.[44] Nearly a decade after Pretoria announced its upgrading plans, by the government's own calculations 86 percent of all African township houses did not have electricity.[45] Ironically, the costs in the 1980s of physical upgrading were so high precisely because the National Party government had, for thirty-five years, been carrying out a policy of denying to the townships the physical infrastructure it now sought to provide.

Housing

The "drag" of apartheid policy on the ability of Pretoria to implement its reform strategy and to deliver on its promise of township upgrading is most starkly manifest in the area of housing. As was discussed in Chapter 2, government policy of freezing new housing starts for Africans in urban areas had, by the mid-1970s, resulted in a disastrous housing shortage in the urban townships. The Riekert Commission, offering a very conservative estimate, calculated the backlog of houses for Africans at 141,000 units, which it said would require an expenditure of R764 million to eliminate.[46] This estimate does not include the shortage of housing in "coloured" townships, which in the mid-1980s was estimated at 100,000 units.[47] During the 1980s, estimates of the housing backlog grew, both because calculations were more realistic and because migration to urban centers continued.* According to one estimate, in 1987 some 7 million black South Africans were living in backyard shacks, garages, self-built tin and plastic shelters, and out in the open. The Urban Foundation, generally thought to provide the most reliable data on black urban areas, calculated that in 1987 the national housing backlog was 1.8 million units.†[48] Jan Lombard, deputy governor of the South African Reserve Bank, calculated that it would cost about R40 billion to eliminate the housing backlog by the year 2000. For the state to achieve such a level of expenditure, it would have to allocate annually to housing during the years 1990–2000 an amount 500 percent greater than it budgeted for that purpose in 1988/89.[49]

Apparently, Pretoria initially intended to finance the immense cost of township upgrading through economic growth. Lombard has noted that a 5 to 7 percent annual rate of GNP growth would be required to cover the costs of upgrading.[50] But unfortunately the combination of structural bottlenecks and the drying up of capital and technology from abroad resulted in economic *decline* in South Africa during the 1980s. Under these circumstances, Pretoria was unwilling and politically unable to finance the immense costs of township upgrading through the state coffer. Thus between 1980 and 1985, the state financed the construction of only about 18,000 housing units per year for African and "coloured" population groups (see Table 4.1). This represents less than 10 percent of what the Urban Foundation has estimated would be needed to eliminate black urban housing shortages over a ten-year period (approximately 200,000 additional housing units per annum).[51]

Unwilling to bear the costs of township upgrading, Pretoria has instead developed its urban policy around the expectation that the private sector can and will finance upgrading, and that township residents can pay for improvements themselves.[52] Such a strategy fit nicely within the National Party's ideological and social agenda. It was consistent with the free enterprise–small government rhetoric that Pretoria adopted in the 1980s as a means to mobilize business energies behind its reform program and, if successful, it would contribute to the creation of a propertied black middle class. This strategy, however, failed to take two important economic realities into account. Business will finance housing construction only when there is a reasonable prospect that the loans it makes will be repaid. And the private sector would rather build fewer large and expensive houses than many cheap ones, since administrative and construction costs are lower in the former case. The black township population is poor, which means that it can afford only relatively small houses, and it represents high risk in respect to repayment of loans. This is not an

---

*Most of this housing shortage has been a long-term problem. It is not, primarily, a result of recent migration from rural areas. A 1988 Urban Foundation study found that within the industrial heartland (the PWV) 68 percent of the black urban residents without access to regular housing accommodations had worked in the PWV for at least five years. Virtually all of these workers had moved to their present locations from other metropolitan locations, not from rural areas. See *Financial Mail*, August 19, 1988).

†Since there is a surplus of housing for whites, this backlog encompasses accommodations for African, "coloured," and Indian population groups. While there is general agreement that the housing backlog is huge, estimates of the number of new units required vary widely. For example, in contrast to the Urban Foundation figure of 1.8 million units, the National Building Research Institute estimates a black housing shortage of some 574,063 units, the non-homeland African component of this figure being in excess of 440,000. See *The Star*, September 9, 1986; *Business Day*, October 6, 1987.

TABLE 4.1.   State-Financed Housing Units,
African and Coloured

Year	African	Coloured	Total
1980	4,260	13,589	17,849
1981	4,583	8,329	12,912
1982	14,549	8,171	22,720
1983	7,437	8,546	15,983
1984	2,834	8,205	11,039
1985	12,702	11,513	24,215
Total	46,365	58,353	104,718

Source: National Building Reasearch Institute, *SA Barometer,* October 10, 1987, p. 245.

environment conducive to galvanizing private enterprise into action. Thus, between 1980 and 1984 the private sector built only 6,756 houses for Africans and 15,091 for "coloureds" throughout South Africa, including the homelands (see Table 4.2). During the same period, the private sector financed some 132,903 units of "white" housing.[53] Although the pace of private-sector "black" housing construction quickened substantially in 1986, in part as a result of the availability of government-subsidized loans, the effort fell far short of housing requirements. One estimate, for example, put the private-sector contribution in 1986 and 1987 at 35,000 units—not an insignificant number but much less than what would be required to deal effectively with the housing backlog.[54] The Urban Foundation estimated in 1989 that fewer than 10 percent of black urban residents could afford a house erected by private builders.[55]

The poverty of township residents also renders moot Pretoria's effort to have the black population pay for upgrading themselves. Government had intended to gener-

TABLE 4.2.   Private-Sector Financed
Housing Units, African and Coloured

Year	African	Coloured	Total
1980	552	2,948	3,500
1981	1,453	2,757	4,210
1982	1,653	3,053	4,706
1983	1,618	2,699	4,317
1984	1,480	3,634	5,114
Total	6,756	15,091	21,847

Source: National Building Research Institute, *SA Barometer,* October 9, 1987, p. 244.

ate resources for housing construction through the sale of existing rental units to their tenants. However, four years after this scheme was launched only 14 percent of the state-owned dwellings on offer had been sold, and the pace of purchases was declining.[56] Only with the introduction of a sharp discount in September 1987, reducing the price of houses by as much as two-thirds, did the pace of purchases pick up. At the end of the year, some 66,247 units, representing 19 percent of total township housing stock, had been sold.[57] Although it produced a substantial increase in the number of black homeowners, this strategy could neither solve the housing shortage nor generate revenues to do so. Since what was being sold was existing and already occupied stock, sales in no way directly contributed to eliminating housing shortages and overcrowding. And because heavy state price subsidization was necessary to enable township residents to afford homes, the sell-off did not generate significant revenue. Moreover, while this scheme helped a substantial number of people to become homeowners, many more could not afford even the subsidized price.

Another impediment to successful implementation of township upgrading was a shortage of available land. To achieve a significant reduction in overcrowding in black residential areas, where on average sixteen persons occupy a small four-room house,[58] new areas for the development of black housing had to be designated under the still existing Group Areas Act. Indeed, the state president, in opening the 1987 session of Parliament, stated that the "provision of housing and land for increasing home ownership" would be a government priority.[59] But the resistance of white local authorities to the allocation of land for black housing led Pretoria to pull back from its verbal commitments. Plans for the development of a giant new township north of Johannesburg, to be called Norweto, were abandoned. Instead the government opted for the development of small "elite" townships. In place of Norweto, Pretoria set aside a "limited area" of 600 hectares for "higher-income black urbanization."[60] Similarly, a new township, to house 4,500 middle-income black families, is planned at Mfueni on the Cape Flats. Pretoria expects the cost of R150 million to be funded by the private sector, with houses selling in the R25,000 to R50,000 range.

Faced with the financial quagmire surrounding the physical upgrading of black townships, Pretoria has moved toward a differentiated approach to black urban residential life. Along with encouraging home construction and ownership for a "new middle class," the state has launched separate and much cheaper "site and service" schemes for the very large low-income segment of the working class. Sites serviced with water, sewerage, roads, and transportation are made available for people to construct their own dwellings, essentially shanties, using readily available building materials. A form of controlled squatting, such schemes face even greater white resistance in regard to available land than does the development of regular townships. Moreover, even if land can be found and sufficient financial resources allocated, residents must be moved out of their existing accommodations within the townships to the new site and service areas. Experience indicates that such relocations are not easily accomplished. It is instructive that few site and service schemes were attempted in the Transvaal, where population is concentrated. In the Western

Cape, however, where land is more readily available, Africans were forced to move to a new site and service area at Khayalitsia when their dwellings in the squatter settlement of Crossroads were razed.

In adopting a policy of upgrading the black townships, Pretoria pursued two political objectives. First, it sought to reduce the general level of political alienation by ameliorating the social conditions which, since the Soweto uprising of 1976, were viewed as conducive to rebellion. Second, it sought to erect a barrier to revolutionary sympathies by facilitating the creation of a black middle class. But Pretoria's ability to successfully pursue township reform was undermined by the limits of both its vision and its resources. Unwilling to completely scrap the Group Areas Act and allow black South Africans to reside wherever they choose, and unable to shoulder the financial burden of social and physical upgrading, Pretoria was incapable, in the decade after 1978, of significantly improving the living conditions of the mass of black urban residents. Consequently, the government focused its attention on the development of a black middle class. This goal, because it targeted fewer individuals, was less costly and thus more easily attained. Home ownership, high school and university enrollment, professional careers, and business opportunities became available to thousands of black South Africans who, prior to 1978, would have been barred from these spheres. Permitting the growth of a black middle class, however, did not automatically guarantee the political co-optation for which Pretoria had hoped. Questions abounded. Would middle class blacks be primarily oriented toward protecting their new-found status; or would they focus on those aspects of the apartheid system that remained in place?* Is the new middle class grateful for reforms, or do the limits of reform make it even more resentful over continuing discrimination and political disenfranchisement? Is cooptation a feasible objective so long as the scrapping of apartheid is only partial and the governing group remains committed to white political supremacy? Pretoria was banking on cooptation, but might partial reform lead instead to greater alienation?

"Deracialization"

State-mandated racial separation in every conceivable sphere is apartheid's most essential formal feature. Whatever benefits the National Party leadership presumed to flow therefrom, officially mandated race segregation also constituted Pretoria's greatest international liability. For the pervasive system of *officially* required race segregation, enshrined in the basic laws of the land, is what distinguished the Republic of South Africa from every other country in the world. Racial and ethnic segregation, discrimination, and domination might exist elsewhere, but only in South Africa were such practices *required* under national law. It is this special

---

*It should be noted that one of the first consequences of lifting some restrictions on black business activity was the formation of several black businessmen's organizations to campaign against remaining discriminatory and other restrictions. See South African Institute of Race Relations (SAIRR), *Social and Economic Update,* no. 4 (1987), p. 13.

feature of the South African system that provided the moral ammunition for those who have sought to render South Africa a pariah in the international community, to isolate it, and to pressure it diplomatically and economically.

In the late 1970s, as South Africa's need for involvement in the international economic and diplomatic system increased and the threat of its isolation intensified, the official racism that had been systematically introduced since 1948 began to look less attractive and far more costly to the leadership of the South African governing group. Not only did official racism appear to preclude international legitimacy but it also came to be viewed as a contributor to intergroup friction. The program of race separation that the National Party since 1948 had trumpeted as the best means for avoiding political conflict in a racially heterogenous society was, after the Soweto uprising of 1976, increasingly seen as producing conflict. Moreover, petit apartheid—the laws mandating segregation in social and personal life—had no direct, or even indirect, role in the maintenance of white political power and material privilege. Rather, as public reflections of the racist worldview that infuses apartheid doctrine, they performed largely symbolic and ideological functions. For the *verligte* politicians who dominated the National Party and government in the late 1970s, and who sought to shore up an increasingly threatened white supremacy, these symbolic and ideological functions of race segregation could not compensate for the domestic and international liabilities that went along with official racism. Thus, from 1979 Pretoria undertook policies directed at "deracializing" the official aspects of personal, social, and public life. It sought to eliminate as much of state-imposed racial separation and discrimination as was consistent with the maintenance of white control over that which the National Party deemed important to the "white community." In 1979 P. W. Botha referred to this as the removal of "unnecessary race discrimination." The Riekert Commission sounded the same theme when it reported that "discriminatory measures should be avoided as far as possible by not drawing any distinction on the ground of race . . . in legislation or administrative rules."[61]

The move to jettison those aspects of officially mandated racism that play little practical role in bolstering white supremacy is most clearly revealed by the abolition of the Prohibition of Mixed Marriages Act and section 16 of the Immorality Act. These laws, which made cross-racial marriage and interracial sexual relations a criminal offense, were repealed in 1986. The long debate that preceded repeal clearly reveals the National Party elite's perception of the necessity to remove those racist laws that exact domestic and international costs without contributing to the maintenance of white power and privilege. In 1980 P. W. Botha told the annual Transvaal Congress of the National Party that he did not believe the survival of his people was dependent on the mixed marriages and immorality legislation. Supporting his position, the pro-government newspaper, *The Citizen*, commented, "We can do without the Mixed Marriages Act and without section 16 of the Immorality Act. . . . The two laws are among the main ones that offend people of colour here and bring the country into disrepute abroad."[62]

The Mixed Marriages and Immorality acts come closest to being the most purely symbolic parts of the apartheid edifice, since they impact upon a very tiny proportion of either white or black South Africans. But because these statutes are so peculiar by international standards, they have had a disproportionate role in generating worldwide opprobrium toward South Africa. Thus, for the National Party political elite intent on creating a situation of international "normalcy," these laws were high on the list of expendable aspects of apartheid. Yet although they affected very few South Africans, it took the government from 1979, when the issue of their appropriateness was first publically raised by P. W. Botha, until 1986 to actually abolish them.

Not surprisingly, those aspects of petit apartheid that impinge on the lives of a greater number of white people, if only marginally, elicited an even more cautious response from the government. Nevertheless, from the late 1970s Pretoria moved to reduce officially mandated race segregation in public amenities—parks, beaches, swimming pools, transportation, hotels, restaurants, and theaters. In keeping with its desire to achieve "normalcy" internationally and to reduce the basis for intra-group "friction" domestically, government officials signaled an intent to move in a non-discriminatory and integrationist direction. As already indicated, in 1979 P. W. Botha announced that the removal of "unnecessary (sic) race discrimination" was a central element in his plans for a future South Africa. In 1983, Minister of Foreign Affairs R. F. (Pik) Botha told a public meeting that there was no justification for racism in South Africa. Things like the Immorality Act were "doing South Africa harm. . . . The government," he stated, "will stand and fight for civilized norms and standards, but . . . will not stand for racism purely on the grounds of the colour of a man's skin."[63] Fanie Botha, minister of manpower, echoed this theme in his parliamentary by-election campaign when he told a meeting that "one of the most important questions facing South Africa was whether there should be discrimination based purely on skin colour."[64] And from the mid-1980s, government officials and advisors spoke of the need to scrap the Reservation of Separate Amenities Act of 1953—the apartheid law that requires strict racial segregation in all public amenities.

The manner in which Pretoria has moved to operationalize these desegregationist signals illuminates both the nature of its reform strategy and the political and ideological limits placed upon it. The government's approach to ending petit apartheid combined two contradictory principles—the elimination of discrimination on the base of race, and the right to race-group exclusivity. According to P. W. Botha, the government wanted to ensure nondiscrimination while at the same time guaranteeing that "facilities may be used within the group context by those who so prefer."[65] This ambivalent orientation produced a hybrid policy; one that allowed for integration within certain specified arenas, while permitting segregation and discrimination to continue in others. Pretoria's method of "desegregating" the state-owned national railway system is a case in point. Until the 1980s passenger railroads were completely segregated according to the officially prescribed race groups, with separate cars for white, black (African), "coloured," and Indian passengers. In the 1980s, when this system was deemed "hurtful," Pretoria did not simply integrate the trains. Instead, it kept the racially exclusive passenger cars for "whites only" and designated the other cars "open" or integrated. Whites, if they chose, could now ride with Africans, Indians, and so-called "coloureds" in the "open" cars. As will be seen, the method that Pretoria applied to its segregated railroads became a template for reform in other areas of petit apartheid as well.

In reforming those aspects of petit apartheid in which administrative control is exercised by local authorities—parks, beaches, swimming pools, public lavatories, buses, sports facilities, and the like—Pretoria combined the concept of the coexistence of amenities that are "open" (racially integrated) and "closed" (racially exclusive), with a second orienting element, the notion of "local option." While not repealing the Reservation of Separation Amenities Act of 1953, Pretoria allowed local authorities to desegregate those public facilities that they administer. On a de facto basis, "local option" replaced the nationally binding Separate Amenities Act.* The result has been an uneven and partial move toward desegregation, since the actions of the different local authorities reflect their particular sociopolitical environment. Thus at one end of the change continuum stands Cape Town, the 'raditional bastion of English-speaking liberalism, where public beaches, swimming pools, parks, and transportation services were desegregated by the early 1980s, while on the other end stands cities like Pretoria, where only minimal steps had been taken toward desegregation by the end of the decade. The norm is typified by cities like Durban, which in late 1987 had seven multiracial "open" beaches, three white beaches, two African beaches, one Indian beach, and one "coloured" beach.[66]

Residential segregation is another area in which Pretoria's reform effort combined the elements of local option along with a combination of integration and continued segregation. The National Party government throughout the 1980s was steadfast in its commitment to retaining residential segregation, as is dictated under the Group Areas Act. Yet for economic reasons (the lack of available housing for black people in the townships), and because residential segregation is bad for South Africa's international image, the government allowed some residential areas to become integrated. At first Pretoria simply ignored the de facto existence of racially mixed neighborhoods, what were termed "grey areas," as black people moved into neighborhoods legally prescribed for whites. Foreign Minister Pik Botha told parliament in 1987 that about 45,000 black people were living in the Johannesburg district of Hillbrow in violation of the law. The fact that these people had not been prosecuted, he said, had "to be seen in the light of the shortage of housing for Africans and the surplus of housing for whites."[67] By the mid 1980s, the population in Johannesburg's three most densely populated "white" residential neighborhoods— Hillbrow, Berea, and Joubert Park—was about one-quarter black. A similar pattern of de facto and technically illegal "grey" residential areas emerged in each of South Africa's major cities: in Durban—Greyville and Claremont; in Port Elizabeth— North End and Korsten; in Cape Town—Woodstock, Salt River, Wynberg, Landsdowne and Obervatory.[68]

In 1987 Pretoria began the process of embedding this coexistence of residential integration and segregation in a reformed legal and policy framework. Under the new reform policy, announced in October 1987 and given legal shape in late 1988, the government committed itself to allowing residential integration in newly devel-

---

*The Separate Amenities Act was finally repealed during the 1990 parliamentary session.

oped suburbs that would be designated "open areas," and in already existing residential areas when established white residents requested that their area be declared "open." At the same time white residential areas could opt to remain "closed," as the vast majority probably would, in which case residential race segregation would continue to be legally enforced. As far as the government was concerned, this arrangement represented a fundamental move away from apartheid in that it allowed for individual choice in respect to living arrangements, and gave primacy to the "local option" rather then to central control.

This hybrid policy stemmed from Pretoria's desire to achieve simultaneously four not necessarily compatible objectives: (1) to remove, or at least reduce, the international stigma of official racism by allowing for multiracial and integrated neighborhoods in the larger South African metropolitan areas; (2) to reduce the housing crisis for black South Africans, and particularly for the black middle class that it was hoped would emerge from the process of socioeconomic reform; (3) to deflect the resistance to any change in the status quo by reassuring whites fearful of racial integration that they would be able to maintain their segregated residential areas; and (4) to maintain a majority of racially homogenous geographic areas that could serve as the basis for territorial, rather than racial, representation in a reformed system of political participation.[69] As P. W. Botha made clear in March 1987: "The devolution of power, the sharing of power, and the protection of minorities [whites] cannot take place without the recognition of own residential areas for different communities."[70] This statement was in accord with Botha's 1979 pledge to end *unnecessary* racial discrimination. In other words, when segregation or discrimination was more than symbolic—when it enhanced the political, economic, and social position of whites, that is, when it involved "the protection of minorities" or "the maintenance of civilized standards"—it was deemed *necessary* and the National Party government was committed to continuing it. F. W. de Klerk, who in 1979 was a member of the cabinet, drew this distinction clearly and succinctly: "Separation that is necessary to maintain self-determination and to protect the rights of minorities will always remain. But separation that is irritating and unnecessary discrimination will go."[71]

Devolution and Decentralization

The third component of Pretoria's reform strategy involved an attempt to achieve the economic, geographic, and political control of the black population by substituting indirect and decentralized means for the coercive apparatus of the central state. Bureaucratization and centralization are perhaps the primary structural characteristics of the apartheid system. They are what distinguishes apartheid as a mode of white supremacy from the system of racial segregation that characterized South Africa before the electoral victory of the Nationalists in 1948.

Prior to 1948 South Africa was a thoroughly segregated society. Practices of racial segregation and domination had, however, evolved piecemeal at the local level over more than a century, and they were largely administered by local authorities and institutions. Consequently, the thoroughness and rigor with which legal segregation was actually enforced tended to vary according to local social history and the political bent of local authorities. The Nationalist government, after 1948, sought to do away with this somewhat haphazard and inconsistent application of racialism. Once in power, they proceeded to rationalize and systematize the already existing practices of racial segregation and domination, and to extend them into every nook and cranny of South African society. Most importantly, they sought the complete centralization of the mechanisms of racial domination, and thus they brought South Africa's myriad racialist practices under the direct control of the central state and its bureaucratic apparatus.

As noted in Chapter 1, the system of centralized social engineering, economic control, and political domination that apartheid represents appeared for at least twenty years to be yielding significant results. But the multiple crises that beset the apartheid state in the 1970s revealed the "downside" to what the National Party had touted as their uniquely effective means of managing a racially heterogeneous society. For the centralization of racial control exacerbated these crises and rendered them more difficult to overcome. Centralization of economic control in Pretoria and the climate of bureaucratization and regulation that went with it had both a stultifying effect on economic growth and an alienating effect on the business community. The former threatened the financial resources required for implementing the Nationalist's total national strategy, and the latter threatened to rob Pretoria of the business support needed to pursue this endeavor. In addition, locating control of the pervasive system of racial discrimination and domination in the bureaucratic apparatus of the central state made the national government a natural and continuous target of black hostility. When the participants in the Soweto uprising sought to obliterate all physical manifestations of the state within the townships, the political cost of centralization was dramatically revealed. What had during the 1950s been seen as the great advantage of apartheid began to look like one of its chief liabilities. The liability lay not only in the intense anger that direct state control generated among the black population, but also in the manner that it affected Pretoria's relations with other countries. The creation of a centrally mandated and controlled system of racial domination marked South Africa as unique among the community of nations, and thus provided legitimation for those who campaigned to have Pretoria treated as a pariah—an outlaw country that should be denied access to the means of national defense and economic growth.

It was in the context of this "triple-threat"—economic stagnation, domestic conflict, international isolation—that Pretoria turned its attention during the immediate post-Soweto years to reducing the direct state role in South Africa's socioeconomic system. In the 1980s "deregulation" and "privatization" replaced "racial separation" as the buzzwords of official rhetoric. With this new emphasis, Pretoria spoke simultaneously to two audiences—the business community within South Africa, which had come to view state economic control as an obstacle to growth, and the increasingly vital international financial community, which in the 1980s trumpeted privatization and deregulation as the elixir for economic health. The emphasis on moving away from state-centric policies, however, went far beyond the organization and regulation of the economy. Far more significant was the effort to substitute indirect means for apartheid's direct methods of controlling the black majority. These indirect means can be divided for analytic purposes into two categories: marketization and indirect rule.

Marketization

At the general level, the use of market mechanisms to both allocate resources and control behavior involves individual or group responses to a particular structure of incentives. "Market-driven" behavior results from calculative decisions rather than authoritative commands. In three important areas, Pretoria's reforms are intended to shift the basis of control from "commandism" to market-type allocation.

Public Amenities

Under apartheid, access to hotels, restaurants, theaters, and cinemas was strictly controlled under the Group Areas Act, the Separate Amenities Act, and various government proclamations. Essentially, establishments were permitted to serve only the racial group that corresponded to the "group area" in which their premises were located. In certain rare instances Pretoria would, upon application, grant "international status" to a hotel or restaurant, allowing it to cater to a multiracial clientele. In 1986, Pretoria utilized its powers of proclamation to lift the Group Areas racial restrictions on hotels and restaurants nationwide. The implications of this action in the view of the Afrikaner political elite were illuminated by the following commentary in the Afrikaans-language newspaper *Die Vaderland:*

> With the unconditional opening of hotels and other licenced business premises for consumers of all races, another step away from constitutional discrimination has been taken. . . . *The reservation of the right of admission and prices are now the methods with which criteria [for access] will be maintained.* That is justifiable.
> The question can rightly be posed who will determine the criteria which must be maintained? . . . The answer is that *criteria are determined according to what people can afford and circumstances in which they feel at home.*[72]

This commentary reveals that while the legal prohibitions against race mixing— "constitutional discrimination"—were being lifted, the National Party elite viewed the economic gap between blacks and whites as a means of maintaining racial segmentation in public facilities such as hotels and restaurants. Moreover, the allocating effect of the market (prices) would presumably be reinforced and backed up by social mores. Proprietors, making their own calculations about what would be good for business, could be expected to limit access to their premises when race mixing, because it violated local mores, might drive away clientele. Thus, the elimination of constitutional discrimination need not mean the end of racial segregation, for in the South African context class criteria, operating through the market and social preferences, can produce the same results as state directives.

Black Trade Unions

In September 1979 the South African government announced with considerable fanfare the granting of formal trade-union rights to African workers. This was a reversal of the apartheid practice of refusing to recognize the right of African workers to organize and bargain collectively, to strike, and to otherwise take part in the statutory industrial relations system of which white trade unions were a part. The September 1979 announcement was a culmination of a process begun with the appointment in 1977 of a government commission of inquiry into existing labor legislation (the Wiehahn Commission). Since the denial of trade-union rights to Africans has generally been considered a core feature of apartheid, the Wiehahn Commission Report, which recommended lifting the prohibition against registration of black unions, and the government action that implemented the report's recommendation, were hailed both domestically and internationally as a major liberalizing step. The intention of both Wiehahn and the government, however, was something quite different.

The primary concern of the government in the late 1970s was how to regain control over a labor situation that appeared increasingly threatening. The return of large-scale labor agitation after the Durban strikes of 1973 posed several interrelated problems for Pretoria. Not only had African laborers shown themselves capable of mounting an effective challenge to apartheid's low-wage system—a challenge that could well be extended into the realm of political change, as the stayaways during the Soweto uprising had shown—but their actions drew international attention to the denial of black trade-union rights in South Africa. Pretoria was especially sensitive to such attention because it tended to galvanize international trade unions, and these were organizations that had the potential to disrupt South Africa's efforts to market its goods worldwide. The period after the Durban strikes had witnessed various forms of pressure from this quarter.[73] The most dramatic instance occurred in 1974. Dockworkers in Alabama and the American Mineworkers Union refused to unload ships carrying South African coal, on the grounds that it was mined under conditions of indentured servitude. In response the South African government abolished the penal provisions of the Masters and Servants Act, which had been part of its law for 120 years.[74]

The introduction to the Wiehahn report reveals that the commission viewed its purpose as providing a solution to the interrelated economic, political, domestic, and international problems posed by the revival of black worker militancy. According to the commission, "Unregistered trade unions for Black workers are becoming a prominent and permanent feature of the industrial relations scene, and from the evidence it is clear that these unions are enjoying financial and moral support on a broad front."[75] The commission continued:

> The fact that their existence is not prohibited, while at the same time they are not registrable . . . serves as an incentive to foreign labour and political organisations to aid them overtly and covertly. Added to this is the fact that other non-labour and political organisations regard these unions as vehicles for change, using them also in matters other than those of a purely labour character.[76]

Later in the report, the commission noted that "the strikes and labour unrest of 1973 brought the position of the Black worker and his organisation under the focus of international attention, giving rise to a preoccupation among pressure groups and various institutions, including trade union organisations, with Black trade unionism and the conditions of employment of Black workers." This situation, the commission remarked, constituted "a development of historical significance."[77]

The related problems of a loss of domestic control, both economic and political, and the costs of international illegitimacy were identified by the Wiehahn Commission as the reason for seeking modifications in the existing apartheid system. The commission considered three options: the status quo, with black unions continuing to exist, grow, and operate outside of and in defiance of the formal system of industrial relations; repression, whereby the new black trade unions would be outlawed; and the extension of full trade-union rights to black workers.[78] The commission dismissed the first option because it deemed the status quo to be increasingly untenable. It noted the rapid increase in numbers of and membership in black trade unions, the location of these unions in all strategic industries, the significant international ties of the new black unions, and the militant orientations that such associations were thought to encourage, and concluded that the developments in black trade unionism, if left unchecked, held ominous economic and political implications.[79] The black trade unions, the commission argued, "enjoy much greater freedom than registered unions, to the extent that they are free if they so wished to participate in politics and to utilise their funds for whatever purposes they see fit."[80] Moreover, the new unions, being outside the statutory industrial relations system, "could within a very short space of time pose a grave danger to industrial peace."[81]

The commission rejected option two, an outright ban on black trade unionism, as being both infeasible and counterproductive. Such a prohibition, Wiehahn argued, would "contribute considerably towards the creation of a climate of industrial unrest."[82] It "would undoubtedly have the effect of driving Black trade unionism underground and uniting Black workers not only against the authorities but . . . also against the system of free enterprise in South Africa."[83] And it "would prepare the ground for confrontation between, on the one hand, employers and their employees—particularly those in multinational enterprises which have already established liaison with the existing unregistered Black unions—and on the other hand the State."[84] Then there was the threat of serious international repercussions should the state use its repressive capabilities to deal with the problem of black trade unionism.

> Apart from the domestic implications . . . the Commission also foresees serious repercussions for the country on the international scene should it be decided to prohibit Black trade unionism by law. It would unite international employers' and workers' organisations in both the Western and Eastern blocs of the world against South Africa. This could only impose an intolerable strain on the country's relations with the international world, inevitably leading to punitive sanctions in the industrial, commercial and communication fields. Finally, such a prohibition would be detrimental to efforts to improve relations between South Africa and the international world.[85]

Having concluded that it would be both impracticable and unwise to either ignore or repress the emergent "wildcat" trade unions, the commission recommended "permitting Black workers to join unions and allowing unions with Black members to be registered."[86] Such a move, the commission argued, would eliminate the unhealthy situation in which the existing but unregistered black unions "enjoy much greater freedom than registered unions." With the extension of full trade-union rights, these black unions would be subject to the "stabilising elements of the system [and] to its essential discipline and control."[87] While bringing the controlling aspects of the existing industrial relations system to bear, government recognition of trade-union rights for black workers would simultaneously bring South Africa labor-relations practices into line with international standards. For "it is self-evident," the commission report stated, "that the denial of recognised trade union rights to the major part of South Africa's work force constitutes a gross departure from internationally accepted standards and practices."[88]

The Wiehahn Commission recognized the "two-edged" character of the extension of trade-union rights. While registration would enhance union organizational capabilities, it would provide the government with significant means of control. As noted in the commission report:

> Registered trade unions are under certain statutory restrictions and obligations designed to protect and nurture a system that has proved its success in practice. The Industrial Conciliation Act, 1956, provides for matters such as the annual auditing of the trade unions' financial affairs; the maintenance of membership registers; the submission of annual reports, statements of income and expenditure and balance sheets to a meeting of members and to the Department of Labour; the strict control of constitutions and memberships; and a prohibition on affiliation with any political party or to a candidate for election to Parliament, a provincial council or any local authority.[89]

Moreover, on the Wiehahn Commission's recommendation the government created a new control mechanism—the National Manpower Commission (NMC). Its purpose is to consult with the industrial registrar on the registration and deregistration of unions, taking into account "a wide spectrum of considerations [including] . . . *the implications for the country as a whole in social, economic, and political contexts.*"[90] Special emphasis was given in the report on the need to reinforce the existing statutory prohibition on political activities by trade unions.[91] The government's white paper that accompanied the issuing of the Wiehahn Report highlighted this recommendation. It indicated that the NMC would be specifically instructed to keep the matter of proscribed political activity "under scrutiny and to make timeous suggestions for any further steps which may be required."[92] Through this and other functions to be performed by the NMC, such as close financial control, a mechanism was created to facilitate the state's intervention in union activities regarded as undesirable by the government. Thus, at the same time that union rights were being extended, a watchdog on labor was created.

Implicit in the Wiehahn Commission's report and the government actions that followed it is a theory of labor control through cooptation. The essential features of this theory are twofold. First, an observation that formal registration (legalization) carries substantial organizational benefits, including checkoff, access to the shop floor, participation in grievance procedures, and the legal right to strike under certain circumstances. Second, an assumption that these benefits are incentives that will encourage trade unions to operate within parameters set by the government, since it is government that through the registration process controls access to them.

In this model of labor control, the state encourages "responsible" unionism by permitting those trade unions that display moderate and apolitical behavior to register, and thereby gain access to opportunities and resources that are crucial to organization-building and maintenance. Registration, and the organizational benefits it brings, is both an incentive toward moderation and an advantage to the moderate unions in their competition with more militant rivals. Once registered, unions can be expected to remain responsible, since leadership will fear the organizational damage that would result should the state withdraw its registration and thus deny them continued access to crucial resources.

What Pretoria was banking on in its reform of the trade-union sector was a version of Robert Michels' Iron Law of Oligarchy—that leadership in worker organizations will act, above all else, to preserve the organizations from which they derive their status and power.[93] In this perspective, an elaborate system of state controls to keep trade unions from becoming economically and politically threatening is unnecessary. The task will be more efficiently and effectively accomplished if a structure of incentives makes "unthreatening" behavior something that is in the self-interest of union leadership. In essence, the message of the Wiehahn Commission, upon which Pretoria acted, was that the South African statutory industrial relations system, with some adjustments, constituted such a structure of incentives. The incorporation of black trade unions into it, rather than racially discriminatory laws, was the way to protect the economy and state from both black worker militancy and international isolation.

Influx Control

Until 1986 a cornerstone of the apartheid edifice had been the system called influx control, whereby the state sought to limit and control the movement of people of African descent into "white" urban areas. Three core elements made up this system: the "seventy-two-hour" clause of the Group Areas Act, which prohibited any African from remaining in a white urban area for more than seventy-two hours without specific official permission; the pass laws, which required every African, on pain of criminal penalty, to carry and produce an identity document that listed their officially approved places of employment and residence; and a network of government labour bureaus that allocated approved employment slots to Africans and vetted such employment and related residential area in the pass documents.

By the late 1970s, there were many signs that this influx-control system was both ineffective and costly. The labor bureaus had for the most part ceased to function as "canalizers" of African labor, and hundreds of thousands of Africans avoided the official system and moved straight to the cities despite the threat of jail and fines. Each year the government spent millions of rand apprehending, prosecuting, imprisoning, and rusticating pass-law violators, and still the black population in urban areas grew. The costs of influx control were not only financial, however, but political as well. Domestically, it ensured the alienation from the state of millions of Africans by rendering them criminals or fugitives. Internationally, it jeopardized South Africa's position since the pass laws, with their devastating effect on African family life, among other deprivations, had become for the global community a central symbol of the odiousness of South Africa's system of racial rule.

A perception within government of the general failure and costs of influx control led to the appointment of the Riekert Commission of Inquiry in 1977. As noted earlier, Riekert concluded that the existing influx-control system produced unacceptable economic distortions, contributed to political conflict ("friction") between race groups, and harmed South Africa's international image. For example, on the matter of the seventy-two-hour law and its enforcement by means of pass laws the Riekert Commission had this to say: "The administration of the 72 hour provision gives rise in practice to numerous practical problems and to arrests which seriously disturb relations between population groups and does great harm to South Africa's image."[94] The commission recommended, therefore, that both the seventy-two-hour provision of the Group Areas Act and the pass laws be scrapped. It did not, however, call for an end to influx control. Indeed, Riekert explicitly rejected the idea that control over the movement of Africans from rural areas into the cities be abandoned. "Control over the rate of [black] urbanisation is, in the light of circumstances in South Africa, an *absolutely essential social security measure,*" stated the commission report.[95] In the commission's view such control was deemed necessary even at the cost of some economic growth: "Even though . . . the abolition of such control would lead to faster economic growth, the price to be paid for it in terms of direct and indirect social costs would be too high."[96] Paradoxically, in the era of reform the governing elite's commitment to the control of rural–urban migration, if anything, increased. In 1982 some 206,022 persons were arrested for violating pass laws, an increase of 43 percent over the 1980 figure of 117,518; convictions in 1982 were up 31 percent over the previous year.[97] This seeming contradiction between a desire to reform influx control and the renewed commitment to enforcing it can be resolved by an appreciation of the logic of Pretoria's reform effort. Those aspects of reform that involved creating a cooptable black middle class through transforming the townships into "established" and "stable" communities required limiting the numbers gaining access to urban areas. Given the limited resources that government was willing to commit to housing and urban infrastructure, the reduction in black urbanization rates became an urgent and essential prerequisite for accomplishing the tasks of township upgrading and cooptation. As Piet Koornhof, one of the most *verligte* government ministers, noted in 1980, "Some form of influx control is essential for good order and the protection of established communities. The alternative is to open the gates to being overwhelmed by hordes of peasants drawn by the hope of a better life."[98] The object of reforms, Koornhof explained, "is to apply [influx control] in such a way that the harassment of the past—demanding passes from Blacks in the streets, persnickety regulations governing their issuance—will come to an end."[99]

It was within this type of reform perspective that the Riekert Commission recommended what it believed to be a more effective, efficient, and less politically damaging method for restricting the number of Africans in urban areas. Instead of a system built upon the seventy-two-hour provision and the pass laws, it urged that "*effective control over employment and housing should be the only criteria for regulating the migration of workers and their families*" into "white" urban areas.[100] This could be accomplished, according to the commission, "without the abandonment of any principles in connection with control over urbanisation or without detriment to the effectiveness of control."[101] Indeed, the commission argued that by shifting the target of enforcement away from the black "illegal" and onto employers of black labor and landlords who provide housing accommodations, the system of control would be both more effective and less costly.

The Riekert Commission reasoned, in essence, that classic influx control—based on pass laws and the seventy-two-hour provision—had failed to deter migration to the urban areas because employers and landlords continued to provide work and shelter outside of official channels.[102] The resultant incentives in respect to access to the means of subsistence outweighed, in this perspective, the sanctions of arrest and prosecution. Accordingly, Riekert proposed that control efforts be focused on the providers of subsistence, the employers and the landlords, with heavy fines imposed on anyone who offered individuals employment or accommodation that had not been officially approved.

> . . . [A]t present the extent of the unlawful employment of Black workers assumes very large proportions. . . . [T]he principal reason for this state of affairs is that it is primarily the employees who are prosecuted in this connection, but that employers are seldom if ever brought to justice for the unlawful employment of Black workers. The only way to bring unlawful employment to an end is to take much stricter action against employers in the future.[103]

Through the imposition of stiff fines and even imprisonment Riekert believed that businesses and landlords could be effectively discouraged from offering blacks jobs and housing that had not been approved by a state agency, such as a labor bureau.[104] In this manner the incentives that supposedly drew black South Africans into the larger urban townships could be choked off. The commission's assumption was that without the existence of a "grey market" for urban jobs and housing, Africans would make a "rational" choice to live elsewhere. They would choose, that is, to live either in the homelands or in new urban centers located at a considerable, but commuting, distance from the major industrial centers.

After 1980 the government devoted substantial resources to the development of just such new-style commuter townships, and it increased the incentives for industry to "decentralize" production away from the PWV industrial heartland. Huge "squatter cities" sprang into existence, such as Winterveldt, inside the borders of "independent" Bophuthatswana but within commuting distance to the Pretoria industrial area. Significantly, in the era of urban reform Pretoria devoted far more resources to low-income housing in homeland "urban areas" than in the "white area." In 1986, for example, R62 million was allocated to low-income housing projects in twenty-two homeland towns compared to R13.9 million for self-build schemes in "white area" townships.[105] The concentration of low-income accommodations in these new commuter townships suggests that they were viewed not only as a means to accommodate workers required by the industrial economy, but also as a means to facilitate the transformation of the large metropolitan townships into "established communities" for the black middle class. With the only significant supply of low-cost accommodations available in commuter townships, low-income workers would presumably voluntarily vacate the overcrowded townships of the "white cities," leaving them to their middle-class compatriots. If, in addition, such working-class towns could be located within the geographic or administrative jurisdiction of homeland governments, migration to them would have the additional effect of reducing the size of the black population within South Africa proper. This in turn would contribute to Pretoria's plans for constitutional reform, as will be discussed later.

The Riekert proposals amounted to what might be called "supply-side" influx control: limiting the availability of jobs and housing was recommended as the method for controlling the movement of the African population. In this vision, the role of the state was to limit supply by structuring the urban job and housing markets through "controlled employment and controlled accommodation."[106] Once availability was effectively limited, rational-calculative market-regarding behavior by individuals would supposedly automatically take over to reduce and channel the stream of urban migrants. As an additional benefit, this approach would theoretically eliminate the need for coercion directed at the black work force, which was such a domestic and international political liability in "old-style" influx control.

Although Pretoria accepted, "in principal," the Riekert Commission recommendations on influx control, the actual changes in law and policy needed to put them into effect were not introduced until 1986, some eight years after the commission issued its report. The delay between recommendations and action indicates that the government was less sanguine than Riekert about the power of market-regarding behavior as a substitute for more directly coercive and racially specific means of control. Nevertheless, in mid-1986 Pretoria announced abolition of influx control and its replacement with a policy of "orderly urbanization." The pass laws as well as the seventy-two-hour provision of the Group Areas Act were abolished, and new penalties were imposed on employers and landlords who provided jobs and shelter to Africans outside of official channels. Simultaneously, Pretoria made it clear that it intended to back up "market" disincentives for urban residents with several coercive measures. Most important of these were the Aliens Act of 1937 and the Prevention of Illegal Squatting Act of 1951. Others included the Trespass Act (no. 6 of 1959), the Slums Act (no. 76 of 1979), and various health and building codes. The Aliens Act requires employers who hire noncitizen workers to comply with a complex registration and approval procedure.* Failure to adhere to these procedures subjects the employer as well as the "illegal alien" employee to harsh penalties (fines of up to R5,000 and two years imprisonment). The government made it clear

*An employer who wishes to hire an "alien" has to approach the divisional inspector of the department of manpower for authorization. In the case of a person who is seeking work for the first time or is changing from one employer to another, the new employer must obtain a "no objection to recruiting" recommendation from the department of manpower. Such a recommendation is based upon the judgment that there is no South African worker available to do the job. Once a "no objection to recruiting" recommendation is obtained, the "alien" must apply to the regional or district office of the Department of Home Affairs for a work permit. See South African Institute of Racial Relations, *Quarterly Countdown*, no. 3 (1986), p. 26–27; see also Riekert Commission Report, par. 5.92, p. 234.

that the provisions of the Alien Act applied to some 7.5 million "citizens" of the four "independent" South African homelands, who for purposes of employment would henceforth be considered aliens under the act.[107] In this manner, access to the labor market for a very large number of black South Africans could continue to be controlled, *but now through the application of a citizenship, rather than a racial, standard.* As Riekert argued in support of using the aliens statutes to control "African influx": "The system of control over the entry and sojourn of citizens of independent states in the Republic of South Africa [found in the Aliens laws] will . . . be conducive to more effective control . . . and will . . . eliminate discrimination on the grounds of colour."[108] Additional means to control the presence of Africans in "white urban areas" were offered by anti-squatting, trespass, and slum laws, which give government the legal means to demolish unapproved dwellings and remove their inhabitants from the urban areas. Health and building codes provided officialdom the means to prevent legal black urban residents from renting to others or otherwise providing accommodations or space in their dwellings.

From Pretoria's vantage point, the Aliens Act, anti-squatting laws, health, and building codes had two virtues. First, they offered a legal means to limit available jobs and accommodation in the urban townships. Second, in contrast to the previous influx-control measures, they were not racially specific. Thus, for example, according to Gerrie van Zyl, the director general of home affairs, after July 1, 1986, the Aliens Act "applied to all aliens *irrespective of their population group, nationality, or country of origin."*[109] Of course, despite the purported universality of the laws in question, the socioeconomic realities of South Africa meant that it was the black population that would end up as their target. The vast majority of people classified as aliens would be black; few whites, but hundreds of thousands of black persons lived in circumstances that qualified under the law as squatting, or resided in dwellings that violated health and building codes. Here, in theory, then, was an ideal solution to Pretoria's problems with influx control: movement into urban areas would continue to be limited, but by market-regarding behavior of individuals rather than through the coercive arm of the state. And people would continue to be removed from the urban townships, at perhaps increasing rates, but this would be done through the application of laws that were non-racial and therefore non-discriminatory. The term "influx control," with its distasteful aura and symbolic liabilities, was replaced by the neutral and seemingly unobjectionable idea of "orderly urbanization." The government's perspective was aptly summed up in the Afrikaans-language newspaper *Oosterlig:*

> The limitations imposed by influx control measures have galled people and caused a great deal of bitterness. South Africa can simply not afford it any more. [In reforming], the sluices are not simply opened. In the case of influx control the emphasis shifts to positive, orderly urbanisation, because urbanisation is a worldwide phenomenon.[110]

Indirect Rule

As should already be clear, a theme that runs through many areas of reform policy is that of administrative devolution, whereby responsibility for control of the black population is transferred away from the central state bureaucracy. The most ambitious and consequential aspect of this policy has been the effort to establish representative local government bodies in the townships that could assume most of the control and extractive functions previously performed by officials of central government.

A year after the outbreak of the Soweto uprising, the South African parliament passed the Community Councils Act of 1977. This marked the beginning of a major reversal in the pattern of administrative control over the affairs of black people living in the townships. It represented the first attempt to introduce in black urban residential areas elected local authority structures to which real executive powers might be granted. Until then black townships had been directly administered by white municipal authorities or, after 1972, by central government administration boards. The participation of black persons in the administration of the townships was limited to advisory boards (created in 1945) and, after 1961, elected urban black councils (UBCs), but these bodies were purely advisory.[111] In the late 1960s and early 1970s, even these limited arenas for black input were viewed as too extensive. The official attitude was expressed in a 1967 report by the deputy secretary of the Department of Bantu Affairs, Dr. P. F. S. J. van Rensburg, who recommended that the UBCs be abolished and replaced by a system of homeland government representation in the townships.[112] In the years that followed, various official moves were made to implement this and other van Rensburg recommendations—administration boards were established to tighten up the enforcement of influx control, and discussions took place with homeland leaders about a role for them in the running of townships.[113]

But the multiple crises that the government faced in the 1970s, most particularly the Soweto uprising, led officialdom to reverse field. With the 1977 decision to establish community councils, government moved in the direction of reliance on self-administration by "responsible" local authorities—elected bodies with real executive powers. The first council was created in November 1977; by March 1982 some 228 had been established. The basic shift in National Party strategy for controlling black residential areas was revealed in a December 1977 radio talk delivered by then Prime Minister John Vorster:

> As far as the urban Black is concerned, I believe that he must be given full autonomy to govern himself as a city dweller—in other words, that he must control and manage his own city, his own town, through elected representatives and that the White must gradually withdraw so that it may ultimately be Black government in every respect.[114]

Two years later, the government minister in charge of implementing the new local government policy, Piet Koornhof, reiterated this message at a meeting of skeptical administration board officials: "Your task is to phase out your role as guardians since there has been a shift of emphasis from direct administration of Black people to a position where Blacks will manage and administer their own communities according to their own abilities."[115]

The Community Councils Act of 1977, which laid the legal foundation for the new direction in township administration, contains important indications of the logic and intent with which Pretoria approached this area of reform. First, the promised local autonomy was ambiguous in nature, in that it combined elements of independence and central government control. On the one hand, the act held out to elected black officials the promise of power and responsibility; on the other hand, it made them completely dependent on the minister of plural relations (previously Bantu administration) and the administration boards for access to that power and responsibility. The minister not only had the authority to establish or remove councils, he also could decide which powers, within a statutorily defined range, would be vested in them. And a power, once granted, could later be withdrawn. Section 5 of the Community Councils Act details the fourteen functions or powers that could be devolved on a council by decision of the minister, in consultation with the relevant administration board. Table 4.3 lists the most important of these powers and matches each with its operational significance.[116] Where necessary a "translation" of the official legalese is provided.

At least three things are especially interesting about the functions slated for devolution to black community councils. They were concentrated in the area of controlling the supply and allocation of housing, which would become one of the twin pillars of new-style influx control; they provided prospective town councillors with significant sources of patronage (access to housing, distribution of building permits, allocation of trading sites, construction contracts, and scholarships); and they involved the councils in key aspects of extraction and enforcement, i.e., rent collection and forced removals.

The Community Council Act also provided for the creation of a "community guard" for "the preservation of the safety of the inhabitants, the maintenance of law and order, the prevention of crime."[117] Thus, basic police functions that had previously been the responsibility of the South African police were slated for devolu-

TABLE 4.3. Community Councils Act: Functional Devolution

Devolved Power	Operational Meaning
1. "Allocation and administration . . . of accommodation to single persons" (translation: control over accommocation for migrant labor)	influx control; patronage
2. "Allocation and administration of the letting of dwellings, buildings, and other structures" (translation: control over family accommodation for those with legal rights to urban residence)	influx control; patronage
3. "Prevention and combating of the unlawful occupation of land and buildings" (translation: enforcement of anti-squatting laws)	influx control
4. "The allocation and administration of sites for . . . trading purposes"	patronage
5. "The approval of building plans of private dwellings and the removal or demolition of unauthorized . . . buildings."	influx control
6. "The award of bursaries" (scholarships)	patronage
7. "The maintenance of services" (refuse removal, water supply, sewerage, roads)	patronage

Source: Riekert Commission Report, pp. 74–75.

Note: Seven additional functions that might be delegated involved either nonspecific responsibilities for things like "sound community development" and "moral and social welfare," or specific but relatively unimportant functions, such as the control of the keeping of animals.

tion to the community councils. Revenue for the councils would come from the rent and service charges that would accrue once a council obtained responsibility for the control of housing, as well as from special levies on township residents.[118]

Within little more than a year after the establishment of black community councils, the Riekert Commission, reporting in August 1978, recommended modifications in the Community Council Act. The commission sought to strengthen "the position of the established Black communities in the White area" by affording them "new and much wider opportunities for decision-making."[119] Riekert was especially concerned that new local government structures would be "free from the historical prejudices" created by "old-style" Bantu administration.[120] This required, according to Riekert, removing the administration boards from a direct role in township governance. The commission noted the reluctance of boards to cooperate in the devolution of what had been their prime functions, and it pointed out the unpopularity of the boards among township residents.[121]

These observations were consistent with the criticism of the already established councils by government opponents, who argued that the new bodies would be powerless against the controlling influence of administration boards and the Department of Cooperation and Development.* Criticism of this kind was particularly salient to the government in the early 1980s because the results of the first round of community council elections, which took place between 1977 and 1980, indicated that most township residents viewed the new assemblies as neither important nor legitimate. In the large townships, where the government's political problems were centered, the voter turnout was very low. In Soweto, only 6 percent of eligible voters went to the polls, considerably below the proportion of residents that had voted for the old UBC advisory body in the 1960s.[122] In the words of one local government study: "[I]f the Councils were intended . . . as a means of stabilising the urban areas in the wake of the 1976 unrest, then the low polls in the major urban centres point to the initial failure of the policy."[123]

It was in this context that Pretoria introduced the Black Local Government Bill in 1980. After much discussion and revision the bill was finally passed into law in 1982 as the Black Local Authorities Act. The act differed from the earlier Community Council Act primarily in that it involved giving the councils in the larger urban townships at least the appearance of autonomy, and it further distanced the hated administration boards from council affairs. Under the 1982 act certain of the existing community councils would be designated as town councils by the minister of cooperation and development, in which case they would by statute be vested with powers to direct local affairs similar to those exercised by "white" municipal councils. While not dependent on the minister to grant specific powers to them, as were the community councils, the town councils remained responsible to the Department of Cooperation and Development. The minister retained discretionary authority in a wide range of matters, including the authority to dissolve a council "for any failure to exercise their powers to his satisfaction."[124] Under the new act, the administration boards were authorized to assist the councils, but the latter were under no legal obligation to avail themselves of such assistance.[125]

---

*The Department of Plural Relations, formerly the Department of Bantu Administration, was subsequently renamed the Department of Cooperation and Development.

With the passage of the Black Local Authorities Act, Pretoria had sought to shift control over the black population living in "white South Africa" from the central government to representatives of the black population, and in so doing reduce the political costs to the state of exercising such control.* Pretoria's political agenda in this respect was explicitly spelled out by a senior official when he explained the rationale for the changes embodied in the Black Local Authorities Act:

> These local authorities will serve to defuse pent-up frustrations and grievances against administration from Pretoria. Local authorities will affect the daily existence of these Black people more directly and intimately than the more removed activities of the central government. In the war in which South Africa is involved and the total onslaught against the country, diffusion of this kind has become an urgent necessity which cannot be postponed much longer.[126]

Summary: Local Government and Reform

The effort to create representative local authority institutions, especially in the larger townships, was a core element in the South African government's reform strategy. Pretoria sought to reap two important benefits from this effort. One was the creation of a forum within the South African state for the political participation of citizens of African descent—something that had been barred by apartheid, at substantial costs internationally. The other was the administrative devolution to black political elites of some of Pretoria's most politically problematic tasks. By making significant resources available to black local authorities, Pretoria could theoretically be assured that (1) Participation in new local government institutions would be valued by black South Africans, for it would bring with it access to a significant measure of power, wealth, and status; (2) The "reliability" of black local government officials could be counted on because of their dependence on central government; for the state would retain the power to provide, curtail, or withdraw the resources available to local government institutions; and (3) The township population could in turn be coopted for it would depend on the favor of local government officials for a variety of basic subsistence needs, such as access to housing. If, in addition to the above, the local government officials were representative, that is, if they were elected by some form of mass franchise, they might be viewed as legitimate both domestically and internationally. *Indirect rule—blacks controlling blacks—would then have been substituted for the coercive fist of the white state.*[127] As such, the alienation that had resulted from the direct administration of townships by white officialdom, and that had been so dramatically revealed to Pretoria by the Soweto uprising, might lessen. Moreover, with control of and extraction from the black population under the direction of elected black representatives, a situation more palatable to the international community would presumably be created.

---

*Displacement from the center was carried a step further in 1985, with the transfer of the administration of black affairs from the ministry level of government to nonelected provincial administrations. Although responsibility for "overall policymaking and co-ordination in respect to devolved functions" would remain with the minister, the provinces were given operational control over black town, community, and village councils, over implementing the Prevention of Illegal Squatting Act, and over the issuing of permits under the Group Areas Act. See *The Star,* October 3, 1986.

A New Political Dispensation

Government can be thought of as society's formal mechanism for the allocation of scarce and valued resources. It is in this political–institutional arena that Pretoria's most fundamental problem is located and in which its maneuverability in respect to change has been most limited. Since the end of World War II and with increasing intensity from the late 1970s onward, South Africa has been beset both domestically and internationally with demands that its governmental system be reorganized through the introduction of a nonracial mass franchise. More than in any other area of the apartheid system, however, change in respect to black political participation strikes at the very foundation of white interests and psychology. Since the arrival of Europeans on the Southern tip of Africa in the mid-seventeenth century, white South Africans have based their social, economic, and cultural security—what they would term their "way of life"—on limiting the political participation and thus access to political power of the far more numerous people of color among whom they lived. This was a central feature of the constitutional agreement between British and Afrikaner that gave birth to the modern South African state in 1910; its maintenance represented the primary political objective of the National Party when it established its governmental hegemony in 1948. And, through at least the decade of the 1980s, white control of the political system continued to represent the central commitment of government.

There is no evidence that the National Party's commitment to reform marked a significant departure from the view that continued control of the political system by a racial minority was essential to the economic, social, and cultural survival of white people in South Africa. In interviews with National Party and government officials in the mid-1980s, South African sociologist Lawrence Schlemmer found that "[T]he principle of political self-determination for racially defined communities is still supported by a clear majority of the party, and very strongly so by party functionaries."[128] A white *determining* voice in the major affairs of state is viewed, Schlemmer reports, as essential for protecting what the political elite terms "white culture." As one Nationalist member of Parliament explained, white political interests required "sufficient control over the allocation of resources and the maintenance of security to ensure the continuation of . . . [their] lifestyle, . . . standards of public order, behavior, and respectability."[129]

How to placate domestic and international demands for black political participation without losing control over the allocation of those resources deemed vital to the "white way of life"—this has been the reform-minded NP elite's most thorny problem. Although movement toward open political participation for black South Africans is a seeming requirement for domestic peace and international legitimacy, simple demographic realities mean that the extension of black participation will eventually spell the end to guaranteed white control of the political system. In the 1980s Pretoria attempted a resolution of this dilemma by proclaiming itself amenable to arrangements for "power sharing" that would not undermine the white group's capacity to control those aspects of the socio-economic system deemed vital—the industrial economy, the system of sociocultural reproduction, and the security apparatus. In the words of P. W. Botha, "We are prepared . . . to share power, but not to relinquish it so we and our children have no future."[130]

In the lexicon of the National Party, the concept of "power sharing" translates into a rejection of the political principle of majority rule. "The so-called one man, one vote system," wrote the party's 1980 Schlebusch Commission of Inquiry into the constitution, "would probably lead to majorities dominating minorities and [therefore] . . . did not offer a solution for the constitutional problems of the Republic."[131] Two years later, the Constitutional Committee of the President's Council reiterated this view. "There is near unanimity," it reported, "on the unworkability of a system of undifferentiated majoritarianism . . . or what is conventionally described as 'one man, one vote, in a single political system' ".[132]

But how to get a favorable reception by the key audiences, black South Africans, and the international community, for a political formula that "shares" power but does not significantly alter who controls the South African political system? In part Pretoria tried to resolve this dilemma by resorting to semantic subterfuge, using normatively attractive terms like "power sharing," "group self-determination," "minority rights," and "avoidance of domination," in an effort to sell the political–institutional aspects of its reform strategy to the international community. But more was involved than simply a campaign of disinformation. The NP leadership hoped that a new black middle class, having attained a higher material standard of living and increased personal freedom as a result of the reform project, would forgo insistence on majority rule rather than risk what it had achieved. Cooptation of black South Africans then becomes the basis for legitimizing both the political reforms and the South African order as a whole in the eyes of the international community.

Consociationalism and Constitutional Engineering

During the 1960s the National Party elite and Afrikaner intellectuals in general were enamored with the idea of partition, or "separate development," as the mechanism for ridding South Africa of the domestic threats and international pressures that flowed from majority disenfranchisement. "Native reserves" would undergo a metamorphosis into ten sovereign states, to which the citizenship of all the country's Africans would be transferred. In the process of creating eleven states out of one, South Africa would thus eliminate its citizens of African descent and erase the problem of minority racial rule.

In the 1970s, enthusiasm for separate development was tempered by the reality that the international community has refused *in toto* to accept the homelands as genuine examples of self-determination. None of the first four "independent" homelands or "national states" received international recognition, other than by the foreign ministry in Pretoria. The Soweto uprising and the diplomatic and economic problems that followed in its wake underlined the reality of separate development's failure to counter the threat to white rule. Consequently Afrikaner intellectuals and the National Party leadership began to search for a new political formula—a new constitutional dispensation—that might succeed where separate development had failed.

In the 1980s, consociationalism replaced separate development as the favored concept at the center of the debate about South Africa's future political order among the intelligentsia associated with the NP.[133] The notion of consociationalism was initially developed by the Dutch political scientist Arendt Lijphart to illuminate the special federal arrangements that exist in a number of European democracies whose societies are "deeply divided" along communal lines.[134] Among the essential elements of Lijphart's model of consociationalism are "segmental autonomy," group rather than individual representation, and a central executive based on a "grand coalition" of segments, each with the power of veto.

It is not difficult to understand why white South Africans are intrigued by the consociational model. "Segmental autonomy" refers to an extreme form of federal devolution whereby constituent communities (segments) retain control over the affairs they consider most vital. It would guarantee to the white group in South Africa control over much that it fears would be eroded under government by a black majority—education, housing, and health care, for example. Emphasis on the representation of groups rather than individuals discounts severely the significance of numbers as the currency of political power. It would thus reduce what South African whites have always feared would be their great disadvantage in a democracy that included the black majority. Finally, the system of mutual vetoes in a cabinet within which all segments are represented ensures that on matters that cannot be handled within the confines of segmental autonomy no policy can be introduced that any constituent community feels violates its interests. When combined with group representation, mutual vetoes in the South African context translates into white codetermination in matters that could not be disaggregated and parceled out to separate communal segments. Thus, under a consociational arrangement economic or social policies perceived as threatening to white interests such as nationalization of major industries, or redistributive taxation and spending policies, could be blocked through the exercise of a group veto. Viewed from Pretoria's vantage point, a consociational arrangement offers the exquisitely attractive combination of a mass franchise without majority rule. One, moreover, that has been accepted as democratic elsewhere.

Constitution of 1983

The first concrete manifestation of the importance of consociationalism in Pretoria's reform strategy was the introduction of a new multiracial constitutional dispensation. The outline of a new constitution for the republic had been made public in 1977. It was extensively debated within higher echelons of the National Party, subject to two high-level governmental inquiries, presented to the public in 1982, and approved in a "whites only" referendum in the November of 1983. As Arendt Lijphart himself recognized, the new constitution had many consociational elements.[135] Five features were of primary importance in the reformed constitutional order:

> 1. A tripartite legislature in which racially separate parliaments for whites, "coloureds," and Indians replaced the whites-only, Westerminster-style parliament that had governed South Africa since 1910.
> 2. The consociational principle of segmental autonomy was embodied in a distinction between "own" and "general" affairs. In respect to the former, exclusive jurisdiction over certain matters, such as education, was reserved to the

racially separate parliaments. In respect to the latter, legislation would require concurrent majorities in each of the three parliaments, reflecting the consociational principle of mutual veto.

3. A powerful and independent executive, consisting of a state president and president's council, replaced the cabinet form of government. Both elements of the executive were indirectly chosen by electors drawn from the three chambers of parliament.

4. The constitutionally prescribed rules for the indirect election of the president and council were heavily weighted in favor of whites. With the number of racially specific electors reflecting the ratio of whites, "coloureds," and Indians in the South African population (4:2:1), white, indeed National Party, control of both the powerful state presidency and president's council was assured.

5. Perhaps the most significant thing about the reformist constitutional dispensation was what it did not include: an opening of the political system to South Africa's citizens of African descent. They were to look to the homeland political structures and the local township councils for the exercise of their political rights.

The general nature of the political reform embodied in the constitution of 1983 was aptly characterized by the Constitutional Committee of the President's Council: "[T]he continuation of the direction of official constitutional policy with regard to Blacks [separate development and partition], combined with a consociational system which includes the White, Coloured, and Indian communities."[136] By opting for this hybrid political reform, Pretoria sought to remove the internationally costly stigma of racism from its constitutional order without threatening white (and National Party) control of the political system. The new constitution replaced a political order defined by white racial exclusivity with one built on multiracial participation. But by limiting the scope of that participation to whites, Indians, and "coloureds," Pretoria ensured that equitable representation in respect to population would provide the largest power bloc to the whites. Moreover, the consociational principles that were embedded in the new constitutional arrangement precluded a situation in which dissident whites could align with "coloureds" and Indians to form a government in which the National Party would be relegated to the position of opposition.

The exclusion of the African population in the new constitutional dispensation reflected the National Party's continued adherence to white political control, despite its commitment to reform. For had Africans been included, say through the addition of a fourth parliamentary chamber, then the principle of proportionality would have provided the African segment with such a large bloc of representatives at all levels—parliament, president's council, and electoral college—that white control would have been placed at risk. As Chris Heunis, minister of constitutional development, explained, if a fourth parliamentary chamber for Africans had been added the population ratios would be 36 blacks [Africans] to 9 whites to 5 "coloureds" to 2 Asians. "What," Heunis asked, "would then remain of the principle of maintaining civilized standards? . . . It [African inclusion] is just not possible. . . . That is why a different path is being followed for blacks."[137] If, instead of excluding Africans from its new dispensation, proportionality had been abandoned so as to ensure a white majority in the electoral college and president's council, the entire constitutional exercise would have been revealed as a farce. Thus Pretoria's objectives limited its maneuverability, leading it to introduce a reform that continued to exclude the African majority from the central political system.

In introducing the 1983 constitution, the government expected to enhance prospects for domestic security by coopting Indians and "coloureds" into the political system. Simultaneously, it hoped to garner international legitimacy by introducing multiracialism into its constitutional order. The fancifulness of such expectations was quickly apparent. Domestic and international audiences focused on what the constitution left out rather than on what it contained. The exclusion of the African majority and the severe limits on the potential power of Indian and "coloured" representatives seemed more significant than the government's conception of "multiracial power sharing." On the domestic front, the decision in 1982 to formally introduce the constitution turned into a stimulus for mass mobilization by government opponents, not only among the excluded Africans, but also within the Indian, "coloured," and white communities (see Chapter 5). Internationally, Pretoria received more condemnation than praise for its efforts, although some tepid support was voiced by the administrations of Ronald Reagan in the United States and Margaret Thatcher in the United Kingdom. Washington called the constitutional reform "a step in the right direction."[138] But even these conservative and sympathetic governments noted the glaring omission of political rights for the African majority.[139]

Constitutional Planning: 1985–89

In the mid-1980s, as domestic political disturbances escalated and threats of international economic sanctions mounted, Pretoria sought to defuse the situation by responding to demands that political rights be extended to Africans. A concerted effort was made, beginning with P. W. Botha's speech to the inaugural session of the tricameral legislature on January 25, 1985, to indicate that the 1983 constitution was only the starting point for political restructuring, and that plans for African political participation would soon be revealed. Although during Botha's remaining four years in office no new major political reform would in fact be introduced, ideas for a "new political dispensation" were the subject of intense discussion within the National Party. Numerous statements by senior officials, as well as several policy actions, indicate the general direction of Pretoria's thinking during the period. Five basic elements can be analytically distinguished in this "new direction."

1. *Accepting the principle of African participation in the central political process.* P. W. Botha's speech on January 25, 1985, was greeted with derision by foes of apartheid. It was short on concrete and comprehendible proposals, they argued, and long on high-sounding phrases that represented double-talk more than new departures.[140] Yet, in that speech Botha abandoned the principle that had guided National Party political thinking and practice for two-and-one-half decades—that Africans had political rights *only* within the homelands. Thus he set a course on unchartered waters.

Referring to Africans who "find themselves outside the national states," Botha declared: "Government has accepted that not all [black] people can express themselves politically via the government's structures of the national states."[141]*

> It has therefore been decided to treat such communities, for constitutional purposes, as entities which in their own right must be given political participation and a say at higher levels. . . . Structures must therefore be developed for black communities outside the national states through which they can themselves decide on their own affairs up to the highest level.[142]

Gerrit Viljoen, chairman of the Afrikaner Broederbond between 1974 and 1980, and a cabinet minister since then, recognized the watershed nature of Botha's statement. Since the president's address to Parliament in 1985, he commented, "the government has completely abandoned [its traditional position] . . . that black people . . . must look [solely] to the national states as their channel for expressing their political rights. This means," he continued, "that power sharing is to be brought about involving and including the black communities both in and outside the national states."[143]

The furor that greeted the exclusion of Africans from the 1983 constitution had apparently convinced the National Party leadership that a new participation formula was required if the hoped-for domestic quiescence and international legitimacy was to be obtained. Thus in 1987 F. W. de Klerk, head of the Transvaal branch of the National Party, and at the time considered one of the more conservative members of the cabinet, commented: "The denial of a political power base to the 10 million blacks who live outside the national states will drive those who seek political change into the hands of revolutionaries. . . . There are blacks who have lived in South Africa all their lives and they and their children will remain here. . . . They cannot stay in South Africa year after year without political representation."[144]

2. *New definition of South African citizenship.* Separate development policy had been conceived by Hendrik Verwoerd as a means to legitimize white power through the redefinition of South African citizenship. Those of African descent would be able to exercise "self-determination" through the transfer of their citizenship to government-created "national states" juridically independent of the South African republic. As it turned out this scheme had the opposite of its intended effect. The transfer of citizenship was interpreted both domestically and internationally as a cynical and self-serving effort by a white oligarchy to "denationalize" South Africa's African majority. It became one of the chief obstacles to Pretoria's legitimation campaign. The National Party elite sought to confront this reality when in September 1985, at a provincial party congress, P. W. Botha declared: "I finally confirm that my party and I are committed to the principle of a united South Africa, one citizenship, and a universal franchise."[145]

Although the language of the state president's declaration suggested a complete abandonment of separate development and the acceptance of the type of majority rule being demanded by government opponents, the reality was something signifi-

'In the mid-1980s Pretoria began referring to homelands as "national states."

cantly different. In the very same declaration, Botha made it clear that by a "united South Africa" he did not mean the dismantling of the four "national states" that had obtained nominal independence from Pretoria between 1976 and 1981, nor did he intend to foreclose the possibility that others of the six remaining "tribal home-lands" might obtain a similar status in the future. Moreover, a senior official pointed out, "common citizenship" did not imply participation in the same political struc-tures.[146] A commitment to a universal franchise did not mean, in other words, acceptance of a system of majority rule.

So what had changed under the National Party's new definition of South African citizenship? First, NP leaders had began to recognize that those who worked perma-nently within the borders of the republic, whose residency rights were being ac-knowledged within the post-Riekert framework, and whose right to some form of political participation was now accepted, ought to be granted citizenship status. However, for those who had lost that status when the four homelands of Transkei, Bophuthatswana, Venda, and Ciskei (called the TBVC national states) became "independent," the situation was ambiguous. The Restoration of South African Citizenship Act was introduced in 1986 to give effect to P. W. Botha's September 1985 declaration on citizenship. Under its terms only an estimated 1.75 million out of the approximately 10 million "citizens" of the TBVC states can qualify to regain their South African citizenship.[147]* In essence, under the act only those who could prove they were born within the republic prior to their homeland's independence, and could show they were continually employed and resident in "white" South Africa since, would be eligible to have their citizenship restored. Presumably the same criteria would apply in the case of future homeland independence. Thus, for what were essentially the erstwhile "Section 10" urban dwellers (i.e., the post-Riekert "urban insiders"), the threat of denationalization was removed. In the words of Minister of Defense Magnus Malan, "The NP government is prepared to give blacks, more particularly *the 5 million or so urban blacks,* full political participation in a future South Africa."[148] Although the *right* to political participation for urban-based Africans was being restored in the late 1980s, the content of that political participation remained very unclear.

3. *City States.* In recognizing the need and legitimacy of African political participation in central government, the National Party elite's focus was primarily on the anomaly of what officialdom termed the "urban blacks." As one senior NP official stated the problem: "The constitutional aspirations of 75% of blacks have been met in either the independent or the self-governing homelands but a formula for the remaining 25% in the white urban areas has to be found."[149] "We must provide for urban blacks," stated F. W. de Klerk in 1987, "own political institu-tions, own political power bases, own legislatures, own executives, so that they get the same degree of self-determination as the homelands blacks and as the whites have within the house of assembly and as the coloured have in their chamber."[150]

Discussions of the "correct" participation formula with which to incorporate the urban-based Africans focused in the late 1980s on a concept that was first mooted a

---

*By the end of 1987, according to the cabinet minister in charge, only 22,006 persons from the TBVC territories had actually had their South African citizenship restored. See *Citizen,* March 3, 1988.

decade earlier: the autonomous "city-state."[151] The Black Local Authorities Act (1982) and the earlier Community Councils Act of 1977, through establishing elected and "representative" institutions at the township level, had paved the way for establishing the black urban area as a unit of representation in central government. In 1980 an official publication explained: "Prime Minister Botha foresaw that these [urban black community councils] would be jointly represented on the council of states proposed as the umbrella body over the confederation he has in mind."[152] When in mid-decade attention focused on the extension of political rights to "urban blacks," the reigning conception was that of urban-African political entities that would be analogous to rural homelands in juridical/political status and functions. The 1987 election manifesto of the National Party envisioned "full autonomy" and even independence for black metropolitan areas as a means for creating "structures of self-determination for communities outside the non-independent homelands."[153] New "city-states" would constitute territorial units that could be represented along with ethnic homelands, and white, "coloured," and Indian racial communities, within a future consociational/federal constitutional dispensation. By this means Africans "in the white area" could be politically represented "at the center" without their superior numbers dominating the distribution of power. Urban blacks, represented as one or more "entities" through autonomous city-states, would be only one among a variety of groups with a say in decisions of common concern. Moreover, within such an arrangement the African majority would be subdivided along urban/rural lines as well as along the ethnic (homeland) dimension.

4. *A New Confederal/Federal/Consociational Dispensation.* Responding to the harsh criticism of its 1983 constitution, Pretoria repeatedly stated that it was considering a new constitutional "dispensation" that would accommodate its post-1985 acceptance of African political participation in central political institutions. Government spokesmen, however, refused to lay out a concrete and specific constitutional plan. They were reluctant to impose such a plan, they said, for it would have to be the product of negotiations between South Africa's population groups. For the purpose of facilitating such negotiations P. W. Botha announced, in 1985, the creation of a National Council that was to include black leaders. Established by legislation a year later as the National Statutory Council, this body was intended to include the heads of homeland governments, township mayors, and urban councillors. Experience with the 1983 constitution had taught the National Party elite that a political formula that allowed for majority participation but severely limited its power would, if simply imposed by the white governing group, be received as illegitimate both domestically and internationally. Thus Pretoria required the agreement of black political leaders to its plans for a new political dispensation. Black officials in the government-created structures of indirect rule were viewed as the solution to this dilemma, and the National Statutory Council was conceived as the forum in which they could legitimate through their approval the NP's constitutional design.

Although officialdom was reticent in respect to specific constitutional proposals, it was expansive about certain principles that would have to be incorporated into any constitutional formula for it to be deemed acceptable by Pretoria. "The National Party has no specific plan on how to accommodate blacks," stated Cabinet Minister

Stoffel van der Merwe in 1987, "but it has preconditions."[154] These, for the most part, involved an insistence that consociational principles be incorporated into any new dispensation. The most important of these, judged by the amount of attention they received in the statements of National Party leaders, were:

The group rather than the individual will provide the basis for political representation and be the primary repository of constitutional rights and protections. "Any future dispensation will have to take place on the basis of group identity," stated F. W. de Klerk in 1987.[155] State President Botha spoke often and at length on what he considered this essential point, as he did to a joint session of the South African parliament in May 1987:

> It is not possible in a multi-cultural country like the Republic of South Africa to talk about the protection of individual rights unless one talks about the protection of its minority rights at the same time. . . . [I]t is [also] impossible to talk about the protection of minority rights unless one talks about the protection of minority groups at the same time . . . [I]t is also not possible to talk about the protection of minority groups and the prevention of domination unless groups enjoy statutory recognition and the relationship among them is regulated constitutionally.

South Africa is a country of minority groups; there is no majority. "South Africa is not a country with a black majority and a small minority of white people," P. W. Botha told the Cape Congress of the National Party in late 1987. The state president said he viewed South Africa as a country of minorities, with the black population, which is often erroneously thought of as a majority, split by tribal rivalries.[156] Within this context, the National Party insisted that ethnic group representation is required to protect the rights of black minorities and to prevent the type of tribal rivalries that allegedly have undermined stability and development elsewhere in Africa.[157]

An emphasis on African ethnic/tribal divisions performs at least two functions for the governing group. First, and most obviously, a constitutional order that incorporates ethnic/tribal representation would divide black South Africans into potentially rival units, thus reducing the likelihood of a majority coalition aligned "against the whites." Second, justifying its constitutional preferences in terms of the need to avoid "tribal conflict" in a post-apartheid South Africa has powerful resonance in the international community. Outside observers have tended to extrapolate from the experience of other sub-Saharan African countries in order to predict the nature of South African politics under a system of majority rule.[158] Ignoring the very significant differences in South Africa's historical experience, socioeconomic development, and political dynamics, these observers focus on "ethnic catastrophes" like the Nigerian civil war or Idi Amin's Uganda and are receptive to constitutional engineering that might avoid the worst manifestations of "tribalism" in a future South Africa. At the same time they are desensitized to the extent to which this constitutional effort to avoid tribal conflict leaves the white minority in control of the political system.

Participation for all without one group dominating another. "The South African government's vision for the future . . . is a system that will not be capable of being manipulated so the majority can enforce its will on the minorities which form part of South Africa."[159] Thus did F. W. de Klerk articulate the central tenet of National Party constitutional thinking in the 1980s: the need to constitutionally protect minority groups from domination by a majority. When combined with the concept of group rather than individual representation, this notion translated into a National Party preference for consociational mechanisms that would neutralize differentials in group size. Minister of Constitutional Planning Chris Heunis explained that "minority protection" was fundamentally different in a "majority model" and in a system of "efficient group participation on the basis of equal power sharing." In the first, "the majority party would dominate government, but *with equal power sharing numbers would not be decisive, and each group would have an effective veto.*"[160]

Community self-determination. The concept of "own affairs" that was built into the 1983 constitution developed by mid-decade into a first-order principle in National Party thinking about the future. "One of the keys to future constitutional development lies with the concept of own affairs," stated F. W. de Klerk during the 1987 parliamentary election campaign. "As with whites, coloured people, and Indians, blacks must get legislative institutions to decide about own affairs, including school, welfare, and community life."[161] "Own affairs," control over which would be lodged in separate institutions, was the basis for "community self-determination." Of course, in the context of South African politics the neutral language of "community self-determination" contains a very important subtext. Community self-determination would, given the way in which Pretoria defines communities, mean that whites can maintain control over many important resources even under circumstances of a universal, nonracial franchise.

The logic embodied in the basic constitutional principles elaborated by National Party spokesmen, as well as the writings of the NP intelligentsia, indicate that the party was groping toward the design of a complex consociational/confederal constitutional structure.* The basic notion was that the South African population would be statutorily differentiated into a variety of groups (white, "coloured," Indian, urban black, ethnic homeland, national state). The groups would participate in central government through representation in an executive institution, within which the principle of "co-determination" (or mutual veto) would govern decision-making. Thus, Chris Heunis explained to a federal congress of the National Party: "With the national council as a forerunner, a joint council of state may be developed in which leaders and other representatives of all the political entities may participate in policy formulation over common interest by means of consensus decision-making."[162] Major areas of decision-making would be reserved for the groups themselves, in keeping with the principle of "own affairs," for which they would have their separate group political institutions—legislatures, executives, bureaucracies, revenue sources, and budgets. The division between own and general affairs might

---

*A book written in 1984 by a leading *verligte* intellectual, Willem de Klerk, *The Second (R)evolution: Afrikanerdom and the Crises of Identity* (Johannesburg: Jonathan Bell Publishers), is especially prescient in regard to the constitutional concepts espoused by officials in the post-1985 period. Willem de Klerk is the brother of F. W. de Klerk.

vary among the entities, with ethnic homelands and independent national states conceived of as self-governing units joined to the center only as part of a common market–type confederation. In 1988 the National Party introduced legislation that substantially expanded the powers of governments in the "self-governing" home-lands, among other things, providing them with their own supreme courts and departments of state. Senior NP members of parliament explained to interviewers that self-governing homelands with their augmented powers would become "re-gional governments" within a federal or confederal system.[163] Thus a constitutional order was being envisioned in which there would exist a federal/consociational core, constituted by white, "coloured," and Indian "communities," along with "black city-states." This core would then be joined to ethnic homeland confederal partners, which would have only a very limited role in central government decision-making.

The arena of constitutional engineering revealed more clearly than any other area of reform both the limit and the most serious weakness of Pretoria's reform strategy. The tortured effort to elaborate a constitutional formula that would deny power to a popular majority exposed the reform strategy's primary objective—to change in order to avoid a loss of control. At the same time, this effort naturally alienated those whom reform was intended to coopt. No more eloquent testimony to this basic contradiction in reform strategy need be found than the response of Gatsha Buthelezi, Chief Minister of the KwaZulu homeland, to claims by senior govern-ment officials that "there is no majority in South Africa, only a collection of minorities." Buthelezi, the individual who was Pretoria's main hope for cooptation and collaboration, declared that "no amount of twisting of words could change the fact that there was a black majority," and said that it would be suicidal "to begin negotiating with the government while it refused to accept the reality of a black majority in South Africa."[164] Likewise, the chief ministers of QwaQwa and Le-bowa, two other key candidates for Pretoria's collaborative efforts, issued a joint statement in which they rejected "the notion that South Africa is a country of minorities" and undertook "not to participate in negotiations aimed at making the country's minorities building blocks of a future constitution."[165]

5. *Multiracial administrative agencies.* While stymied in its efforts to introduce multiracial power sharing to the constitutional/political arena, Pretoria moved in the administrative/provincial sphere—what it termed "second-tier" government. The vehicles for "power sharing" were new administrative agencies called regional services councils (RSCs). Introduced in 1987 and 1988, these bodies were given administrative responsibility for basic services (water, sewerage, electricity, trans-portation) whose distributional infrastructure crosscut the racial and political bound-aries that divide the white municipalities from their surrounding black townships. Besides rationalizing the distribution of these services by acknowledging their re-gional character, the RSCs were intended as a means to reduce the financial burden on the central state of township upgrading.[166] In theory, with the authority to impose new taxes within their jurisdictions, such as a business levy on salaries, the RSCs were to subsidize the cost of service delivery to the low-income townships. But critics are skeptical that these agencies can in fact mobilize adequate resources to maintain, let alone improve, the heavily subsidized services that have been devolved on them.[167]

Whatever their prospects in respect to the provision of services, the RSCs were intended to perform a political-legitimation function, as well. When fully operational, each municipality will be represented on the RSCs, with town councillors representing the black townships alongside the mayors and city council members representing the white cities. Pretoria can then point to the RSCs as examples of multiracial power-sharing in the "new South Africa." Thus, Ambassador to the United States Piet Koornhof, in his May 1988 monthly newsletter to Americans, made note of the new administrative structures: "Today, blacks participate in local and state-level government. . . . They serve alongside whites on the Executive Councils which govern the four provinces."[168]

While the participation of blacks along with whites in decision-making bodies was something new, the manner in which voting power is distributed within the RSCs demonstrated Pretoria's commitment to the notion of power-sharing without a loss of control. Voting strength was to be determined not by a local authority area's population size, but by the amount of bulk services (water, electricity, sewage disposal) that the local authority buys from the RSC.[169] Consequently, the larger and poorer black townships have fewer votes than the smaller but wealthier white municipalities: "black" Soweto, with more than twice the population of "white" Johannesburg, has 12.7 percent of the voting power on the Central Witwatersrand RSC compared to the latter's 48.5 percent.[170] The organization of the RSCs provides a prime example of how a history of racial discrimination in the allocation of material resources has provided a foundation for the white oligarchy to shift the basis of power from race to class without significantly altering the distribution of power.

Summary

In this chapter I have tried to do more than simply describe the South African government's reform effort. Pretoria's reforms have been revealed to possess an "inner logic." Each core aspect of reform can be seen to be oriented to a set of three interrelated goals—the reestablishment of domestic security, the attainment of international legitimacy, and the return to a trajectory of rapid economic growth. Moreover, the various aspects of reform fit together and reinforce each other. For example, permanent urban residential rights and township upgrading are vital to the creation of "reliable" third-tier government within the terms of the Black Local Authorities Act. The act, and the town councils to which it gave legal standing are, in turn, vital to the creation of autonomous "city-states." The city-states, and the established "bourgeois" communities that are supposed to constitute their population (and to which township upgrading and urban residency rights will supposedly give rise), are vital to a political/constitutional vision that would permit South African whites to share power without losing their control of the political system.

Not only is there a fit among the core elements of reform, but there exists a pronounced consistency over time to Pretoria's reform ideas. True, government showed great hesitancy in introducing reforms that were either vociferously opposed by its constituency or that carry significant risks in respect to its continued control.

Yet when reforms are finally introduced, often to divert domestic and/or international pressures, as was the case in 1985, they reflect concepts that were advanced at the earliest stages of the reform effort. Virtually every alteration in the apartheid system that occurred during the 1980s had been foreshadowed by proposals put forth by the National Party leadership in the late 1970s. This is so even in the arena of political/constitutional reform, the area in which Pretoria appeared most inconsistent, even floundering. Thus in October 1980 the Afrikaans-language newspaper, *Die Transvaler,* described the National Party's constitutional plans this way:

> The basic reasoning could be formulated as a "confederation" of the RSA with Black States; the recognition of the urban Blacks as an entity with a say in such a union of interests in a confederal framework; a joint general citizenship; and the development of the common interests of Coloured, White and Asian in the South African Parliament.[171]

Eight years later the NP leadership was describing its vision of the political future in precisely the same manner.

To adopt a coherent strategy and even to apply it consistently does not lead necessarily to the achievement of strategic objectives. The reality to which the strategy is directed is rarely under the strategist's complete control. As a result his actions can have unintended consequences, producing results that may be even the opposite of those pursued. In this chapter it has been my concern to lay before the reader Pretoria's intentions and the strategy it adopted to attain them. I have focused on *purposes,* only in passing noting the actual *consequences* of Pretoria's reform policies. These, the results or consequences of South African government reform policy, will be the primary concern of succeeding chapters.

Notes

1. Steven Friedman, "Yet Another 'Grand Plan,'" *Weekly Mail,* July 29–August 4, 1988, p. 18.

2. See *South African Digest,* August 24, 1979, pp. 3–4.

3. For the predictive potential of these early government statements on its reform intentions see Robert M. Price, "The Meaning of Government-Led Reform," in Robert Price and Carl Rosberg, eds. *The Apartheid Regime* (Berkeley: Institute of International Studies, 1980), pp. 297–332.

4. See Friedman, "Yet Another 'Grand Plan,'" p. 18.

5. Republic of South Africa, *Report of the Commission of Inquiry Into the Riots at Soweto and Elsewhere* (Cillie Commission Report) (Pretoria: Government Printer, 1980), pp. 606, 605–614, passim.

6. Republic of South Africa, *Report of the Commission of Inquiry into Legislation Affecting the Utilisation of Manpower* (Riekert Commission Report) (Pretoria: Government Printer, 1979).

7. Quoted in South African Institute of Race Relations (SAIRR), *Social and Economic Update,* #4 (1987), p. 1.

8. Riekert Commission Report, p. 5.

9. Republic of South Africa, *White Paper on the Report of the Commission of Inquiry into Legislation Affecting the Utilisation of Manpower,* WP T-1979 (Pretoria: Government Printer, 1979), p. 1, par. 5.

10. *Sunday Times,* August 12, 1979; repr. in *South African Digest,* August 17, 1979, p. 23.

11. Riekert Commission Report, chapter 6, I., p. 245.

12. Ibid., par. 6.4, pp. 245–46 (emphasis added).

13. Ibid., par. 6.5, p. 245 (emphasis added).

14. Ibid.

15. Ibid., par. 6.7.

16. Ibid., par. 614(p)(i), p. 250 (emphasis added).

17. Ibid., pp. 248–52, inter alia.

18. For an early and low estimate of the number of "urban insiders," see Steve Friedman and John Kane-Berman, "Pretoria's Plan for the Black Elite," *Manchester Guardian Weekly,* June 3, 1979, p. 8; for a larger estimate by a government official see quote from Magnus Malan, reprinted in *Quarterly Countdown Five,* South African Institute of Race Relations, 1987, p. 7.

19. Quoted in Friedman and Kane-Berman, p. 8.

20. Simon Bekker and Richard Humphries, *From Control to Confusion* (Pietermaritzburg: Shuter & Shooter, 1985), p. 43.

21. See ibid.

22. See SAIRR, *Quarterly Countdown Eight* (1987), p. 24.

23. Ibid.

24. Ibid.

25. See *The Sowetan,* November 17, 1987; see also SAIRR, *Quarterly Countdown Eight* (1987), p. 24.

26. South African Institute of Race Relations (SAIRR), *Race Relations Survey 1988/89,* (Johannesburg: Institute of Race Relations, 1990), p. 206.

27. Ibid.

28. See SAIRR, *Social and Economic Update, #2* (1987), p. 6; SAIRR, *Quarterly Countdown Eight* (1987), p. 27; *Weekly Mail,* July 29–August 4, 1988, p. 20.

29. SAIRR, *Race Relations Survey, 1988/89,* p. 341.

30. SAIRR, *Social and Economic Update, #2* (1987), p. 6.

31. SAIRR, *Race Relations Survey, 1988/89,* p. 341.

32. See John A. Marcum, "Black Education in South Africa: Key or Chimera? *CSIS Africa Notes,* no. 41 (April 15, 1985), p. 4.

33. John A. Marcum, *Education, Race, and Social Change in South Africa* (Berkeley: University of California Press, 1982), p. 5.

34. See *SA Barometer,* August 14, 1987, pp. 184–185.

35. Marcum, *Education, Race, and Social Change in South Africa,* p. 22; and C. T. Verwey et al., eds., *Education and Manpower Production* (Bloemfontein: University of the Orange Free State, no. 2, 1982), p. 5.

36. SAIRR, *Race Relations Survey, 1988/89,* p. 242.

37. See John A. Marcum, "Black Education in South Africa," p. 2.

38. See David R. Smock, "Black Education in South Africa: The Current Situation" (paper presented to Conference on U.S. Education and Training Initiatives for South Africans and Namibians, Michigan State University, African Studies Center November 1986), p. 10.

39. See Marcum, *Education, Race, and Social Change in South Africa,* p. 4.

40. See *Weekly Mail,* April 28–May 4, 1989, p. 34.

41. Ibid.

42. Quoted in *Fact Sheet on the Republic of South Africa*, South African Embassy, Washington, D.C., 1982, p. 4.

43. See study by University of Cape Town researcher Charles Dingley. Reported in SAIRR, *Social and Economic Update, #4* (1987), p. 24.

44. *Business Day*, October 30, 1986.

45. *Natal Witness*, March 5, 1987; SAIRR, *Social and Economic Update, #1* (1987), p. 9.

46. Riekert Commission Report, par. 3.616, p. 111.

47. *The Star*, October 22, 1987.

48. See *Financial Mail*, August 8, 1988.

49. See Hilary Joffe, "The Housing One in Ten Can Afford," *Weekly Mail*, March 10–16, 1989, p. 15; and also, Hilary Joffe, "This Time, Expect No Talk of Social Remedies," *Weekly Mail*, March 10–16, 1989, p. 14.

50. Quoted in Mark Swilling and Mark Phillips, "The X Factor," *Weekly Mail*, September 2–8, 1988, p. 9.

51. See *The Citizen*, November 17, 1987.

52. See statement by Minister Chris Heunis, *The Citizen*, September 26, 1986.

53. *SA Barometer*, vol. 1, no. 16 (October 9, 1987), p. 244.

54. See Mark Swilling and Mark Phillips, *Weekly Mail*, September 2–8, 1988, p. 9.

55. "The Housing One in Ten Can Afford," *Weekly Mail*, March 10–16, 1989, p. 15.

56. See *Business Day*, October 6, 1986.

57. SAIRR, *Social and Economic Update, #4* (1987), p. 40.

58. *South African Builder*, September 1986.

59. *Business Day*, May 26, 1987.

60. *The Star*, March 6, 1988.

61. Riekert Commission Report, par. 1.9(g), p. 2.

62. *The Citizen*, April 23, 1983.

63. Quoted in *Rand Daily Mail*, April 30, 1983.

64. Ibid.

65. *Business Day*, October 6, 1987.

66. SAIRR, *Quarterly Countdown Three* (1986), p. 21.

67. Pik Botha, quoted in *The Citizen*, March 24, 1987.

68. A report by team of Rands Afrikaans University researchers, in *The Star*, March 26, 1987.

69. For an insightful analysis of the logic underlying Pretoria's plan for reform of residential segregation see Steven Friedman, "Dropping Pebbles in the Path of the Flood," *Weekly Mail*, May 5–12, 1988, p. 12.

70. *The Star*, March 26, 1987; and SAIRR, *Quarterly Countdown Five* (1987), p. 7.

71. Quoted in Shaun Johnson, "In Search of the Real FW," *Weekly Mail*, August 18–24, 1989, p. 2.

72. *Die Vaderland*, April 10, 1986; reprinted in *South African Digest*, April 18, 1986, p. 342 (emphasis added).

73. See Philip Bonner, "Black Trade Unions in South Africa Since World War II," in Price and Rosberg, eds., *The Apartheid Regime*, p. 190.

74. Ibid.

75. N. E. Wiehahn, *The Complete Wiehahn Report* (Johannesburg: Lex Patria Publishers, 1982), par. 1.10, p. 3.

76. Ibid.

77. Ibid., par. 3.27(ii), p. 30.

78. Ibid., par. 3.34, p. 32.

79. Ibid., par. 3.35–3.35.14, p. 32–35.

80. Ibid., par. 3.35.5, p. 33.

81. Ibid., par. 3.35.14, p. 35.

82. Ibid., par. 3.36.7, p. 36.

83. Ibid., par. 3.36.6, p. 36.

84. Ibid., par. 3.36.3, p. 36.

85. Ibid., par. 3.36.8, p. 36.

86. Ibid., par. 3.38, p. 37.

87. Ibid., par. 3.35.5, p. 33.

88. Ibid., par. 3.41, p. 38.

89. Ibid., par. 3.35.4, p. 33.

90. Ibid., par. 3.71, p. 55.

91. Ibid., par. 3.110, p. 72.

92. White paper on part I of Wiehahn Commission Report, reprinted in Wiehahn, p. 134.

93. Robert Michels, *Political Parties: A Sociological Study of the Oligarchic Tendencies of Modern Democracy* (New York: Dover Publications, 1959).

94. Riekert Commission Report, par. 4.204(h), p. 168.

95. Riekert Commission Report, par. 4.204(f), p. 167 (emphasis added).

96. Ibid.

97. See South African Institute of Race Relations (SAIRR), *Survey of Race Relations, 1983* (Johannesburg: Institute of Race Relations, 1984), p. 262–63.

98. Quoted in *To The Point,* November 7, 1980, p. 18.

99. Ibid.

100. Riekert Commission Report, par. 4.204 (emphasis added).

101. Ibid., par. 4.204(j), p. 168.

102. See Ibid., par. 4.152, p. 155.

103. Ibid., par. 4.152(c), p. 156.

104. See Ibid., par. 4.153, p. 156.

105. See SAIRR, *Social and Economic Update, #1,* First Quarter 1987, p. 15.

106. Riekert Commission Report, par. 4.152(e), p. 156.

107. See SAIRR, *Quarterly Countdown Three* (1986), p. 26–27.

108. Riekert Commission Report, par. 5.92(c), p. 234.

109. Quoted in ibid., p. 26.

110. Reprinted in *South African Digest,* September 20, 1985, p. 866.

111. See Bekker and Humphries, *From Control to Confusion,* pp. 96–97.

112. Ibid., p. 97.

113. Ibid., p. 98.

114. Quoted in Riekert Commission Report, par. 4.393, p. 203.

115. Quoted in ibid., p. 101.

116. The specific legal language is taken from the Riekert Commission Report, par. 3.316, p. 74.

117. Ibid., par. 3.317, p. 75.

118. Bekker and Humphries, *From Control to Confusion,* p. 100.

119. Riekert Commission Report, par. 6.23, p. 253.

120. Ibid.

121. Ibid., par. 4.398(5) and (7), p. 204.

122. Bekker and Humphries, *From Control to Confusion,* p. 104.

123. Ibid., p. 105.

124. Ibid., p. 113.

125. Ibid., 114.

126. Dr. P. J. Riekert, chief director of the Western Transvaal Administration Board, quoted in ibid., p. 111.

127. The idea that Pretoria had adopted a strategy of replacing direct state control of the black population with a form of indirect rule was introduced by Andre du Toit in 1979. See "Emerging Strategies for Political Control," in Price and Rosberg, eds., *The Apartheid Regime,* pp. 1–14.

128. In Peter L. Berger and Bobby Godsell, eds., *A Future South Africa: Visions, Strategies, and Realities* (Boulder: Westview Press, 1988), p. 26.

129. See ibid., p. 27.

130. Quoted in *The Citizen,* May 1, 1987.

131. Quoted in Republic of South Africa, *First Report of the Constitutional Committee of the President's Council* (Cape Town: Government Printer, 1982), p. 3.

132. Ibid., 9.

133. See, for example, ibid., passim, especially par. 2.8(d), p. 9; see also "Consociational Democracy in SA—The Only Option?" *The South Africa Foundation News,* vol. 6, no. 6 (June 1980), p. 2.

134. See Arendt Lijphart, *The Politics of Accommodation: Pluralism and Democracy in the Netherlands* (Berkeley: University of California Press, 1968).

135. See "Federal, Confederal and Consociational Options for the South African Plural Society," in R. Rotberg and J. Barratt, eds., *Conflict and Compromise in South Africa* (Cape Town: David Philip, 1980), p. 67.

136. *First Report of the Constitutional Committee,* p. 40.

137. Quoted in "South African Bars a Black Role in 3-House Parliamentary System," *New York Times,* November 10, 1982, p. 6.

138. See John de St. Jorre, "A Vote to Modernize Apartheid's Edifice," *New York Times,* November 7, 1983, p. 23.

139. See SAIRR, *Survey of Race Relations in South Africa, 1983* (Johannesburg: Institute of Race Relations, 1984), p. 91.

140. See, for example, "Botha's Old Hat," *Solidarity News Service: From the Frontline,* no. 2 (January 29, 1985), p. 1.

141. Quoted in ibid., p. 1.

142. Ibid.

143. SAIRR, *Quarterly Countdown Five* (1987), p. 5.

144. Ibid., p. 6.

145. See "Botha Sets Out His 'Agenda' for Racial Changes," *New York Times,* October 4, 1985, p. 1.

146. Ibid.

147. See SAIRR, *Quarterly Countdown Three* (1986) p. 23.

148. Quoted in SAIRR, *Quarterly Countdown Five* (1987), p. 7 (emphasis added).

149. Statement by Kobie Coetsee, quoted in *The Citizen,* March 24, 1987, p. 8.

150. BBC interview with F. W. de Klerk, quoted in SAIRR, *Quarterly Countdown Five* (1987), p. 9.

151. See "New Plans for Blacks," *Die Burger,* August 13, 1979; reprinted in *South African Digest,* August 17, 1979, p. 21; see also Robert M. Price, "Apartheid and White Supremacy: The Meaning of Government-Led Reform," in Price and Rosberg, eds., *The Apartheid Regime,* p. 327.

152. See "Urban Blacks Still at the Root of the Problem," *To The Point,* November 7, 1980, p. 18.

153. See SAIRR, *Quarterly Countdown Five* (1987), p. 13.

154. *The Star,* March 10, 1987, p. 8.

155. Quoted in SAIRR, *Quarterly Countdown Five* (1987), p. 7.

156. SAIRR, *Quarterly Countdown Eight* (1987), p. 5.

157. See, for example, Willem de Klerk, *The Second (R)evolution: Afrikanerdom and the Crises of Identity* (Johannesburg: Jonathan Ball Publishers, 1984), p. 34–35.

158. See, for example, Arendt Lijphart, *Power-Sharing in South Africa* (Berkeley: Institute of International Studies, 1985), pp. 20–21; see also Henry Kissinger, "What To Do for Southern Africa: Three Principles," *Washington Post,* September, 7, 1986, section C, p. 8.

159. Interview by the BBC, reported in *The Star,* March 16, 1987; also quoted in SAIRR, *Quarterly Countdown Five* (1987), p. 8.

160. Quoted in SAIRR, *Quarterly Countdown Eight* (1987), p. 11 (emphasis added).

161. Quoted in *Cape Times,* March 17, 1987; reprinted in SAIRR, *Quarterly Countdown Five* (1987), pp. 7–8.

162. *The Citizen,* August 13, 1986.

163. See SAIRR, *Quarterly Countdown Nine* (1988), p. 14.

164. Quoted in SAIRR, *Quarterly Countdown Eight* (1987), p. 11.

165. Quoted in SAIRR, *Quarterly Countdown Nine* (1988), p. 10; see also *The Star,* February 15, 1988.

166. See SAIRR, *Social and Economic Update,* #1 (1987), p. 18.

167. Ibid.

168. "A Letter From South Africa," no. 5 (Washington, D.C.: South African Embassy, May 26, 1988), p. 1.

169. See SAIRR, *Quarterly Countdown Six* (1987), p. 10.

170. SAIRR, *Quarterly Countdown Six* (1987), p. 10.

171. *Die Transvaler,* October 6, 1980.

5

From Reform to Insurrection

"The most dangerous moment for a bad government is usually that when it enters upon the work of reform."[1]

ALEXIS DE TOCQUEVILLE

Toward the end of the decade of the 1970s, the South African government fashioned what it termed a "a total national strategy," whose intent was to restore domestic political peace, end international isolation, and return the economy to a path of sustained growth. The centerpiece of this strategy was a program of domestic reform whereby the governing group sought to dismantle much of the edifice of racial separation and control that it had constructed over a thirty-year period. But by the middle of the 1980s, some seven years into the reform program, the country was engulfed by a black uprising that was more radical, more violent, more widespread, and more sustained than anything witnessed in modern South African history. It also faced a more hostile international environment and was subject to substantially more damaging foreign economic pressures than anything previously experienced. Outlawed organizations and imprisoned leaders were openly revered; tens of thousands cheered as the flag of the ANC, the red banner of the South African Communist Party, and pictures of Nelson Mandela were held aloft. Prominent members of the business establishment and white clergymen defied the government, traveling to Lusaka, Zambia, to discuss the future of South Africa with the top echelon of the African National Congress. The political initiative had seemingly slipped from Pretoria and passed to its most radical opponents. Pretoria had expected reform to elicit sympathy, if not kudos, from the international community, and acquiescence, if not appreciation, from the urban black population. It produced neither. Instead, reform appeared to have unleashed political forces that were beyond the state's ability to control. What had happened?

Autocratic regimes that move down the path of reform, allowing the deprived access to valued societal resources that had once been denied to them, face a common danger. From the vantage point of the ruling elite reform is, in effect, an

152

effort to intervene in a dynamic process of societal transformation so as to slow it down, blunt its impact, and lessen the threat to established power and privilege. But the social forces driving the transformation, which led the autocracy to seek reform in the first place, do not disappear at the announcement of the regime's reformist intentions. Reform takes place in a highly dynamic sociopolitical situation, something that the reform strategy is unlikely to take sufficiently into account. The demands and grievances that are salient when the elite begins to contemplate reform may not be the ones that are most intensely felt when changes are actually introduced. Moreover, the evolving grievances, as well as the shape, direction, and power of the social forces pushing for change from "below," are influenced by the reform program itself, and in not easily predictable ways. For this reason, the adage "too little, too late" is a frequent epitaph of elite-sponsored reform programs.

The reformer is in the position of a rifleman trying to hit a moving target whose speed he does not know and whose future direction and velocity will be affected by the flight of his own bullet in ways he does not comprehend. For the riflemen this means that he is very unlikely to hit his target; for the reformer it means that the changes he introduces are likely to have unanticipated consequences that undermine the achievement of his goals. The reformer can counter these "negative" outcomes in two basic ways. He can adapt his policies as his knowledge of the sociopolitical dynamic in which he finds himself grows; and he can use repression, as discussed in Chapter 3, to shape the dynamics of sociopolitical change and to blunt or eliminate unintended effects as they emerge. But, the freedom of action of a ruling elite is not unlimited. Its ability to act is constrained by its own interests, by the actual or anticipated reactions of domestic constituencies upon which it relies, and/or by powerful external actors who can affect its fortunes. In other words, in a world of complex interdependencies a reformer's latitude for adaptation and for the use of repression is often limited. The dynamic sociopolitical environment he seeks to alter will, as a result, often move beyond his capability for control.

Reform and Alienation

In reforming apartheid, Pretoria was, in part, seeking to ameliorate the deprivations of black urban life so as to reduce the level of grievance and alienation that— according to the Cillie, Wiehahn, and Riekert commissions, among others—had produced the Soweto uprising. Intentions apart, however, the era of reformism coincided with an increasing, not decreasing, sense of grievance and alienation. Evidence of this can be found in a series of attitude surveys conducted between 1977 and 1985 among black urban residents. In each of these surveys, respondents were asked to locate on a five-point scale "the way most African people like yourself [in your township] feel about life in South Africa now." The five options available to the respondent ranged from "very happy" at one end, through "not happy but also not unhappy" in the middle, to "angry and impatient" at the other end. Table 5.1 presents the data from the surveys. A response of "angry and impatient" is taken to indicate a condition of alienation, while "unhappy" signifies a "prealienated" state of grievance. Not surprisingly, these data reveal widespread dissatisfaction with the existing state of affairs—over six out of ten urban Africans expressed some form of

TABLE 5.1.   Level of Alienation (Urban Africans)

	1977[a]	1979[b]	1984[c]	1985[d]
Alienated ("angry")	39%	44%	50%	66%
Prealienated (unhappy)	25%	17%	16%	—
Number of respondents	(592)	(422)	(551)	(800)

[a]Theodor Hanf et al., *South Africa: The Prospects Peaceful Change* (London: Rex Collings, 1981), p. 442.
[b]Lawrence Schlemmer, in Hanf et al. p., 442.
[c]Lawrence Schlemmer, "Black Attitudes, Capitalism and Investment in South Africa" (Centre for Applied Social Science, University of Natal, Durban, August 1984), p. 10.
[d]Mark Orkin, *The Struggle and the Future* (Johannesburg, Raven Press, 1986), p. 34.

unhappiness. What *is* startling is that this data reveal a steep and steady movement toward alienation during the first nine years of Pretoria's reform program—from 39 percent of the urban African population immediately after the Soweto uprising in 1977 to 66 percent in 1985. Another indication of the increasing alienation that characterized the era of reform is provided by the answers to a question posed during 1984* and 1985 surveys: "Think of the present time in South Africa— everything that is happening. Is life for you improving, staying the same, or getting worse?" In 1984, 60 percent of township residents answered that life is "getting worse," compared to only 16 percent who saw an improvement.[2] By 1985, three-quarters of the urban residents felt that their quality of life was deteriorating.[3] Ironically, those Africans who would appear to be the major beneficiaries of reforms—workers who are members of trade unions and the educated/professional/ white-collar middle class—registered more alienation than the average respondent. In 1979, 58 percent of the black middle-class respondents expressed "anger and impatience" with their situation, compared to 44 percent of the entire sample of black urbanites;[4] in 1984 some 76 percent of black trade unionists were alienated compared to 66 percent of the overall sample.[5]

Pretoria's reform strategy was based on the notion that the level of black aliena-tion could be reduced through an improvement in the conditions of black urban life. This premise itself rested on a basic assumption about political behavior—that political alienation and opposition is a function of the absolute level of access to societal values: the better off an individual or group, the greater the acceptance of the status quo; the worse off, the more likely it is to support movements of radical opposition. On a common-sense basis this would seem a persuasive notion, and if it were indeed valid reform would be a far less precarious enterprise for ruling elites. But historians and theorists of revolution have long recognized that human behavior

---

*Interviews were conducted in early 1984, prior to the outbreak of insurrection that began in the townships of the Vaal Triangle in late August.

does not, in fact, conform to this seemingly logical notion.[6] Marx, for example, pointed out that social tension in capitalist society arises not from the absolute level of worker deprivation, but rather from increases in the social welfare of the proletariat that do not keep pace with the rise in wealth of the bourgeoisie.

> [A]lthough the enjoyments of the workers have risen [with the rapid growth of productive capital], the social satisfaction that they feel has fallen in comparison with the increased enjoyments of the capitalists, which are inaccessible to the worker. . . . *Our desires and pleasures spring from society; we measure them, therefore, by society and not by the objects which serve for their satisfaction. Because they are of a social nature, they are of a relative nature.*[7]

"Relative deprivation," a central concept of contemporary theories of revolution and radical mass movements, is similar to Marx's idea.[8] In this formulation, what gives rise to political alienation and opposition is not the absolute level of a group or individual's deprivation, but rather the gap between expectations of what society will provide and what it actually does provide. Populations that experience abject and long-term deprivation are unlikely to have expectations that differ significantly from their lot. But the once abjectly deprived who experience improvement in their lot will alter upward their level of expectations. They will become prime raw material for movements of mass opposition if the change in their level of expectations is greater than the change in their material conditions.

Although Alexis de Tocqueville did not think in the conceptual language of contemporary political psychology, the significance of what we now term relative deprivation is the central thesis of the nineteenth-century historian's classic study of the French Revolution. After showing that the revolution occurred during a century of unprecedented socioeconomic growth and in those regions of France experiencing the most improvement, de Tocqueville concludes:

> [I]t is not always when things are going from bad to worse that revolutions break out. On the contrary, it oftener happens that when a people which has put up with an oppressive rule over a long period without protest suddenly finds the government relaxing its pressure, it takes up arms against it. . . . Patiently endured so long as it seemed beyond redress, a grievance comes to appear intolerable once the possibility of removing it crosses men's minds. . . . [P]eople may suffer less, but their sensibility is exacerbated.[9]

Herein lies the "Achilles' heel" of the autocratic reformer. Introducing change, he raises expectations of what is possible. The level of absolute deprivation may well decline, but the level of relative deprivation simultaneously increases. And it is the latter, not the former, that is politically significant. For the oppressed will now focus on what they are still denied, not what they have been given. Thus de Tocqueville's warning that "the most perilous moment for a bad government is one when it seeks to mend its ways."

> Only consummate statecraft can enable a King to save his throne when after a long spell of oppressive rule he sets to improving the lot of his subjects. . . . For the

mere fact that certain abuses have been remedied draws attention to the others and they now appear more galling. . . . In the reign of Louis XVI the most trivial pinpricks of arbitrary power caused more resentment than the thoroughgoing despotism of Louis XIV.[10]

De Tocqueville's discourse on eighteenth-century France, provides a key to understanding why the alienation felt by black South Africans increased at the same time that Pretoria opted to jettison much of apartheid. From 1978 onward, promises of reform and change were repeatedly and loudly proclaimed, raising the expectations of South African blacks that a new deal was in the offing. Black politics "was full of optimism," reminisced black political leader Patrick Lekota, of the early 1980s. "The government was talking about change and everybody was talking about change."[11]

Increased levels of expectation resulted not just from officialdom's zealous efforts to make its "new deal" known to the world, but also from the indirect consequences of Pretoria's early reform actions. The township political dynamics set off by the introduction of elected community councils is of particular significance. Since a majority of township residents greeted the new councils with suspicion and cynicism, the black politicians who sought election to them were in a precarious position. In order to create credibility for themselves, and legitimacy for the newly created councils, they often adopted populist platforms, promising rapid improvements in living conditions. In Mamelodi, outside Pretoria, the Vukani Vulahmelo People's Party (VVPP) campaigned successfully on a platform to oppose high rents, prevent "slum demolition," and introduce low-cost housing. In Soweto, the Sofasonke Party promised rents cuts, leniency to rent defaulters, permanent home ownership, and an end to influx control. In Alexandra, a Johannesburg township slated for demolition, the populist appeal of the aspiring community councillors was reflected in the name of their political party, the Save Alexandra Party.* It promised to fight the scheduled demolition of the township and announced alternative "development plans" for a reprieved Alexandra.[12]

Because Pretoria was largely unable to meet the expectations created by its own words and actions an increasingly large gap developed between black expectation and reality. The government was constrained in at least three ways from moving effectively to close this gap. First, there were the limits inherent in the *verligte* ruling group's vision of appropriate change. As shown in Chapter 4, the governing group excluded from its reformist orientation those elements of the South African system that were necessary to maintain the "white way of life." At the very least this meant continuing race segregation and thus discrimination in respect to residence, education, and health-care delivery; maintaining a system of influx control for most people of African descent, albeit by new methods; avoiding a radical redistribution of material resources that might spell a decline in white living stan-

---

*Even with the populist appeals made by the candidates for community council seats, only a minority, and usually a small minority, of township residents voted in local government elections. In 1983 the voter turnout in Mamelodi was 28 percent, and in Soweto 10 percent (up from 8 percent in 1978).

dards; and, most important of all for it represented the ultimate guarantee of the "white way of life," maintaining white control of the political system. Thus, while proclaiming that "apartheid is dead," the "zone of exclusion" envisioned by Pretoria for South Africa's people of color remained substantial, even if reform were to be fully implemented.

Not surprisingly, Pretoria did not dwell publicly on this zone of exclusion, but rather talked loudly but unspecifically about its plans for change. The fact that the international community was an important audience for reform, indeed a constituency whose collaboration was required if the resources to finance reform were to become available, contributed to Pretoria's tendency to exaggerate the extent of its commitment to change. Had it been more modest about what it intended to alter it would have been less likely to dramatically raise expectations at home. Had it done so, however, the required collaboration from abroad was unlikely to be forthcoming. The conflict between Pretoria's international and domestic requirements thus becomes apparent.

A second constraint on Pretoria's reformist action was the conservative pull of its own Afrikaner political constituency. The National Party leadership had to worry about its electoral constituency, which had for thirty years been fed an ideological doctrine defining that which the elite now claimed to be destroying as a just, indeed a sacred, social and political order. It also had to worry about the impact of reform on the Afrikaner public servants, who made up the National Party's core body of political supporters. They had been the chief beneficiaries of the apartheid regime's commitment to central administrative control. If building apartheid had meant the creation of thousands of government jobs to be filled with an emergent Afrikaner middle class, would dismantling apartheid mean Afrikaner unemployment, downward mobility, and a loss to the National Party of its patronage base? These concerns limited the speed with which Pretoria could implement even those reforms that fit within its limited vision. Thus, although an outline for a new constitution was prepared by a parliamentary committee in 1977, the new political dispensation was not introduced until 1984. The Riekert recommendation to abolish the pass laws was made and accepted in 1978—but not implemented until 1986, some eight years later. Public discussion by government leaders about repealing the Mixed Marriages and Immorality acts began in 1980, but these laws remained on the books until 1986. Thus, even within the limited parameters of Pretoria's vision for change, the time lag imposed on the government by the realities of "white politics" exacerbated the gap between promised reform and its delivery. And, furthermore, once Pretoria belatedly acted to alter law and policy, the inevitable bureaucratic sabotage ensued. The government was relying, after all, on a public bureaucracy whose members were either ideologically hostile to the changes being introduced or potentially threatened by them.[13] Consequently, they naturally acted so as to reduce the actual as opposed to the apparent impact of altered policy.

A third constraint on Pretoria's ability to move on its reform promises was financial. As already discussed, the cost of ameliorating the physical and social conditions of urban black life was very high, and Pretoria expected to pay for its plan to upgrade black townships out of revenues generated by economic growth. But for a variety of reasons—OPEC-orchestrated oil price increases, a petroleum embargo by Arab oil-producing countries, international economic recession, falling gold prices, structural impediments in the South African economy, international economic isolation following Soweto—the 1980s were a period of stagnation and decline for the South African economy.

Figure 5.1 depicts the performance of the economy through changes in real gross domestic product per capita. As can be seen, the last three years of the 1970s were a period in which the South African economy gradually recovered from the recession associated with the Soweto uprising. The year 1980 marked a high point of this growth period, with a nearly 5 percent increase in per capita GDP, placing South Africa among the most rapidly growing economies in the world. Interestingly, it was in 1980 and 1981 that the more grandiose plans for the physical upgrading of the townships and expanding primary and secondary education were launched. But 1980 turned out to be a short-term aberration; the late 1970s recovery was a misleading prelude to a much more profound and long-lasting decline that would mark the entire next decade. As one authority summarized, "Regardless of one's vantage point, the South African economy in the 1980s was in severe difficulty. . . . [T]he aggregate performance during this decade has been dismal."[14] In the five years between the end of 1980 and the beginning of 1986 GDP increased a total of less than 4 percent, while population was increasing by more than 12 percent. In relation to the size of South Africa's population, GDP had thus shrunk

Index of Real GDP/capita

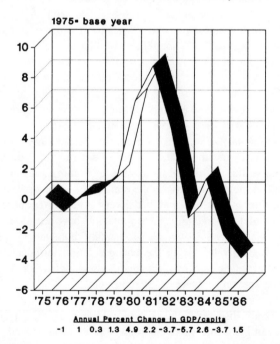

1975= base year

Annual Percent Change in GDP/capita
-1   1   0.3   1.3   4.9   2.2   -3.7   -5.7   2.6   -3.7   1.5

FIG. 5.1. Performance of the South African economy, 1976–1986 (Source: *Weekly Mail*, December 2–8, 1988, p. 19)

by nearly 8 percent. In other words, just as Pretoria announced its grand plans for turning the black townships into established middle-class communities, with electricity, indoor plumbing, paved streets, recreation facilities, schools, and adequate housing, the anticipated means of finance disappeared. Thus, even within an arena of reform already limited by the government's own vision and the conservative pull of its Afrikaner constituency, economic and financial exigencies undermined Pretoria's ability to deliver on the expectations it had created.

If the primary political consequence of economic stagnation was to limit the government's ability to make good on its reform promises, a secondary consequence was a possible *decline* in the absolute level of black living standards.[15] After a period of improvement in wages and employment opportunities in the 1970s, the recession of the 1980s brought increased levels of unemployment, high rates of inflation, and stagnating wages to the urban black population. When asked, in early 1984, what things had gotten worse, black urban residents most frequently mentioned inflation, wages, and unemployment.[16]

Rent increases were another threat to the living standards of township residents. During the 1970s the financial situation of townships administration neared crisis proportions. Costs, driven by inflation, escalated; Pretoria, seeking to end state subsidization of township administration, pursued a policy of township self-financing; and township-based revenues, generated largely by liquor taxes and rents, lagged behind expenditures.[17] By the end of the decade the administrations of the large townships were essentially bankrupt.[18] There was a great deal of pressure, therefore, to raise rents in order to cover the costs of electricity, water, refuse collection, sewerage, and the like. Additionally, Pretoria also hoped to get the township residents to pay for township upgrading themselves. As a result, escalating rents were a salient feature of township life in the early 80s.[19] In the townships of the Vaal triangle, for example, rents were increased more than 400 percent between 1978 and the end of 1983.[20] The government's reform policies, in essence, added directly to the deteriorating economic situation facing black township residents in the early 1980s.

There was developing what theorists of mass movements refer to as a "J-curve" situation. A period of improving material conditions produces a trajectory of rising expectations, when a sudden economic downturn creates a rapidly widening gap between expectations and actual experience. Comparative historical evidence suggests that such moments are politically explosive.[21] In the South African case, the J-curve phenomenon extended the gap between expectations and reality created by the announcement of reform in the late 1970s, enhancing the situational conditions for mass political opposition.

Reform, Mobilization, and Organization

Within the communities of South Africa's urban townships, the early 1980s were a time of organizational effervescence, as well as political alienation. The period witnessed a veritable explosion in associational life. It gave birth to new organizations of every variety—community, youth, women's, labor, student, political— which by mid-decade honeycombed the social fabric of all but the smallest and most remote of the townships. Incorporating the young and old, students and unemployed youths, workers and the bourgeoisie, the employed and the jobless; emphasizing a grass-roots "bottom-up" form of association; these new organizations while serving somewhat different geographical, class, gender, or functional constituencies, shared a central and all-important feature—they mobilized their members in opposition to the limited form of inclusion that was Pretoria's vision of a reformed South Africa. The emergence of this rich labyrinth of associational life constituted, by mid-decade, the organizational foundation for a sustainable, multi-class, nationwide movement of liberation.

As was the case with the psychology of alienation, the organizational efferves-cence of the early 1980s was, in part, an unintended consequence of reform. Although certainly uninterested in the existence of strong and autonomous organiza-tions in the black community, Pretoria through its reform strategy contributed never-theless to their emergence. Government policies in the era of reform provided both the stimulus for mass opposition, and the latitude for that opposition to effectively organize. In the case of trade unions the impact of reform policy was direct, since the post-Wiehahn industrial relations laws made provision for labor organizations with black members. The role of reform in the emergence of other forms of associa-tion was indirect, and worked in two ways. First, the reform policies themselves, falling short of the expectations that government itself had helped create, gave rise to grievances. These became the stimulus for the formation of new organizations, as well as the fuel for their efforts at mass mobilization. Second, and more indirectly, the reform strategy limited government's latitude in acting repressively against opposition organizations once they had emerged. This constraint was built into the logic of Pretoria's total strategy, which sought to overcome international isolation by presenting South Africa to the world in an enlightened and thus acceptable light. Since government's ability to finance reform was dependent on a robust economy, which, in turn, required access to foreign capital, technology, and markets, the achievement of international acceptability had to occur simultaneously with the unfolding of the reform program. This was a crucial weak point of total strategy. It limited Pretoria's ability to use repression against the emergent organizations of opposition in the early 1980s. For to ban newly created organizations, to outlaw their potential successors, and to put a blanket restriction on all political expression by the majority would have made it impossible to convince the international com-munity of the seriousness of the South African government's intentions. It would thus have made much less likely the foreign business involvement required for high rates of economic growth.

This sort of constraint was especially intense in the early 1980s, the very period of organizational effervescence in the townships. Political developments outside of South Africa, particularly in the United States, were propitious for the achievement of the international acceptability Pretoria sought. The winner of the 1980 U.S. presidential election, Ronald Reagan, was someone whose ideological proclivities, public statements, and political associations indicated sympathy for Pretoria's situa-tion. Under Reagan's policy of "constructive engagement," announced early in his administration, the United States would eschew the hostile acts and rhetoric that characterized the Carter presidency and instead seek a normal, active, and positive relationship with South Africa.

This was, potentially, the international breakthrough that Pretoria required. But it was also an opportunity that would limit Pretoria's ability to act against the unintended and undesired mushrooming of opposition organizations. For constructive engagement was predicated on the assumption that the government of P. W. Botha would move forward with reform, and that such reform was gradually creating a society acceptable to Americans. Only if the credibility of this assumption were established could the Reagan administration expect to sell constructive engagement politically at home. Pretoria was told as much by U.S. Secretary of State Alexander Haig when he met South African Foreign Minister P. K. Botha in May 1981. A briefing paper prepared for Secretary Haig laid out the crucial link between a friendly U.S. policy and the credibility of Pretoria's domestic actions:

> We [the U.S.] cannot condone a system of institutionalized racial differentiation, [but] we can cooperate with a society undergoing constructive change. Your Government's explicit commitment in this direction will enable us to work with you. You must help to make this approach credible. You should also recognize that this period represents *your best shot,* a rare opportunity, because of . . . our desire to turn a new leaf in bilateral relations.[22]

The advent of the Reagan presidency in 1980 thus exposed the weak link in Pretoria's total strategy. As noted in Chapter 3, repression and reform can be thought of as opposite sides of the same coin. Repression can make the success of reform more likely by eliminating any political alternative to cooptation on the ruling regime's terms. But this abstract theorizing assumes that repression has no significant costs for the regime. The example of Pretoria's total strategy indicates, however, that such costs can enter the equation. Required to satisfy an international audience in order to make reform financially feasible, Pretoria found that it could not act with impunity against those who rejected its form of inclusion.

This does not mean that Pretoria simply abandoned political repression. Indeed, in the early 1980s it continued to jail political activists and labor organizers, ban political meetings, and interfere with the activities of organizations it deemed too radical. By normal democratic standards it was still a highly repressive regime. But in the reform environment of the early 1980s the use of repression was far less systematic and complete than the regime was capable of imposing, or that it would impose after mid-1986.[23] Opposition political activists were jailed, but in insufficient numbers to deplete the cadre of potential organizational leaders; force was used to disrupt mass meetings but not in sufficient quantity to prevent such meetings from taking place; organizations were harassed but their activities were not banned and so they continued to function. Pretoria's international concerns acted as a drag on its repressive proclivities, making it hesitate here, behave inconsistently there.[24] As a result, despite a still highly repressive political environment, the reform dynamic of the early 1980s opened up sufficient social space for new organizations of opposition to take root. And, ironically, the use of "limited" repression facilitated such a process by adding to the grievances that fueled mass mobilization and organization.

Trade Unions

One of the earliest, most dramatic, and most important instances of reform-driven organizational development was the trade unionization of black workers. Control of the workplace is one of the few levers of power potentially available to South Africa's resource-poor black population. With an economy utterly dependent on black labor, the organization of large and autonomous trade unions would represent a significant shift in the South African balance of power. Obviously this would not constitute a reversal in the majority–minority power relationship, but clearly it would mean a significant movement away from the unhindered power of the white minority.

After the Durban strikes of 1973 trade-union organizations for black workers had once again become a fact of South African industrial life, albeit an informal one. With the passage of the Wiehahn labor reform laws in 1979, the membership of black workers in new, predominately black trade unions burgeoned. In 1978 there were only thirty-nine nonracial trade unions, with a total membership of 206,000. By 1986 nonracial unions numbered 109 and had a membership of nearly 900,000.*[25] A study by South African labor economist Eddie Webster found that by 1983 the new independent unions had an organizing presence in 756 workplaces, and had signed formal agreements with management in 420 of these.[26] By 1985 the number of workplaces in which organizing was occurring reached 3,400![27] The organizational core of the emergent unions—over 6,000 shop stewards,[28] most of whom were under thirty-five years of age—represented a new generation of worker activists.[29]

The growth in black trade-union organization can be said to have been anticipated, if not exactly welcomed, by Pretoria when it moved in 1979 to deracialize the arena of industrial relations. The policy of deracialization was intended to enmesh the emergent independent trade unions within the state's statutory industrial relations system, reduce their autonomy, and in so doing prevent them from becoming militant and political. Data on strike activity, displayed in Figure 5.2, reveals that the labor reforms did not have the intended effect. Instead, the annual level of strike activity climbed rapidly, doubling in 1980 and then doubling again by the end of 1982. The number of workers involved in strike action increased from 23,000 in the year of the reform action to 182,000 in 1984. In the industrial sector the increase was from 250 per 100,000 workers in 1979 to approximately 2,000 per 100,000 in 1984. Production losses due to strike activity, as measured in "man-days" of labor

---

*Technically, use of the term "nonracial" to refer to the new union movement is incorrect. A minority of the new unions, following Black Consciousness philosophy, defined their membership as exclusively black, and can thus be considered "racial" unions. In contrast, most of the new unions, with an overwhelmingly black rank and file, defined membership in class rather than race terms, and were open to whites as members, organizers, and staff. I will, unless context suggests otherwise, use the term "independent unions" to refer to both the Black Consciousness and nonracial unions. Both types were independent of the state and of the establishment unions that existed prior to the Wiehahn labor reforms.

TRADE UNION MILITANCY
1977–1986

Number of Workers Involved in Strikes

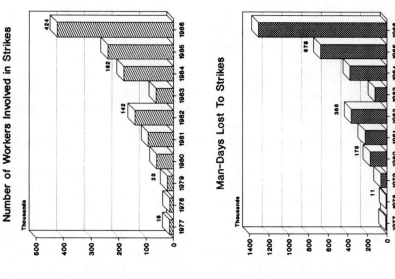

Man-Days Lost To Strikes

Strike Actions

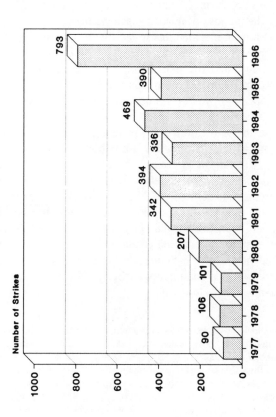

Fig. 5.2. Strike activity, 1977–1986 (*Source*: South Africa, Department of Manpower and National Manpower Commission, Annual Reports, in *SA Barometer* vol. 1 no. 5 [May 8, 1987], pp. 67–70; and *SA Barometer*, vol. 1, no. 9 [July 3, 1987], pp. 131–33)

lost, doubled in 1980 compared to 1979, doubled again in 1982, and doubled yet again in 1985. Man-days of labor lost to strike activity in 1985 were thus over ten times greater than the annual average in the immediate pre-reform years.*

In addition to its heightened militancy, the emergent trade-union movement in the post-Wiehahn era was marked by a process of increasing politicization. This development was contrary to Pretoria's expectations and to orthodox industrial relations theory, which holds that once labor unions become "established" they focus increasingly on workplace issues and eschew general sociopolitical agendas. However, in the South African case narrow "bread and butter" unionism—what Lenin called "economism"—rapidly gave way to involvement in community and political struggles.

At first the question of political involvement by trade-union organizations was indeed salient and divisive. Some activists argued for an exclusive workplace focus. A larger grouping accepted that political action was required, but held that organizational autonomy from multi-class populist political movements must be maintained if worker interests were to be protected. A third grouping argued, from the outset, for involvement in community-based political struggles and alliances with political movements.[30] The conditions of life for black workers in South Africa militates in favor of the third position. So much of the apartheid-shaped social system had been designed for the purpose of making black people cheap, movable, and dispensable parts of an industrial machine that it is difficult if not impossible to separate workplace from broader social issues, such as housing, group areas, forced removals, citizenship rights, and the like. Moreover, since race, not class, has been the primary basis for social discrimination and economic deprivation in South Africa, the political appeal of multi-class coalitions seeking liberation from racial oppression is very powerful.†

Not surprisingly, therefore, the worker purists, or "workerists" as they are called in South Africa, have remained a rather small grouping, largely made up of intellectuals. The largest grouping, those who sought autonomy from political movements for fear of damaging their fledgling labor organizations, accepted from the beginning that trade unions would be involved in broad community and political struggles. What they insisted on, however, was that in such struggles the unions remain separate, worker-controlled bodies that would set their own strategies and tactics rather than follow the lead of multi-class "populist" movements.[31] But just as the special nature of the South African social system rendered the boundary between workplace and community artificial and nonviable, it eroded this commitment to organizational aloofness.

---

*These statistics on strike activity are drawn from Department of Manpower and National Manpower Commission annual reports. They underestimate worker militancy, because of the manner in which the government collects this data. Employers are required to notify the government only about work stoppages that result from disputes over terms of employment or where there is a "legal" strike as defined by the Labour Relations Act. Consequently, sympathy strikes, work slowdowns, and political strikes are not officially recorded. See *SA Barometer,* vol. 1, no. 5, (May 8, 1987), p. 67.

†It is only the theoreticians and intellectuals who remain resistent to such appeals, for their grand abstractions permit them "to see" the "essential" class dynamics of the South African social system irrespective of existential realities.

It was not until 1985 that the main body of independent trade unions unequivocally joined the political struggle as affiliates of a broad political movement, but there were harbingers of this development in earlier years. In 1981 a new form of worker organization, shop steward councils, emerged in the townships. Formed as a means for established unions to penetrate unorganized plants and as a way to organize the unemployed, these new associations were a hybrid union–community organization. Especially active among migrant workers living in the East Rand hostels, the councils were pulled toward mobilizing around the "nonproduction" type issues that were central to the lives of this particular segment of the working class—housing, removals, unemployment benefits, and family rights. They were also natural allies of community groups that were already organizing campaigns on the same issues.[32]

Another harbinger of the involvement of unions in community-based actions were several instances of prominent trade-union victories that relied on the mobilization of consumer boycotts. In 1979 a seven-month strike at Fattis and Monis in Cape Town was won with the support of a product boycott by black consumers. The threat of a consumer boycott was also an important factor in what was possibly the most important trade-union victory of 1981, a successful strike at Colgate over the union's demand that negotiations take place at plant level.[33]

And from 1979 onward trade-union activists played a prominent role in the formation and leadership of township "civic" associations that mushroomed into existence in the early 1980s. The orthodox theory of trade-union economism relies on the presumption that trade-union leadership will eschew non-workplace agendas and extra-union political involvements for fear that these will threaten the workplace organizations from which their newfound status and power flows. In the peculiar South Africa socioeconomic context, however, such a dynamic did not apply. The realities of township existence meant that many of the labor union leaders were also community leaders, and thus they were not likely to keep their union organizations aloof from community-based organizations.

The economically strategic position of black industrial workers makes clear the potential political significance of union organization among the black working class. Yet that potential is undermined by, among other things, the tendency for organizational rivalry and division. Such tendencies were clearly in evidence in the early 1980s. While one of the strengths of the independent trade unions was their "shop-floor" form of organization, it was also a source of political weakness. Unions formed around the shop floor tended to be small plant-based organizations. A collection of relatively small, locally focused associations is not conducive to large-scale political action. The emergent trade unions were also often divided on issues of principle, especially that of racialism. Some unions adopted the Black Consciousness position of insisting on black exclusivity in membership and extraorganizational affiliation. A larger number followed the precept of non-racialism. Although their membership was made up predominantly of black workers, they were open at both rank-and-file and leadership levels to individuals regardless of race, and were willing to establish political affiliations with organizations without requiring a racial "litmus test."

Although these divisions were deep and difficult to overcome, the early 1980s were a period of unity building as well militancy and politicization for the emergent trade-union movement. Between 1981 and 1984 six "summit meetings" of the independent trade unions were held to discuss means of building unity.[34] Unions in the period were faced simultaneously with the reformist and repressive dimensions of Pretoria's total strategy. On the one hand, the process of official registration now opened to them held the potential for cooptation; on the other hand, their leadership cadre was constantly faced with the threat of arrest and detention. In response the fledgling union movement was searching for a common survival strategy. The formation of a giant labor federation, an umbrella organization for all independent trade unions, came to be seen as the best option, but this proved an extremely difficult idea to operationalize, given the differences that divided the trade-union movement. Nevertheless, the move to unity through federation was still rapid and significant. It culminated in the December 1985 launch of the giant Congress of South African Trade Unions (Cosatu), which grouped together trade unions representing a majority of organized black workers, and from the outset committed itself to a national political struggle for black social, political, and economic rights. The power potential of this type of unity had been foreshadowed more than three years earlier, when the independent trade unions, with only two days notice, mobilized over 100,000 workers for a work stoppage to protest the death in police detention of Dr. Neil Aggett, Transvaal organizer of the Food and Canning Workers Union.

Community Organizations

In contrast to the situation that followed Sharpeville, the repression of the Soweto uprising was rapidly followed by a new wave of mass mobilization and organization. A prominent feature of the new organizational landscape was the emergence of numerous "civic" associations—organizations that sought to defend the interests of the residents of specific urban communities. They were often joined within the townships by locally organized student and youth associations.

The contrast between the post-Sharpeville and post-Soweto eras stemmed from a number of factors. First, the Soweto generation was less naive about the harshness of Pretoria's security apparatus than were the participants in the anti-apartheid mobilizations of the 1950s. The township residents of two decades later had been "educated" by the 1960s state of emergency and the realities of urban life in apartheid South Africa. Thus, when faced with the state's repression of the Soweto uprising they were already immunized against the type of political trauma that had immobilized an entire generation after Sharpeville. While a "culture of acquiescence" was the legacy of Sharpeville, the legacy of Soweto was an incipient "culture of resistance." Second, several new sources of community leadership were present in the townships of the early 1980s. Many of the young activists who had fled into exile and joined the African National Congress in late 1976 had completed their training and were slipping back into South Africa. At the same time a number of the seasoned activists of the 1950s, imprisoned since the Sharpeville repression, were completing their sentences in the late 1970s and returning to their urban communities. They would become available to contribute to the leadership cadre of the emergent civic organizations.[35] Simultaneously, the independent trade-union movement, begun in 1973 and growing rapidly in the late 1970s, provided a forum for the training of hundreds of grass-roots organizers and potential leaders. They too would represent an important resource for the new civic associations. Third, there was the unintended contribution of Pretoria's total strategy, which constrained its repressive capability. "The government," Lawrence Schlemmer noted, "had shifted its position away from comprehensive repression towards partial repression under the impact of human rights protest in the media which had gained momentum after the 1976–1977 disturbances."[36] Consequently, as has already been noted, the black community had some sociopolitical "space" for autonomous organization.

While concern with undermining its efforts at projecting an enlightened image to the world kept Pretoria from acting decisively against the fledgling community organizations, its reform program had the ironic effect of generating the grievances around which the organizations were formed. Take, for example, the arena of secondary school education in the townships. Here the implementation of reform represented an ideal formula for perpetuating the school as a cauldron of anger, alienation, and mobilization. Pupil enrollments were dramatically increased after 1977, but insufficient resources were committed to new buildings and teacher training. The result was overcrowding and a probable decline in the already dubious quality of the education offered to black South Africans. Certainly both the number and proportion of students experiencing academic failure increased dramatically. The percentage of African high school students failing their matriculation exams rose each year after reform was initiated—from 24 percent in 1978 to 52 percent in 1983. Given the increase in the numbers of students sitting for exams as a result of educational expansion, these results translated into a very large pool of disappointed and aggrieved young adults. In 1978 the number in this pool amounted to only 2,336; in 1983 it was 41,627![37] At the same time, while Pretoria proclaimed its reformist intent, the curriculum of Bantu education and the centralized control of the Department of Education and Training (DET) was maintained, with the result that grievances over class size and educational quality, as well as anger about widespread academic failure, naturally became intermeshed with general political hostility directed at the state.

In this atmosphere, the student organizations that had been banned during the repression of the Soweto uprising soon reappeared. The Congress of South African Students (COSAS), a national federation of student groups at secondary schools throughout the country, was launched in 1979. In just two years from the end of the Soweto rebellion students had achieved an organizational potential for coordinated nationwide actions that had not been conceivable a half-decade earlier.

By the end of 1979 student militancy had reappeared as well. In Soweto students began to protest against state policies of excluding older pupils who had failed their matriculation examinations and of employing white ex-servicemen as teachers.[38] Then, in February in 1980, school boycotts broke out in "coloured" and Indian schools in the Western Cape. Again, the employment of SADF veterans as teachers, and the demand for the readmission of barred older pupils, were the issues that sparked the student actions. The boycott quickly spread to the Transvaal and Eastern Cape and to the DET-controlled schools in the African townships. As a result the government closed some seventy-seven township schools from 1980 to 1981.

Clashes between students and police in the Eastern Cape townships in July 1980 led to a virtual collapse of the school system in that region for the remainder of the year.[39]

Although organized around education-related issues, the student groups of the early 1980s rapidly moved to broaden their scope of concern and activity. For example, in the Eastern Cape townships, where many residents had originally come from areas within the Ciskei or Transkei homelands, boycotting students in 1980 demanded an end to compulsory homeland citizenship.[40] The broadening of student activism beyond purely educational or school-based issues could also be seen in the willingness of student organizations to mobilize in support of other community groups. In the Western Cape during 1980 student groups mobilized to boycott the purchase of meat in support of striking meat workers. And political broadening could be seen in the effort to organize youth who were not students. In May 1982 a COSAS national conference resolved to establish organizations for young workers and unemployed youth. Within the year some twenty youth organizations were launched. Some, like the Alexandra Youth Organization and the Soweto Youth Congress, were township-based; others, like the Cape Youth Congress and Port Elizabeth Youth Congress, were federations with branches in a number of townships.[41]

"Orderly urbanization," with its policy of removal of urban blacks to commuter townships was another aspect of reform that generated grievances, stimulated mobilization, and facilitated organization. Following Riekert there was a renewed emphasis on urban deconcentration; the creation of large townships located no more than seventy kilometers from industrial zones, and ideally within homeland borders, from which people would commute to work. Thus between 1977 and 1983 the number of daily commuters to "white" cities from within the homelands increased by 36 percent, from 567,000 to 773,000.[42] This policy of urban deconcentration inspired numerous protests.[43] Commuters were especially resistant to paying the increased costs of transportation from their new residences to their places of work. In 1982 and 1983 fare increases triggered bus boycotts organized by commuters in townships that serve as "bedroom" communities for Durban and East London. In both cases the boycott weapon forced a rollback in fares.[44]

The most significant generator of grievances, and stimulator of mobilization and organization, was the reform policy of administrative devolution to local community councils. When townships were run directly by state bureaucratic agencies, township administrators were socially, psychologically, and physically separate and remote from the township residents. With the introduction of "indirect rule" through administrative devolution to elected councils, the agents with formal responsibility for township conditions lived and operated within the urban black communities. Hence, compared to the officials of old-style apartheid, the councillors and their councils constituted a greater irritant because they were more visible, and a more attractive and accessible target for mobilized political hostility. The nature of the responsibilities devolved by government to the new councils ensured, moreover, that such hostility would be plentiful.

As has already been noted, by the end of the 1970s township administration was in a financial shambles. From 1972, when township administration boards had to pay for water, sewerage, refuse collection, and the like, the costs of running the townships outstripped the income generated by the service charges (rents) collected from township residents. Since Pretoria was unwilling to subsidize township administration—something that would have involved a transfer of resources from white to black population groups—the pressure on the administration boards to raise rents, their major source of revenue, was substantial. With the creation of black community councils in 1978 and 1979, this pressure mounted even further.

The Community Councils Act of 1977 had established the new councils as financially self-supporting entities. Thus they faced the same predicament as the administration boards; they needed new revenue sources to pay inherited debts and cover current deficits. The extent of this financial squeeze is depicted in Tables 5.2 and 5.3, which present data on the deficit in the township "housing account," i.e., the negative balance between the expenditure for services paid by township administration and the income received from housing rents. Table 5.4 reveals the steep rent increases that would be required to make township administration self-financing by bringing the service charges that are part of resident's rent payments into line with the actual cost of services.

The new community councils were actually under greater pressure to raise rents than the administration boards were during the 1970s, for the township upgrading that was part of reform strategy added a new type of expenditure. In 1982–83, for example, capital projects totaling R227 million were budgeted for Soweto, and R74 million in capital expenditure was planned for townships in the East Rand.[45] As Pretoria sought to push the financial burden of urban upgrading onto the township residents themselves, the Community Councils were to be the vehicle to accomplish this task. "Community Councils," wrote an official of the Eastern Transvaal Administration Board, "can play an important role . . . in making the leaders in these communities realise that the more comprehensive role they now play in the management of their own affairs needs to be accompanied by greater responsibility. . . .

TABLE 5.2. Housing Account Deficits
(aggregated), 1971–79

Year	Deficit (in rand)
1971–72	1,096,000
1972–73	666,000
1973–74	4,079,000
1974–75	7,947,000
1975–76	11,389
1976–77	9,094,000
1977–78	11,500,000
1978–79	10,590,000
Total	56,361,000

Source: Simon Bekker and Richard Humphries, From Control to Confusion (Pietermaritzburg: Shuter & Shooter, 1985), p. 141. Reprinted by permission.

TABLE 5.3.　Housing Account Deficits
of Selected Administration Boards,
1979–82 (in rand)

Board	1979–80	1980–81	1981–82
West Cape	3,247,264	4,704,066	7,217,398
East Cape	3,174,246	4,838,212	6,603,078
West Tvl	2,959,190	3,458,190	2,565,885
Central Tvl	4,756,922	2,411,131	4,411,198
Port Natal	3,747,162	3,019,212	4,000,000

Source: Bekker and Humphires, *From Control to Confusion*, p. 142. Reprinted by permission.

TABLE 5.4.　Difference Between Actual
and "Economic" Service Charge (in rand)

Township	Service Charge (rent)	Economic Charge (real cost)	% Increase required
Western Cape (1981–82)			
Ashton	7.24	30.16	316.6%
Ceres	11.90	44.65	275.2
Mfuleni	8.99	62.37	593.8
Hermanus	10.58	48.70	360.3
Paarl	7.73	40.20	420.1
Penninsula	13.52	53.50	295.7
Robertson	7.39	36.34	391.7
Stellenbosch	11.09	65.25	488.4
Worcester	5.18	35.05	576.6
Western Transvaal (1982–83)			
Bloemhof	13.50	20.03	48%
Carletonville	22.00	46.27	110
Christiana	8.70	24.88	186
Klerksdorp	25.00	54.31	117
Koster	13.50	32.02	137
Orkney	23.00	68.40	197
Potchefstroom	25.00	44.67	79
Sannieshof	5.50	40.08	629
Stilfontein	20.00	41.54	108
Wolmaransstad	13.50	14.52	8
Zeerust	13.50	22.84	69

Source: Bekker and Humphries, *From Control to Confusion*, pp. 154–56 (compiled
from data supplied by departments of finance, Western Cape and Western Transvaal
administration boards).

This implies that they need to convince their own people of the need to make greater contributions so as to improve living standards, particularly those relating to housing, services, and recreation facilities."[46]

In addition to the pressure emanating from Pretoria, many councillors were motivated to fund new programs as a means of enhancing their power and prestige. The only significant mechanism of paying for the contracts and larger staffs that this implied was to further jack up housing rents. The councillors were not unmindful of the political costs attendant upon the drastic increases in rent that were required to bring their budgets into balance. Indeed, recognizing the political salience of the rent issue, some candidates for council seats campaigned on a platform of reducing rents. In some instances councils were successful in temporarily holding off the demands of Pretoria and its administrative boards for rent increases. But, given Pretoria's limited willingness to subsidize township costs, financial exigencies contained a kind of inexorable logic, making the move to general rent increases in South Africa's black townships inevitable. As a result, escalating rent charges, both actual and threatened, were a salient feature of township life in the late 1970s and early 1980s. The Soweto Community Council, for example, announced in August 1979 that rents were to be raised by 88 percent.[47] In Kathlehong, southeast of Johannesburg, rent rose 60 percent in 1978–80.[48] Residents of Lamontville, in Natal, faced a 63 percent rent hike of 1982.[49] Between 1978 and the end of 1983 rents in the Vaal Triangle rose by over 400 percent.[50]

It was, then, an environment of increasing material hardship, shaped to a significant degree by the unintended consequences of Pretoria's reform strategy, that provided the impetus for a mushrooming of community organizations in the townships. Table 5.5, which provides information on some of the more prominent civic associations, reveals the wide range within which the government's strategy of change stimulated the organization of opposition. Noteworthy, in addition to the prominence of rent increases as a formative issue, is the geographic spread of the "civic phenomenon." The housing and rent crisis that gripped South Africa was so general that it stimulated widespread organized opposition. Moreover, Pretoria's commitment to "new style" removals and to administratively incorporating "rural" townships into homelands triggered an extension of community organization into even small rural towns that rarely experience oppositional politics. Solidly based and militant civic associations sprang up in quiet towns such as Cradock (Lingelihle), as well as in metropolitan centers such as Johannesburg (Soweto); they appeared in the "coloured" townships and Indian group areas of the Western Cape as well as in the African communities of the Transvaal.

This organizational effervescence represented, initially, the spontaneous response of separate township communities to what appeared to be new threats to their already meager living standards. Thus at the beginning the "new civics" could be said to be parochial in two senses—their organizational bases and reach were localized, and their political vision was narrow in that it focused on some partial aspects of urban life: rent, bus fares, evictions, and the like. But from these common parochial origins the civic associations rapidly underwent parallel developmental transformations which turned them into constituent units in a political struggle to restructure the South African polity and society "root and branch." Figure 5.3

TABLE 5.5.   Black Community Organizations

Organization	When Formed	Area	Region	Formative Issue
Committee of Ten	June 1977	Soweto	Transvaal	community councils
Soweto Civic Assoc. (SCA)	September 1979	Soweto	Transvaal	rent increases
Port Elizabeth Black Civic Organization (PEBCO)	October 1980	Port Elizabeth Townships	Eastern Cape	rent increases; forced removals
Durban Housing Action Committee	1979	Durban Townships	Natal	rent increases
Cape Areas Housing Action Committee (CAHAC)	September 1980	Western Cape Colored and African towns	Western Cape	rent increases
Border Civic Organization	1980	Uitenhage Grahamstown	Eastern Cape	rent increases
Bus Boycott Committee	1982	Lamontville (Durban)	Natal	transportation costs
Joint Rent Action Committee (JORAC)	1983	Durban Townships	Natal	rent increases
Ekangala Action Committee	1983	East Rand	Transvaal	bus fares; incorporation
Cradock Residents Association	1983	Lingelihle (Cradock)	E. Cape (Great Karoo)	rent increases; council elections
Vaal Civic Association	1983	Sebokeng Sharpeville	Vaal Triangle	rent increases; council elections

provides a schematic representation of this transformation. In the space of just a few years, fledgling civic associations moved, at differing paces, through four developmental phases, with each phase involving a different mix of political and mobilizational orientations.*

In phase 1, "genesis," state policies in regard to rents, removals, transportation fees, and the like, posed a new threat to material welfare. Local residents organized, often informally, in neighborhood associations, to petition the authorities (community council or administration board) for redress of a specific grievance, i.e., a roll back of rents, a reduction in bus fares, or a rescinding of removal orders. Typical of developments at this first stage was the situation in the relatively small and impoverished community of Zwide, one of Port Elizabeth's five black townships.[51] At the end of 1978 residents were paying monthly rentals of R11 for dilapidated "houses," often little more than packing cases. In early 1979 the government destroyed dwellings for Africans at nearby Ford Village in order to make room for a new "elite" township. Many of the displaced inhabitants were moved into the

*The excellent empirical and analytic work of Mark Swilling and his colleagues at the Center for Policy Studies, University of Witswaterstrand, provides an essential foundation for understanding the evolution of grass-roots politics in South Africa's townships during the 1980s.

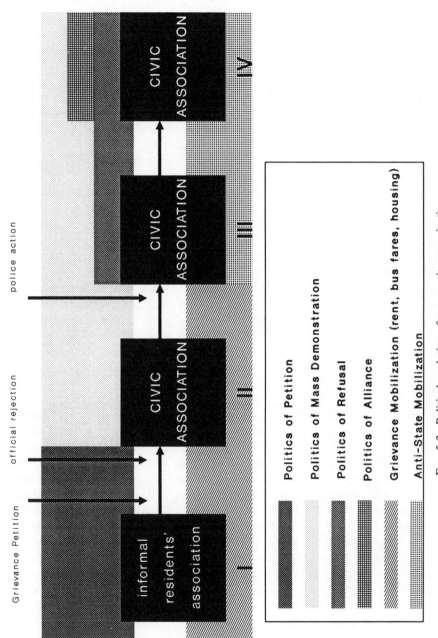

FIG. 5.3. Political evolution of community organizations

already overcrowded Zwide. At the same time it was announced that a new rent schedule would be introduced, ranging from a minimum of R20 to a high of R41, depending on the quality of the house and the income of the resident. In other words, rent increases were to be introduced ranging from nearly 100 to 400 percent. In addition, at about the same time, water meters were installed in the township so that residents could be charged a separate water rate.

In September 1979 the Zwide Residents' Association was formed in order to petition the community council and Eastern Cape Administration Board.[52] A similar association had been formed a month earlier by residents of the nearby township of Kwaford, who also faced steep rent increases. A combined delegation of the two residents' associations approached the community council and administration board with a letter demanding the abolition of water payments and a reduction in house rentals to a uniform R15.[53] Neither the council nor the board would or could meet the community's demand. Although a delay of several months in the assessment of water rates was granted, and a scheme for partial reduction in rental payments for some categories of residents was announced, the meters and increased rents for most residents would remain in force.

The official rebuke of the Zwide Residents' Association was typical of the response to petitions by local residents' associations by authorities throughout South Africa during the early 1980s. Mark Swilling, who has conducted a comparative study of community organization in some thirty townships, concluded that "In case after case around the country the authorities either ignored, rebuked or repudiated the petitioners."[54] Community councillors typically either said they could do nothing because the real decisions were made by administration boards,* or they made promises on which they then failed to deliver. The boards typically responded with one or another form of "bureaucratese" (i.e., they were powerless because real power lay with the community councils; problems were under study and patience was required; the petition had to be dealt with by higher authority; the residents' association was unrepresentative or lacked legal status).[55]

This official obfuscation usually initiated phase 2 of organizational development: community groups turned to mass mobilization and demonstration to gain the attention of officialdom and force redress of their local grievances. Often this coincided with a broadening of localized, informal, and essentially neighborhood organizations into formally structured civic associations mobilizing and organizing in several adjacent townships. When individual townships already had residents' associations, federations were formed. The Port Elizabeth townships again provide an illustration. In October 1980, after the rejection of their petition, the residents' associations of Zwide and Kwaford formed the Port Elizabeth Black Civic Organization (PEBCO). The new organization was launched at a mass meeting of between eight and nine thousand people who resolved to fight until demands for rent and water-rate relief were met.[56]

The state's harsh response to the mobilizational politics of civic associations—detention of leaders, deployment of police to break up demonstrations—led to phase 3 of organizational development, in which community groups expanded their

*After 1983 these were renamed development boards.

focus beyond the specific urban grievances of high rents, transport fees, and residential insecurity to include demands for the release of detainees and the removal of the police presence from the townships. Most important, the repressive response served to undermine whatever minimal credibility the community councils had been able to muster. As they were the most basic and visible point of the state apparatus, the anger of township residents was turned on the councillors. They were assailed for their refusal to redress residents' grievances, and for the detentions and police harassment with which efforts to express grievances were met. Moreover, the councillors' exercise of newly acquired patronage powers and their enjoyment of material perquisites of office, at a time of increasing hardship for most township residents, served to tar the councils and their members with the brush of corruption. The town councillors "never cut the rents the way they spelled it during the elections," wrote a resident of Sebokeng, in the industrial zone south of Johannesburg. Instead, they "went on to take good care of themselves. . . . [T]hey soon owned shops and many other things."[57]

In the early 1980s a common political dynamic had developed in South Africa's black townships: increased material hardship produced organization and protest, which was met by official intransigence and repression, which in turn generated more organization and protest. Caught within this dynamic, the community councillors were increasingly viewed as corrupt collaborators of the white regime; as individuals who had sold out the township residents for their own material gain. It was thus a natural evolution for the civic associations to call for the abolition of community councils. In doing so, however, they were challenging a cornerstone of the state's total strategy, an essential feature of Pretoria's design for a domestically and internationally palatable form of administrative and political control. In short, the use of repression against the new community organizations by the white government and its local agents of indirect rule precipitated a transition from a rather narrow "grievance mobilization" to an "antistate mobilization."

A second transformation spurred by the government's repressive response to community-based mass mobilization was the adoption by community organizations of what has been termed the "politics of refusal"—consumer boycotts, school boycotts, rent strikes, political stayaways, bus boycotts, and the like. Unlike mass demonstration, these forms of mass action can impose direct costs on the state or those it relies on, such as the business community, and thus they represent potentially more efficacious means for asserting demands.

Campaigns of "refusal," if they are to be successful, require broad and sustained commitment by community members on a day-in, day-out basis. Hence the civic organizations, when they began to mount such campaigns, were led naturally into broad alliances with other associations in their communities—youth and student organizations, women's organizations, trade unions and, after 1983, with national political movements. The move to alliance politics in opposition to the presence of the state in the townships represents phase 4 in the evolution of community organizations. Although the transition to antistate mobilization and alliance politics was driven by the internal logic of urban political dynamics, it was also facilitated, unwittingly, by Pretoria's decision to move forward in 1983 with its agenda for political reform.

Political Organization—United Democratic Front

From the early 1960s until the mid-1980s South Africa's political landscape had been characterized by the absence of a nationally organized movement of black political opposition. From the vantage point of apartheid's architects this was, of course, one of their great "successes." The Black Consciousness movement had political implications and consequences, but it was essentially cultural. The Soweto uprising had almost no organizational base at all; the little coordination that existed was provided by a loose alliance of student councils. The growth of community organizations in the early 1980s, as has been discussed, represented a common response of local communities to similar problems.

In 1983 this feature of South Africa's political terrain changed dramatically, with the birth of the first nationally organized mass movement of black opposition since the banning of the ANC and PAC in 1960. The immediate impetus for this development was the decision by Pretoria to move ahead with its agenda for political reform. The Black Local Authorities Act, under discussion since the Riekert Commission's report and intended to upgrade the powers of the community councils, came into effect at the beginning of August 1983. Elections for twenty-nine "new" councils, established under the act, were scheduled for November and December, with elections for an additional eighty-four councils planned for 1984, and the anticipation that elections in the remaining 119 township areas would take place within two to three years.[58] In September 1983 the Republic of South Africa Constitution Act, making provision for a new tricameral legislature representing white, Indian, and "Coloured" communities, was passed by Parliament. The state president announced that a referendum for white voters on the new constitution would be held on November 2, 1983. In the event of a positive vote, elections for the new parliamentary chambers were anticipated for mid-1984.

In contrast to the urban-oriented reforms introduced in the previous several years, these reforms elicited a response that was explicitly political in nature and organizationally national in scope. Pretoria saw the reforms as representing a sharing of power with "non-white" population groups; they were an example of reform as increasing "inclusion." The reaction of the black population, however, was a classic case of an already partially mobilized population focusing on what was still "excluded." The new constitution was viewed as a means of divide and rule; providing participation without significant power to the Indians and "coloureds" so as to gain their collaboration against the still excluded Africans. It infuriated even "moderates" like Gatsha Buthelezi, because it provided a clear sign that the ruling National Party had no intention of allowing Africans to participate in national politics. Upgrading the increasingly discredited community councils as a substitute for participation in central politics had the effect of adding insult to injury. It reemphasized the minimal political role that Pretoria intended for the African population. As one African observer put it, under the new arrangement Africans would be placed in charge of "polishing their own chains." The introduction of the reformed constitution, the passage of the Black Local Authorities Act, and the announcement of new elections for the community councils produced a wave of anger that swept African, Indian, and "coloured" communities. Observers of black politics noted in late 1983 that the constitution had "sparked black resistance on a scale not seen in South Africa since the mid-1970s."[59] And, by the very nature of the reforms to which the populous was responding, this resistance was directed at the broadest political target: the nature of participation in and distribution of state power.

The political reforms of 1983 had an especially profound impact because, along with sparking new levels of anger, they provided the impetus for a country-wide campaign of political mobilization. Pretoria's intent was to generate electoral support for its new structures of power sharing as a means to legitimate its vision of a reformed South Africa. But ironically, by providing this occasion for electoral campaigns, it also created the opportunity for "counter-campaigns" against that vision and the structures that it spawned. Pretoria placed itself in the position of having to allow opposition campaigning lest the entire exercise in political reform take on the appearance of a farce. As such, Pretoria's actions had the unanticipated and, from its point of view, certainly undesirable consequence of encouraging the formation of an opposition movement that, unlike the community mobilizations against local grievances, was national in scope.

The notion that localized struggles and disparate community organizations might provide the basis for a nationwide movement was not something entirely new to opposition activists in 1983.[60] But the announcement of the new constitutional dispensation, and of a national referendum and elections, provided an immediate issue for such a movement to rally around. The reforms thus had a galvanizing effect. At a political gathering in January 1983, the Reverend Allan Boesak, a "coloured" minister and president of the World Alliance of Reformed Churches, was the first to publicly call for a united movement of community organizations in opposition to the constitutional reforms. "There is . . . no reason," stated Boesak, "why the churches, civic associations, trade unions, student organizations and sports bodies should not unite on this issue, pool our resources, inform people of the fraud that is about to be perpetuated in their name and, on the day of the election, expose their plans for what they are."[61]

As an initial response to Boesak's call, united fronts were organized on a regional basis, and soon thereafter a decision was made to combine these into a national United Democratic Front (UDF). Although conceived as a means to oppose Pretoria's constitutional plans more effectively, the founders of the new organization from the outset defined its mandate in much broader and politically more consequential terms. The guidelines for the new organization stated that the UDF would be dedicated to the "creation of a non-racial, unitary state undiluted by racial or ethnic considerations."[62] On August 20, 1983, at a meeting in a "coloured" township outside Cape Town, the UDF was nationally launched. One thousand delegates, representing some 575 organizations, were in attendance at this founding conference. They passed a declaration committing the UDF to "uniting all our people, wherever they may be in the cities and countryside, the factories and mines, schools, colleges, and universities, houses and sports fields, churches, mosques and temples, to fight for our freedom."[63] The conference resolved to oppose the Black Local Authorities Act as a means devised by the government to deprive African people of their birthright, and to reject the government's constitutional proposals as "yet another undemocratic constitution" for South Africa.[64] It pledged to extend grass-roots organizational activity; to help strengthen community-based organizations where they already existed; to educate people about the "coming dangers"; and to "unite in action" against the constitution, the community councils, and other day-to-day problems of the people.[65] The conference culminated in a mass rally attended by an estimated 10,000 people.

Although Pretoria's political reforms created the situational stimulus for the formation of the UDF, its foundation had been created by the phenomenal growth of township associational life during the previous four years. Only because of this was it possible to establish, in the space of less than eight months, a national political movement that reached down organizationally into practically every black community, and that had links with virtually any significant functionally organized social group. Table 5.6 provides a breakdown of the 575 organizations that were represented at the UDF's founding conference in August 1983. As can be seen, the community-based civics, student organizations, and youth associations, virtually all of which had been established since 1979, provided the core of the UDF's organizational base; nearly 80 percent of the affiliated organizations. The support of the newly formed trade unions was also substantial, although this was not reflected in formal UDF membership. Many unions, concerned about the autonomy and survivability of their fledgling organizations, at first resisted formal membership in the political alliance.

The geographic spread of the UDF was also impressive. If one sets aside the large number of youth groups from the Western Cape that sent representatives, organizational affiliates were drawn in roughly equal measure from the Transvaal, Natal, and the Eastern and Western Cape. The inclusive nature of the UDF is also reflected in the social heterodoxy of its leadership strata. Typical was the composition of the Duncan Village Residents Association's central committee. The nine members included, in 1985, a receptionist and a matron at the local hospital, an unskilled factory worker, two teachers, a community worker, a Catholic priest, a nurse, and a clerk.[66] As can be seen in Table 5.7, this heterodox social profile is also found in the UDF's regional and national executive committees. Essentially, UDF leaders and activists were drawn from all social strata and significant functional groups within black society, save the small commercial petty bourgeoisie. The latter was closely identified with the new community council system, through which it obtained the licenses, contracts, and trading sites that made commercial activity in the townships possible. In many cases these were distributed as patronage to the relatives and friends of councillors, or to the councillors themselves, so that the

TABLE 5.6.   Founding Affiliates of the United Democratic Front

| | | | Type of Organization | | | | |
Civic	Student	Youth	Worker	Women	Religious	Political	Other
82	33	338*	18	32	16	27	29

Source: South African Institute of Race Relations, *Survey of Race Relations in South Africa,* 1983 (Johannesburg: Institute of Race Relations, 1984), pp. 68–69.
*Includes many local affiliates of youth congresses.

TABLE 5.7.   United Democratic Front
Leadership

Age		Occupation	
20s	6	Professional	11
30s	17	White-Collar	14
40s	11	Clergy	3
50s	4	Worker	17
60s	10	Activist	6
Race		Past Political Affiliation	
African	46	ANC	5
"Coloured"	8	Indian Congress	4
Indian	6	Liberal Party	2
White	5	Col/Lab. Party	2
		Black Consciousness	6
		Unity Movement	1

Source: Compiled from Tom Lodge, "UDF," in J. D. Brewer,
ed., Can South Africa Survive?, (London: Macmillan press,
1989), p. 207.
Note: N = 66, but background not available in every case.

township petty bourgeoisie and the community council political elite overlapped to a
significant degree.

The fact that the UDF was a conglomeration of preexisting grass-roots organizations constituted both its strength and its weakness. The strengths were primarily
two fold: (1) the network of civic, student, youth, women's, and worker associations provided the new organization with multiple means of communication and
mobilization reaching right into the social arenas in which people worked and lived.
(2) the foundation of affiliate grass-roots organizations offered a certain resiliency in
the face of state repression. The UDF could not be completely crippled by the
detention of its national leaders, for its operational strength lay at the affiliate level.
Moreover, the grass-roots activity of these affiliates constituted a training ground for
an ever expanding cadre of leaders. From the vantage point of the state, the UDF
was like a weed with deep roots. To eliminate it would require removing more than
just the top or even the roots immediately below the surface, but burrowing deep
into the soil. The task of removing this movement from South Africa's domestic
landscape would, consequently, prove far more difficult than had been the case with
the ANC and the PAC in the 1960s.

While the affiliate form of organization provided strength in the face of state
repression and considerable capability in the area of mass mobilization, it was not
conducive to coordination and discipline. The tendency of preexisting units to resist
relinquishing their autonomy is inherent in any "congress"-type organization. Indeed, this reality was recognized and accepted by the UDF leadership from the start.
The working principles set forth at the UDF founding conference stated that affiliat-

ed organizations had "complete independence provided their actions and policies were not inconsistent with those of the UDF."[67] The UDF was born, then, as a sociopolitical coalition that rested on constituent units whose strength and leadership were essentially independent of the central organization.

The UDF's "Ideological" Contribution

Although the UDF drew its strength and shape from its affiliates, it was more than the sum of its parts. One can understand its distinctive contribution by employing the concepts of "pure" and "practical" ideology, a distinction drawn by Franz Schurmann in *Ideology and Organization in Communist China*, his seminal work on the Chinese Communist revolution.[68] Pure ideology molds consciousness and identity; it ties otherwise mundane human acts to moral values, imbuing them with transcendent purpose. Practical ideology provides a guide to action. By providing its affiliates with both "pure" and "practical" ideology the UDF enhanced and transformed them, turning localized and parochial efforts into constituent parts of a movement for national liberation and political power. As such the UDF contributed significantly to the growing strength of black opposition to white rule.

Analyses of the UDF's ideology typically stress the ambiguity, even confusion, that derived from the organization's heterodox social base.[69] Such analyses, which commonly focus exclusively on ideology as doctrine, examine the extent of intellectual elaboration and consistency, and find the UDF's contribution severely limited. Whatever the validity of such observations, they miss important areas in which the UDF's ideology, however rudimentary and ambiguous as doctrine, made a significant contribution to the development of a movement of liberation. In the area of "pure ideology," the UDF contribution lay in the provision of political symbols and political culture rather than in the elaboration of a specific belief system or "ism." The UDF articulated a "culture of liberation" in which local struggles for the redress of specific grievances were portrayed as the basic components in a nationwide struggle to end white minority rule. It thus imbued these local struggles with a larger meaning, giving participants the sense that their local actions contributed to the complete liberation of South Africa, not just to decreasing rents or bus fares, or to removing some corrupt collaborator from his position as town councillor.

The UDF provided a linkage for ongoing local struggles, not only forward to a "liberated and democratic" South Africa, but also backward to the tradition of the multiracial freedom struggle associated with the Congress Alliance of the 1950s, the Freedom Charter, and the ANC.* This commitment to the congress and charterist tradition was not something explicitly or prominently featured at first. Indeed some leaders explicitly denied a connection.[70] But the charterist signals at the UDF founding were nonetheless clear. They were there in the identity of those elected as

---

*The crowning event in this tradition had been the Congress of the People. Following on its success with mass mobilization during the Defiance Campaign of 1952, the ANC in June 1955 convened a congress of all organizations opposed to apartheid. Delegates from throughout the country and representing organizations of all races attended, and together formed an anti-apartheid united front or Congress Alliance. The Freedom Charter, emphasizing democratic, socialist, and multiracial principles, was drafted and adopted at the congress as the alliance's manifesto.

"patrons" and officers at the organization's inaugural conference—stalwarts of the ANC, the Defiance Campaign and the Congress of the People: Nelson Mandela, Albertina Sisulu, Helen Joseph, Francis Baard, Oscar Mpetha, Henry Fazzie, and Archie Gumede; veterans of the Umkhonto we Sizwe sabotage campaign of the early 1960s: Dennis Goldberg, Steve Tshwete, and national chairman Curnick Ndhlovu; and the mother of Umkhonto hero and ANC martyr Solomon Mahlangu.[71] They were also there in the slogans and songs that punctuated the inaugural conference and mass rally that followed. This connection to the charterist tradition would gradually become more explicit, until it was made official in 1985 when the Freedom Charter was adopted as embodying the organization's guiding principles. But even at the beginning "charterism" played a significant role in providing the fledgling UDF and its affiliates with a fully developed panoply of symbols, freedom songs, heroes, and legends. By tying current acts to a historical tradition it ennobled them, infusing the daily efforts of local activists and their sympathizers with moral and emotional weightiness. It is this kind of "culture of liberation" that makes large numbers of people willing to risk all, to lay down their lives for a cause; something that an effort merely to lower rents is unlikely to do. As such the creation of a culture of liberation is an essential prerequisite for the emergence of an insurrectionary and revolutionary social condition.

With respect to "practical ideology" the UDF made at least three significant contributions. The first relates to the principle of nonracialism. The charterist tendency of the UDF represented the reemergence of "multiracialism," what in the 1980s came to be termed "nonracialism," to a dominant position within black politics. This was a development of considerable strategic significance. If black South Africans were to successfully pursue a political struggle they would need to drive a wedge between many whites and the existing state, and they would require the support and collaboration of the industrial countries of the West. Such was unlikely to occur if the political struggle was waged in the racially exclusivist terms of Black Consciousness. By adopting the multiracialism of the charterist tradition, the UDF, either fortuitously or by design, positioned itself to be able to deal constructively with two constituencies that would be vital to its prospects, white South Africans and white people in Europe and North America.

A second contribution in the area of practical ideology involved "issue linkage." While the UDF linked local struggles to the future and the past through its pure ideology, its practical ideology articulated the essential linkage between worker, rent, transport, group area, community council, and other local issues. One of the chief characteristics of UDF activity in the year following its formation was an effort to educate the population on the common element in their individual grievances. As Murphy Morobe, the UDF publicity secretary explained at a trade-union conference:

> We know how it is for people to go to work in the morning and find their shack demolished when they come back home. To such people it is completely artificial to build a Chinese wall between trade unions and community organisations. . . . Therefore who would deny the patent symbiotic relationship between the rent boycott and struggle for high wages?[72]

UDF pamphlets distributed in Soweto and Alexandra in support of rent strikes are other examples of the organization's "issue-linkage" practical ideology:

> AN EVICTION TO ONE IS AN EVICTION TO ALL. . . . Because of low wages, unemployment, retrenchment, rent [should] be reduced to an affordable amount. [Boycott all] shops, garages, cinemas, dry cleaners, funeral parlours, etc. [owned by councillors].[73]

> WORKERS, WE CAN'T ESCAPE WITHOUT BOYCOTT. THE SYSTEM IS PROFITS, HIGH RENT, SLUMS, OPPRESSION BY SOLDIERS, DONKEY WORK FOR THE BOSSES. BE UNITED, WORKERS. RESIDENTS OF ALEXANDRA, HOLD THE BOYCOTT. DONT PAY RENT.[74]

UDF practical ideology also made a contribution in the area of "democratic values." One of the most remarkable features of UDF organizational culture was the stress placed on the accountability of leaders to their constituents. The grass-roots, "bottom-up" quality that marked the organizational effervescence of the early 1980s produced a great deal of emphasis on the requirement that leaders receive a popular mandate through continuous mass meetings and "report backs." This could be observed first in the organizing efforts of the trade-union movement, and was carried over into the civic associations.

Political "Tremors"

During 1983 the tempo of black political resistance quickened: the number of civic, youth, and student organizations increased exponentially; the militancy of opposition intensified; and mobilization spilled over from one issue and geographic area into another. In part this was a consequence of a new wave of rent hikes; in part it was a function of the radicalizing effect of Pretoria's political reforms; and in part it was a result of the national and political focus imparted to local struggles by the newly formed UDF. It is impossible to disentangle these various strands and weigh their relative importance. But the evidence of their interactive effect in producing increased organization, politicization, mobilization, and militancy is clear.

Soon after its national launch the UDF began an intensive campaign for a boycott of the upcoming township council elections and against the new constitution. House to house campaigns were undertaken in the townships, and numerous rallies were staged. These efforts succeeded in denying Pretoria the legitimation for which it had planned. Only 21 percent of registered voters went to the polls in the community council elections of November and December 1983, down from 30 percent in 1978.* In fourteen of the twenty-one townships in which elections were held in both years, voter turnout was lower in 1983 than in 1978.[75] A similar pattern

---

*The UDF claimed that since so many people were not on the voting rolls the overall percentage of adults who cast ballots was even lower than that reported by the government. For example, in Kagiso only 18,000 persons out of an adult population of approximately 34,000 were actually registered to vote. Since only 1,016 people voted, the UDF argued, a mere 3 percent of the adult population participated, not 36.6 percent, as reported by the authorities. See South African Institute of Race Relations, *Survey of Race Relations, 1983*, p. 260.

held in the August 1984 elections for the new "coloured" and Indian chambers of parliament. Only 31 percent of "coloured" voters went to the polls according to the official tally, with the percentage lowering to 11 percent in the Cape peninsula, where the "coloured" population is most heavily concentrated. (If measured by the number of eligible rather than registered voters, the turnout overall was only 18 percent.)[76] And just one in five Indian adults cast ballots. The successful election boycotts were important in that they gave the UDF and its affiliates a sense of efficacy and confidence. They were also a blow to Pretoria's reform strategy, not only domestically but also internationally. But the most politically consequential thing about the boycotts is not found in the voting results per se, but rather in the mobilizational and organizational developments that the boycott campaigns contributed to within the township communities.

The UDF's anti–community council campaigns contributed significantly to the already phenomenal growth of civic associations. In many areas, UDF-affiliated community groups were organized to press for the boycott of upcoming elections. Since rents were also skyrocketing during this same period, the new civic associations typically combined the anti-rent and anti-council issues as a mobilizational base. Such was the case, for example, with the Vaal Civic Association and the Cradock Residents' Association, two community organizations that were destined to play a prominent role in future political events.

The UDF's "issue linkage" became one of the general features of mobilization politics during 1983, as did what might be termed "crossover mobilization"—the combination and interaction of mobilization campaigns within different social and issue spheres. This was most dramatically manifest in the resurgence of student activism. During 1983 some 10,000 pupils in all four provinces took part in classroom boycotts.[77] Given focus and coordination by the UDF-affiliated Congress of South African Students, school protests and strikes increased in intensity into 1984. By the beginning of April some 13,107 pupils in Atteridgeville (Pretoria), Alexandra (Johannesburg), and the eastern Cape townships were boycotting classes. By July student strikes had spread to the East Rand and Orange Free State, and more than 30,000 were refusing to attend class.[78] Although initially concerned with educational issues, this wave of school protests and boycotts rapidly took up wider community demands. The Institute of Race Relations report for 1984 remarked of the student protests: "[R]ising political consciousness among pupils led them to believe that their grievances with the education system were not isolated from the grievances expressed by other sectors of society."[79] Student organizations thus joined civic associations and trade unions in protesting against rent increases, hikes in transport fares, community councils, and the elections to the tricameral parliament.

The spread of protests, boycotts, and strikes during 1983 was accompanied by increased violence. This involved both the use of violent repression—tear gas, sjamboks (rawhide whips), and sometimes firearms—by the state against community protests, and attacks by members of the township communities on people who were perceived as agents of the state, particularly the town councillors. Threats against the lives of council members and petrol-bomb attacks on their houses escalated in late 1983 and early 1984. The newspaper *Sowetan* described the situation in the East Rand as a "reign of terror" against councillors.[80]

In retrospect the township political struggles of 1983 and early 1984 were like the tremors that are felt prior to a volcanic eruption. They were signs of a buildup of political pressure that would eventually be released with tremendous force. Events of August–November in the East Rand townships of South Africa's industrial core—the Vaal Triangle—are generally accepted as a watershed in contemporary South African history. The Vaal Triangle townships of Sebokeng, Sharpeville, Boipatong, Bophelong (Vereeniging/Vanderbijlpark), and Zamdela (Sasolburg) had been hit hard by the post-1981 recession. Unemployment was high, as was inflation, and rents had been raised more steeply than in any other area. The five townships come under the jurisdiction of the Lekoa Town council. "Elected" after its power had been enhanced by the passage of the Black Local Authorities Act, the council in 1984 was again facing extensive deficits, despite the rent increases of the previous three years. Consequently, in August it announced yet another rent increase. Angry residents mounted large protests, refused to pay the increases, and demanded that rents be reduced by one-half and that the town councillors resign.

At this point events in the East Rand would not have appeared different from the mobilization and protests that had intermittently characterized townships across the country during the previous several years. But the developments during that period, the increased sense of grievance, the establishment of a labyrinth of grass-roots organizations, the formation of the UDF, the politicization of township anger, and the spread of a "political culture of liberation," had created the conditions for the transformation of intermittent episodes of "unrest" into a full-blown insurrection.

When the Lekoa Town Council refused to scrap the rent increases, the Vaal Civic Association called for a general strike of workers and students in the townships of the East Rand. An estimated 60 percent of the area's workers and 93,000 students heeded the call.[81] When police moved against the demonstrators it touched off a month-long battle between residents and the authorities. Thousands were detained, R30 million in property was destroyed, and 60 people were killed, including four councillors who died at the hands of angry residents.[82] These events, in turn, touched off a series of urban uprisings across South Africa. For the next two years a civil war would rage for the physical and political control of South Africa's black townships.

Summary

Pretoria had entered the decade of the 1980s with a design for restoring peace and stability to its domestic political landscape. Within five years, however, that landscape was torn up more thoroughly than at any time in the history of the modern South African state. Reform and repression were supposed to produce cooptation, and its twin manifestations, collaboration and acquiescence. Instead it produced insurrection. State policy had the following basic design: repression against radicals would serve to lower expectations, and the amelioration of black living conditions through improved material standards and greater social security would serve to reduce levels of grievance, lessen alienation, and gain acceptance of something less than political, social, and economic equality. State policy, however, was introduced into a dynamic socioeconomic and political environment that both limited the state's

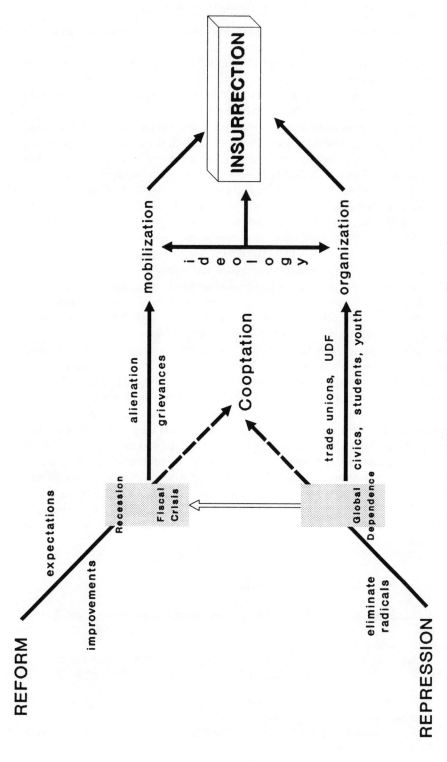

Fig. 5.4. Background to insurrection: reform and repression

ability to implement policy as designed, and produced consequences that were unanticipated by the policy's architects.

Figure 5.4 presents a diagrammatic representation of the manner in which state policies of reform and repression interacted with the South African "policy environment." Pretoria's reformist rhetoric and actions raised expectations. Its ability to fulfill these was, however, undermined by the very economic and political/strategic contradictions that pushed Pretoria to reform apartheid in the first place. The structure of the South African economy produced recession in the face of rising oil and declining gold prices on international markets. Economic stagnation was made more pronounced and prolonged because Pretoria's global political isolation interfered with its economy's access to foreign markets for capital, technology, and the export of manufactured goods. A fiscal crisis ensued in which the state found itself lacking the resources to pay for reform. The result was increased black alienation as the gap between expectations, often created by reform, and the ability of the state to deliver on its promises grew wider. The deteriorating conditions of urban life, both relative and absolute, aggravated by recession and reform, provided the raw material for popular mobilization to seek redress of material grievances. It also provided the conditions for the rapid and wide-scale formation of grass-roots organizations.

At the same time, the state's ability to move against organizations that favored the radical redistribution of society's resources and privileges was constrained by its political/strategic contradiction. The success of reform depended upon adequate financial resources; which necessitated a healthy rate of economic growth; which required unfettered access to international markets; which could be obtained only if reform was accepted as credible; which would not occur if black organizations were massively repressed. As a result, at the time when the organizations of black opposition were most vulnerable to state action—when they were new and inexperienced—Pretoria's use of repression was erratic, haphazard, and inconsistent.

Organizational development, partially shielded from the state by the dynamics of Pretoria's international contradiction, coincided with an ideological change that transformed mobilization from issue-specific protests to a generalized attack on the state presence in the urban townships. By mid-1984 the situational, organizational, and ideological conditions for an insurrectionary upheaval were again present in the black urban areas of South Africa.

Notes

1. Alexis de Tocqueville, *The Old Regime and the French Revolution,* trans. by J. P. Mayer, in *Alexis de Tocqueville: A Biographical Study in Political Science* (New York: Harper & Brothers, 1960), p. 74.

2. See Lawrence Schlemmer, "Black Attitudes, Capitalism and Investment in South Africa" (Centre for Applied Social Science, University of Natal, Durban, August 1984), p. 12.

3. See Mark Orkin, *The Struggle and the Future: What Black South Africans Really Think* (Johannesburg: Raven Press, 1986), p. 34.

4. See Theodor Hanf et al., *South Africa: The Prospects of Peaceful Change* (London: Rex Collings, 1981), p. 442.

5. Schlemmer, "Black Attitudes," p. 11.

6. See James C. Davies, "Toward a Theory of Revolution," *American Sociology Review,* vol. 27, no. 1 (February 1962), p. 5.

7. Karl Marx and Frederick Engels, "Wage Labour and Capital," *Selected Works in Two Volumes,* vol. 1 (Moscow: Foreign Languages Publishing House, 1955), p. 94 (emphasis added).

8. See, in particular, Ted Robert Gurr, *Why Men Rebel* (Princeton: Princeton University Press, 1970), passim.

9. Alexis de Tocqueville, *The Old Regime and the French Revolution,* trans. by Stuart Gilbert (Garden City, N.Y.: Anchor Books, 1955), pp. 176–77.

10. Ibid., p. 177.

11. Testimony at Delmas Treason Trial, p. 15,472.

12. See Jeremy Seekings, "Political Mobilization in the Black Townships of the Transvaal," in Philip Frankel, Noam Pines, and Mark Swilling, eds., *State, Resistance and Change in South Africa* (London: Croom Helm, 1988), p. 208.

13. See, for example, Simon Bekker and Richard Humphries, *From Control to Confusion* (Pietermaritzburg: Shuter & Shooter, 1985), p. 100.

14. Stephen R. Lewis, *Apartheid's Economics: Realities of the South African System* (New York: Council on Foreign Relations), introduction, p. 1.

15. See Jeremy Seekings, "The Origins of Political Mobilization in PWV Townships, 1980–1984," in William Cobbett and Robin Cohen, eds., *Popular Struggles in South Africa* (London: James Currey, 1988), pp. 60–61.

16. Schlemmer, "Black Attitudes," p. 13.

17. See Republic of South Africa, *Report of the Commission of Inquiry into Legislation Affecting the Utilisation of Manpower* (Riekert Commission Report) (Pretoria: Government Printer, 1979), pp. 68–78.

18. See Bekker and Humphries, *From Control to Confusion,* pp. 139–70.

19. See Seekings, "Political Mobilization," pp. 203–04.

20. Ibid., p. 214.

21. Davies, "Toward a Theory of Revolution," passim.

22. Memorandum ("Scope Paper") from Chester A. Crocker to Secretary of State Alexander Haig, for "Your Meeting With South African Foreign Minister Botha," May 14, 1981, reprinted in *CounterSpy,* August–October 1981, p. 56 (emphasis in original).

23. South African Institute of Race Relations (SAIRR), *Survey of Race Relations in South Africa, 1983* (Johannesburg: Institute of Race Relations, 1984), p. 545.

24. See Lawrence Schlemmer, "South Africa's National Party Government," in Bobby Godsell and Peter Berger, *A Future South Africa* (Boulder, Colo.: Westview Press, 1988), p. 16–17.

25. *SA Barometer,* vol. 1, no. 1 (March 11, 1987), p. 15.

26. Eddie Webster, "New Force on the Shop Floor," in *South African Review II* (Johannesburg: Raven Press, 1984), p. 81.

27. See Eddie Webster, "The Rise of Social-Movement Unionism: The Two Faces of the Black Trace Union Movement in South Africa," in Philip Frankel et al., eds., *State, Resistance and Change in South Africa* (London: Croom Helm, 1988), p. 193.

28. Ibid.

29. Ibid.

30. Ibid., pp. 174–76.

31. Ibid., pp. 185–88.

32. Ibid., p. 183.

33. Ibid., p. 182.

34. Quoted in Doug Hindson, "Union Unity," in *South African Review II* (Johannesburg: Raven Press, 1984), passim.

35. See Mark Swilling, "The United Democratic Front and Township Revolt," in Cobbett and Cohen, eds., pp. 95–96.

36. Schlemmer, "South Africa's National Party Government," p. 16.

37. SAIRR, *Survey of Race Relations, 1983*, p. 439.

38. See Theodor Hanf, Heribert Weiland and Gerda Vierdag, *South Africa: The Prospects of Peaceful Change* (London: Rex Collings, 1981), p. 430.

39. See Jonathan Hyslop, "School Student Movements and State Education Policy: 1972–87," in Cobbett and Cohen, eds., p. 188.

40. Ibid.

41. SAIRR, *Survey of Race Relations, 1983*, p. 62.

42. See Elaine Unterhalter, *Forced Removals* (London: International Defence and Aid Fund for Southern Africa, 1987), p. 147.

43. Ibid., pp. 122–41.

44. See Jeff McCarthy and Mark Swilling, "Transport and Political Resistance," in *South African Review II*, pp. 34–41.

45. Bekker and Humphries, *From Control to Confusion*, p. 146.

46. Quoted in ibid., p. 149.

47. See Seekings, "Political Mobilization in the Black Townships of the Transvaal," pp. 203–04.

48. Ibid., p. 204.

49. See Jeremy Grest and Heather Hughes, "State Strategy and Popular Response at the Local Level," in *South African Review II*, p. 55.

50. Ibid., p. 214.

51. Material on Zwide is drawn primarily from Carole Cooper and Linda Ensor, *PEBCO: A Black Mass Movement* (Johannesburg: Institute of Race Relations, 1981).

52. Ibid., pp. 7–10; see also Mark Swilling, "UDF Local Government in Port Elizabeth," in *Monitor, The Journal of the Human Rights Trust*, October 1988, p. 44.

53. Cooper and Ensor, *PEBCO*, p. 7.

54. Swilling, "UDF Local government in Port Elizabeth," p. 45.

55. See ibid.

56. Cooper and Ensor, *PEBCO*, pp. 27–28.

57. See Joannes Rantete, "Frank Talk," *Rand Daily Mail*, January 17, 1984, quoted in SAIRR, *Race Relations Survey, 1984* (Johannesburg: Institute of Race Relations, 1985), p. 72.

58. SAIRR, *Survey of Race Relations, 1983*, p. 158.

59. See Paul Van Slambrouck, "Black South Africans Lash Out at White 'Reform,'" *Christian Science Monitor*, October 31, 1983.

60. See speech by N. G. Patel, quoted in Howard Barrell, "The United Democratic Front and National Forum: Their Emergence, Composition and Trends," in *South African Review II*, p. 9.

61. Quoted in ibid., p. 9.

62. Quoted in ibid., p. 10.

63. Quoted in ibid., p. 13.

64. See SAIRR, *Survey of Race Relations, 1983*, p. 58.

65. See ibid.

66. See Mark Swilling, "Local-Level Negotiations: Case Studies and Implications," Centre for Policy Studies, University of Witwatersrand, August 1987, p. 29.

67. Quoted in Barrell, p. 13.

68. On the distinction between pure and practical ideology see Franz Schurmann, *Ideology and Organization in Communist China* (Berkeley: University of California Press, 1968), pp. 22–45.

69. See Lodge, "The United Democratic Front: Leadership and Ideology," in John D. Brewer, ed., *Can South Africa Survive?* (London: Macmillan Press, 1989), pp. 210–20; and Swilling, "The United Democratic Front and Township Revolt," pp. 96–100.

70. See Lodge, p. 210.

71. See SAIRR, *Survey of Race Relations, 1983*, p. 58; and Swilling, "The UDF and Township Revolt," pp. 95–96.

72. Quoted in Swilling, "The UDF and Township Revolt," p. 99.

73. Ibid., p. 99.

74. Ibid.

75. SAIRR, *Survey of Race Relations, 1983*, pp. 25–59.

76. SAIRR, *Survey of Race Relations, 1984*, p. 128.

77. SAIRR, *Survey of Race Relations, 1983*, p. 465.

78. SAIRR, *Survey of Race Relations, 1984*, p. 671.

79. Ibid., p. 672.

80. *Sowetan*, August 4, 1983, quoted in Grest and Hughes, op. cit., p. 54.

81. SAIRR, *Survey of Race Relations, 1984*, p. 71.

82. Ibid.

6

Chaos and Transformation: The Insurrectionary Process

> We are talking about a challenge to the whole system . . . not a piecemeal challenge. We are not attempting to reform unreformable structures, but are fighting for complete social transformation. The people of S. Africa have never governed the country: we are fighting to realise this most basic right, the right to self-determination. Therefore ours is not a *civil rights* struggle. It is a struggle for NATIONAL LIBERATION.
>
> INTERNAL UDF DISCUSSION PAPER, MAY 1985[1]

Since World War II the politics of mass opposition to white rule has moved through three developmental stages. The first is represented by the anti-apartheid mobilizations of the 1950s, which initiated a black mass movement of opposition that was country-wide in scope. In contrast to the ANC's pre–World War II opposition, which relied primarily on petition campaigns by a small urban African educated elite, the activists of the 1950s sought to mobilize a mass following and to stage large demonstrations as a means of putting pressure on the government. Although willing to violate "immoral" laws and to make aspects of the existing sociopolitical system unworkable through civil disobedience, the leaders of these campaigns did not *directly* seek a fundamental restructuring of state power, nor did they represent a threat to the general system of "law and order." In a certain respect the mass movement of the time had, implicitly "bought into" the existing system, for at least in part the protests against new apartheid laws were intended to appeal to certain moral values that the Union of South Africa was presumed to embody. The state's uninhibited and brutal response thus caught a still hopeful population unawares, politically anesthetized an entire generation, and brought this first stage of mass political opposition to an end.

The second developmental stage, that of rebellion, began with the Soweto uprising. Unlike the movement of the 1950s which, while protesting specific laws, was respectful of the state's authority in general, this mass uprising attacked all the visible signs and symbols of the state. It frontally assaulted the "law and order" of established authority. But although Soweto was characterized by a powerful eruption of mass alienation and anger, it was not a movement consciously directed at restructuring or replacing the existing state. This is what distinguishes it from the third developmental stage—that of insurrection—which was initiated by the events in the Vaal Triangle in August 1984.

Insurrection can be distinguished from rebellion in that it nullifies state power in a portion of the state's territory and inserts a new system of domination in its place. If the new system of domination expands to encompass the entire territory of the pre-existing state, then insurrection is transformed into revolution.* More often then not, however, the limited geographic reach of the insurrectionary process allows the state to crush the insurrectionists and reassert its authority.

One of the extraordinary things about episodes of insurrection in the modern era is that across time and space they are characterized by a common leitmotiv. There exists a historical repetition which, as the political theorist Hannah Arendt noted, is "unaccounted for by any conscious imitation or even mere remembrance of the past."

> . . . a swift disintegration of the old power, the sudden loss of control over the means of violence, and, at the same time, the amazing formation of a new power structure which owed its existence to nothing but the organizational impulses of the people themselves.[2]

Between mid-1984 and mid-1986 the black townships of South Africa would experience this leitmotiv of insurrection, moving along a path of political development strikingly similar to that associated with such uprisings as the Paris Commune in 1871, Russia in 1905, and Hungary in 1956.

Insurrections can be seen to contain two linked but distinct processes, what I will term "chaos" and "transformation." The first is associated with the obliteration of established authority: the existing system of domination is overwhelmed and trampled by a seemingly uncontrollable convulsion of mass anger. In what could be mistaken for a description of South Africa in 1984–86, Leon Trotsky wrote of the sociopolitical convulsion in Russia of 1905:

> Having freed itself from inherited fears and imaginary obstacles, the mass did not want to, and could not see the real obstacles in its path. Therein lay its weakness, and also its strength. It rushed forward like the ocean tide whipped by a storm. . . . Workers' strikes, incessant meetings, street processions, wreckings of country estates. . . . Everything disintegrated, everything turned to chaos.[3]

*Revolution, the seizure of state power, can of course take other routes, including armed revolt, conspiracy, and coup d'etat. Insurrection differs from these means of toppling an established government in that its defining feature is mass mobilization. It is not unusual, however, for revolutionaries to combine insurrection with another method of defeating state power. Many students of twentieth-century revolution view guerrilla warfare as a combination of armed revolt and rural insurrection. One authority on the Chinese revolution thus dubbed the guerrilla phenomenon "militarized mass insurrection." See Chalmers Johnson, *Revolution and the Social System*, Hoover Institution Series #3 (Stanford, Calif.: Hoover Institute, 1964), p. 57.

For most contemporaneous observers chaos is what defines the insurrectionary phenomenon. They are so mesmerized by its violence, the scale of its disruptions, and the awesome power of unleashed social forces, that they take the part for the whole. They fail to see the other crucial element in the insurrectionary process: transformation. As social space is liberated, as the old system of domination is smashed by the insurrectionary convulsion, a new structure of domination begins to form in its place. A new system of authority arises where the old is destroyed. Historical evidence reveals this transformation to be as much a leitmotiv of insurrection as chaos. Trotsky, in chronicling the events of 1905, again describes a process uncannily similar to that which would occur some eighty years later in the black townships of South Africa.

> [W]ithin this chaos there arose a need for a new order, and elements within that order began to crystallize. Regularly recurring meetings in themselves introduced the principle of organization. The meetings elected deputations, the deputations grew into representative assemblies.[4]

The Insurrection of 1984–86

"Ungovernability"

The South African insurrection of 1984–86 began with the events in the Vaal Triangle and spread rapidly outward, rising in intensity as it swept from one area to the next, from the industrial centers of the Transvaal and the Eastern Cape to the rural towns of the Great Karoo, from the "coloured" townships of the Western Cape to the commuter shantytowns of Bophuthatswana and the Ciskei. By 1985 the situation in the black townships took on the character of a civil war as residents sought to drive the state out of their communities. When early in the year the ANC, from its exile headquarters in Lusaka, called upon the populace to "make the townships ungovernable," what had initially simply been a consequence of the ferocity of the mass uprising became a conscious short-term insurrectionary goal. By midyear Pretoria indirectly acknowledged that this goal had been achieved, at least in some areas, when it began to refer to the townships of the Eastern Cape as "no-go areas"—places that were too dangerous for the South African police to enter except in convoys of armoured personel carriers.

The barricades of the South African insurrection were manned by the township youth, for the most part teenagers, who dubbed themselves "comrades." In roving bands, utilizing the hit-and-run tactics of the guerrilla, armed with petrol bombs, paving stones, and the occasional gun, they sought to nullify Pretoria's control of the townships. At first glance, these actions appeared similar to what had occurred eight years earlier during the Soweto uprising.

But the 1984–86 uprising contained aspects that mark it as a qualitative transformation in black opposition politics. Two of these aspects were its geographic reach and social depth. Soweto was a phenomenon of the large urban centers, and had been essentially a youth rebellion. The insurrection of 1984–86 gripped virtually the entire black population outside of remote rural areas. While the young comrades were its militant vanguard, the insurrection drew support and participation from virtually the entire social spectrum of black South Africa, save the tiny commercial petit bourgeoisie. The rich associational life that had characterized the townships during the early 1980s and the existence of the UDF which linked together geographically and functionally diverse associational elements and gave them a national political orientation, laid the organizational foundation for this aspect of the insurrection.

The organizational development of the previous half-decade had also prepared the way for another distinguishing feature of the 1984–86 period—multiple forms of mass resistance and protest interacted and reinforced each other. Simultaneous waves of school boycotts, political strikes, consumer boycotts, rent strikes, and huge community rallies combined with escalating armed sabotage by the ANC and determined street battles by young comrades to turn protest and resistance into insurrection. Figure 6.1 reveals how four of these elements—deaths associated with street battles, guerrilla sabotage by the ANC, school boycotts, and political strikes by the independent trade unions—simultaneously escalated between September 1984 and July 1986. The number of attacks by armed guerrillas on police stations, government offices, public amenities, "collaborators," and the like, for the most part carried out by ANC cadre, tripled between 1981–83 and 1984–86. The 230 attacks in 1986 alone represented a 300 percent increase over insurgent activity in 1983, the year prior to the outbreak of insurrection. Along with an increase in aggregate numbers, the nature of the insurgent attacks changed. The use of assault rifles increased steeply, and hand-grenade attacks jumped from seven in the two years prior to September 1984 to 122 in the ensuing two years.[5] Land mines were introduced by insurgents for the first time in 1985.[6] A shift to attacks on "soft" targets (those that lead to loss of life and injury) in contrast to "hard" targets (those that damage property) also characterized the period after 1983. According to the government, 12 percent of insurgent attacks in 1981 were against so-called soft targets; in 1986 the figure had risen to 80.7 percent.[7]

In two-and-one-half years, between August 1984 and the end of 1986, four times more political work stoppages or "stayaways" were staged than in the entire preceding three-and-one-half decades. This escalation in the use of the general-strike weapon for political ends coincided with a huge escalation in conventional industrial disputes. The workdays lost to strikes over "economic" issues jumped over 200 percent between 1983 and 1984, then increased by 80 percent in 1985 and 93 percent in 1986 (see Figure 5.2). A comparison of the total number of workdays lost to industrial disputes in 1983 and 1986 reveals an increase of 950 percent. When one considers that in 1986 workdays lost to industrial strikes constituted only 22 percent of the total workdays lost, the remaining 78 percent being a result of political stayaways,[8] the extraordinary turmoil wrought on the South African industrial economy during the 1984–86 insurrection is apparent. Concurrently, the number of students boycotting school increased from approximately 10,000 in 1983 to almost 700,000 in 1985, swelling the ranks of militant youth available to "man the barricades."

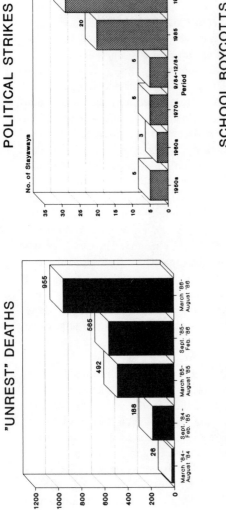

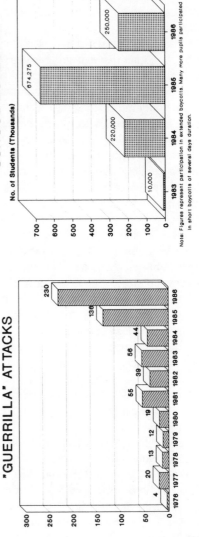

Fig. 6.1. Level of insurrectionary activity (*Source: SA Barometer*, vol. 1, no. 1 [March 11, 1987], p. 12; South African Institute of Race Relations, *Survey of Race Relations, 1984*, p. 66; *SA Barometer*, vol. 1, no. 5 [May 8, 1987], pp. 70–72; *SA Barometer*, vol. 1, no. 7 [June 5, 1987], p. 101)

Rent strikes represented another dimension of insurrectionary action. Initiated in five Vaal Triangle townships in September 1984, they had spread to some 53 townships countrywide by September 1986.[9] A research group at the University of Witwatersrand found that by then 300,000 African households were not paying rent, and that the consequent loss in government revenue was approximately five hundred million rand.[10] In July the Urban Councils Association of South Africa reported that thirty-five community councils had collapsed because rent strikes had eliminated their sources of revenue for running the townships.[11] Paralleling the spread of rent strikes, consumer boycotts were launched against white-owned businesses, as well as against the commercial establishments of perceived black collaborators. The Institute of Race Relations listed some thirty-six towns and cities in all four of South Africa's provinces that were affected by such actions. Organized for the most part by UDF affiliates, consumer boycotts were viewed by some as a means to pressure the business community into getting the government to meet local and national political demands.[12] Others viewed it as a means to weaken the state through undermining the economy. Illustrative of this latter position is the following ANC commentary on Radio Freedom:

> There is no doubt that a co-ordinated national consumer boycott can and will succeed to reinforce the people's struggle for the destruction of the monstrous apartheid system. . . . We have it within our means now to use the might of buying power. We must simply refuse to buy from the white-owned and puppet-owned shops in townships and cities. A nation-wide consumer boycott would be our own version of economic sanctions, because we would be crippling the economy from within.[13]

This insurrectionary process of catalyzing, interacting, and reinforcing forms of resistance emerged fully in the Transvaal during September–October 1984, and set a pattern which was to be repeated over and over again across South Africa in the subsequent twenty-two months: The UDF-affiliated Vaal Civic Association initiated the process. In order to support an ongoing rent strike that had been called to force the reduction of rental charges and the resignation of the Lekoa Town Council, the civic association called for a school boycott and work stayaway. With approximately 100,000 students and about 60 percent of the work force in the area heeding the call, clashes took place between police and demonstrators. The student boycott then spread to all schools in the East Rand, and violent clashes over the next four weeks resulted in sixty deaths, hundreds of injuries, and thousands of arrests.[14] Two weeks after the Vaal stayaway, the Release Mandela Committee (RMC), a UDF affiliate based in Soweto, called for a two-day work stoppage in Johannesburg in order to express solidarity with the residents in the Vaal Triangle and to protest police action in the townships.[15] High school students, who had been boycotting school in Soweto for a week, joined in the stayaway campaign. Attempts by some residents of the township to defy the RMC strike call, as well as efforts by the police to protect them from strike-enforcers, resulted in violent clashes and initiated a phase of general chaos—the stoning of police and commercial vehicles, the burning of homes of community councillors, and an extension and expansion of the school boycott. The residents of the nearby East Rand township of KwaThema responded to the student boycott that had spread from Soweto by organizing a parent-student committee that demanded, among other things, the release of all detained students, the withdrawal of police and army from the townships, and the resignation of all African councillors. A one-day work stoppage in support of the demands was backed by the major unions in the area and honored by 80 percent of the township's workers.[16] By mid-October, then, the black population centers of South Africa's industrial heartland were engulfed in what the government and the media euphemistically called "unrest."

Toward the end of October, Pretoria attempted to reestablish "law and order" with a show of force. It sent the army into the Vaal Triangle. The townships were cordoned off with armored personnel carriers and troops searched house to house for political activists, making many arrests.[17] This repressive response served only to intensify the revolt. In order to answer the government's move, the Congress of South African Students (COSAS) approached the trade unions with plans to organize a Transvaal-wide work stoppage. An ad hoc committee representing thirty-six political, community, student, and trade-union organizations called for a two-day stayaway in support of a list of demands that included withdrawal of the police and the army from the townships, the resignation of community councillors, the scrapping of all rent and bus-fare increases, and the release of all detainees and political prisoners.[18] The call was apparently widely heeded, for the South African Federated Chambers of Commerce reported very light attendance at work throughout the Transvaal on November 5 and 6, the days of the stayaway. Some 800,000 striking workers were joined by some 400,000 boycotting students.

The alienation and discontent in the Transvaal townships, which had manifested itself in separate eruptions over a two-and-one-half month period, thus came together in the November general strike. The Institute of Race Relations observed, "schoolchildren, local groups, and trade unions . . . united to express their discontent in the largest political stayaway on record."[19] A spokesman for FOSATU (Federation of South African Trade Unions), the biggest federation of independent trade unions and the forerunner of COSATU said that the stayaway was "a very effective and major protest . . . against a totally unacceptable situation."[20] The chairman of the Transvaal regional stayaway committee declared:

> We as oppressed and struggling masses have power and we can use it the way we like. . . . We can determine the future of this country's economy and the economy of a country is its backbone, no matter how powerful it might be politically. . . . [W]e have power in our hands . . . that can bring the machinery of this country to a standstill.[21]

Following the successful stayaway, the UDF called upon all South Africans to observe a "black Christmas"—a nationwide consumer boycott in commemoration of those who had been killed, injured, or detained in the "unrest" of the previous four months.[22] This was followed in December by a COSAS statement that students would not return to school for the new term beginning in January until their demands had been met.[23] The stage was set for a continuation of the mass insurrection in the Transvaal and for its spread during 1985 and 1986 to the Eastern and Western Cape.

For decades Pretoria had been able to hold the costs of maintaining political control over the black population to a feasibly low level by the extensive use of collaborators. Black policemen were used to patrol the townships, and the existence of an elaborate network of informers was an open secret. The poverty of the township communities meant that minimal material incentives would ensure an adequate supply of people willing to collaborate. The community councils that were introduced during the reform era represented, in some sense, a more sophisticated form of this strategy of control through collaboration. Another distinctive facet of the 1984–86 insurrection is that it turned with a fury on these agents of state control within the black community itself. The houses and businesses of community councillors were burned, as were the homes of black policemen. Community councillors and even their relatives were beaten and sometimes killed by angry mobs. Suspected police informers were executed by means of "the necklace"—an especially gruesome death in which a gasoline-soaked automobile tire was placed around the person's neck and then set afire.

Between September 1984 and May 1986, some twelve councillors and a larger number of black township policemen were killed, and many more were injured.[24] Over 200 councillors lost either their homes or businesses; 124 such structures were burned down during the first nine months of the insurrection.[25] The homes of at least 814 black policemen were destroyed.[26] Fearing for their lives, many councillors gave up their offices. By the beginning of May 1985, some 257 community and town councillors had resigned, including many mayors and council chairmen.[27] The newspaper *Sowetan* reported in July 1985 that only five of the thirty-eight councils that had been upgraded under the Black Local Authority Act were still functioning.[28] Many councillors and black policemen fled the townships, retreating with their families to specially arranged accommodations provided by the government. Often enclosed by barbed wire, these were located on the grounds of police stations, or outside the townships altogether.[29] While it is clear that the insurrection effectively nullified Pretoria's effort at indirect rule—rendering many of the most important black local authorities inoperative—its impact on Pretoria's ability to penetrate the community with informers cannot easily be gauged. Certainly, however, the highly visible "necklacing" of accused informers must have been a powerful disincentive to individuals who might otherwise have considered assisting Pretoria's security apparatus.

A New Political Culture

In rendering the townships ungovernable, the insurrection of 1984–86 operated not just at the level of physical control (fighting the police and army, eliminating informers, disrupting community council administration, and the like), but also on the level of political psychology. Insurrectionary activity produced a transformation in political identity and orientation; a liberation of political consciousness as well as of territory. Two closely related processes were work, that of radicalization and that of legitimation. In the throes of the insurrectionary upheaval the populace of the townships became more and more willing to lend its active support to militant, even extreme, acts against Pretoria. In mid-1985 a research institute surveyed a representative sample of township residents, asking them what strategies should be used to pressure the government for change. Nearly 70 percent supported the use of "direct action by blacks . . . such as strikes, boycotts of white businesses and protests against high rents and unequal education." Almost 40 percent approved the use of "armed struggle" and over one-quarter thought that attacks on blacks who worked for the system were "justified."[30] When asked about how "the apartheid system can brought to an end," 80 percent rejected a power-sharing compromise—a federal solution in which Africans would be given some limited representation—in favor of a unitary state based upon the principle one-person, one-vote.[31]

Support for armed struggle, and the widespread perception that the goal of black politics was the restructuring of the South African polity along majoritarian lines, reflected the emergence of the African National Congress as the dominant political force in black politics. From its exile and marginalization during the 1960s, the ANC began to reenter domestic black politics during the Soweto uprising. In the insurrection of 1984–86, it became the embodiment of the tradition of liberation and the leading organization in the struggle to overthrow apartheid and white minority power.

Identification with the ANC occurred at both individual and organizational levels. Since endorsement of the ANC was, at the time, a serious offense under South African law, opinion surveys of individuals cannot be taken as accurate reflections of the depth of ANC support. Nevertheless, surveys of black urban residents reveal that of those willing to state a political preference the proportion of respondents stating they backed the ANC went from less than 20 percent in 1977 to 41 percent in 1985.[32] Similarly, although a 1977 survey of urban Africans found 44 percent voicing support for the Inkatha movement of Chief Gatsha Buthelezi,[33] by mid-1985 the level of support for the ANC was at least three times greater than that for any other political tendency or organization.[34] Support for Inkatha and Buthelezi, the representative of the so-called "moderate" position in black politics, had dropped to only 8 percent nationwide.[35] Only in Buthelezi's ethnic/regional base in Zulu-speaking Natal was any significant support retained. Even there he received the backing of only one-third of Zulu-speaking urban residents in mid-1985. Outside Natal, in the PWV, three times as many Zulu-speakers preferred the ANC to Inkatha.[36] Thus the insurrection of 1984–86 contained a political transformation not only in terms of the rise in popular allegiance to the African National Congress, but also in respect to the collapse of the "collaborationist–moderate" center in black politics.

The ANC's leading position in black politics was also reflected at the level of organization. The UDF, COSATU, and the National Union of Mineworkers (NUM), the largest and most powerful of South Africa's trade unions, all moved during the mid-1980s to publicly identify themselves with a struggle for political liberation in which the ANC was acknowledged as the leading organization. In 1985, the UDF made explicit what was implicit and ambiguous at its inception—its association with the Freedom Charter as a statement of basic political principles. In South Africa, where membership in the ANC was illegal, an association with the Freedom Charter—the ANC's official "guiding document"—had great symbolic significance. It was tantamount to a declaration of the ANC's leading role in the struggle for a new South Africa.

In March 1986, three months after its founding, a delegation of top COSATU officials traveled to Lusaka to meet with the ANC leadership. At the conclusion of the talks a joint communique was issued which, among other things, included this significant passage:

> [I]t was recognised that the fundamental problem facing our country, the question of political power, cannot be resolved without the full participation of the ANC, which is regarded by the vast majority of the people of South Africa as their overall leader and genuine representative.[37]

Nine months later, the giant mineworkers union, the largest of COSATU's constituent units, separately associated itself with the ANC when it formally adopted the Freedom Charter "as a guiding document in our struggle from national oppression and economic exploitation."[38]

The ANC's emergence as the leading organization in black politics did not mean that it could count on a mass following that would subject itself to organizational discipline. Rather, in the political culture that was being forged in the caldron of insurrection, the ANC had been endowed with a broad political legitimacy, providing it with the "right" to give general direction to the struggle against white rule, and to play a central role in shaping a post-apartheid South Africa. This meant, at the very least, that those who considered themselves part of the "liberation struggle" or "mass democratic movement" would consult with the ANC leadership on all important matters, and would adopt the ANC's broad political agenda as laid out in the Freedom Charter. The latter implied a commitment to three basic elements: nonracialism, majority rule (defined as one-person, one-vote in a unitary state), and an economy with a strong socialist element. In the language of the ANC–COSATU communique of March 1986 the program of the liberation movement, led by the ANC, involves "the establishment of a system of majority rule in a united democratic and non-racial South Africa."[39]

Funerals and the Transformation of Consciousness

The main vehicle for the insurrectionary transformation of political consciousness was the mass funeral for those killed in clashes with the security forces. Attended by thousands, sometimes tens of thousands, these "funerals" were actually community-wide political gatherings. By late 1985 they had become ubiquitous features of township life and generators of insurrectionary culture.* Table 6.1 provides an indication of the frequency and size of this "funeral phenomenon," as well as of the types of events they set in motion.

---

*Pretoria sought during 1985 to end the insurrection by banning outdoor political meetings in much of South Africa. In response, township activists began to use the funerals of "unrest victims" as surrogate political rallies. Gradually, during the year, these funerals were held with greater regularity, and developed into a kind of insurrectionary institution.

TABLE 6.1.   Political Funerals, 1985–86

Date, Location	Attendance	Repercussions
4/85, Port Elizabeth	7,000	Police disperse mourners
7/85, KwaThema (E. Rand)	50,000	
7/85, KwaThema	30,000	
7/85, DaveyTown (E. Rand)	4,000	Clashes w/police, 4 dead, 17 wounded
8/85, Duncan Village (E. Lon.)	50,000	Clashes w/police, 19 dead, 138 wounded
9/85, Guguletu (Cape Town)	20,000	Clashes w/police, 2 dead
12/85, Soweto	—	Clashes w/police, 4 dead
1/86, Soweto	—	Tear gas
1/86, Soshanguve (Pretoria)	20,000	Tear gas
2/86, Alexandra (J'berg)	13,000	Tear gas, clashes w/police, 3 dead
2/86, Atteridgeville (Pretoria)	5,000	Water cannon, tear gas, many injuries
3/86, Alexandra	70,000	Peaceful
3/86, Guguletu	—	Tear gas
3/86, Soweto	—	Tear gas
3/86, Zwide (P. Elizabeth)	30,000	Tear gas
3/86, Lebowa	—	Clashes w/police, 6 dead
3/86, Khuma (W. Transvaal)	—	Tear gas
3/86, Atteridgeville	—	Police charge mourners, scores injured
4/86, Vosloorus (Boksburg)	—	Clashes w/police, streets barricaded
4/86, New Brighton	—	Tear gas, general melee
5/86, Soweto	—	Clashes w/police, tear gas
5/86, Tembisa	—	Clashes w/police
5/86, Zwide	—	Peaceful
6/86, Guguletu	—	Tear gas, clashes w/police

Source: SAIRR, *Race Relations Survey, 1985* (Johannesburg: Institute of Race Relations, 1986) and SAIRR, *Race Relations Survey, 1986* (Johannesburg: Institute of Race Relations, 1987).

While themselves products of the insurrection, the political funerals, in turn, made three important contributions to its development. First they served as an engine of the insurrectionary process. Almost invariably the police or army would teargas the funeral gathering or the "mourners" as they departed, resulting in a general melee during which the police would fire on the crowd. Any deaths would be cause for yet another funeral. This cycle, with its attendant heightening of tension and militancy, was replayed again and again.

Events of early 1986 in the Johannesburg township of Alexandra illustrate the role of the political funeral in driving the insurrectionary process forward.[40] In mid-February, a funeral attended by 13,000 people was held at the Alexandra sports stadium to commemorate a local student leader who had been shot. Police tear-gassed the mourners as they left the stadium. A general melee ensued as thousands fled the scene, while others barricaded the streets with burning tires. For the next

several weeks the township was in turmoil. In the five-hour battle that raged immediately after the funeral three people were killed by security forces. This was
followed by widespread violence in which township residents attacked alleged
"collaborators" and "agents of the system." Some thirty people, mostly community
councillors and black policemen, were killed by gunfire and an additional seventy
were injured. Three days after the disrupted funeral there was a work stayaway and
school boycott in Alexandra, culminating in a rally of 40,000 people. On March 5,
nineteen days after the funeral that had sparked the township turmoil, another
funeral was held; this time for seventeen people killed by security forces in the
subsequent events. It is estimated that seventy thousand people were in attendance.
The level of militancy and defiance that gripped the Alexandra township was sym-
bolized when, of the many political banners raised at the "funeral," the flag of the
Soviet Union was unfurled.[41]

The political funeral also served to build community solidarity. The mass gatherings gave tens of thousands of individuals a common political language and set of
political symbols, a group of shared goals and, most important, a sense that they
were part of a huge and irresistible force. The funerals were occasions for political
speeches, the display of revolutionary symbols, and the singing of liberation songs.
Since the modern history of resistance to white rule in South Africa is predominantly an ANC history, and since the ANC's apparatus for the generation of ideology, art, and music is elaborate by comparison with any of its potential rivals, it
was natural that the political ideas, symbols, and songs that made up the funeral
"services" were predominantly those of the African National Congress. Thus, the
political funerals acted as a mechanism through which the urban masses were
drawn, more by process than design, into the tradition of the ANC and the Freedom
Charter.

The funerals with their revolutionary pageantry, symbols, and rhetoric were in
themselves powerful acts of opposition to Pretoria's authority. Both the gatherings
themselves and what went on at them were forbidden under South African law. But
much more was involved than simple defiance. By displaying the picture of Nelson
Mandela, by draping coffins with the gold, green, and black colors of the ANC, by
hoisting the red flag of the South African Communist Party or the hammer and
sickle of the USSR, the township residents were demonstrating that they had indeed
rendered the townships "ungovernable"; that in respect to black South Africa,
Pretoria could no longer propose and dispose at will. According to the black clinical
psychologist Professor Chabani Manganyi, 1985 "was a watershed. . . . There was
a dramatic broadening of resistance, and *blacks finally broke the psychological
barrier of thinking that the whites were all-powerful* and could not be challenged."[42]

Collective defiance also produced the kind of profound and exquisite emotional
uplift so often recalled by participants in revolutionary upheavals—a combined
sense of community, purpose, and hope. "You go to a funeral or meeting in the
townships," a white political activist told a journalist in May 1986, "and for a few
hours black, brown and white share the most exhilarating comradeship you can ever
imagine."[43] Having shed its old fears and inhibitions, and having thwarted Pretoria
in the process, the township populace developed a belief in its own power vis-à-vis

the government; a confidence in its ability to deliver its own "liberation." As a knowledgeable and experienced commentator on South African affairs observed about the atmosphere in black politics in mid-1986:

> [I]n their quest to remove apartheid and achieve political power, most [black South Africans] know there is a long, painful road to travel. But they also have the visceral knowledge that, after centuries of defeats, humiliation and countless false dawns, the final phase is under way.[44]

Early 1986, then, witnessed the full flowering in South Africa's black townships of a "political culture of liberation." The seeds were present in the "culture of resistance" that was the legacy of the Soweto uprising. They began to sprout with the formation of the UDF in 1983. They came into full bloom in the hothouse of insurrection during 1985.

Transformation

The violence, disruption, and seeming unpredictability that accompanies the breakdown of established authority—the symptoms of ungovernability—are the things observed most often about insurrectionary action. But in South Africa in the mid-1980s, as with popular uprisings in other times and places, incipient order of a new type was hidden within the chaos of insurrection. Ungovernability soon gave rise to new forms of governance, or what the UDF leadership termed "alternative structures of people's power." In March 1986 Zwelakhe Sisulu, a distinguished journalist and UDF leader, described for the first time to a national audience a process of transformation that had been ongoing in the country's black townships for the past several months.

> There is a growing tendency for ungovernability to be transformed into elementary forms of people's power. . . . [The security forces] couldn't stop the people in some townships from taking power under their very noses, by starting to run those townships in different ways. . . . [T]he struggles which the people had fought, and the resulting situation of ungovernability, created the possibilities for the exercise of people's power.[45]

These "elementary forms of people's power" referred to by Sisulu were apparently forged out of a combination of grass-roots spontaneity and the designs of political leadership. It is not possible to disentangle and weigh the relative importance of each in creating these alternative structures of governance. What can be observed is that at both grass-roots and leadership levels there developed, nearly simultaneously, a common response to somewhat different aspects of the conditions created by "ungovernability." The grass-roots, or bottom-up, response involved coming to grips with the breakdown in urban services that followed the collapse of the local government apparatus. What should be done about crime once the police had fled the townships or were totally preoccupied by "security" matters? Who would remove night soil, dispose of trash, provide intercity transportation, repair water pipes? These immediate and palpable problems arose directly out of the insurrection's successful assault on the local manifestations of the state. A need for their solution prompted new grass-roots organizational initiatives, and afforded leaders new opportunities to elevate the movement for black liberation to a new level. Available evidence suggests that at least some elements within the UDF leadership perceived, in these insurrection-created problems of urban living, the possibility of transforming what was essentially a broad movement of protest and resistance into something that would pose a fundamental challenge to the minority-controlled state. A confidential UDF discussion paper circulated in May 1985, and titled "From Protest to Challenge," contained the following significant passage:

> Having established the illegitimacy of the S. African regime, it is necessary to project a popular alternative. . . . Where the apartheid puppets are no longer able to effectively function, a stage could be reached where the people's organisation assumed responsibility for organising the community to govern itself in a variety of ways from setting up health clinics to crime prevention. This will make people fully understand our vision of a future democratic South Africa.[46]

For the UDF leadership, new forms of governance were also needed to stem the threat to organization and discipline that flowed inevitably from the social and emotional forces unleashed by insurrectionary mobilization.[47] By its very nature insurrection breaks down existing forms of cultural constraint and social control, as well as of political domination. It is inherently hostile to convention, discipline, and organization. In the midst of an insurrectionary upheaval that was partially of its own making, the UDF leadership confronted a situation that threatened to spin out of control. "We have been unable to respond effectively to the spontaneous waves of militancy around the country," noted a discussion document circulated by the UDF's Transvaal Education Forum May 1985.[48] UDF leaders might well have recognized their predicament in Leon Trotsky's description of the 1905 Russian insurrection: "[J]ust as spontaneous indignation outpaced the work of political consciousness, so the desire for action left the feverish attempts at organization far behind. Therein lies the weakness of the revolution—any revolution—but therein also lies its strength."[49] In May 1985, a UDF analysis of the current situation described, although in more prosaic terms, the identical predicament:

> The brief period since the front [UDF] was launched has seen the flowering of organisations throughout the country. Yet in the same period we have seen relatively spontaneous mass mobilisation sweep the country like wildfire. The relationship between the processes of mobilisation and organisation is a very complex and dynamic one. One thing is clear, however: *the process of mobilization has far outstripped that of organisation.*[50]

Of particular concern to the UDF leadership was the tendency of militant young comrades to take matters into their own hands, and especially to use intimidation to advance the insurrectionary struggle. The "necklace" killing of suspected informers by what amounted to insurrectionary lynch mobs was especially troubling. To the

UDF leadership the ultramilitant tendencies of the comrades violated their conception of accountability. Reflecting this concern, Zwelakhe Sisulu, in March 1986,
warned a national UDF conference:

> Struggles over the past few months demonstrate that it is of absolute importance that
> we don't confuse coercion, the use of force *against* the community, with people's
> power, the collective strength of the community. . . . In times of ungover-
> nability . . . undisciplined individual action can have very negative con-
> sequences.[51]

Ultramilitancy, and especially the "necklace," also threatened to alienate important
sources of UDF support within the international community, as well as among the
small faction of south Africa's white population that identified with the struggle for
majority emancipation.

The UDF's civic, youth, and student organizations, with the mass rally as their
main activity, were not especially well suited for dealing with the situation; they
were effective instruments of mobilization but not of coordination and discipline.
Hence, the natural dynamic of insurrection with its drive toward "pure action",
provided the catalyst for leadership to develop new forms of organization that might
bring focus and discipline to the waves of insurrectionary activity. "We want to
strengthen unity, not divide the community," stated Albertina Sisulu, the UDF's
copresident, "and we do not want to confuse people's power with coercion, which
is undemocratic. . . . We must get on with [building new forms of organiza-
tion]. . . . Our crime is too high, many of the youths are undisciplined, some of our
efforts lack a focus and community support."[52]

In seeking to supplement their mass organizations, the UDF leadership was not
operating in a conceptual vacuum. In 1953, the ANC National Executive Committee had issued what it called the M-Plan as a means to compensate for the weaknesses of mass-type organizations.[53] Authored by Nelson Mandela, the M-Plan
bears a striking resemblance to the alternative structures of governance that were
constructed in the townships more than thirty years later. This is hardly surprising,
given that by mid-1985 the ANC underground was flourishing, ANC cadre could be
counted among the UDF leaders, and the ANC and Nelson Mandela had emerged as
the focus of political legitimacy within black politics. Thus, it is highly likely that in
constructing their "alternative structures," community activists were inspired by the
M-Plan.

The Street Committee System

Out of this mix of grass-roots militancy and leadership efforts to adapt to conditions
created by ungovernability there emerged new organizational arrangements that
began to perform representative, adjudicative, and control functions within the
black townships. Most prominent and potentially significant of these was what
came to be termed "the street committee system." This involved organizing each
township on the basis of small geographic constituencies that could serve as units of
political participation, representation, and control (see Figure 6.2). The develop-

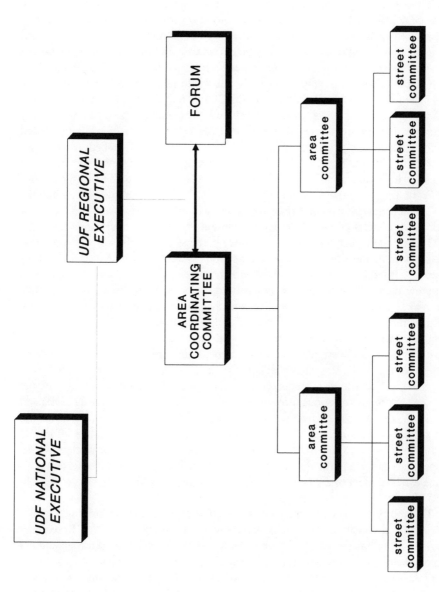

Fig. 6.2. Street committee system

ment of street committees was initiated in the townships of the Eastern Cape, and it was there that they reached their fullest development. The African townships of Port Elizabeth, containing at least 400,000 people, provide a good example of the institutional development that took place.[54] In the latter half of 1985, leaders of the local UDF-affiliated civic associations set out to organize their townships street by street, with each street represented by an elected committee. In turn, the townships were subdivided into areas, each with an area committee of sixteen to twenty members, elected by the street committees within its zone. The area committees each elected two representatives (usually one youth and one older person) to what was called the Area Committee Council (ACC). It met three to four times monthly and was the apex of a system of geographic representation. Also created was the Forum, which brought together representatives from the existing UDF-affiliated youth, student, civic, and women's organizations: the Port Elizabeth Youth Congress (PEYCO), the Port Elizabeth Students Congress (PESCO), the Port Elizabeth Black Civic Organization (PEBCO), and the Port Elizabeth Women's Organizations (PEWO). The Forum was the main policymaking body for the township, while the ACC dealt primarily with managing the delivery of urban services and administering social and political control. Through the system of area and street committees, the ACC dealt with such problems as crime, garbage and night-soil disposal, and breakdowns in the sewerage and water-supply systems. Its managerial concerns extended, in addition, to things like the appropriate operating hours for shebeens (drinking bars), the settlement of domestic disputes, the conversion of empty lots into parks, and the reinstatement of tenants evicted by agents of the state. Directly political matters such as the handling of police informers, the logistical arrangements for large rallies or mass funerals, and the organization and enforcement of consumer boycotts, were also dealt with through the street committees, area committees, or the ACC. Research conducted in the Port Elizabeth townships indicates that the level at which a matter was handled depended upon the nature of the problem.[55] The more serious the problem the higher the level. Thus petty crime and family disputes would be dealt with in meetings of the street committees, while the punishment of civil crimes like murder and political crimes like police informing would be referred to the ACC. The ACC was also responsible for matters whose scope transcended a particular street or area, like the rupture of a major water main, or the establishment of a 9:00 P.M. curfew for all township shebeens, as occurred in 1985.[56]

The ability of this committee system to act as a governing authority was exhibited during a consumer boycott of white-owned businesses in 1986. Researcher Mark Swilling has described how, in order to ensure that black shop owners did not exploit their boycott-created oligopoly, the Forum and ACC established price controls. A list of fixed prices was distributed to shop keepers, who were told that if they violated the posted prices their shops would also be boycotted. Street committees were made responsible for monitoring prices; violations were reported to the ACC, which placed the offending shop on the boycott list. According to Swilling, no major contravention of the price controls occurred during the several months of the boycott.[57] At the same time that it established price controls, the street committee system also was able to regulate economic transactions between the informal

sector within Port Elizabeth's townships and the white-owned businesses that supplied it with goods. Any trader who wished to purchase goods for resale from city
businesses had to obtain "buy cards." These were yellow documents which on one
side contained a photograph of the trader and information about him—his name and
trading location, the goods he traded in, and his supplier. On the other side was
printed the Freedom Charter.

As the street committee system was taking shape in the Port Elizabeth townships
a similar process was producing the same basic structures in other Eastern Cape
townships. For example, a journalist visiting Langa, a township of 50,000 serving
the industrial city of Uitenhage, learned of an elaborate new representative system
that residents explained was "the basis for a people's government."

> Langa's dozens of street committees are united by a structure of 20 area commit-
> tees, each administering about 10 street committees. Above them, there is an
> overall coordinating committee, which in turn works under the regional branch of
> the United Democratic Front.[58]

Pervasive in the Eastern Cape by the beginning of 1986, the street committee
system spread rapidly to the townships of the Transvaal and Western Cape.
Mamelodi, outside of Pretoria, and the Johannesburg township of Alexandra established well-developed committee networks based on the Eastern Cape model. In the
largest of South Africa's black townships, Soweto, organization of street committees did not begin in earnest until the second half of 1986.

Why the alternative structures of governance took the specific form they did is
not entirely clear. Part of the answer may lie in the fact that an incipient form of
street committee predated leadership's effort to respond to the turbulence of insurrection. Groups of youthful comrades tended to divide up the townships into "turf,"
within which each would seek to control crime, administer discipline (some would
say intimidate), and remake the urban landscape through "clean-up" campaigns,
(the building of small parks, and the renaming of streets, buildings, and parks with
"appropriate" revolutionary labels—i.e., Mandela School, Tambo Street, AK47
Avenue, Unity is Strength Park).[59] In seeking to bring some organizational discipline to the ultramilitant comrades, the UDF leadership, in part, built a new pyra-
midal structure on top of the comrades' "turf organization." In so doing the UDF
formalized the incipient street committees, introduced more mature political leadership into their operation, and knit them into a community-wide, and potentially
country-wide structure.

Whatever its inspiration, it is clear that the activists viewed the street committee
system as far more than simply a means to deal with immediate problems of
sanitation, crime, and indiscipline, or even as a means to launch and sustain effective rent strikes and consumer boycotts. Rather, they viewed these formalized
manifestations of people's power as a new structure of government, first for the
townships that they believed were being liberated from Pretoria's control, and
eventually for all of South Africa. A leading activist in Graaf-Reinet described his
community's effort to create organs of "people's power" in the following manner:

[W]e realize that we are not just coming together to sing freedom songs and to discuss this [or that], we are preparing ourselves for a complete takeover. Therefore, if we make decisions and talk about organisations, we are talking about . . . how we are going to run Graaf-Reinet, how we are going to run Cradock. We will be in charge. The people of those areas will be in charge of governing the area and we are governing ourselves right now.[60]

A year later, a reporter for the *Los Angeles Times* was told by the president of a street committee in Uitenhage's Langa township:

We are already taking over, and that's no boast but fact. We have made ourselves ungovernable by the apartheid regime, and now we are starting to implement people's power. . . . The community council has been brought down, the police have been forced to leave and the informers have been isolated, driven out or in some cases killed. Political power is shifting to the hands of the people's own organizations, and we can begin to think about forming our own people's government.[61]

The activists were not alone in seeing their alternative structures as proto-local governments. Local businessmen in the "white" cities, hurt by consumer boycotts and by the workplace disruptions that were a ubiquitous aspect of the insurrection, began to enter into negotiations with representatives of the UDF's "organs of people's power." Eventually white local government officials who, like the businessmen in their area, desired a restoration of "order," were drawn into these negotiations. A study by the Centre for Policy Studies at the University of Witswatersrand describes twenty separate cases of such negotiations that took place during 1985–86.[62] Issues under discussion ran the gamut of concerns that had catalyzed mass protests since the early 1980s—from bus fares, housing, and removals to the potential for new nonracial forms of municipal government.

By seeking to solve their problems through negotiations with UDF-created structures, rather than by calling upon the state's political and administrative agencies, the locally based political and economic establishment indicated the profound nature of the political change ushered in by the insurrection. White businessmen and elected officials were, in effect, recognizing the ability of the UDF's structures to control the townships, and in so doing they informally granted the status of governing authority to the new "organs of people's power." However, these negotiations could not succeed without the acquiescence of central government. But recognizing that bolstering autonomous structures of black power was a basic threat to its strategy of change, Pretoria was decidedly unenthusiastic about these local negotiations. Eventually the central government intervened to nullify every one of the local-level initiatives.[63]

In South Africa's street committee system we can observe a recapitulation of one of the more remarkable leitmotivs of modern revolutionary situations. As Hannah Arendt noted in *On Revolution,* no social or political theory can "account for the regular emergence and reemergence of the council system ever since the French Revolution."[64] These "organs of action and germs of a new state," as she refers to them, provided the basis of the Paris Commune in 1871, were embodied in the soviets of the Russian revolutions of 1905 and 1917, and were a predominate feature of the Hungarian Revolution of 1956.[65] Arendt has noted of the Russian and Hungarian revolts: "In both instances councils or soviets had sprung up everywhere: councils of workers', soldiers', peasants', students', youths', neighborhoods', and so on."[66] Arendt continues:

> The most striking aspect of these spontaneous developments is that in both instances it took these independent and highly disparate organs no more than a few weeks . . . to begin a process of coordination and integration through the formation of higher councils of a regional or provincial character, from which finally delegates to an assembly representing the whole country could be chosen.[67]

The very same dynamic process could be observed in the black townships of South Africa, where the newly created "councils" spread outward from the Eastern Cape in an uneven but rapid and seemingly inexorable process of political transformation. Just when it seemed both natural and imminent that the township coordinating committees would link up, via the regional executives of the UDF, into a representative national political structure, Pretoria put an end to the process, at least temporarily, with its declaration of a state of emergency on June 12, 1986.

Functionally Specific Structures

In addition to the street committee system, the turmoil of 1984–86 also served as a catalyst for the formation of functionally specific alternative structures in the areas of law, education, and health.

People's Courts
"People's courts," the most controversial of the new organizational formations, emerged prior to the formalization by UDF activists of the street committee system. Evidence suggests that initially these "courts" were created by militant youths, or "comrades," when they began to assume a social control function for the streets and neighborhoods in which they lived. As local teenagers began to substitute for the police, apprehending thieves, rapists, muggers, and the like, a mechanism was required to decide upon and administer punishment. The need was filled by informally gathered groups of youths, who dubbed themselves "people's courts" or "discipline committees."[68] A reporter covering the phenomenon in the Pretoria township of Mamelodi found that "courts" could be held at any time, whenever there is a plaintiff and an accused. Petty thieves were sentenced to community service such as painting and watering parks, whereas corporal punishment was meted out to more serious offenders. Rape or robbery, for example, were punishable by twenty-five to thirty lashes with a sjambok or whip.[69] "The punishment is carried out on the spot," said a young woman court member. "You have to see this from our point of view. . . . The community must be the judge and must see that justice is done."[70] Another member of the court added, "Here we do not concern ourselves with legal technicalities like in the Magistrate's Courts where, if you have a good lawyer, you can get off."[71]

Although they may initially have been created to deal with criminal offenses of a civil nature, people's courts soon were also engaged in trying "political crimes" ranging from lack of enthusiasm for "the struggle" to informing to the security police. It is generally believed that many "necklace" deaths were the result of sentences by people's courts, although this has been denied by court participants.[72] The harshness of people's courts, as well as the opportunity for abuse inherent in the rough and ready nature of street justice, generated considerable criticism from UDF activists at both local and national levels. For example, Mike Seloane, the twenty-six-year-old general secretary of the Mamelodi Youth Organisation (Mayo), told a reporter for the South African *Weekly Mail* that people's courts were formed to deal with petty crime, but that "this led to other elements using the courts to settle personal feuds." Sometimes, "disciplinary courts would try the person in absentia without caring to listen to the other side of the story. . . . Some people took advantage of this type of undemocratic procedure and would fabricate charges against people they had a dislike for."[73] The remarks of Zwelakhe Sisulu, delivered in a keynote address to a UDF conference, were even more trenchant: "[W]hen bands of youth set up so-called 'kangaroo courts' and give out punishments, under the control of no-one with no democratic mandate from the community, this is *not* people's power."[74]

In some townships it was the abuses inherent in the comrades' "street justice" that was a major stimulus for the formation of a formal street committee system. By institutionalizing and formalizing the incipient street organizations of the youthful comrades, the UDF was able to fold the people's courts into a larger structure. This resulted in the naming of more mature court members and opened up the possibility of greater discipline through both control from above and accountability from below. Sisulu was speaking of this incorporation of people's courts within the UDF street committee system when he stated:

> When disciplined, organised youth, together with other older people participate in
> the exercise of people's justice and the setting up of people's courts; when these
> structures are acting on a mandate from the community and are under the democrat-
> ic control of the community, this is an example of people's power.[75]

Through the institutionalization of the street committee system, the kangaroo courts of which Sisulu spoke were, in many of the townships, transformed into a rudimentary criminal justice system. Typically, those accused of crimes, including political offenses, would be brought before twenty to thirty neighborhood residents in a trial presided over by the street committee president.[76] The decision would then be reviewed by an appeals court. A middle-aged schoolteacher in Kagiso, northwest of Johannesburg, who sat on an appeals court of "elders," explained: "We hear the cases again and weigh the evidence a little more carefully. Usually, we confirm the community's judgment but reduce the sentences."[77] Another striking element in the development of people's courts was the drafting of "codes of conduct" which stressed the need for due process, the right to a defense, and the right of appeal.[78]

Like the creation of the street committee system itself, the developmental process in respect to people's courts was an uneven one. Given the conditions of insurrection within which they were born and operated, it would be naive to believe that even where people's courts were most developed and institutionalized abuses did not frequently occur. Moreover, the process of institutionalization did not begin every-where simultaneously, move at the same rate, or reproduce itself in identical fashion within each of the townships. Nevertheless, there was an unmistakable developmental process occurring, however uneven and imperfect its manifestations. An alternative structure performing the functions of a criminal justice system was emerging out of the chaos of insurrection.

National Education Crisis Committee

As the South African insurrection extended into a second year, the extensive school boycotts posed a dilemma for the UDF leadership. On the one hand, there was little doubt that the boycotting students had been the spearhead of the unfolding liberation movement. On the other hand, the open-ended nature of the turmoil within which they were operating could mean that an entire generation of black South Africans might receive its only education in the streets. In their revolt against Bantu education, the students had raised the battle cry "Liberation Before Education." But for parents, who recognized the distance yet to be traveled before liberation, the implication of this slogan was the creation of a generation of illiterates. For the UDF leadership, who in a sociological sense were representative of parents and who therefore shared their concerns, the open-ended school boycotts contained the danger that an entire generation would lack the intellectual and technical skills needed to build a new South Africa. For these reasons, many adult South Africans preferred even the despised system of Bantu education to no formal education whatsoever.

The first organizational manifestation of adult concern about the educational crisis was the Soweto Parents Crisis Committee (SPCC), formed by the UDF-affiliated Soweto Civic Association in October 1985. The crisis committee immediately entered into discussions with senior officials of the Ministry of Education in an ultimately unsuccessful effort to get Pretoria to accede to student demands as a basis for ending the school boycott.[79] In December the SPCC convened a conference of 16 organizations involved in education throughout the country. In addition to what by then had become the standard resolutions demanding the withdrawal of the security forces from the townships and the release of detainees, the delegates issued four key resolutions: that all students should return to school at the beginning of the new term in January; that a national parents' crisis committee be formed; that parent-teacher-student structures be created at all schools; and that another conference to assess the situation be convened in March 1986. Finally, the delegates declared that apartheid education was "totally unacceptable to the oppressed people," and resolved to strive for what it termed "people's education" for all South Africa.[80]

The resolution at the SPCC conference calling upon students to return to school had relatively little impact on attendance.[81] Other resolutions, however, especially those pertaining to the creation of a national education organization, did play a role in shaping the ongoing insurrectionary process. In March 1986 the National Education Crisis Committee (NECC) was founded at a conference attended by 1,500 delegates representing UDF-affiliated civic, youth, student, and labor organizations. This meeting marked both a formalization of the activities that had been ongoing since the SPCC conference the preceding December, and a shift in emphasis from the need to end the school boycott to the need to devise and implement an alternative system of education. An indication of this shift is found in the contents of the conference's keynote address by Zwelakhe Sisulu. Out of a thirty-page text, six were devoted to defining "people's education," and not a single sentence dealt with the need for terminating the school boycotts.[82]

For the UDF leadership, now grappling with the educational crisis through the newly formed NECC, getting students back into school posed a dilemma. It was neither practical nor, for them, ideologically tolerable to call for the students return to a system defined by Bantu education. Could students really be expected to heed such a call? How could such a call be made consistent with UDF claims to be part of a popular movement of liberation from Pretoria's system of racial rule? Would it not instead be an act of collaboration? This dilemma, like so many others created by the turbulence of insurrection, posed an opportunity as well as a problem. If getting on with the task of education was essential, and if asking students to return to Bantu education was out of the question, than a new form of education that was consistent with the movement for liberation had to be offered the students. At its inaugural conference in March 1986 the NECC leadership articulated such a vision of an alternative education and took on the task of its design and implementation. To the students' cry of "Liberation Before Education," the NECC counterpoised the slogan "Education FOR Liberation!" In other words, the NECC was asserting that the introduction of "a free, democratic, compulsory and non-racial education,"[83] what it dubbed "people's education," need not await the era of full political liberation. "In effect," Sisulu told the March conference, "this means taking over the schools, transforming them from institutions of oppression into zones of progress and people's power." Sisulu acknowledged that this was a long-term endeavor but asserted "we have already begun this process."[84] As with the other forms of people's power—the street committees and people's courts—people's education could be introduced because insurrectionary turbulence kept the white minority state at bay. If a form of education with a clear liberatory content could be introduced outside of Pretoria's control, then a return to school would be consistent with pushing forward the struggle for "people's power." Under such circumstances a call to end the school boycotts might strike a responsive chord.

In the NECC vision the project of creating "people's education" involved several analytically distinct tasks, beginning with the de facto, if not de jure, transfer of control from the government's Department of Education and Training (DET) to representative organs "of the people." "The struggle to implement people's education," stated the NECC chairman, Vusi Khanyile, "involves people's organisations taking control of the administration of education in the interests of the people."[85] General educational policy would be set by the NECC, while individual schools would be run by parent-teacher-student associations.[86] The model for such associations was found in the parent crisis committees that had spring up in many communities after the SPCC educational conference in December 1985.

Teachers in the township schools, who had because of their positions as government employees occupied an ambiguous role in regard to the UDF and its affiliated student organizations, would be drawn into the effort to construct people's education.[87] And a new curriculum would be developed and a new democratic style of teaching would replace the authoritarian and rote-learning methods of the DET and Bantu education. In the social sciences and humanities curricula materials were to reflect the conditions and perspectives of South Africa's deprived majority, as well as the political values embodied in the "struggle for liberation and people's power." Thus, according to Eric Molobi, a member of the NECC executive committee:

> People's Education is . . . decidedly political and partisan with regard to oppression and exploitation. . . . [I]t is fundamentally different from . . . programmes that shun the reality of the conflict in South Africa [and seek] the depoliticisation of education. . . . People's Education, by contrast, becomes an integral part of the struggle for a non-racial, democratic South Africa."[88]

The overall task set by the NECC vision of people's education was a daunting one. Aside from the question of how long the insurrectionary forces could hold off Pretoria's efforts to reassert control over township schools, there was the problem of resources. Whatever the creative power of the insurrection might be, it did not have the resources to maintain an educational system country-wide. Assuming the unlikely, that the state could be held at bay indefinitely, who would pay the teachers now providing people's education? The NECC leadership offered a pragmatic answer. Vusi Khanyile, the NECC chairman, explained that

> [T]he state must continue financing education, providing and maintaining the necessary infrastructure. . . . What we reject is the authoritarian structure of the DET, the content of its curriculum and the teaching methods employed. We must be sure that we can formulate an alternative in all these areas.

But, as many within the political opposition pointed out, it was unrealistic to believe that the state in its existing configuration would pay for such an alternative. Nonetheless, the project of creating people's education moved forward impressively in the few months before the imposition of the state of emergency in June 1986 stymied such efforts.

In May 1986, Khanyile announced the formation of a commission to rewrite the English and history curricula, and he indicated that during 1987 the NECC planned to rewrite curricula for all grades. Seven months later he announced that the job of creating alternative history and English syllabi was nearly complete.[89] In those townships where the state's control had been reduced to a minimum, elements of the NECC program were introduced at once. Aubrey Matshiqi of the National Education Union of South Africa (NEUSA), an organization of radical teachers affiliated with the UDF, claimed that by May 1986 in many Soweto and Eastern Cape schools Wednesday and Friday were set aside for the teaching of alternative education.[90] His assessment was corroborated by the liaison officer of the DET, who said that in Port Alfred and East London (both in the Eastern Cape) teachers had been removed from the department's payroll for following an alternative program.[91] These teachers were apparently being supported by funds raised by the communities themselves. In mid-May, one month before the state of emergency crackdown, the Port Elizabeth parent-teacher-student crisis committee announced that it would take over the administration of DET schools within a month. The committee said that it planned to renovate school buildings, since the DET had refused to repair African schools until the townships returned to "normal."[92]

It is easy to romanticize the developments associated with the NECC. Like other aspects of "people's power," the alternative educational structures introduced in the midst of insurrectionary turbulence were uneven in their geographical distribution, imperfect in their operation, and only partially elaborated. There was a good deal of confusion over how people's education should be implemented, and ambiguity about the contents of a "people's curriculum." But to expect anything else under the conditions in which the NECC operated would be absurd. What is important is that within South Africa in the mid-1980s there was developing under the general aegis of the UDF and NECC a new system of cultural reproduction. The National Party government had introduced Bantu education in the 1950s for the expressed purpose of ensuring a politically quiescent and compliant African majority. Now, insurrection had spawned a rival form of education whose purpose was the opposite.* And, to a limited but meaningful extent, the organizational apparatus of insurrection had begun to put that idea into practice, forming in the NECC what was in effect an alternative Ministry of Education.

National Medical and Dental Association (NAMDA)

As with the areas of public order and education, the insurrection raised a set of new health-care problems that stimulated creative, community-based responses. People injured in battles with the security forces required treatment, as did those who had suffered physical and psychological abuse while under police detention. The state-run clinics were at best of dubious value to people whose injuries were related to insurrectionary activities, especially when the security forces began to use clinic treatment records as a source of information about political activists, as occurred in 1985. In response, UDF-affiliated health professionals began to treat patients extra-curricularly and to train community workers in first aid. NAMDA, a UDF-affiliated medical association formed in 1982, began to give this effort a national focus by sponsoring emergency service groups and groups for treating detainees in at least twenty townships.[93]

The creation of alternative structures in the health area went less far during the duration of the insurrection than was the case with people's courts and people's education. But a similar pattern had begun to emerge, which continued into the period following the imposition of the state of emergency. By early 1987 NAMDA was describing itself as "a powerful National Health Organization which has as-

---

*Actually the idea was first broached by Nelson Mandela in his 1953 presidential address to the annual conference of the Transvaal ANC. In the same speech in which he introduced the M-plan, Mandela outlined a response to the impending introduction of Bantu education. It bears a striking resemblance to the concept of "people's education" as developed by the NECC—"Establish your own community schools where the right kind of education will be given to our children. If it becomes dangerous or impossible to have these alternative schools, then again you must make every home, every shack or rickety structure a centre of learning for children." See Nelson Mandela, *The Struggle Is My Life* (New York: Pathfinder Press, 1986), pp. 40–41.

sumed its rightful place alongside other progressive organisations in the struggle for change in South Africa."[94] It was engaged in "the development of a range of supportive measures to victims of apartheid. . . . These include care of detainees, support for detainee's [sic] families, health provision for communities in crisis (eg workers on strike) . . ."[95] That NAMDA came to view itself as a proto-alternative ministry of health is indicated by the theme of its 1987 conference, "Towards a National Health Service," as well as by the fact that it began planning for the implementation of a national health-care system to serve the black population. Meetings with major foundations and donors were held to explore external funding for a program of training in primary health care.* In these sessions NAMDA's objectives were described as to "provide needed health care today" and to "lay the foundations for a national primary health care system in a future South Africa."[96]

Summary: From Protest to Challenge

During 1985 the UDF National Executive Committee set as a theme for its activities "moving from protest to challenge." The construction of "alternative structures of people's power" was the practical expression of this theme. The emergence of fledgling organs of people's power represented a new stage in the development of black opposition politics; one whose "markings" would be familiar to the student of comparative revolution. In the words of Leon Trotsky:

> The historic preparation of a revolution brings about, in the pre-revolutionary period, a situation in which the class which is called to realize the new social system, although not yet master of the country, has actually concentrated in its hands a significant share of the state power, while the official apparatus of the government is still in the hands of the old lords.[97]

Trotsky called this phenomenon dual power; others have referred to it as the creation of a revolutionary infrastructure. The great political significance of institutions of dual power— "alternative structures" in the South African parlance—lies in the fact that they constitute a transformation in society's structure of domination, i.e., the system whereby a state maintains control over its citizens.

Any system of domination involves a mix of three forms of compliance: normative, which is based on moral obligation and is usually associated with legitimacy; utilitarian, which is based on instrumental rewards and is usually associated with a relationship of dependency/cooptation; and coercive, which is based on fear, usually of physical punishment. The South African state, for obvious reasons, has never rested on a grant of legitimacy from the black majority. Just as obviously coercion has always played an important role in maintaining a system of domination defined by white power. But one of the most anomalous things about the South African system is that despite the great political, social, and economic inequities

---

*Meetings were held in New York City on June 19, co-hosted by the Kaiser Foundation and the Carnegie Corporation.

that are associated with minority racial rule the state had for decades maintained sociopolitical peace while keeping the costs of coercion within feasible limits. "The South African social system," wrote the anthropologist Max Gluckman, "has become increasingly, a horrible one, morally. . . . But it worked and works, in total and in its parts."[98] This is because South Africa's minority racial rule has not, at least in the twentieth century, rested primarily on coercion but rather on a highly efficacious structure of utilitarian compliance. There have been two key elements to this structure: the African majority has been kept at a marginal level of material existence, and it has increasingly had to rely upon the state for its access to subsistence, however meager. One of the functions performed by apartheid has been to adapt this peculiarly South African structure of utilitarian compliance to the conditions of modern industrialism as these emerged after World War II. The form of centralized control introduced by the National Party as part of its apartheid project made the black population totally dependent on the state for the essential means of biological subsistence and social advance. Jobs, education, health care, housing, and the ability to live where these were available, were all doled out by the apartheid apparatus. What was given could, of course, be taken away. To fall afoul of officialdom was to risk one's access to the city, which given the economic destitution of the homelands could spell disaster for oneself and one's family.

The alternative structures of "people's power" that emerged in the midst of insurrection struck at the very foundation of this system of state control. They had begun to offer to the urban black populace the resources for survival and security that had previously been available only through agents of the state. In so doing they began to shift the basis of domination, threatening Pretoria's hold over the majority and thus weakening the state. When the people's courts, street committees, and NECC were taking on the functions of governance, more was involved than simply the emergence of an alternative state in the formal sense. A new system of domination was being forged. It contained elements of utilitarian and coercive compliance, and with the legitimacy bestowed on the ANC, an important element of normative compliance as well.

In this analytic treatment of the insurrection of 1984–86 I have, for the most part, ignored the divisions within black politics as well as the very real organizational and ideological weaknesses that marked the insurrectionary movement. Old differences between Africanist and nonracial political tendencies persisted, and more recent ones between national populists and class-oriented "workerists" intensified. Some influential organizations and individuals who lost ground to the spreading ANC/UDF alternative structures reacted bitterly and even violently to the dimunition of their influence. At the ideological level, the UDF's concepts of democracy, people's power, people's education, and the like were vague, and its ability to impose its vision on the more militant activists was always problematic. At the organizational level, the developmental process in respect to "organs of people's power" was uneven from region to region. The potential for a cohesive national structure of "dual power" existed in the street committees, area committees, township coordinating committees, UDF regional executives, and the UDF national executive, but was never completely realized before the insurrectionary phase came to an end in mid-1986. And, of course, because the ANC/UDF lacked an armed force that could take on the state's security forces it could neither complete the insurrectionary process through a revolutionary seizure of power, nor protect its terrain once the state decided to act decisively against it.

These divisions and weaknesses were neither new nor remarkable. That political differences persisted and produced conflict within the black community is hardly surprising. What is remarkable is how rapidly the ANC/UDF tendency became the "center of gravity" of black community politics. Increasingly bitter conflict with tendencies that are losing ground is the inevitable "flip side" to such an ideological and organizational consolidation. It is also not surprising that alternative structures were unevenly and incompletely developed. Again, what is remarkable is their existence at all, the rapidity of their spread, and the extent to which they were able even temporarily and incompletely to check and replace the state's structure of domination. It is these things—the power of insurrectionary action, the dominant position established by the ANC/UDF in black politics, and the emergence of an alternative structure of governance—that impacted on the cohesiveness and strength of the South African state and thus contributed to the erosion of minority rule.

Notes

1. "Protest to Challenge?" Transvaal Education Forum, May 1985, unsigned and unpublished (Karis-Gerhart papers, Graduate Center of the City University of New York), p. 1.

2. Hannah Arendt, *On Revolution* (New York: Viking Press, 1963), p. 260.

3. Leon Trotsky, *1905* (New York: Random House, 1971), p. 198.

4. Ibid.

5. South African Institute of Race Relations (SAIRR), *Race Relations Survey, 1985* (Johannesburg: Institute of Race Relations, 1986), p. 542.

6. Ibid.

7. Ibid., p. 543.

8. *SA Barometer*, vol. 1, no. 5 (May 8, 1987), p. 71.

9. SAIRR, *Race Relations Survey, 1986* (Johannesburg: Institute of Race Relations, 1987), p. 372.

10. Ibid.

11. Ibid., p. 373.

12. See SAIRR, *Race Relations Survey, 1985*, p. 556.

13. Quoted in SAIRR, *Race Relations Survey, 1986*, p. 554.

14. SAIRR, *Survey of Race Relations, 1984*, (Johannesburg: Institute of Race Relations, 1985), pp. 71–72.

15. Ibid., p. 73.

16. Ibid., pp. 75–76.

17. Ibid., p. 75.

18. Ibid., pp. 75–76.

19. Ibid., p. 64.

20. Quoted in ibid., p. 76.

21. Quoted in ibid., p. 76.

22. Ibid., p. 78.

23. Ibid., p. 79.

24. Data on township political violence and casualties is drawn from the 1984, 1985, and 1986 volumes of the South African Institute of Race Relations, *Race Relations Survey*.

25. SAIRR, *Race Relations Survey, 1984*, p. 88.

26. Ibid., p. 545.

27. Ibid.

28. Ibid., p. 89.

29. SAIRR, *Race Relations Survey 1986*, pp. 532–33.

30. See Mark Orkin, *The Struggle and the Future* (Johannesburg: Raven Press, 1986), p. 33.

31. Ibid., p. 50.

32. Percentages calculated from data presented in Theodor Hanf, Heribert Weiland, and Gerda Vierdag, *South Africa: The Prospects of Peaceful Change* (London: Rex Collings, 1981), pp. 351–60; and Orkin, p. 35. On this subject, see also Mark Swilling, "The UDF and Township Revolt," in W. Cobbett, and R. Cohen, eds., *Popular Struggles in South Africa* (London: James Currey, 1988), p. 107.

33. Hanf et al., *South Africa*, p. 352.

34. Orkin, *The Struggle and the Future*, pp. 35–36.

35. Ibid.

36. Ibid., p. 40.

37. Repr. in *Fact and Reports*, vol. 16, no. E (March 14, 1986), p. 2.

38. NUM Congress, political resolution. Reprinted in *South African Labour Bulletin*, vol. 12, no. 3 (March/April 1987), p. 48.

39. *Facts and Reports*, March 14, 1986, p. 2.

40. For a description of events see SAIRR, *Race Relations Survey, 1986*, pp. 521–22.

41. Ibid., p. 522.

42. Quoted in John de St. Jorre, "The Final Phase," *The Observer*, May 4, 1986, p. 17 (emphasis added).

43. Ibid.

44. Ibid.

45. Zwelakhe Sisulu, keynote address, National Education Crisis Committee, Second National Consultative Conference, March 29, 1986, mimeo, pp. 14–15.

46. "Protest to Challenge; What does the NEC mean when it talks about the UDF moving from 'Protest to Challenge,' " unsigned, May 1985 (Karis/Gerhart papers, Graduate Center of the City University of New York), p. 4.

47. Swilling, "The UDF and Township Revolt," p. 103.

48. Internal discussion document, UDF Transvaal Education Forum, unpublished, May 1985 (Karis/Gerhart papers), p. 5.

49. Trotsky, p. 198.

50. UDF internal discussion document, p. 5 (emphasis added).

51. Sisulu, keynote address, p. 17.

52. Interviewed by Michael Parks and quoted in " 'Street' Groups Spur Fight to End Apartheid," *Los Angeles Times*, April 17, 1986, Part I-A, p. 2.

53. See "No Easy Walk to Freedom," presidential address by Mandela to the ANC (Transvaal) Conference, September 21, 1953, reprinted in Nelson Mandela, *The Struggle Is My Life* (New York: Pathfinder Press, 1986), p. 40.

54. Material on the political organization of Port Elizabeth comes, primarily, from Mark Swilling, "Local Level Negotiations: Case Studies and Implications" (Centre for Policy Studies, University of Witwatersrand), August 1987, pp. 37–43.

55. Ibid., p. 39.

56. Ibid., p. 39.

57. Ibid., pp. 39–40.

58. Parks, " 'Street' Groups," p. 2.

59. Peter Honey, "Street Committees: People Power or Kangaroo courts?," *Weekly Mail*, May 9–15, 1986, p. 9.

60. Reverend Nissan, speech to an April 1985 conference in Cape Town, quoted by Swilling, "Local Level Negotiations," p. 12.

61. Quoted in Michael Parks, "'Street' Groups," p. 2.

62. Swilling, "Local Level Negotiations," passim.

63. Ibid., p. 55.

64. Arendt, *On Revolution*, p. 265.

65. Ibid., pp. 263–64.

66. Ibid., p. 270.

67. Ibid., p. 271.

68. See Peter Honey, "Street Committees: People Power or Kangaroo Courts?" *Weekly Mail*, May 9–15, 1986, p. 9; see also Alister Sparks, "The Comrades Take Over in Alex," London *Observer*, February 23, 1986.

69. Honey, "Street Committees"; see also Tom Lodge, "The United Democratic Front," in J. D. Brewer, *Can South Africa Survive?* (London: MacMillan Press, 1989), p. 222.

70. Quoted in Honey, "Street Committees."

71. Quoted in ibid.

72. See Honey, "Street Committees."

73. Ibid.

74. Sisulu, Keynote address, p. 17 (emphasis in original).

75. Ibid.

76. Parks, "'Street' Groups," p. 3.

77. Ibid.

78. Ibid.

79. See SAIRR, *Race Relations Survey, 1985*, p. 381.

80. Ibid., p. 395.

81. SAIRR, *Race Relations Survey, 1986*, p. 448.

82. See Sisulu, keynote address, pp. 20–26.

83. Ibid., p. 18.

84. Ibid., p. 25.

85. Quoted in SAIRR, *Race Relations Survey, 1986*, p. 425.

86. See ibid., pp. 18 and 23; and Jonathan Hyslop, "School Student Movements and Educational Policy," in Cobbett and Cohen, eds., *Popular Struggles in South Africa*, p. 202.

87. Sisulu, keynote address, pp. 22–23.

88. Eric Molobi, "From Bantu Education to People's Education," in Cobbett and Cohen, eds., *Popular Struggles in South Africa*, pp. 158–59.

89. Ibid., pp. 424–25.

90. Ibid., p. 425.

91. Ibid., p. 426.

92. Ibid., p. 452.

93. See NAMDA, *Annual Report, 1986/7*, presented at the 4th annual general meeting, April 5, 1987, passim.

94. See NAMDA, *Primary Health Care*, reports presented at the consultative meeting held on April 6, 1987, in Cape Town, p. 1.

95. Ibid.

96. Letter of invitation to U.S. meeting participants from the Carnegie Corporation.

97. Leon Trotsky, *The History of the Russian Revolution* (Ann Arbor: University of Michigan Press, 1957), p. 207.

98. See "The Tribal Area in South and Central Africa," in Leo Kuper and M. G. Smith, *Pluralism in Africa* (Berkeley: University of California Press, 1971), pp. 374–75.

7

International Reaction and Domestic Realignment

As with the other historical instances of insurrection whose leitmotiv it shared—the Paris Commune of 1871, the Russian revolution of 1905, and the Hungarian uprising of 1956—the South African insurrection of 1984–86 was unable to bring down and replace the existing state. For its epitaph one could take the observation of Leon Trotsky who, upon pondering the fate of the 1905 Russian revolution which he had led, wrote: "At a certain moment in revolution the crucial question becomes: on which side are the soldiers—their sympathies and their bayonets?"[1] Once it was prepared to absorb the domestic and international costs of massive repression, Pretoria, its security forces loyal and intact, was in a position to throttle the township insurrection. But while having fallen short of a revolutionary seizure of power the insurrection did have a significant impact on the medium- to long-term strength and viability of white minority rule. It profoundly affected the international situation of the South African state, reinforcing its diplomatic and economic isolation and escalating the threats to economic growth, thus further jeopardizing the resources required for the implementation of reform. The direct and indirect reverberations of the upheaval threatened white security and material standards, and splintered the cohesion of white politics. Having nullified Pretoria's attempt to obtain domestic security and international legitimacy through reform, the insurrection produced a counterthrust by the state in the form of repression and autarky.

"A Sanctions Environment"

In March 1984, just two months prior to the outbreak of insurrection in the townships of the Vaal Triangle, South Africa's economic and political establishment was hailing what it believed was a breakout from the diplomatic and economic isolation that had undermined the economy since the Soweto uprising. Pretoria had just signed the Nkomati Accord of "non-aggression and good neighborliness" with the government of Mozambique. The direct result of South Africa's nine-year-long

220

policy of destabilization, military assault, and economic leverage, the accord was the first fruit of Pretoria's strategy of regional hegemony. Abroad, the signing of the Nkomati Accord was lauded, even by some of Pretoria's harshest critics, as representing a basic reorientation toward moderation, accommodation, and compromise.[2] At home, it was hailed as a "platform" from which South Africa's return to international respectability could be launched and, relatedly, as creating the circumstances in which the threat of international economic sanctions* would be nullified. A leading English-language newspaper, the *Sunday Times* of Johannesburg, usually critical of Pretoria, applauded P. W. Botha's foreign policy success the day following the signing of the accord: "The new alliances in Southern Africa will have a valuable spin-off benefit in the international arena by making the prospect of economic sanctions against South Africa—ever present for two decades—more remote."[3]

Diplomatic benefits to Pretoria of Nkomati were not long in arriving. One month after the signing of the accord, Prime Minister Botha was invited for official visits to Portugal, West Germany, and Great Britain. Botha's tour, which took place in June 1984 and eventually involved stops in six countries, represented the first time in over twenty years that a South African head of government had paid an official visit to Europe, and was the most extensive such trip since the National Party came to power some thirty-seven years earlier. "The fruits from the Nkomati Accord are beginning to ripen," declared one South African newspaper. Celebrating the implications of Pretoria's diplomatic breakthrough, it observed: "A completely new . . . game is under way and with so many new teams in the league it should be clear to all but the most dense of overseas observers that there is just no place on the field for purveyors of sanctions, boycotts, and disinvestment."[4]

Yet such optimism was wide of the mark. When in August 1984, just two months after the prime minister's European trip, the black townships of the Vaal erupted, the "fruits of Nkomati" shriveled. With political unrest returning on a massive scale to South Africa's townships, and with images of insurrectionary action and police response broadcast to the world via the electronic media, international attention swung rapidly away from Pretoria's regional policy and toward South Africa's domestic sociopolitical arrangement. The international response was swift and more intense than it had been after either Sharpeville or Soweto.

Anti-apartheid organizations in the industrial West, particularly in the United States and Great Britain, mobilized domestic support for public and private policies of economic pressure on South Africa. This response was especially rapid because the organizational infrastructure for such mobilization had been created at the time of Soweto. By the early months of 1985, anti-apartheid groups, particularly in the

---

*Technically, economic sanctions are *governmental* measures adopted by one state to achieve a political result in another state. Private actors can also make economic decisions which are intended to achieve political ends. Both public and private decisions of this kind constitute economic pressure. In contemporary discussions of South Africa, this technical distinction tends to disappear. The term sanctions is used as a synonym for economic pressure, and it encompasses both governmental *and* private acts. In this book, the term sanctions will be used to encompass any economic action of a state or a private actor, such as a business corporation, which is intended to put pressure on Pretoria in order to achieve some political result.

United States, were successfully pressuring large institutional investors like universities, churches, and city and state governments to shift the stock holdings of their endowment and pension funds away from corporations with operations in South Africa. By the end of 1988, dozens of colleges, twenty-three states, and over seventy U.S. cities had adopted "divestment" policies aimed at reducing or eliminating South African–related stock from their equity portfolios.[5]

Although American corporations with operations in South Africa were not directly affected by the divestment movement, these campaigns helped create a political climate in the U.S. conducive to severing business ties with the apartheid state. One result of this new political climate were procurement laws passed by various states and some of the largest cities. These prohibited the purchase by public agencies of goods and services from companies with South African operations. Since procurement restrictions threatened to exclude South Africa–tied companies from sizable sales markets, they constituted a significant addition to the opportunity costs of investing in or maintaining a South African exposure.

At the national level, too, pressure was building for the U.S. government to adopt sterner measures against Pretoria. By mid-1985 Congress was moving toward the passage of a relatively stringent sanctions bill, prompting President Reagan in September 1985 to issue an executive order containing milder measures—a prohibition on the sale of gold Krugerrands in the United States; a prohibition on the transfer of nuclear technology; a prohibition on computer sales to agencies that enforce apartheid; and a prohibition on new bank loans to the South African government. Although these were very mild measures—for the most part they prohibited things that had already ceased to occur*—the Reagan executive order represented an excellent barometer of the direction U.S. politics was moving on the South African issue. A president who was adamantly opposed to sanctions had been forced by the realities of popular and congressional politics to introduce punative sanctions measures.

Movement toward economic sanctions also characterized the Western European reaction to the South African insurrection. On September 10, 1985, exactly one day after the Reagan executive order, the European Economic Community adopted measures constraining economic intercourse between member states and South Africa. Nuclear collaboration, the sale of oil, and the export of computers to the security services were banned, and new scientific agreements were discouraged.

The actions taken by governments in mid-1985, although very significant as indicators of the posture that Western industrial states would increasingly take toward Pretoria, had less immediate impact than the lending policies adopted by private financial institutions. In July 1985 Chase Manhattan Bank informed its South African corporate borrowers that, contrary to customary practice, their short- and medium-term loans would not be renewed. Consequently, payment of the full principal as well as interest on outstanding debt was expected at the expiration of existing loans. A month later all the major international banks raced to follow suit.

*For example, loans by U.S. banks to the South African public sector had already fallen from $623 million in June 1982 to $217 million in June 1985.

By refusing to roll over their loans, the banks created both an immediate balance of payments crisis for Pretoria, since the central bank lacked sufficient foreign reserve to cover outstanding external obligations, and a nearly insurmountable barrier to new borrowing. The global economy's reaction to this predicament was a sharp drop of confidence in the South African economy, as was reflected in a nearly instantaneous decline of over 50 percent in the rand's value relative to the U.S. dollar.

As the South African insurrection continued into 1986, the governments of the industrial democracies of Western Europe and North America moved beyond the largely symbolic measures they had adopted in 1985 and significantly turned up the economic pressure on Pretoria. During July and August the U.S. Congress debated and then passed the Comprehensive Anti-Apartheid Act (CAAA). Among other things, this legislation prohibited U.S. firms from making new investments in or bank loans to the South African economy, and placed a U.S. embargo on the importation of several South African–produced goods. An attempt by President Reagan to block the intensification of sanctions by vetoing the CAAA was thwarted when the necessary two-thirds majority of both congressional houses was mustered in support of the bill. Particularly interesting as an indication of the support for economic sanctions in the United States was the fact that the Senate Republican leadership and a group of conservative Republican members of the House of Representatives joined with the Democratic majority to override the Reagan veto. Sanctions, which had represented a "left" political position in 1984 had, by mid-1986, become the dominant U.S. policy orientation toward South Africa. As noted in a speech to the Senate by Nancy Kassenbaum, Republican senator and chair of the upper house's subcommittee on Africa:

> Whatever the shortcomings [of sanctions legislation] . . . they are far less onerous than a failure to respond to the challenge of the present moment . . . to correct the South African misperception that it has tacit Western approval for its course of gradualist reform without political change, . . . to show white South Africans that intransigence will have tangible costs for them . . . [6]

At the same time that the U.S. Congress was ratcheting up the economic pressure on Pretoria, the European countries and the Commonwealth of Nations were doing likewise. In July and in October 1986 the European Parliament adopted a number of measures that paralleled the actions of the U.S. Congress. During the same period the governments of the Nordic countries took similar actions. Table 7.1 summarizes the range of sanctions adopted by industrial states by late 1986. Since the EEC and Commonwealth states differed in their political commitment to imposing sanctions, with some, such as Great Britain, adamantly opposed, these measures were unevenly implemented. Nonetheless, they represented both an intensification of the sanctions environment and an indication of the direction in which the political climate within industrial states was moving.

The diplomatic and domestic pressures that had produced the 1986 measures could be expected to push toward the implementation of sanctions in "laggard" countries. The South African National Union of Mines (NUM), for example, se-

TABLE 7.1. Government Economic Sanctions Against South Africa, 1986

Country	Direct Investment	Loans to SA Gov't.	Loans to Companies	IMF Loans	Import Embargo	Export Embargo
United States	banned	banned	banned	opposed	coal, steel, agric. prod., gold coins, uranium, textiles	computers for security force
European Community (voluntary)	banned	banned		opposed	coal, steel, agric. prod., gold coins	oil, computers for security force
Nordic Countries	banned	banned	banned	opposed	coal (Sweden), gold coins (all), agric. prod. (Norway) (Sweden), uranium (all)	oil (Norway) (Denmark), computers (all)
Commonwealth Countries (except U.K.)	banned	banned	banned		coal, steel, gold coins, agric. prod., uranium	oil, computers for security forces
Japan	banned	discouraged			coal, steel, uranium, gold coins	computers for security force

Source: Facts and Reports, October 1986.

cured the support of the Miners' International Federation (MIF) to strengthen implementation of the EEC's ban on South African coal imports.[7] Three Italian trade-union federations said they would block any local efforts to import coal from South Africa.[8] The possibility of "secondary boycotts" also affected South Africa's international economic situation by threatening actors who circumvented sanctions. The three largest Swiss banks, for example, were shut out of a big Euro-loan to Canada because they continued lending to South Africa after 1986.[9] Even Japan, usually seen as a primary means for Pretoria to circumvent the sanctions of the Western democracies, moved in the late 1980s to join the sanctions environment. The Japanese government, apparently sensitive to the fact that Japan had become South Africa's principal trading partner, urged all companies dealing with South Africa to exercise "self-restraint." In response, Japan's electricity supply companies, which had purchased 11 percent of their uranium ore from South Africa in 1987, announced in 1988 that they would phase out all uranium imports from the apartheid state.[10] A year later, a major South African uranium oxide producer announced it would cease operations because an unnamed customer, known to be Japan, had given written notice of termination of its agreement to purchase uranium oxide.[11]

Impact of Sanctions

By the end of 1986 South Africa was effectively cut off from international capital markets, and faced selective embargoes against some important foreign-exchange-generating exports. The South African economy had attracted no significant new inflow of direct investment during the entire decade of the 1980s, and after 1984 international bank loans, which had become the only real source of new foreign capital, began to dry up. Outstanding loans by U.S. banks to South Africa, which had increased from $3.7 billion to $5 billion between June 1982 and September 1984, decreased to just under $3 billion by the end of 1986, a drop of 41 percent. Lending by British banks also declined but by a much less dramatic rate.[12] Even the availability of commercial credits to South African importers was drastically curtailed, despite the fact that such trade financing was generally exempt from the lending prohibitions of government-imposed sanctions. As a trading economy with a relatively high proportion of its gross domestic product accounted for by exports and imports, South Africa requires short-term trade credits to offset variations in its foreign receipts and expenditures.[13] The shutdown of the commercial credit spigot, such as is revealed in Table 7.2, thus contained especially costly implications for the economy's ability to sustain necessary imports.

At the same time that South Africa's access to new capital was being drastically curtailed, foreign capital already within the South African economy began a quick exodus. Of the various means by which capital has left the South African economy, disinvestment, which has received the most attention, has had the least impact. Although between 1984 and 1989 some 184 U.S. firms and approximately 125 firms of other countries had pulled out of South Africa, the consequent loss of capital to the economy has been minimal. For the sale of these firms assets to South Africans has usually involved an arrangement for the extended repayment of the purchase price out of future profits. Hence the value of U.S. direct investment in

TABLE 7.2.   U.S. Commercial Credit to
South Africa (in millions of dollars)

Year	Letters of Credit	Nonbank credits
1983	$123	$142
1984	110	128
1985	112	80
1986	42	50
1987	11	76

Source: Report to Congress, *South Africa: Trends in Trade,
Lending and Investment* (Washington, D.C.: U.S. General
Accounting Office, 1988), p. 28.

South Africa was reduced by only 10 percent between 1982 and 1986, despite the significant degree of disinvestment.*

Nonetheless, while disinvesting firms have not withdrawn significant amounts of their capital from South Africa, the shedding of their South African subsidiaries makes it unlikely that they will put new money into the country. In addition, the extensive movement to disinvestment likely had a significant psychological impact with economic implications. This psychological effect on the economy cannot be easily measured, but the "disinvestment spectacle"—the apparent abandonment of South Africa by many of the world's leading industrial firms—helped cast a pall over South Africa's economic future and thus probably contributed significantly to an undermining of investor confidence.

Of far greater consequence then disinvestment was the decision by major international banks to recall their outstanding short-term loans to South African borrowers. Given that the actions of foreign governments and the preferences of private actors precluded access to the alternative sources of foreign capital that had been available in the early 1980s, the impact on net capital movement was devastating for the South African economy. Figure 7.1 shows the effect of the 1984–86 insurrection on the net flow of loan capital. As can be seen, the cumulative loss to the economy between 1984 and 1987—the result of loan repayments without the recourse to counterbalancing new lending—was over $4 billion. The total loss of capital from all sources during the same period was more than twice as large—25.2 billion rand, or approximately $10 billion at the 1989 rate of rand/dollar exchange (see Figure 7.2).

The economic strains created by a situation of accelerated debt repayment combined with blocked access to new foreign capital were exacerbated by trade

*The value in dollars of U.S. direct investment in South Africa dropped from $2.28 billion to $1.14 billion between 1982 and 1986. But this decline is almost entirely a function of the drastically devalued South African currency after August 1985. If the impact of exchange-rate changes on the value of investments is removed the decline was only to $2.10 billion in 1986. See Report to Congressional Requesters, *South Africa: Trends in Trade, Lending, and Investment* (Washington, D.C.: U.S. General Accounting Office, 1988), p. 29.

MOVEMENT OF INTERNATIONAL LOAN CAPITAL

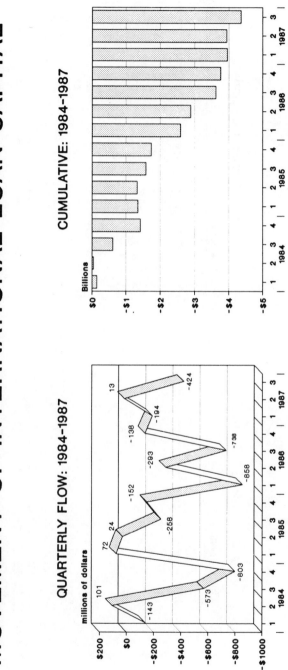

FIG. 7.1. Foreign exchange burden of debt repayment, 1984–1987 (*Source: South Africa: Trends in Trade, Lending and Investment* (Washington, D.C.: U.S. General Accounting Office, 1988), p. 25

FLOW OF CAPITAL FROM SOUTH AFRICA

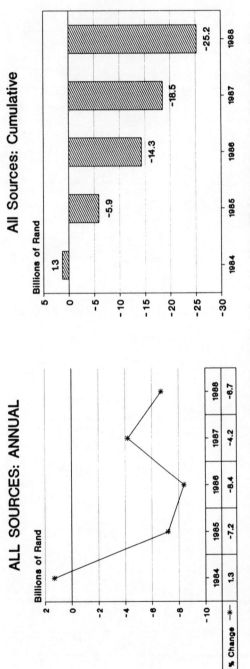

FIG. 7.2. Capital flight, 1984–1988 (*Source: Weekly Mail*, December 2–8, 1988, p. 19; *Weekly Mail*, March 17–23, 1989, p. 16)

sanctions. Embargoes on South African exports, although highly selective in respect to products and very unevenly implemented, nevertheless cost the economy in the form of foregone earnings and the loss of desperately needed foreign exchange. South African exports to the United States were cut by $624 million in the first nine months of 1987 alone.[14] Nedbank, a major financial house, estimated that in 1988 the adverse effect of trade sanctions was about 5 percent of export receipts.[15] The managing director of one of South Africa's major banks estimated that by mid-1988 the economy had lost $5 billion in export earnings as a result of trade sanctions.[16] Over time the impact of trade sanctions could be expected to increase. Derek Keys, the executive chairman of Gencor, South Africa's second largest mining-finance house, noted that coal sanctions could be expected to have only a limited short-term impact, since it takes time for competitors to gear up to displace South Africa from its overseas coal markets. "However," he pointed out, "longer term sanctions will, if nothing else, deprive us of the kind of growth we could otherwise have expected." Prior to the era of coal sanctions, studies had shown South Africa's future exports of steam coal doubling within a decade. "That," according to Keys, "is now at risk: other sources will probably supply that demand."[17]

The impact of economic sanctions imposed in response to the 1984–86 insurrection was exacerbated by the constrained state of the economy at the time the new wave of international pressure hit. Several constraints were a residue of sanctions imposed at the time of Soweto. For example, billions were invested in coal-to-oil synfuel plants in an effort to shield the economy from an international oil embargo,[18] in effect since 1979.* Additionally, billions were spent on premium prices charged by suppliers to evade the embargo, as well as on domestically produced synfuel, which cost nearly three times the world-market petroleum price in the mid-1980s. In 1986 Pretoria acknowledged that the oil embargo was costing the South African economy between one and two billion dollars per year, and a total of $22 billion since its imposition.[19]

Sizeable outflows of foreign capital, because they took place in the context of blocked access to new foreign capital, and in conditions of constrained export earnings and artificially high energy costs, undermined South Africa's prospects for economic growth. First, the economy was denied the new capital required for expansion. Of course, domestic savings could, in principle, substitute for lost foreign capital as a source of new investment. But problems inherent in a hostile international economic environment clouded future economic prospects, increasing the risks for investors whatever their nationality.† In the 1980s, South African investors appear to have become reluctant to undertake the risk involved in gambling on the country's future. "We should be opening more mines, putting up more plants . . . " the chairman of Gencor told *Leadership* magazine. "That we haven't . . . is because uncertainty has produced a lack of confidence."[20] Data on

*An embargo was announced by the Arab oil-producing states in 1973, but it lacked effectiveness until 1979 when, with the fall of the Shah, Iran joined in the embargo effort.

†In the semiannual rankings of credit reliability published by *Institutional Investor,* South Africa dropped by 49 percent between 1981 and 1987, from 62 on a 100-point scale to 31. *Institutional Investor,* a financial periodical, ranks 100 countries based upon anonymous ratings from the world's largest banking institutions. See *Weekly Mail,* February 2, 1989, pp. 26–27.

TABLE 7.3.   Growth in Real Domestic
Investment (percent)

1982	1983	1984	1985	1986	1987
−2	−3.7	−1.4	−7.2	−17.6	−2.8

Source: South Africa Reserve Bank Quarterly Bulletin, reported
in *Financial Mail*, April 17, 1989.

domestic investment reveal a consistent decline since 1981 (see Table 7.3). According to the South African Reserve Bank, real gross domestic fixed investment was 31
percent lower in 1987 than in 1981.[21] Capital investment as a proportion of total
output fell from 27.5 percent in 1982 to only 18.5 percent in 1987.[22] "Very few
investors are prepared to take a view of longer than two to three years," noted a
South African economist. "Risk taking investors cannot easily discount a future as
murky as ours."[23] One South African publication referred to a process of "domestic
disinvestment," noting that local companies "are not ploughing money back into
productive investment, and [are] reducing the value of their existing plant and
stocks,"[24] while at the same time they were investing billions abroad.* Thus,
because of the psychological impact of international economic sanctions—the sense
of pessimism and risk they cast over the future—the South African economy in the
1980s was not able to adequately substitute domestic for lost foreign investment.
The impact of sanctions which blocked South Africa's access to international capital
markets was consequently greater than just the loss of foreign capital.

A second growth-retarding consequence of post-1984 economic sanctions was
created by pressure on South Africa's balance of payments. The South African
economy depends heavily on imported producer goods and industrial components.
For growth to take place, the economy must have a surplus of foreign exchange with
which to pay for these vital high-tech items. Sanctions, however, struck at all of the
mechanisms available to obtain foreign exchange—new foreign direct investment,
access to foreign loans, and earnings from exports. With its foreign exchange
generating capacity limited by sanctions, Pretoria in the late 1980s had difficulty
simply meeting the demands of foreign banks for loan repayment. A foreign exchange surplus adequate to support sustained economic growth was thus
unavailable.

The external economic squeeze, in combination with the structural characteristics of the South African economy, produced a decade of economic stagnation
and decline. Figure 7.3 provides several indicators of this poor economic performance. From 1982 to 1987 average annual growth in GDP was only 1 percent,

*The largest such foreign investment involved Anglo-American's R12.5 billion 1987 takeover bid for
Consolidated Goldfields. South African firms do not count this as a form of disinvestment because the
capital being invested is not being earned in South Africa and therefore represents no loss to the country.
Yet, if these funds were brought "home" by the South African corporations they would certainly serve as
an economic stimulant. The failure of local firms to do this appears indicitive of their lack of confidence
in the long-term prospects of the South African economy.

ANNUAL RATE OF ECONOMIC GROWTH
REAL GDP PER CAPITA

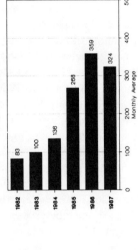

BUSINESS INSOLVENCIES
MONTHLY AVERAGE

REAL PER CAPITA INCOME
Index: 1975–1987

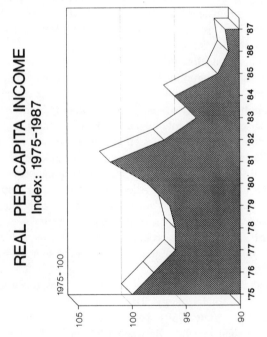

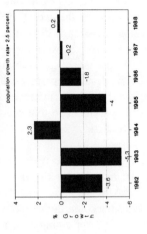

FIG. 7.3. Economic decline in the 1980s (*Source:* ABECOR, *Country Report—South Africa*, August 1988; *Weekly Mail*, August 5–11, 1988, p. 20; *Weekly Mail*, December 2–8, 1988, p. 19; *Weekly Mail*, February 10–16, 1989, p. 34)

considerably below the population growth rate of about 2.5 percent per annum. In three of these six years the economy actually shrunk, declining by more than 2 percent in 1985 alone.[25] Given the rate of population increase, the impact of stagnant aggregate GDP on personal incomes was dramatic. Per capita income slid downward after 1981, declining by 8.3 percent in real terms by the end of 1987.[26]

Micro-level indicators of economic crises and decline are equally dramatic. The average number of business insolvencies, as shown in Figure 7.3, were more than three times greater in 1986 and 1987 than in 1983. Employment generation and unemployment were also, not surprisingly, affected by the desultory performance of the economy. Between June 1984 and June 1987 the number of jobs in manufacturing declined by some 75,800, or 5 percent of total employment in that sector.[27] According to a 1986 report of the Central Bureau of Statistics, 291,000 jobs had been lost in the manufacturing and construction industries in less than ten years.[28] The actual unemployment situation is difficult to measure, since there is little agreement over numbers. The government's data is disputed by university researchers who place the actual unemployment rate for Africans at as much twelve times the official rate.[29] Nevertheless, the official data give some indication of the steep climb in unemployment rates in the post-1984 period. In a single year, between March 1985 and March 1986, the number of persons looking for full-time employment and those seeking part-time work both increased by nearly 80 percent,[30] The increase in "registered unemployment"* from 1984 to 1985 was 55 percent for people classified as African, 145 percent for Asians, 156 percent for "coloureds," and 114 percent for whites.[31]

South Africa's economic decline in the context of increasing international isolation contained several significant political implications. First, it held the potential to alter the white minority's "risk calculus" in respect to the issue of majority versus minority rule. Black political participation has been feared by South African whites in large measure because they view rule by the majority as a threat to their material standard of living; minority rule has been seen as a guarantee against such a threat. But in the mid-1980s international economic sanctions rendered minority rule a threat to white material well being, and made black political inclusion the condition for economic benefits in the future. The risks associated with majority rule have thus been relativized: the peril to white "standards" that was associated with a loss of white political control now becomes something that exists *because* of white control. In other words, sanctions that produce economic decline serve to bring the "fear of the future," under conditions of majority rule, into balance with the "threat of the present," under minority rule.

Second, economic stagnation has denied Pretoria the resources to adequately pursue all elements of its total strategy. The costs of its domestic and regional security policies soared in the late 1980s. The budget allocation for defense in 1987 was 218 percent higher than in 1984. Between 1986 and 1989 alone the defense budget grew at over thirty times the economic growth rate and twice the rate of inflation.[32] This brought the allocation for security to nearly one fourth of the total

*Out-of-work individuals who register with the government constitute only a small fraction of the total unemployed. In particular, African unemployed are in most cases unlikely to have registered.

national budget.[33] Given the desultory performance of the economy this high level of security spending jeopardized the other aspects of total strategy, especially domestic reform in which plans for physical upgrading, housing, and education require large-scale government outlays.

The reform effort, the financial cost of which was officially estimated to require an annual economic growth rate of from 5 to 7 percent,[34] is thus a third area where economic stagnation has had substantial political implications. Specifically, the lack of funds for school construction, housing projects, township electrification, and the like nullified the strategy of coopting a black middle class as a buffer against the forces pushing for majority rule. Likewise, the government was unable to follow through on its plans to reduce the political alienation of the black urban masses through an amelioration of their squalid living conditions. The latter situation is especially noteworthy, both in regard to its magnitude and in its relationship to the socioeconomic conditions conducive to outbreaks of insurrectionary activity. Given an annual increase in the labor force of more than 3 percent, estimates show that the economy needs to grow at more than 5 percent per annum if there is to be a reduction in the proportion of the labor force unemployed, and at over 6 percent for the absolute number of unemployed to be reduced.[35] The stagnating economy of the 1980s produced a situation in which unemployment among black South Africans, which stood at between 20 and 30 percent in the mid-1980s, could reach 50 percent by the turn of the century.[36]

We can see here the interactive nature of the trialectic of change: militant political opposition ("unrest") on the domestic front stimulates the introduction of international pressures, which through their impact on the economy help perpetuate the conditions conducive to future outbreaks of insurrectionary action. This process, as will be discussed later, threatens white living standards, and in so doing undermines the cohesiveness of support for minority racial rule, and saps the power and strength of the white state. In this manner a slow but steady redressing of the power imbalance between the organized expression of the black majority and the government of white minority rule was taking place.

"Positive" Measures

It is not by economic sanctions alone that the international community has played a role in altering the disparity in power between South Africa's majority and minority. Measures of diplomatic, financial, and technical support for organizations of the black majority also serve that end. Like the escalation of economic sanctions, an extension of such measures was part of the international community's response to the insurrection of 1984–86. Governments, business corporations, and private philanthropic foundations began to provide assistance to South African blacks. In 1984 the U.S. Agency for International Development (AID) initiated a South African program targeted specifically on the black population. In the first four years of its existence the program made some 500 grants, totaling $66 million, to projects mainly in the areas of legal defense, entrepreneurial training, and educational advancement.[37] The European Community acted similarly, channeling funds to a South African–based foundation, the Kagiso Trust, "to assist the victims of apartheid."[38] The Japanese government followed suit in 1987 with a modest contribution to Kagiso of approximately $400,000.[39] Founded in 1986 with R5 million, a staff of two, and approximately twenty-five projects, Kagiso—with its foreign funding— expanded rapidly. By 1989 it had an annual budget of some R30 million, a staff of twenty-four, offices in Johannesburg and three other cities, and was supporting approximately 1,300 projects.

Funding by foreign governments represented the largest component of new resources directed at South Africa's black community. But the funding of "social" and educational programs by business corporations, and the support for new community-based organizational initiatives by foundations like Ford, Carnegie, and Rockefeller in the United States, and Friedrich-Ebert-Stiftung in Germany, also increased substantially after 1984. The Ford Foundation alone contributed $3 million in 1987 and $5 million in 1989.[40] During 1987 about $250 million in grants and other forms of financial assistance came into South Africa from governments, multinational corporations, churches, and foundations to support a range of activities in the black community.[41]

Foreign funding for "victims of apartheid" has been a highly controversial subject within black politics. Critics have charged, among other things, that funding agencies are motivated by a desire to avoid imposing economic sanctions; that under the guise of being "nonpolitical," programs are designed to produce an educated professional black middle class and hence contribute to Pretoria's strategy of cooptation; and that donors are attempting to shape the political allegiances, social orientations, and economic values of recipients so as to facilitate the emergence of a politically "moderate" and capitalist-oriented black leadership stratum. Undoubtedly these criticisms are accurate to some degree, especially in respect to corporate funding. Nevertheless, the net effect of foreign funding has been to strengthen black opposition. It has increased the resources available to autonomous community-based organizations and provided technical training to a stratum of secondary leadership. These effects have taken place irrespective of the initial motives or designs of donors. For funding agencies, whether they be corporations, governments, private foundations, foreign universities, trade unions, and the like, were caught up in a political process that they could not control and which often shaped the nature of their funding of South African programs. In a sense, the "victims of apartheid" themselves began to define the nature of the assistance being offered.

Undoubtedly, many governments and business firms viewed "positive measures" of support to apartheid's victims as an alternative to sanctions,[42] but the record demonstrates that the pressure for sanctions was not effectively diverted in this way. Whatever the intent, "positive measures" turned out to operate in tandem with sanctions, rather than as an alternative to them. In respect to the "politicization" of external funding, foreign governments, as well as private foundations and institutions like universities, were indeed concerned that their activities within South Africa be "nonpolitical." They were also initially oriented to channeling their resources into large, established South African institutions with which they had a natural affinity. This translated into an early proclivity to look to "liberal" organizations of the white community, such as the English-speaking universities, as the agents for aiding the "victims of apartheid."

EMIGRATION/IMMIGRATION

1981 – 1986

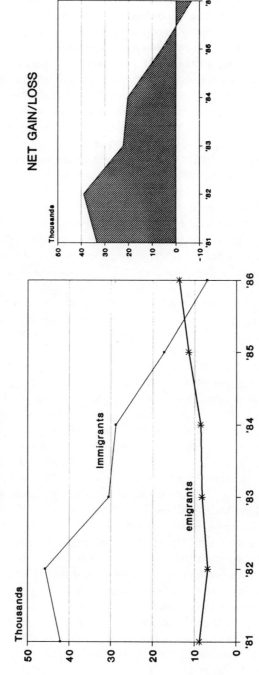

Fig. 7.4. Insurrection and white emigration (*Source: SA Barometer*, vol. 1, no. 2 [March 27, 1987], p. 26)

insurrection there occurred an upsurge in emigration, with the number of people departing the republic reaching 11,401 in 1985 and 13,711 in 1986. Immigration of whites into South Africa simultaneously fell dramatically, so that in 1986 emigration exceed immigration, producing a net loss of 6,717 persons.

For an economy and military already strapped for skilled manpower these trends had ominous implications. Not surprisingly, the people who were most likely to emigrate were professionals and technicians who could find a market for their skills abroad. This was largely the case in 1985 and 1986,[53] with the net loss of professionals (emigration over immigration) in 1986 amounting to 1,215.[54] Surveys conducted at South Africa's universities during 1987 reveal the extent of an emigration orientation among the young educated and professional sector of white society. At the University of Natal, some 32 percent of the students said they had decided to emigrate, and an additional 35 percent said they were considering doing so. At Rhodes University 57 percent of the white male students had either decided to leave South Africa or were contemplating emigration. In the business school at the University of Witswatersrand, some 80 percent of the 1988 graduating class were contemplating leaving, as were 100 of 220 graduates of the university's medical school. When asked why they might choose to emigrate, the main reasons cited by students were "political instability" (77.6 percent) and military conscription (56.1 percent).[55]

The latter finding points to another new, significant, and apparently rather extensive phenomenon in post-insurrection South Africa—the unwillingness of young white males to serve in the military. The South African government does not make the number of "draft evaders" public, but there are many indications that these numbers began increasing after 1984. The minister of defense revealed in 1989 that one-quarter of the citizen force and commando members called up to attend camps applied for deferment, while an additional 15 percent failed to report. He also said that 38 percent of citizen-force troops requested exemption from township duty.[56] The extent of resistance to military service among white males is also indicated by the seriousness with which officialdom treated the End Conscription Campaign (ECC). This white, UDF-affiliated organization seeking to encourage young men to refuse military service was denounced as a national threat by General Magnus Malan, the minister of defense. Speaking before Parliament in 1986, General Malan declared that "leftist radicals in South Africa with their anti-conscription campaign were doing the SADF, the country, and its people a great disservice and should stop the 'devilish' onslaught against the SADF."[57]

Rising emigration rates and reluctance to serve in the armed forces are indirect measures of a weakening confidence in the South African state. During the mid-1980s there were also many direct reflections of this increasing breakdown in the cohesion of the ruling white minority. One of the most dramatic of these was the birth of a new and unprecedented phenomenon in South African politics: the "trek to Lusaka." Delegations of prominent South Africans, respected members of the white social, economic, and political elite traveled outside the country for discussions about the future of South Africa with the exiled ANC leadership. What would become a recurring phenomena was initiated by a September 1985 meeting in Zambia between several executives of South Africa's largest industrial firms and the most senior members of the ANC's National Executive Committee. The discussions that took place, about the shape of South Africa's government and economy after the demise of apartheid, were described by one of the members of the business delegation as "amicable." While there was some disagreement on nationalization, he noted, "there was an overall feeling of South Africanism and, when we could not agree at least we agreed to disagree."[58]

Significantly, it was the business community, the segment of South African white society upon whom the indirect economic effects of insurrection had the most immediate impact, that led the way in initiating contacts with the ANC. But other segments of the white "establishment" soon followed. As indicated in Table 7.4, in relatively short order, delegations containing prominent clergymen, academics, politicians, journalists, students, farmers, professionals, and sportsmen left South Africa to meet with high-level ANC officials, discussing subjects ranging from the future of the universities to constitutional designs for a post-apartheid South Africa. At first, participants were primarily from the English-speaking segment of white society and delegations were small. But by the end of 1986 Afrikaners were joining the "trek to Lusaka" in increasing numbers, and the small meetings were being replaced by large conferences, such as the July 1989 parley in which over 100 white South Africans traveled to Lusaka to confer with senior members of the ANC.

Not surprisingly, Pretoria vehemently opposed these talks between prominent members of the white establishment and senior officials of an organization whose promotion it had made a criminal offense and whose members it had branded terrorists and murderers. When in November of 1985 a group of clergymen representing various branches of the Afrikaans Dutch Reformed Church announced a planned meeting with the ANC, State President P. W. Botha subjected them to harsh public criticism. "If these naive discussions with this terrorist organisation continue in spite of the appeals by the head of state and his ministers," he warned, "it will amount to a defiance of the state's authority."[59] Through indirect and direct pressure on individuals, such as by threatening to withdraw passports, Pretoria was able to prevent several planned meetings from taking place. But what is really significant is that Pretoria's efforts to intimidate potential participants, at first somewhat successful, particularly among Afrikaners, had utterly failed in its objectives by 1987, as Table 7.4 reveals. South Africans from virtually all segments of white society were trekking in greater numbers and with increasing frequency to meet with ANC officials.

The political consequences of the "trek to Lusaka" were several. First, the meetings with ANC officials served to alter in a favorable direction the attitudes of at least some whites toward the dominant political group among black South Africans. The participants in virtually every meeting returned to South Africa with reports of frank but cordial discussions, and of a deep and positive emotional experience. The "trek" thus demystified and "de-demonologized" the ANC, reducing white apprehension about the prospect of the ANC playing a significant role in South Africa's future, and correlatively rendering less threatening a restructured political system based upon some form of majority rule. Of course, only a tiny percentage of the white population actually undertook the "trek," but those who did were important political actors and/or opinion leaders in the white community.

TABLE 7.4. The "Trek to Lusaka" Meetings with the ANC

Date	Delegation
September 1985	Major industrialists and journalists: Gavin Relly (Anglo-Ameircan), Zac De Beer (LTA Construction), Tony Bloom (Premier Milling), Peter Sorour (South African Foundation), Hugh Murray (publisher, *Leadership*), Harald Pakendorf (editor, *Valderland*), Terius Myburgh, (editor, *Sunday Times*)
November 1985	Progressive Federal Party: Dr. Frederik van Zyl Slabbert (party leader), Colin Eglin (foreign affairs spokemen), Peter Gastrow (member of parliament), Dr. Alex Broaine (deputy leader)
November 1985	University of Stellenbosch students: Student Representative Council (SRC) president, student newspaper editor, Dutch reformed church minister, student chaplain. Meeting cancelled when passports are withdrawn prior to departure from South Africa. Dutch Reformed Church: six ministers. Meeting cancelled when government says passports will be denied.
December 1985	Thirty-seven South Africans: mostly church leaders (including the Anglican and Roman Catholic archbishops of Cape Town) but also including five Stellenbosch University students and four University of Cape Town students.
January 1986	Federated Chamber of Industries (FCI)
March 1986	National Union of South African Students (NUSAS): eight-member delegation, including students from seven English-speaking campuses and one Afrikaans-speaking campus.
April 1986	Southern African Catholic Bishops Conference: four-person delegation led by Archbishop Denis Hurley.
September 1986	Joint delegation from University of Cape Town (UCT) and University of the Western Cape (UWC): including the vice chancellor, deputy vice chancellor, and dean of the medical school at UCT; and the rector and vice rector of UWC.
January 1987	Afrikaans Legal Scholars: professors Henning Viljoen and Johann van der Westhuizen of University of Pretoria, and Professor Derek van der Merwe of Rand Afrikaans University (RAU). Government pressure leads to cancellation.
May 1987	International Business Executives
July 1987	Institute for a Democratic Alternative in South Africa (IDASA) organized delegation of fifty, mostly Afrikaans-speakers: including members of Parliament, academics, journalists, teachers, artists, and a farmer.
September 1987	Prominent white South Africans: including Dennis Worral, former NP member of Parliament and ambassador to Great Britain; Tommy Bedford, former Sringbok rugby player; and Richard Steyn, editor of the *Natal Witness*.
July 1989	Four Freedoms Forum: 130 white South Africans

Source: S.A. Barometer, vol. 1, no. 15 (September 25, 1987), pp. 227–30.

The "trek" phenomenon also served to nullify Pretoria's objective of isolating the ANC domestically and internationally. By picturing the ANC as a communist and terrorist organization, Pretoria sought to push the organization, and those associated with it, beyond the pale of respectable political discourse both inside and outside of South Africa. The most significant blow to this strategy was struck during the insurrection of 1984–86, when the ANC emerged as the leading organization of opposition to white rule. Then, when the "trek" phenomenon resulted in respected white "moderates," powerful industrialists, and prominent churchmen publicly acknowledging the significance of the ANC in South Africa's future, and describing ANC officials in respectful and cordial terms, the spectrum of political discourse within white politics was widened. What had been unmentionable, if not unthinkable, now became a viable position within white politics. A press release issued at the conclusion of a meeting with the ANC by fifty, mostly Afrikaans-speaking, white South Africans captured the essence of this new stance: "What we share . . . is a common belief that serious discussions with the ANC must form part of the search for the resolution of conflict and the transition towards a peaceful and just future."[60]

In addition to fostering pluralism in South African politics, the meetings between ANC leadership and establishment white South Africans facilitated the ANC's legitimation internationally. Did it make sense for the U.S. government, for example, to shun the ANC when the CEOs of South Africa's largest corporations and leaders of major religious organizations were acknowledging the organization's centrality to their country's future. Thus, Pretoria's effort to render the ANC a PLO-like political leper in Western diplomatic circles was undermined.

A third significant aspect of the "trek" phenomenon is that it both reflected and fostered an erosion of government control. The efforts of Pretoria to stop the meetings—efforts that included public denunciations that amounted to charges of treason*—revealed the state as unable to control the manner in which white South Africa would deal with the growing black opposition. The spectacle of some defying government threats gave others courage to do likewise. When P. W. Botha warned a group of clerics that if they met with the ANC "it will amount to a defiance of the state's authority," he failed to stop future meetings. Instead, he inadvertently defined the situation in such a way that the "trek" phenomenon was transformed from simply a cordial meeting with Pretoria's opponents into both an indication and an instrument of the erosion of state authority.

The presence of Afrikaners at talks with the ANC meant that in addition to the general pluralization of white politics, the "trek to Lusaka" was also indicative of a disintegration in the cohesiveness of Afrikaner political unity as embodied by the National Party. Afrikanerdom had experienced a significant split "to the right" in 1982 when hostility to the reform of apartheid led to the formation of the Conser-

---

*A planned meeting between Stellenbosch University students and members of the ANC Youth League led P. W. Botha to appeal to all South Africans not to lend credibility and status to the ANC. "If they proceed with their plans," the president said of the student leaders, "they would at least owe an explanation to the security forces on the borders and inside the country who fight and die for the maintenance and enhancement of the principles of democratic governing structures, freedom, and justice." See *S.A. Barometer*, vol. 1, no. 15 (September 25, 1987), p. 227.

vative Party. The impact of the insurrection on white politics contributed to a split "to the left," as prominent Afrikaners began to doubt the viability of the NP's vision of reform. "The NP cannot transform South Africa from its present state of stagnation, crises, structural inequality, international isolation and apartheid into a country of prosperity, international respectability, fairness and good hope for all its people"—so wrote a man who until early 1987 was a respected Afrikaner academic and a leading National Party intellectual.[61]

One manifestation of this disintegration in Afrikaner unity and NP cohesiveness was the emergence, in 1985, of "New Nats," a circle of Nationalist members of Parliament who were willing to entertain discussion of a future based upon majority rule, and even suggest that the ANC would be part of that future. Several would bolt the party in 1987 to run against National Party candidates as independents in that year's parliamentary elections. Another manifestation of the "split to the left," was the public abandonment of the NP by several dozen prominent Afrikaner intellectuals and academics prior to the 1987 parliamentary elections. This rupture in National Party ranks began with the resignation from the party of Sampie Terreblanche and James Fourie, two of the most respected Afrikaner academics and both professors at Stellenbosch University. Terreblanche, an economist, eminent party theoretician, close advisor to the minister of constitutional development, and vice chairman of the state's South African Broadcasting Corporation, said in his resignation statement: "For many years I placed my academic freedom and integrity at risk in order to lend credibility to the Government's alleged reforms. . . . [Now] I have become convinced that the Government does not possess the will or the vision to bring about appropriate reforms."[62] The NP suffered another significant defection when Dawid de Villiers announced he would support the party's opponents in the 1987 election. De Villiers had been managing director of Nasionale Pers, a powerful Afrikaans newspaper company and ally of the governing party. In the late 1960s he had led South Africa's legal team at the World Court in defense of South African rule over Namibia.[63]

The pluralization and fluidity that the insurrection directly and indirectly produced in white politics was also reflected in the arena of parliamentary electoral politics. Figures 7.5 and 7.6 display changes in white parliamentary representation and electoral politics. The ruling National Party, whose political hegemony seemed unchallengeable in the beginning of the 1980s, had by decade's end lost substantial ground in both popular vote, and parliamentary seats. In 1989 the NP faced two main challengers. To its right was the Conservative Party, which had broken away from the NP in 1982, and which stood for a return to unreconstructed, i.e., unreformed, apartheid. On the NP's left stood the Democratic Party (DP). It had been launched in 1989 out of merger between the Progressive Federal Party (PFP)—the party of "English-speaking liberalism"—and two very minor political parties that were essentially the personal vehicles of dissident Nationalists who had abandoned the NP in 1987. The PFP dissolved itself in favor of the Democratic Party in an attempt to resuscitate the opposition within Parliament, to attract what were believed to be increasingly large numbers of disaffected Nationalist Afrikaners, and to build a better relationship with the extraparliamentary opposition. The DP envisioned a South African political order featuring a "universal adult franchise in a

PARLIAMENTARY ELECTION RESULTS
Percent of Seats and Votes, by Party

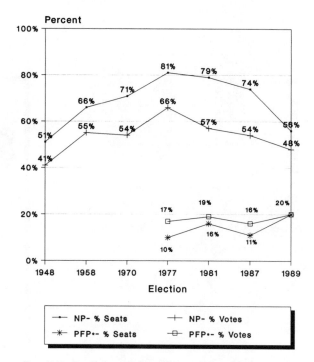

FIG. 7.5. Declining National Party electoral hegemony

federal system," in which the federal units would be based on "regional and demographic divisions, . . . not on race." Proportional representation was favored "to ensure that minority political interests were also given expression."[64]

In the 1989 general election the NP lost ground to both the Conservative and Democratic parties. It emerged from the election with its smallest parliamentary majority since its initial victory in 1948, and with a minority of the popular vote (see Figure 7.5). In contrast, the electoral performance of the Democratic Party strengthened the position of the "liberal" opposition to white supremacy. Its 20 percent share of parliamentary seats and of the popular vote represented an increase over the showing of the Progressive Federal Party (PFP) in the 1987 general election. It should be noted however, that the increase in proportion of total vote received by the DP was only one percent higher than had been obtained by the PFP in 1981. If, as seems reasonable, the DP can be considered to have stood for more substantial political change than did the NP in 1989, then these results did not indicate a groundswell of white opinion in favor significant and rapid alteration of the status quo.

Figure 7.6 examines this data from another perspective. The column graphs distribute parliamentary seats and popular vote in respect to three positions on the continuum of political change, and allow a comparison between the situations in

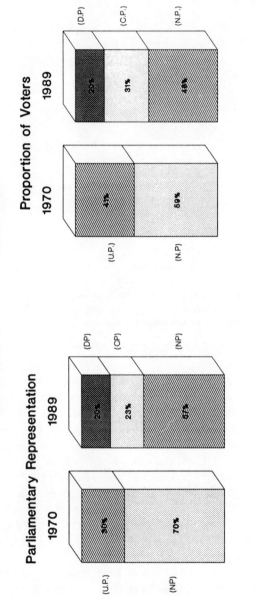

SHIFTING POLITICAL ORIENTATIONS
Positions on White Rule

Parliamentary Representation

1970

1989

(U.P.)

30%

(DP)

20%

(NP)

70%

(CP)

23%

(NP)

57%

Proportion of Voters

1970

1989

(D.P.)

20%

41%

(C.P.)

31%

(U.P.)

(N.P)

59%

(N.P.)

48%

Majority Rule/
Minority Guarantees

Change/white
Control

Pure
Apartheid

Fig. 7.6. Minority vs. majority rule in South African electoral politics

1970 and 1989. The pluralization that has occurred in white politics can be clearly observed. In 1970, fully 70 percent of the members of parliament and almost 60 percent of the voters supported pure apartheid (the National Party position). The remaining seats in Parliament and share of the popular vote, which went to the erstwhile United Party (UP), can be associated with a desire to change away from apartheid, but in a manner that would preserve white control of the political system.* In 1970, there was no parliamentary contingent that favored majority rule, even with extensive protection for the white minority. The contrast in 1989 was stark: the majority-rule position, as embodied in the Democratic Party, was represented in one out of five parliamentary seats and a like percentage of popular votes. The "change while maintaining white control" position, associated with the opposition United Party in 1970, was represented in 1989 by the ruling National Party, with nearly 57 percent of the seats in parliament and 48 percent of the popular vote. And a commitment to unreconstructed apartheid, which was professed by 70 percent of MPs and almost 69 percent of the voters in 1970, was in 1989 relegated to only 23 percent of parliamentary representation and less than one-third of the electorate. A position associated with unfettered majority rule, however, was still absent from the parliamentary spectrum.†

Summary

The insurrection of 1984–86, and the international repercussions that it wrought, introduced a pluralism and fluidity into white politics that did not exist a decade earlier. The process of breakdown in the political cohesion of Afrikanerdom, and in the tacit acceptance of the socioeconomic and political status quo by much of the rest of white society, had begun with the shock of the Soweto uprising. It was greatly accelerated by the insurrection of 1984–86 and its international repercussions. Yet it would be a mistake to read an end of consensus as constituting a major transformation in white political orientations, i.e., as the emergence of a new consensus in favor of majority rule.

At the end of the 1980s fears of the implications of majority rule continued to run high among the white population. A 1988 survey revealed that over 80 percent of white urbanites believed majority rule, in which blacks could form the government, would threaten the property and physical safety of whites, produce a decline in white living standards, lead to discrimination against whites, escalate crime, and undermine law and order.[65] The basic thrust of white political attitudes in the late 1980s appeared to be less a commitment to a vision of an altered South African sociopolitical future, than a longing for a return to stability, "law and order," and prosperity. At any particular moment, the strategy that appeared best able to deliver

*The United Party favored a "qualified franchise" for people of color. The application of income and educational qualification to the right to vote had been the basis of black political incorporation in the Cape Colony during the nineteenth century.

†Of course the tripartate division of white opinion, while it may accurately reflect the center of gravity of the political parties, does not reflect variations within the parties. Pluralism was thus more extensive and probably wider in scope than was represented in Figure 7.6.

these received support. Thus, Pretoria's imposition of a state of emergency in 1986 was broadly supported within the white community, and by some of the most reform-minded business people. Likewise, the National Party, running on a platform of guaranteeing white *security,* scored an impressive victory in the 1987 parliamentary elections. Two years later, when these promises proved hollow, the NP suffered one of its greatest electoral setbacks.

Thus the opening up of the South African political arena to new positions, and the weakening of the National Party's grip on the Afrikaner community, did not translate into a new consensus on the need for fundamental political change, at least as that was defined by most black political groupings. The demand for a nonracial democracy, based upon one-person, one-vote majority rule in a unitary state, was eschewed by all organizations within the spectrum of parliamentary politics. The preference of the parliamentary "left" during the 1980s, as before, was for federalism, in which the strong central state that characterized the period of minority rule would be replaced by a weak central state in the event of majority rule. This suggests that the basic thrust of the parliamentary left during the 1980s was to search for a formally nonracial means to guarantee established white privileges under conditions of a mass franchise. While a new pluralism emerged in white politics during the 1980s, a new consensus had not formed to replace the disintegrating consensus on white rule and apartheid.

Notes

1. See Leon Trotsky, *1905* (New York: Random House, 1971), p. 102.

2. See, for example, Flora Lewis, "South Africa Watershed," *New York Times,* March 22, 1984, p. 23; and, also Stephen S. Rosenfeld, "Clark Kent in Africa," *Washington Post,* March 23, 1984, p. 15. For the official U.S. view of the changes wrought by Nkomati, see Chester A. Crocker, testimony before the Subcommittee on African Affairs of the Senate Foreign Relations Committee," reprinted in *Current Policy,* no. 619 (September 12, 1984), Department of State, Bureau of Public Affairs, p. 4.

3. *Sunday Times,* March 18, 1984, reprinted in *South African Digest,* March 23, 1984, p. 21.

4. *Natal Mercury,* May 5, 1984, reprinted in *South African Digest,* May 11, 1984, p. 21.

5. See Ann Micou and Sheila McLean, *U.S. Support Organizations Raising Money for South Africa Causes,* South African Information Exchange Working Paper #6, Institute for International Education, May 1989, p. 3.

6. Quoted in Pauline Baker, *The United States and South Africa: The Reagan Years* (New York: Ford Foundation-Foreign Policy Association, 1989), p. 44.

7. See *Southscan* (South Africa), March 15, 1989.

8. See *Southscan,* November 11, 1989; see also, *New Nation* (South Africa), November 17, 1988.

9. See *Star,* March 2, 1989.

10. See *Financial Times* (UK), November 3, 1988, p. 6.

11. See *Star,* November 21, 1988.

12. See United States General Accounting Office, Report to Congressional Requesters,

South Africa: Trends in Trade, Lending and Investment (Washington, D.C.: General Accounting Office, 1988), p. 25.

13. See Stephen R. Lewis, *The Economics of Apartheid,* (New York: Council on Foreign Relations Press, 1990), pp. 71–72.

14. See *Financial Times* (UK), June 25, 1988, p. 2.

15. "Chairman's Annual Statement," in *Leadership,* vol. 7, no. 6 (1988), p. 48.

16. See Roger Thurow, "South Africa Facing a No-Growth Future," *Wall Street Journal,* July 26, 1988, p. 31.

17. Interview, *Leadership,* vol. 7, no. 6 (1988), p. 30.

18. See Lewis, pp. 103–04; see also *Sunday Star,* April 16, 1989.

19. See Lewis, p. 103.

20. Interview, *Leadership,* vol. 7, no. 6 (1988), p. 32.

21. See Ronald Bethlehem, "High Stakes," *Leadership,* 2nd ed., 1989, p. 9.

22. South African Reserve Bank, Annual Economic Review, quoted in *Weekly Mail,* September 2, 1988, p. 14.

23. Edward Greller, "The Crystal Ball's too Murky to Tempt Big Risk-Takers," *Weekly Mail,* March 31–April 7, 1988, p. 16.

24. See *Weekly Mail,* January 16–22, 1987, p. 13.

25. See *Weekly Mail,* March 31–April 7, 1988, p. 16.

26. *Weekly Mail,* December 2–8, 1988, p. 19.

27. See *Weekly Mail,* March 17, 1989, p. 16.

28. See South African Institute of Race Relations (SAIRR), *Race Relations Survey, 1986* (Johannesburg: Institute of Race Relations, 1987), p. 718.

29. Ibid.

30. Ibid.

31. SAIRR, *Race Relations Survey, 1985* (Johannesburg: Institute of Race Relations, 1986), p. 134.

32. See *Weekly Mail,* Special Supplement, "Focus on Human Rights," December 9–15, 1988, p. 11.

33. Ibid.

34. Estimate by Jan Lombard, deputy governor of the South African Reserve Bank, quoted in Mark Swilling and March Phillips, "The X Factor," *Weekly Mail,* September 2, 1988, p. 9.

35. Pieter Le Roux, "The Economics of Conflict and Negotiation," in Peter Berger and Brian Godsell, *A Future South Africa* (Boulder: Westview Press, 1988), p. 228.

36. Ibid.

37. See *American Grantmaking in South Africa: A Conference Report* (Washington, D.C.: Council on Foundations and Henry J. Kaiser Family Foundation, June 6 and 7, 1988), p. 21.

38. See Martin Holland, *The European Community and South Africa* (London: Pinter Publishers, 1988), p. 118.

39. Ibid., p. 121.

40. See, Sheila McLean and Rona Kluger, *U.S. Foundation Giving To Enhance Educational Opportunities for Black South Africans,* South African Information Exchange, working paper #1, Institute of International Education, November 1987, p. 3; and interview with Ann Micou, South African Programs, South African Information Exchange, Institute of International Education, October 5, 1989.

41. See *Washington Times,* March 14, 1988, p. B8.

42. See Holland, *The European Community and South Africa,* p. 116.

43. Guidelines Adopted by the Carnegie Corporation Meeting on 16 October 1985 for the

Provision of Aid from American Foundations and Universities to Education Institutions in South Africa, unpublished.

44. See "Black South Africans Propose Guidelines for Aid," *The Chronicle of Higher Education,* December 10, 1986, p. 1.

45. See ibid.

46. Ibid., p. 118.

47. See Ann Micou, *U.S.-Related Corporate Trusts in South Africa,* South African Information Exchange, working paper #5, Institute of International Education, May 1989, pp. 7–12.

48. Ibid., p. 8.

49. Ibid., p. 11.

50. Ibid., p. 12.

51. *Washington Times,* March 14, 1988, p. B8.

52. See *S.A. Barometer,* vol. 1, no. 7 (June 7, 1987), p. 101.

53. See *Weekly Mail,* October 31–November 6, 1986, p. 4.

54. *S.A. Barometer,* vol. 1, no. 2 (March 27, 1987), p. 26.

55. See *Weekly Mail,* December 9–15, 1988, special supplement, p. 11.

56. See *BBC Monitoring Reports,* April 21, 1989; repr. in *ANC Newsbriefing,* April 23, 1989, p. 6.

57. *Hansard,* (A) 7 cols 2160–2161, quoted in SAIRR, *Race Relations Survey, 1986,* p. 808.

58. *S.A. Barometer,* vol. 1, no. 15 (September 25, 1987), p. 227.

59. Ibid.

60. "Dakar Press Statement," *Democracy in Action,* news bulletin of the Institute for a Democratic Alternative for South Africa, August 1987, p. 3.

61. Sampie Terreblanche, "A New Government," *Leadership,* vol. 6, no. 2, 1987, p. 18.

62. *Financial Times* (Br), February 23, 1987, p. 3.

63. *Guardian* (Br), March 22, 1987.

64. See SAIRR, *Race Relations Survey, 1988/89* (Johannesburg: Institute of Race Relations, 1989), pp. 659–65.

65. *Financial Mail,* October 7, 1988.

8

Pretoria's Response: From Autarky and Counterrevolution to Negotiations

"Total strategy" had been Pretoria's response to the Soweto uprising and the altered politico-economic environment of the 1970s. The reform of apartheid, the center-piece of that strategy, was supposed to eliminate the socio-economic conditions that gave rise to political unrest, while simultaneously insulating South Africa from diplomatic pressure and economic sanctions by bringing the country's social order into line with international standards. The failure to achieve these goals in the mid-1980s produced a policy response from Pretoria that, many have argued, indicated an abandonment of the South African government's total strategy and an about-face on its reform orientation. As will become clear, Pretoria's policy response to the insurrection of 1984–86 can be viewed instead as a tactical shift; an alteration in emphasis within a strategic vision whose basic assumptions and goals remained the same.

Its desire to escape international isolation, and the related need to stem external efforts to impose costly economic sanctions, constrained Pretoria's instinct to confront the mass uprising with the full force of its repressive capability. The general unpreparedness of the security forces to deal with the scale and ferocity of the uprising also contributed to the inconsistent and haphazard manner in which repression was initially used against the insurrection. The result of this combination of factors was that Pretoria's use of the police to restore "law and order" was sufficient only to act as an irritant in the situation, and served to expand and accelerate insurrectionary action. Thus the insurrection reached its height of militancy and achieved it most stunning organizational successes—the creation of the structures of "people's power"—during the partial state of emergency that was imposed in July 1985 and lasted through March of the following year.

While widespread detention of political activists and the deployment of police and even army units in the townships failed to impose "order," producing instead an escalation of "disorder," South Africa's international dilemma intensified. As occurred in the aftermath of both Sharpeville and Soweto, militant black opposition and heightened repression at home intensified the threat of sanctions from abroad. The imposition of the July 1985 state of emergency was not only a disastrously unsuccessful effort to control the mass uprising, it also galvanized European and American elites into pushing for economic sanctions. "The recent declaration of a state of emergency in South Africa," wrote Congressman Stephen Solarz, a senior member of the U.S. House of Representatives' Foreign Affairs Committee, "should have removed any lingering doubts that we can gently persuade the South African Government to abandon apartheid, and instead advance racial justice by joining other countries in applying economic pressure against South Africa."[1]

For twenty-two months after the breakout of insurrection in August 1984, the South African government adhered closely to the course it had adopted at the beginning of the decade. It hastened to introduce promised but long-stalled reforms in an effort to convince "moderate blacks" and the international community of the credibility of its commitment to change. More reform policies were introduced in the eighteen months between January 1985 and July 1986 than during the previous six-year period.[2] And the changes introduced in the midst of insurrection represented the major items on the reform agenda that had been under discussion since the late 1970s. The pass laws and the influx control sections of the Group Areas Act were abolished, as was the Immorality and Mixed Marriages acts and the Prohibition of Political Interference acts. Other reforms of this period included opening the central business districts of major cities to all races, the extension of freehold land ownership to urban Africans, the repeal of the limits on African residence and employment in the Western Cape, the official commitment to stop the practice of forced removals, and the relaxation by the central government of forced race segregation in hotels, restaurants, and public amenities.

In introducing reforms, Pretoria was as much attempting to thwart the intensifying movement for international sanctions as it was seeking to defuse the insurrection.* But it had little more success with its international audience than with its domestic one. Pretoria's dilemma was the same as it had been for the past decade. Its limited vision in respect to what it would change, and the conservative pull of much of the Afrikaner community, produced reforms that—while constituting real changes—fell far short of the expectations of the black community. And these were rising rapidly as a by-product of the spreading mass uprising. Thus the announcement in February 1986 that the pass laws and much of the group areas influx-control measures were being scrapped was received with relative indifference by the black opposition. Its attention was now on political change, and Pretoria's promises in that respect were so ambiguous, limited, and hedged as to have no impact. When in January 1986, P. W. Botha had announced the establishment of a multiracial National Statutory Council to serve as a forum for negotiating a new constitutional order, even so-called moderate black "leaders"—homeland officials and township

---

*Pretoria's efforts to convince the Western industrial democracies of the credibility of its commitment to genuine change included a live television broadcast to Europe and America of P. W. Botha's address to the annual Natal Congress of the National Party. Dubbed the "Rubicon" speech by officials, this August 1985 address was supposed to indicate to the world the crossing of a major threshold in respect to change.

mayors—refused to serve. Having failed to persuade significant elements of the black political leadership to endorse its reform program, Pretoria's efforts to dissuade the international community from sanctions were nullified. Even the conservative Reagan administration had told Pretoria in August 1985 that if sanctions were to be avoided "your country's blacks must perceive the forthcoming racial reform as promising real progress."[3]

Altering Course

Amid escalating insurrection and intensified sanctions, Pretoria's calculus of the costs of repression changed. Two elements were involved. First, once sanctions became a reality, the constraining effect of trying to avoid their imposition disappeared. And second, at a certain point, the threat to the state's authority was perceived as entailing greater costs than would be imposed by threatened international pressure. By mid-1986, with the insurrection increasingly characterized by alternative governing structures and a psychology of revolutionary euphoria, and with new sanctions by the United States and Europe apparently unavoidable, that point of transition in Pretoria's cost calculus was reached. The new perspective can be observed in the following editorial that appeared in early June in *The Citizen,* a newspaper with close ties to the government:

> We say the challenge to the authority of the State has become too real, too dangerous, for anyone to believe that the forces of insurrection can be fought with kid gloves. . . . *[Government] must do what has to be done without worrying any more about the effect on overseas opinion.*[4]

Four months later, after the U.S. Congress overrode President Reagan's veto of the Comprehensive Anti-Apartheid Act, *The Citizen,* in an editorial titled "Free at Last" revealed how the reality of sanctions as opposed to the their threat, altered Pretoria's calculus in respect to domestic repression.

> Now that severe sanctions are our lot . . . there are some things we don't have to do any longer.
> We don't have to look over our shoulders to see whether what we do pleases or displeases the United States or other Western governments.
> Doves in the Government have cautioned. "Don't do this or that because the Americans will think we're cruel, nasty, oppressive and will impose stiff sanctions against us." Now we don't have to worry any longer whether the Americans understand us, or accept our bona fides. . . . *Sanctions, bitter though they are, have freed us from the restraints imposed by those who wished to placate the United States, to placate the West, to buy more time, to avoid tough action against us.*[5]

From Repression to Counterrevolution

As *The Citizen* editorial indicates, faced with an increasingly powerful insurrection and the inevitability of sanctions, influence within the South African government shifted away from those ministries most sensitive to the international repercussions of Pretoria's actions. Government agencies and ministries responsible for security—military and civilian intelligence organizations, the police and the army, the ministries of law and order, interior, and justice—ascended to a dominant position within Pretoria's policymaking apparatus. Their organizational mission, the reestablishment of domestic security, became the government's top priority. The National Security Management System (NSMS), in development since the late 1970s, was made operational (see Chapter 3). After mid-1986 the State Security Council (SSC), upon which sat the chiefs of the major security agencies, emerged as the most powerful government policy body. It had responsibility for developing a broad strategy for reimposing "order," and it had sufficient control over the state's bureaucratic and financial resources to translate that strategy into policy.

In essence, the South African government under the direction of the "securocrats," as the personnel of the NSMS would come to be called, began to take seriously the dictum set forth by Samuel Huntington in a 1981 address to the Political Science Association of South Africa: "reform and repression may proceed hand-in-hand."[6] Effective repression, in this view, enhances the prospects for change under state auspices. It reduces the appeal of radicals by rendering their cause costly, if not hopeless, while diminishing the appeal of reactionaries by demonstrating the government's ability to maintain order.[7] In this way the basis is laid for acceptance of reform on the state's terms.

The securocrats' strategy was neither antithetical to, nor a reversal of, the reform program adopted in the late 1970s. Rather, it emphasized that there were political prerequisites for the success of that program that required an intensified, focused, and carefully designed companion program of repression. But the political situation in which this dual reform-repression program had to be introduced meant that the securocrat's conception of required policy went considerably beyond Huntington's notions about the "limited" use of repression against radicals. Under conditions of widespread mass insurrection, as existed in South Africa by 1986, the commitment to heightened repression was folded into a broad and systematically conceived counterrevolutionary "security regime."

The first major manifestation of this new "regime" was the imposition, on June 12, 1986, of the second state of emergency to be imposed since the beginning of the insurrection. It differed in many significant respects from the earlier version. At the most basic, the definition of the task to be accomplished was different. The first emergency represented, essentially, an ad hoc police attempt to prevent large public manifestations of mass mobilization. The second involved an explicit and multifaceted state strategy of counterrevolution. Although the state's use of coercive power would escalate substantially after June 12, Pretoria's security planners, consciously following the lessons taught by successful theorists and practitioners of twentieth-century revolution,* viewed repression as the foundation of a strategy that

---

*In May 1988, the State Security Council distributed a pamphlet to politicians and functionaries of the NSMS entitled *The Art of Counter-Revolutionary Warfare*. Its introduction contains the observation: "A governing power can defeat any revolutionary movement if it adapts the revolutionary strategy and principles and applies them in reverse." See Mark Swilling, "Whamming the Radicals," *Weekly Mail*, May 20–26, 1988, p. 15.

was also socioeconomic and political in scope. "There should be absolute inte-grated action between security and so-called welfare," noted Roelf Meyer, deputy minister of law and order, during a discussion of the government strategy in the post–June 12 period. "Security and welfare are really integrated as far as counter-revolutionary activities are concerned. . . . If one studies revolutionary struggles elsewhere in the world," he pointed out, "[one learns] that the two must be ad-dressed simultaneously and totally to achieve success."[8]

An examination of statements by officials and documents written and distributed by the NSMS indicate that the South African version of counterrevolutionary doc-trine had four basic elements: "The first step," according to the SSC's manual *The Art of Counter-Revolutionary War,* is the "annihilation" of the enemy, which "involves the relatively simple task of seeking out the enemy and destroying him."[9] The second step involves removing the socioeconomic basis for alienation among the masses. Major General Bert Wandrag of the South African Riot Police Unit put this point succinctly: "Drastic action must be taken to eliminate the underlying social and economic factors which have caused unhappiness in the population. . . . The only way to render the enemy powerless is to nip the revolution in the bud by ensuring there is no fertile soil in which the seeds of revolution can germinate."[10] The third step is to "win the hearts and minds" of the masses. This is done through the creation of a "good working relationship between the administration and the masses," that is sustained by identifying "problems locally . . . and implementing corrective measures." It also involves extensive programs to train "loyal leaders," and "the youth" for local administration.[11] The fourth and final step is the creation of "counterorganization" at the community level, which is "the main weapon against revolutionaries. . . . The government must take the lead in all groups, classes, clubs and societies with the organisation of social, career, sport, education, medical, religious and military activities. . . . The population must become in-volved and identify with the group's activities."[12]

The SSC was the "brain" of the counterrevolutionary security regime, and its operational arms constituted the other basic elements of the NSMS. The working committees and secretariat provided coordination among government ministries, departments, and agencies, and in principle had the political clout to break through bureaucratic rivalry and inertia so as to mobilize required resources and deliver them in a timely fashion. The far-flung network of Joint Management Centres (JMCs), each headed by a military or police officer, were the "line organizations" of the counterrevolution—they were to adapt counterrevolutionary doctrine to particular local conditions and integrate repressive, socioeconomic, psychological, and ideo-logical policies "on the ground." An example of how this was supposed to work is provided by a researcher who described the response of the Cape Town JMC to the "revolutionary climate" in the "coloured" township of Atlantis:

> The JMC was given the task of formulating a counter-strategy [to the UDF-affiliat-ed resident's association]. It accordingly organised food parcels for the hungry, soccer tours for the children. The communications committee organised pamphlets and newspaper coverage. The social, economic, and political committee ensured that local politicians in the formal system were seen at the forefront; i.e., the ("coloured") management committee was given the credit—but it was simply a front.[13]

The National Security Management System, according to Major General C. J. Lloyd, chairman of the SSC secretariat, had been developed "to manage and marshall the resources of the country" for a counterrevolutionary strategy at the national, regional, and local levels. It was concerned, Lloyd noted, with three basic targets—the government (self-criticism and correcting shortcomings); the enemy ("command, coerce, and eliminate"); and the "masses" (whose support had to be won through communication and education).[14]

Stripped of doctrinal rhetoric, Pretoria sought to accomplish four interrelated objectives with the security regime it initiated in June 1986: to eliminate the radical black opposition that was represented domestically by the UDF and its affiliates; to upgrade the physical and social infrastructure of selected townships; to reintroduce and legitimate community and town councils; and to gain the participation of "moderate" (some would term them "collaborationist") black leaders in the National Statutory Council through which a new political/constitutional dispensation would emerge. These objectives can be inferred from government policy under the state of emergency. They can also be found in the statements of important government officials. Take, for example, the minister of law and order's summary of the state of emergency's "main goals": "[I]mposing security police actions to bring short-term stability to black townships; upgrading living conditions for blacks, and finding a political solution that will give South Africa's 23 million blacks a role in governing the country."[15]

The directly repressive aspect of the new security regime attacked the black opposition at the mobilizational, organizational, and psychological levels. The state sought to eradicate the successful mobilization campaigns that had characterized the insurrection. This meant not just preventing mass political meetings and funerals, as had been the focus of the 1985 emergency, but eliminating worker stayaways, consumer boycotts, school boycotts, and rent strikes. Hence in December 1986 Pretoria introduced emergency regulations that made it illegal to "encourage members of the public . . . to take part in a boycott action against any firm . . . [or] any particular product, . . . [or] against any particular educational institution." In the same emergency regulation, encouraging people to refuse to pay rent or to participate in a political stayaway was declared a subversive act.[16] To choke off any communication that might spread or facilitate mobilizational activities, Pretoria declared it illegal

> to publish news or comment on . . . any "restricted gathering" [i.e., any public political meeting] insofar as such news or comment discloses at any time before the gathering takes place the time, date, place and purpose of the gathering.[17]

Also illegal was publishing news or comment about

> any boycott . . . insofar as such news or comment discloses particulars of the extent to which such boycott is successful or the manner in which members of the public are intimidated, incited or encouraged to take part in or to support such action or boycott.[18]

In cracking down on the mobilizational aspects of black opposition, however, Pretoria was striking at the symptoms of the insurrection. What the government really desired was to crush the uprising's organizational base. Consequently, the security apparatus zeroed in on the structures of "people's power." The government, said Adriaan Vlok, minister of law and order, will pay particular attention to dismantling the "alternative governmental structures—[including] people's courts, protest education, street committees and para-police groups." These "governments within the government" he added, posed the "most serious threat to law and order."[19] In the words of P. W. Botha, "It's subversive to create alternative organizations in South Africa for the education of people, for local government, for proper economic development."[20] In keeping with Botha's view, the state sought to have participation in alternative structures punished as the ultimate political crime. UDF community leaders from the Transvaal township of Alexandra were charged with treason for their roles in organizing and operating organs of "people's power." At their trial the state prosecutor laid before the court the extent of their treasonable deeds:

> For the first time in our history people took it upon themselves to create unconstitutional courts of law. From backyards in Alexandra the so-called comrades usurped the functions of the police with anti-crime campaigns, and from local authorities by re-naming streets and schools and by setting up alternative structures of self-government, and the judiciary by operating "democratic people's courts."[21]

Although in this instance the judge rejected Pretoria's definition of treason and acquitted the UDF activists, the state was able under its emergency regulations to subject those organizing and participating in alternative structures to the lesser but still very serious criminal charge of subversion. Under emergency regulations adopted in December 1986 it became an act of subversion to, among other things, "exert power and authority in specific areas by way of structures purporting to be structures of local government, . . . or to establish such structures, or to support such structures."[22] It was also deemed subversive "to subject [oneself] to the authority of [alternative] structures, or to make payments due to local authorities to such structures."[23] Because the National Education Crisis Committee's effort to introduce "people's education" directly threatened the counterrevolutionary goal of "winning hearts and minds," the alternative structures in the education field were of particular concern to the securocrats. According to Adriaan Vlok, "If you look at the type of education they want for South Africa, this is the kind of revolutionary thing they are trying to spread. . . . We don't have any fight with black people who want to change their education system, but they must do it in an orderly way *with the government*."[24] The concern of the securocrats is reflected in two emergency decrees directed specifically at the NECC's program. One outlawed all but officially approved courses; the other forbade all meetings held under NECC auspices where people's education was discussed.[25]

The new security order established under the legal umbrella of the state of emergency was also intended to deal with the psychological dimension of the insurrectionary upheaval; to undermine the revolutionary euphoria that had, by 1986, swept the black community. The ruthless use of the state's repressive apparatus was intended to lower expectations. The lesson Pretoria hoped to teach was that South Africa was not on the verge of majority rule or "liberation" and that therefore a less complete form of political inclusion should be accepted. According to Stoffel van der Merwe, minister of constitutional planning, the state's security actions under the state of emergency "are meant to send out signals to show that we are prepared to go [up to] a certain point in the move towards power-sharing and no further. . . . We are saying to those who now refuse to negotiate that if they want to have a part of the power, they are going to have to compromise."[26]

The second basic objective of the security regime, to physically upgrade black townships, was of course identical with a major objective of the reform program initiated in 1978. The difference is that under the counterrevolutionary strategy, goals were to be made consistent with fiscal realities, and control of the upgrading process by local JMCs would supposedly cut through the usual inertia and turf battles of government bureaucracy. Rather than spread scarce resources countrywide, funds for upgrading would be channeled to several dozen of the worst urban "trouble spots." During 1987–88, R3.2 billion reportedly was spent on some thirty-four selected townships. P. W. Botha, in a speech to parliament, indicated that there were plans to spend an additional R16 billion on improving another 200 townships.[27] By concentrating resources and operating a "crash program" of coordinated interagency action, rapid and dramatic improvements would supposedly be made, permitting Pretoria to finally demonstrate the benefits of its reform program to the alienated majority. In at least some of the townships slated for special treatment the physical evidence of this approach was quickly apparent. In Alexandra, for instance, an observer noted in early 1989:

> Amid the mess [of the huge Alexandra slum], there are signs that real progress is being made. . . . Bulldozers, mechanical diggers and teams of labourers dig trenches for water and sewers and blocks of candy-coloured flats are beginning to spring up among the shanties. An extension to the township has sprung up— hundreds of spanking new houses which . . . would not be out of place in many commercial township developments in Britain.[28]

The new security regime's emphasis on effectiveness and efficiency in the upgrading process represented a new twist to a decade-long strategy; but the political assumptions were still those that had dominated NP thinking since the 1979 Riekert Commission Report. First, upgrading urban slums into stable ghettos of black middle-class homeowners was supposed to produce a sociological buffer against radicals and revolutionaries. "We believe that if a person owns his own house," explained Colonel Goeffrey Holland-Muter, head of the Alexandra JMC, "he will not tolerate stonethrowing, or petrol-bombing in the vicinity."[29] Second, control of the sale and rental of residences was seen as a crucial source of revenues and patronage for local government structures. Eddie Makeba, the mayor of Duncan Village, to which he had recently returned after having fled in August 1985, waxed enthusiastic about the situation in early 1987: "We are very pleased with the way in which the upgrading is going," he explained to a visiting journalist.[30] The scene that the journalist described outside the mayor's office may explain his ebullience:

> Outside the office of Eddie Makeba, there is always a long line of supplicants. They may wait for hours, even the whole day, without seeing Makeba. . . . But if he

does not come, they will have to return the next day, or the next. *For anything from a house to a burial plot, residents have to get his personal approval.*[31]

In giving community councillors credit for upgrading and providing them with control over resources, Pretoria sought to reintroduce the town councils and establish them as viable local government units. The achievement of this, the third objective of the post–June 12 security regime, was threatened by rent strikes that had begun in the Vaal Triangle in 1984 and which had spread to at least fifty-seven townships by the end of 1986.[32] By mid-1986 the state had lost over R250 million in withheld rents.[33] Since rents were the major source of town council finance, restoring proper rent payment was a prerequisite for their viability. Moreover, the refusal to pay rents represented an overt rejection of council authority by township residents. Not surprisingly, therefore, breaking the rent strikes was a priority of the security regime. A JMC document, entitled "Strategy for the Collection of Arrear Rental and Service Charges," describes how "local collection action groups" made up of councillors, policemen, and JMC officials will be formed "to use all available means to collect rentals in arrears."[34] The document stresses that in ending rent strikes "no acknowledgement through negotiations must be given to revolutionary groups or organizations. . . . All actions are to be taken in mini-*Gesamentlike Bestuursentrums* [local constituencies] and [in that] context . . . within the ambit of the National Security Management System."[35]

The elimination of radicals by repression, the lowering of revolutionary expectations, the establishment of viable local government authorities—these would provide the foundation for achieving the fourth objective of the security regime. Town councillors would now, presumably, be willing to come forward and join homeland leaders on the government's National Statutory Council. Supported by a "depoliticized" new urban middle class, and with radical critics silenced, these moderate "black leaders" could "negotiate" a power-sharing constitution with Pretoria that would be accepted as legitimate by the international community. Such, at least, was the logic of the counterrevolutionary policies adopted by Pretoria to deal with the insurrection.

"Annihilating the Enemy"

Although the counterrevolution had four interrelated objectives, the success of the first objective—repression of the black opposition—was the essential prerequisite for the achievement of the other three. Consequently, the securocrats focused primarily on the elimination of insurrectionary action, the destruction of alternative structures, and the deflation of liberatory expectations. Their systematic campaign of repression combined a number of elements that in both their intensity and combination were new to the South African scene.

First, the manpower available for deployment in the townships to enforce the state of emergency was expanded. Mainline troops of the South African Defence Force assumed a major and permanent role in township control, in some cases surpassing the police as the primary enforcers of "law and order." The most highly politicized of the townships and the ones in which UDF organization was most extensive were placed under virtual military occupation, with troops patrolling streets and occupying school grounds.[36] During the emergency, Pretoria also accelerated its plans to provide local government structures with their own municipal police forces. As military occupation of the townships provided cover for the return of the community councillors, thousands of new municipal police were put at their disposal. By late 1987 there were over 9,000 of them, of which at least 4,000 had been recruited after the declaration of the 1986 state of emergency.[37] The latter, called *kitskonstabels* (instant police) by the township residents because of the meager training they received, were recruited from the rural areas so that they lacked social ties with the urban population. Intended to provide the shield against urban unrest that the councillors had lacked in 1984–85, the *kitskonstabels* quickly developed a reputation for extreme brutality and indiscipline as they assisted in reimposing community council rule on the urban areas.[38]

A second element of the heightened repression under the new state of emergency was an intensified campaign to apprehend and detain political activists. In the eight months between the imposition of the emergency and the end of 1986, more than 29,000 persons* were placed in detention.[39] The extensiveness and vehemence of this repressive surge can be gauged by comparing what occurred in mid-1986 with earlier repressive episodes in South African history. Figure 8.1 offers such a comparison. If detentions can be considered a measure of the extent of state repression, then the 1986 emergency was almost three times more repressive than the period following Sharpeville, twelve times more repressive than the immediate post-Soweto period, and nearly four times greater than that experienced during the 1985 state of emergency. The significance of these detentions lay not just in their number, but also in who was being imprisoned. Essentially, Pretoria sought to eliminate both the leadership core of the insurrection and the rank-and-file personnel of its organizational base. A security-force "dragnet" was thrown over the townships in an attempt to snare the members of the UDF regional and national bodies, the leaders of its affiliated functional and civic associations, and the young comrade activists of the street committees and people's courts. Over 75 percent of detainees in 1986 and 1987 were from the UDF and its affiliates, and 40 percent were persons under the age of eighteen.[40] According to the Port Elizabeth Human Rights Trust, the minister of law and order attributed a majority of detentions to membership in street and area committees, with the second largest category of detentions relating to participation in people's courts.[41]

A third element of heightened repression in the period after June 1986 involved what was in effect the banning of numerous UDF-affiliated organizations.† Already severely disrupted by security-force operations and by the detention of much of their personnel, opposition organizations were struck another blow in early 1988 when

---

*This is the estimate of the Detainees' Parents Support Committee (DPSC), the organization generally thought of as the most reliable monitoring agent of political detentions. The government's figure for detainees is several thousand lower, because it does not include those detained for fewer than thirty days. The total figure for detainees includes approximately 25,000 persons detained under emergency regulations and 4,132 persons detained under provisions of the Internal Security Act. See *S.A. Barometer*, vol. 2, no. 3 (February 26, 1988), pp. 36–37.

†Several black opposition organizations associated with Black Consciousness philosophy and the Pan Africanist Congress were also targets of government restriction.

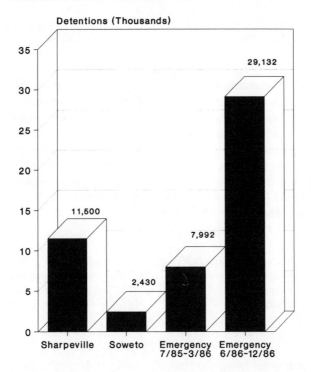

Detentions (Thousands)

FIG. 8.1. Periods of repression—number of persons detained (*Source: SA Barometer*, vol. 1, no. 1, p. 10; *SA Barometer*, vol. 2, no. 3, p. 37; South African Institute of Race Relations, *Race Relations Survey, 1985*, p. 517)

Pretoria, acting under the Public Safety Act, restricted virtually all their activities. Thirty-two organizations, including the UDF national and regional bodies and the NECC were prohibited from "carry on or performing any acts whatsoever,"[42] other than routine bookkeeping functions. At the same time COSATU, while not limited to the same extent as other popular organizations, was restricted from engaging in what a police spokesman called "external political activities."[43] The list of "restricted" organizations encompassed the country's main civic associations, youth and student groups, associations for the support of detainees, independent organizations of teachers in state schools, and the End Conscription Campaign. Minister of Law and Order Vlok explained that the new restrictions were necessary because "revolutionaries and other activists, realising that confrontation and violent revolution could not succeed, had created alternative strategies for achieving their goals."[44]Since other repressive actions had already curtailed the mass mobilization aspects of the insurrection, Vlok was apparently referring to the continued influence of the UDF on the political psychology of the township populace. In an interview some months earlier, he had outlined officialdom's perception of the problem:

> Only the visible signs of unrest—the stone throwing, the petrol bombing and so on—have died down. *But the propaganda war is continuing.* . . . Although we

have been able to curb the visible signs of unrest, the revolutionaries have stepped up their propaganda war against the country. We have seen this in the townships.[45]

Evidence that the "revolutionary political atmosphere" of the townships had remained relatively unchanged—to Pretoria, the result of a successful "propaganda war"—was found in the failure to achieve officialdom's main medium-term political goals. Despite the fact that by the beginning of 1988 the townships had been under a state of siege for nineteen months, there was little evidence that town councillors were being accepted as legitimate and credible community leaders, or that the anticipated willingness of homeland leaders to participate in a national negotiating forum had materialized. Stoffel Botha, minister of home affairs and Natal leader of the National Party, alluded to this political failure of the security regime when he argued in late 1987 for the introduction of further restrictions on the spread of "revolutionary propaganda" via the media:

We have fully committed ourselves to giving black people a say in government. How it is to be done is a matter for negotiation. Government is appealing to black people to come and sit around the table and talk. The door has been thrown wide open, but the radicals are not interested. . . . They are only interested in the total overthrow of the system. The media regulations are part of our efforts to stabilize the situation so that we can carry on with our reform programme.[46]

The new and severe restriction measures were meant to facilitate a more receptive environment for Pretoria's perspective on political change. With the main community-based organization rendered inoperative, their potent impact on the political orientation of township residents would, in theory, be nullified.[47] In other words, restricting the UDF organizational infrastructure was a means to eliminate the political culture of liberation as a necessary step to its replacement by a culture of cooptation.

Pretoria's assault on anti-apartheid organizations was supplemented by a campaign of covert harassment, disruption, and assassinations. According to the South African Human Rights Commission, between 1984 and the beginning of 1989 there were 113 attacks—bombings, arson, and burglaries—against opposition organizations or the buildings in which they have their offices.[48] Most of these attacks occurred after the declaration of a state of emergency in June 1986. The most dramatic was the powerful bomb blast that destroyed COSATU House, the Johannesburg headquarters of the Congress of South African Trade Unions, on May 7, 1987. The government denied involvement in this and any of the other bombings, fires, or thefts. But the fact that these attacks occurred when the targeted organizations were under close security-force surveillance, and the fact that not a single arrest was made, provides strong circumstantial evidence for state involvement in the covert war against the anti-apartheid opposition. So too did the state's failure to make a single arrest in a string of deaths, under mysterious circumstances, of prominent anti-apartheid activists, both within South Africa and abroad. The existence of a covert war against the state's opponents was publically revealed in early 1990, when retired officers in military intelligence disclosed their involvement in a secret campaign of political assassinations, under the auspices of the euphemistically named Civilian Cooperation Bureau.

In the counterrevolutionary doctrine adopted by the NSMS, preventing mass meetings, detaining individuals, and banning people's organizations was only one side of the repression coin. The other side involved creating grass-roots "counterorganizations" to occupy the social space vacated by the routed "people's" organizations. Operating at "street level" like the UDF's street and area committees, such organizations were better suited than the security police to thoroughly root out radicals and serve as a check against their reemergence. Thus the SSC's counterrevolutionary manual speaks of the counterorganization as "the main weapon against revolutionaries," and explains that "self-defense militias" are the "most important part of counter-organisation of the masses." The militias were intended to serve as a "bridge between the administration and the masses and . . . should therefore be politically oriented, [in order to] influence/mobilize the masses."[49]

The doctrinal notion of counterorganization was operationalized through a phenomenon that anti-apartheid activists termed vigilantism. Under the umbrella of the 1986 state of emergency, loosely organized mobs rampaged through many black townships in search of known UDF sympathizers, members of street and area committees, and participants in people's courts. Smashing, burning, beating, and killing, the vigilantes moved from house to house, block to block, driving many comrades into hiding and terrorizing the local population into providing information on the identity and whereabouts of activists who had eluded the security forces. A detailed personal account of events in Kwanobuhle, a township outside of the Eastern Cape industrial city of Uitenhage, is provided by the wife of a UDF area committee member. She recounted that a van pulled up outside her house and about eight people got out.

> They broke every pane of glass in the house . . . they took out my six piece lounge suite, the room divider, TV, generator, hi-fi, double bed, children's beds, all my linen, curtains, blankets, sheets, lamps and ornaments. They chopped these up with axes, and the furniture they could not remove—such as the wardrobes and the fridge—they smashed up inside with axes. . . . They removed all my husband's clothing . . . and made a pile of all our smashed belongings on the pavement outside. [Then two more vehicles pulled up, men alighted and] took paraffin from my primus stove, poured it over my smashed belongings and lit them.[50]

The Port Elizabeth Human Rights Trust, on the basis of close observation and over forty eyewitness affidavits, issued a report about the Kwanobuhle events. It concluded:

> Kwanobuhle has been plunged into month after month of murder and assault by the Ama-Afrika vigilantes who appear to be immune from prosecution. Statement after statement confirms their commitment to assault after assault—but, somehow, despite any number of witnesses, assaults and murders by the Ama-Afrika continue as the police make no effort to prosecute the organisation they have sponsored to power in their attempt to immobilise the UDF.[51]

The working relationship between vigilantes and the security forces, implied in the above, is a recurring theme of eyewitness reports wherever vigilante activities have occurred. Typical are the following observations of Tony Weaver, a reporter for the *Cape Times,* covering the attack by the *Witoeke* vigilantes on the KTC squatter camp outside Cape Town:

> I watched as three Casspirs and two Hippos [popular names for armored personnel carriers used by security forces] moved in front of a crowd of more than 1000 vigilantes and led them into KTC for the attack. . . .

> With police moving in front, the vigilantes first attacked the Zolani Centre, focal point of aid distribution to the estimated 33,000 refugees. . . .

> I watched as the police stood by and observed the vigilantes torching the Zolani Centre. . . .

> I watched later in the day as police Casspirs moved ahead of vigilantes, firing teargas and birdshot at KTC residents trying to defend their homes against vigilantes. . . .

> I watched as the vigilantes milled around the Casspirs and the police waved to them and cracked jokes.[52]

The sociopolitical basis for the vigilante phenomenon was created by the intra-black community conflicts that were submerged within the insurrectionary challenge to the state. Vigilante leaders and activists emerged from the ranks of those groups that lost out in the drastic social and political changes that insurrection wrought within the township communities: black policemen who saw their colleagues killed, their homes burned, and their social status destroyed; urban gangsters who once controlled the township streets at night, and whose power and livelihood were undermined by the young comrades and their street committees; local notables and influentials, many of whom were part of the community council system, who were pushed aside in the rise of alternative structures of people's power; councillors and mayors who had their lives threatened and property destroyed by militant youth; small businessmen who were allied with the community councillors, and who experienced the brunt of the class conflict aspects of the insurrection; traditional authorities who were ignored by the UDF popular organizations, and whose bases of authority and organizational control were directly threatened by the spread of UDF legitimacy and organization; and, sometimes, erstwhile UDF supporters who lost out to rivals during the process of political development that characterized the insurrection.

The particular social identity of the vigilante leadership varied from area to area. In the Kwanobuhle township a local businessman whose shop had been burned in 1985 emerged as the leader of Ama-Afrika. There was also a connection there to the displaced town councillors, as was revealed by the graffiti that Ama-Afrika scrawled on the gutted ruins of the house of Kinikini, a councillor who had been killed by the "necklace" in 1985— "Kinikini Is Alive & Coming to Revenge."[53] In the Western Cape the *Witoeke* were formed and led by a local influential who had earlier supported the UDF. In Natal's Durban and Pietermaritzberg townships the vigilantes were organized by the Inkatha movement of the KwaZulu homeland government, led by Inkatha warlords and staffed by "impis," the vigilante movement's paramilitary wing. Probably nowhere else in South Africa had the insurrection pitted modern legitimacy against traditional authority as it did in the Zulu-speaking area of Natal. The spread of UDF organizations into the Natal urban areas had weakened, and threatened to displace, the powerful Inkatha political machine. In this way the UDF's success threatened to deny Chief Buthelezi and the Inkatha leadership the uncontested political base among Natal's Zulu population that was essential if they were to claim a role in South Africa's political future. The state of emergency offered Inkatha an opportunity to retake lost ground, as it could rely upon the tacit cooperation of the state in the pursuit of a shared objective: the destruction of the UDF structures.[54]

The insurrection was a revolutionary assault on the state and on the privileges of white society, but it was also a revolution *within* the social system of the black townships. Like all revolutions this one had its losers: people who suffer drastic losses in power, status, and wealth. It was from these that Pretoria recruited its leadership for the "self-defense militias" or vigilantes. The ranks of counterorganizations like Ama-Afrika and the *Witoeke* were filled, as far as can be determined, by individuals who resented the reign of the comrades and their proclivity for intimidation, and especially by the numerous uneducated and unemployed street toughs—the real "lumpen proletariat" of South African society. Ironically, many of this latter element had earlier swelled the ranks of the comrades, and probably was responsible for much of the insurrectionary intimidation and bullying that alienated community members and worried the UDF leadership. Caring more for the excitement of action and the opportunity to intimidate and brutalize than for political goals or ideology, this essentially antisocial element of township society rapidly switched from comrade to vigilante when the June 12 state of emergency offered opportunities for the latter and imposed great costs on the former.

Countering International Pressure

At the same time that it moved aggressively against the insurrection and the organizational infrastructure of domestic opposition, Pretoria sought to insulate itself from global pressure. This involved attempts to limit the degree to which domestic events catalyzed international actions, to reduce the impact of the trade embargoes imposed during 1986, and to restructure the South African economy so as to reduce its vulnerability to future sanctions.

Breaking the Media Connection

Aware that anti-apartheid politics in North America and Western Europe was fueled by media images of revolt and repression within South Africa, Pretoria sought to prevent these images from being transmitted. In this way the connection between domestic unrest and international reaction could be short-circuited. Before the state of emergency went into effect, restrictions on the press were extensive, but as one legal expert on South African censorship put it, "The rules were harsh but the Press could work within them, and often get the story out."[55] The issuance of emergency media regulations (EMR) after June 1986 altered this game fundamentally, making getting the story out difficult and dangerous, if not impossible. Under the EMR the media was legally barred from covering the mass political movement and the actions of the security forces in response to it. Specifically, journalists, photographers, and news organizations were prohibited from being at or near the scene of "unrest"; reporting on the actions and conduct of the security force (military, police, and municipal police); publishing so-called "subversive statements," defined to include descriptions of consumer boycotts, rent strikes, political stayaways and school boycotts; publishing any information relating to the treatment and condition of detainees; and publishing articles and statements whose content "encourages revolution." Transgression of the EMR could lead to a fine of R20,000 or a ten-year prison sentence, and the seizure or suspension of the offending publication.[56] Pretoria also refused to issue visas and work permits to foreign journalists whose coverage it deemed threatening to its interests.

The clampdown on the press accomplished its immediate objective: within several months foreign press and especially television coverage of South Africa dropped dramatically.* An important link in the connection between Pretoria's domestic political problems and its international economic difficulties appeared to have been cut.

Evading the Cost of Sanctions

While blocking the flow of information abroad was a means of avoiding an escalation of international pressure, Pretoria's primary concern was with limiting the impact of economic sanctions. Partly, this involved devising mechanisms to evade trade embargoes. A new government unit devoted to "sanctions busting" was created; efforts were made to shift trade toward countries in Asia and Latin America whose domestic politics made their adherence to sanctions unlikely; and "dummy" firms, which could be used for the trans-shipment of goods, were established in third countries. Such policies represented an intensification of efforts that had begun in the early 1980s, when the fallout from Soweto raised the specter of trade sanctions.[57]

What was new in the post-1986 response to the sanctions environment was an effort to reduce South Africa's dependence on the international economy and thus to limit Pretoria's future vulnerability to global pressure. Economic autarky, or self-sufficiency, would nullify the international community's power in respect to South Africa's domestic situation; it would constitute an escape from the pincer effect of domestic and international pressure that had prevailed since the late 1970s. The method for achieving this objective was an economic strategy that Pretoria termed *"inward industrialization."*

---

*It is difficult to determine how much of the drop in press coverage can be attributed to the media regulations, and how much resulted from the successful repression of mass mobilization. In part the reduction in foreign media coverage was undoubtedly a result of the fact that the situation in South Africa was now less "newsworthy."

Economic sanctions, already blocking access to international sources of capital and potentially threatening imports of technology-embedded producer goods, were now viewed as providing South African business with the incentive for import substituting industrialization. Government enhanced the incentives for domestic capital formation by fiscal and monetary policy, and sought to enlist the energies and resources of the private sector in the new development effort with promises of deregulation and privatization. As producer-goods import substitution would provide a new lease on life to manufacturing, which had been in the doldrums since the mid-1970s, the move away from traditional statist economic policy was supposed to stimulate the informal economy within the black townships. A thriving informal sector would provide lucrative business opportunities for a new black middle class, and would soak up some of the endemic black urban unemployment. In Rhodesia during the late 1960s and early 1970s sanctions had stimulated rapid economic growth; in South Africa in the late 1980s sanctions would stimulate not only growth but the restructuring of the economy away from international dependence and toward greater autonomy. Inward industrialization would, in this way, subvert the goal of the sanctioners by turning their pressure into the occasion for reducing vulnerability. Such, at least, was the hope.

Repression + Inward Industrialization: The Result

The eighteen months between January 1987 and mid-1988 were a period of consid-´erable optimism within South Africa's political and economic establishment. The security regime introduced in mid-1986 had reimposed "order" on the black townships. The mass mobilization that had characterized the urban townships for more than twenty-two months had been brought to an end. Overt mass attacks on and resistance to authority declined sharply. A surface calm returned to the urban areas. The international media, under strict censorship and without the drama of mass insurrection to report, gradually lost interest in the South African story. The stage was thus set for the lessening of international economic isolation, as had occurred after Sharpeville and Soweto. The government's new policies of inward industrialization and deregulation, along with the end of the insurrection, bolstered confidence in the business sector. Modest but real economic growth in 1987 and early 1988, between 2 and 3 percent, fed optimism and encouraged a stance of near bravura in respect to international pressure. Sanctions were not working, the South African population was told by both its governmental and business elite.

But by mid-1988 an abrupt reversal occurred in elite mood. Economic prognoses turned decidedly gloomy, precipitating a successful revolt within the cabinet against the state president and his securocrat allies. What had happened in essence is that the fundamental contradiction between Pretoria's domestic goals and international requirements, which inward industrialization could not instantly resolve, worked to undermine its latest attempt to secure the regime of white supremacy. Two things were involved: the failure of the security regime to achieve the more substantial of its goals; and the failure of inward industrialization to sustain a pattern of economic growth. The two failures were not unrelated, for the absence of economic growth undermined security objectives, while the continuation of repression rendered inward industrialization little more than a utopian fantasy.

The Failure of Repression

While the repression associated with the security regime had succeeded in ending sustained insurrectionary mobilization and in rendering inoperative the alternative structures of governance, the accomplishment of its more profound security goals eluded Pretoria. When the state of emergency was renewed in June 1988, a full two years of harsh repression had not succeeded either in eliminating the UDF's community-based organizational infrastructure, or in transforming the township political environment from a liberatory to a cooptive political culture. The revolutionary euphoria that characterized the townships in early 1986 had been replaced by a more sober outlook, but allegiance to and legitimacy of UDF/ANC leadership remained, as did utter hostility and cynicism toward the government and its overtures.

Although significantly weakened in their capability to launch a wholesale assault on state authority, the UDF organizations were still able to defy the state in focused areas. For example, when in October 1988 Pretoria held township elections in order to legitimize the recently reimposed community councils, the UDF launched a successful boycott. Despite an unprecedented government effort to ensure a large voter turnout—a huge propaganda campaign to stimulate public interest, a sharp increase in detentions prior to election day, the banning of anti-election campaigning—only 10 percent of the eligible voters cast ballots, representing no significant increase over the previous effort at council legitimation in 1983. In Soweto, the country's most populous township, only 11 percent of registered voters, about 2.8 percent of adult residents, went to the polls.[58] A British reporter who visited Soweto's polling stations described these voters as predominately "the old, the meek, and the bewildered."[59] Over half the council seats countrywide went uncontested, and for 138 seats there were no candidates at all, as Pretoria experienced difficulty in getting people to come forward and stand for election.[60] Some of the worst results, from Pretoria's vantage point, were in townships that had been singled out for special counterrevolutionary treatment. In Alexandra, KwaNobuhle, and Langa, all subject to major upgrading efforts, there were too few candidates to even hold an election, and all nominees were returned unopposed. In the Eastern Cape township of Lingehile, which also underwent massive upgrading, not a single candidate stepped forward.[61] The British newspaper *Independent* summed up the meaning of the election this way: "For the second time in five years, the overwhelming majority of blacks in South Africa's townships were . . . delivering a decisive vote of no confidence in Pretoria's power-sharing schemes."[62]

Another example of the continued vitality of the radical opposition was the security regime's inability to break the township rent strikes, despite the high priority it gave to the matter. In December 1988 the Bureau of Information reported that a total of R475 million in rent arrears was owed to black local authorities.[63] This is nearly double the amount of rent that Pretoria had reported as unpaid when the state of emergency was imposed in 1986. By May 1989 the total of rent arrears attributable to rent strikes amounted to R551 million.[64] In Soweto, the extent of continued support for the rent strike was indicated by the township's chief electrical engineer in July 1988 when he warned that the council cannot continue "supplying 95 percent of people for free."[65] Transvaal officials acknowledged in early 1989 that only R3 million out of a total potential monthly rent income of R13 million was being collected.[66] In the Pretoria township of Mamelodi, a special target of JMC counterrevolutionary action, residents had not paid rent since 1985.[67] In an attempt to end the most costly of the rent strikes, that in Soweto, officials were forced to violate one of the cardinal principles of the SSC's counterrevolutionary doctrine: during 1988 they began a series of negotiations with Soweto's UDF-affiliated community leaders. In so doing they revealed that despite the deprivations of the security regime, UDF leadership and not the councillors continued to exercise real—that is, operative—authority within the township.

The readiness of the township population for renewed mobilization as well as the capability of popular organizations to launch it were revealed wherever "cracks" appeared in the security regime. One such "crack" was the protection afforded COSATU by its strategic role in the economy. Repression against it was less complete than for other community-based organizations because an attempt to eliminate trade union organization could result in industrial chaos, undermining both the policy of inward industrialization and the alliance with business that that policy was predicated on. Thus, in the midst of the state of emergency, trade-union militancy, as reflected in strike actions, escalated sharply. Strike activity in 1987 compared to 1986 was up 144 percent, the number of workers involved had increased 139 percent, and the number of workdays lost jumped 444 percent.[68] The ability of the workers' movement to launch militant collective actions was also evident in the explicitly political sphere, as trade unions continued staging dramatic political stayaways. In June 1988, in commemoration of the Soweto uprising, COSATU launched what the South African Institute of Race Relations called the biggest national stayaway in the country's history. The three-day general strike, 70 percent effective in the manufacturing sector, is estimated by the Chamber of Commerce to have cost the South African economy approximately R500 million.[69] Nine months later a stayaway in the Eastern Cape townships, commemorating the Sharpeville shootings, produced 100 percent absenteeism in many of the area's largest industrial enterprises, including Volkswagen, Goodyear, and S.A. Breweries.[70]

Another "crack" in the security regime developed when the Conservative Party won control of several Rand towns in the 1987 municipal elections. Immediately, the Conservative local government reimposed the segregationist apartheid laws that had been abandoned over the previous decade. In response the black population of the area launched an effective consumer boycott against white businesses in the area. The Chamber of Commerce of Carltonville, for example, reported that 98 percent of the 330 businesses it had surveyed had been adversely affected, with drops in turnover ranging between 10 and 100 percent. Twenty-three businesses said they might be forced to close.[71] The boycott action was illegal under the security regime's emergency regulations, but Pretoria, interested in teaching the right-wing Conservative Party and its supporters a painful lesson, ignored the matter. There was, however, another lesson in these developments. The rapidity and effectiveness with which the boycotts were organized, and the broad support they received from the area's black populace, indicated that neither the organizational capability nor popular inclination to engage in militant forms of collective action had been destroyed by two years of harsh repression.

A third, "crack" in the security regime was created by the tactical creativity of the UDF opposition itself. Two campaigns were undertaken that sought to turn the detention weapon—the core of Pretoria's repressive arsenal—into a domestic and international liability. One campaign called attention to the plight of children being held, often without access to attorneys, under the emergency regulations. The other was a coordinated and disciplined hunger strike launched in February 1989 by UDF activists who had been held in prisons across South Africa for lengthy periods without being brought to trial.[72] Hunger strikes had been undertaken by prisoners throughout the period of the emergency. These had been essentially individual or small group actions intended to force prison authorities to redress specific grievances. The campaign begun in 1989 differed from earlier efforts in both the extent of participation and the nature of the strikers' demands. Over 600 prisoners took part, demanding not the amelioration of prison conditions, but their immediate release from detention.[73] The government initially scoffed at this action, calling it a publicity stunt. But as the strike wore on and as over 100 hunger strikers, having suffered serious physical deterioration, had to be admitted to hospitals, international attention focused on the plight of South Africa's detainees. Fears that deaths of hunger strikers might create the basis for renewed domestic mobilization and an intensification of international sanctions led the government to back away from its repressive tactic of massive detention without trial. In April, nine weeks after the hunger strike began, some 900 of 1,100 detainees were released.[74] Most of those released were served with "restriction orders," which sought to place severe limits on their activities and required them to report daily to police stations. But the fact that they were now back in their communities across South Africa meant that Pretoria's ability to limit their political activities was far less than when they had been in prison. Thus, by blunting the "detention weapon" the anti-apartheid activists had rendered the state of emergency less effective, and increased their mobilizational and organizational capabilities.

One of the true ironies of the security regime was that the physical security of the white population underwent significant deterioration after the imposition of the state of emergency. According to government statistics, the ANC increased the number of its military attacks inside South Africa by 700 percent between 1984 and the beginning of 1989. Most of this escalation occurred after 1986, and included an increasing number of attacks on civilian or "soft" targets.[75] A research and monitoring unit at the University of Natal reported that 1988 was the "worst" year in South African history for guerrilla activity.[76] Figure 8.2 shows the sharp increase in ANC military attacks that coincided with the establishment of the counterrevolutionary security regime. It should be noted that the sense of danger and insecurity produced by the limpet mines placed in office buildings and shopping centers was far greater than the probability of being killed. The ANC campaign introduced white South African society to the ubiquitous metal detector and sandbagged build-

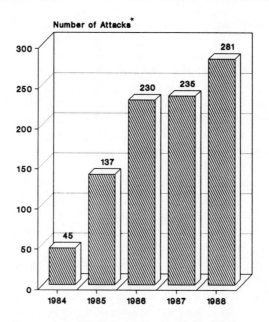

Number of Attacks[*]

*within "white" South Africa. Does not include TBVC

FIG. 8.2. ANC military attacks, 1984–1988 (*Source: Weekly Mail*, October 28, 1988, p. 14; South African Institute of Race Relations [SAIRR], *Race Relations Survey 1988/89* [Johannesburg: Institute of Race Relations, 1989], pp. 610–16.)

ing, as well as to the atmosphere of constant danger in public and crowded places. It robbed white South Africans of the strongly held sense that they lived in what was probably the safest and most peaceful industrial society in the world. In that way the ANC's military campaign did more to impact directly on the quality of life for white South Africans than had the insurrection, from which they had been largely insulated.

The second strand of the counterrevolutionary program—eliminating socioeconomic grievances in order to undermine radical opposition and legitimate "moderate" leaders—appears to have met with even less success than the effort to root out the infrastructure of "revolutionary" organizations. Just as in the pre-1986 period, the combination of a desultory economic situation, the related constraint on available government revenues, and the massive nature of socioeconomic problems combined to render politically marginal the efforts at improvement that were undertaken. Pretoria's dilemma was most dramatically manifest in the area of unemployment. Given a rate of increase in the labor force of more than 3 percent per year, economists estimate that the economy would need a growth rate of 6 percent for the absolute numbers of unemployed to decline.[77] In other words, at the rates of growth achieved by inward industrialization in 1986 and 1987, South Africa's economic and *political* problem with black unemployment was getting more rather than less severe.

Education was another sphere in which "improvements" produced little in the way of amelioration of grievance. Overcrowding, shortage of qualified teachers, poor results on the matriculation examinations, anger over the detention of students and teachers, and the occupation of school grounds by security forces continued to generate intermittent protests within South Africa's schools. According to the government agency in charge of African education, 97 of its 368 secondary schools experienced "unrest or disruption" in 1987.[78] The following year, according to government reports, 400,000 black high school pupils engaged in classroom boycotts and 255 secondary and 662 primary schools experienced "unrest and disruption."[79] In the Western Cape over 90,000 students, close to 90 percent of the total pupil population, boycotted classes in April 1988 in support of a set of education-related demands. In sum, despite government undertakings in the education sector, student, parent, and teacher alienation continued to fester. And, in spite of the state of emergency, that alienation intermittently erupted in pupil boycotts throughout the country. In 1986 the government had announced a "ten-year plan" for racial parity in education. Three years later F. W. de Klerk, the then minister of education, announced that the plan's goals had not been met because the annual economic growth rate had not reached the requisite 4.1 percent.[80]

The amelioration of grievance in the areas of urban housing and services was equally problematic. The crash program of housing construction undertaken within the security regime, even if it had the cooptive political results Pretoria anticipated, was directed at only a very small segment of the African population—the prospective middle-class homeowner. And because in most cases the construction of these new homes for the relatively privileged entailed a parallel displacement of the less fortunate, this counterrevolutionary upgrading was likely to create increased grievance among those not targeted for its benefits. Moreover, the number of those who suffered from upgrading was usually greater than those who benefited. In Alexandra, for example, the scheme to build a middle-class suburb for about 23,000 people entailed a plan to dispossess some 37,000 and remove them from the township.[81]

The limits on housing construction were part of the larger problem of township finance that had been endemic since the mid-1970s, and that had been such a major element in creating the basis for insurrectionary mobilization in 1984. With the imposition of the state of emergency in mid-1986, Pretoria sought to take the pressure off African municipal governments by providing "bridging finance." By late 1988, however, the burden this created on the central treasury led to a reduction in the amount of such support and black municipalities were informed that this type of aid would soon end.[82] Pretoria's plan was to have newly created regional service councils solve the township financial crisis by providing cheaper bulk services and raising new revenues through a corporate tax. However, knowledgeable observers expressed considerable skepticism that this new arrangement would have the requisite impact.[83]

Pretoria's inability to allay the grievances among South Africa's black population is revealed in a series of surveys conducted between twelve and eighteen months after the imposition of the June 12 state of emergency.[84] A random sample of residents in Port Elizabeth's African and "coloured" townships were asked

TABLE 8.1   Grievances of Township Residents, 1988 (percent)

	African Townships			"Coloured" Townships		
	Problem	No problem	Don't know	Problem	No problem	Don't know
Lack of jobs	100	0	0	90.6	5.2	4.2
Low wages	100	0	0	90.6	4.0	5.4
Poor housing	97	0.5	2.5	81.0	14.4	4.6
Shortage of housing	97	2.5	0.5	97.0	2.0	1.0
High rent	98	0.5	1.0	90.8	7.0	2.2
Black Educ. system	73	3.5	23.5	55.0	15.6	29.4
Poor schools	87	11.5	1.5	41.4	48.8	9.8
Police violence	85	1.5	13.5	53.2	5.8	41.0

Source: Human Rights Trust/Port Elizabeth, *Monitor,* June 1988, p. 70, and October 1988, p. 56.

"What do you think are the main problems or grievances of black people in Port Elizabeth?" Respondents were read a list of some twenty-four types of grievances the security regime was supposed to ameliorate, and instructed to indicate whether they thought each was still "a problem" or "a small issue or no problem at all." Table 8.1 lists the responses.

The socioeconomic grievances that Pretoria perceived as the causes of insurrection, and which its counterrevolutionary doctrine had targeted for amelioration—unemployment, housing, and education—were the problems most frequently mentioned by survey respondents.* And, asked to differentiate *major* problems from those that were simply problems, 92 percent of African township residents indicated unemployment, 87 percent high rent, 86 percent poor housing, 83 percent a shortage of housing, and 64 percent poor schools.[85]

The same surveys provide data that allow an assessment of the security regime's ability to shift political support from the UDF-affiliated community organizations to the community councils and their representatives. What emerges from these surveys is the overwhelming support that UDF-affiliated organizations continued to enjoy despite the efforts of the security regime. And, correlatively, how little in the way of a positive orientation existed for the groups that were supposed to be the beneficiaries of Pretoria's effort at "winning the hearts and minds" of township residents. Respondents were presented with a list of nine organizations—four UDF community associations, the Ibhayi City Council, the government development board, the "vigilante" group Ama-Afrika, AZAPO (a Black Consciousness organization), and Idamasa, a fraternal organization of black religious leaders—and were then asked: "Which of these local organizations do you think tries to help solve the problems and grievances of black people, and which doesn't help at all?" Nearly 90 percent of the sample indicated they thought each of the four UDF organizations tried to help

*The "coloured" respondents considered education-related issues to be a problem about half as frequently as did African respondents. This is not surprising, in that the education system for "coloureds" has traditionally been superior to the Bantu education offered to Africans.

solve their problems. The UDF's Port Elizabeth Civic Organization (PEBCO) received the highest number of positive responses, 94 percent. In contrast, the city
council and the government's development board were considered helpful by only 3
percent of township residents, and Ama-Afrika, Pretoria's attempt at grass-roots
"counterorganization," was perceived as helpful by only 2 percent. When asked
which of the helpful organizations tries the hardest to solve black people's problems, only the four UDF organizations and Idamasa were named. Again, the largest
proportion of township residents considered the main UDF organization, PEBCO,
as the organization that "tries the hardest to help."[86] When asked to indicate which
organization helps the least, respondents named AZAPO, the city council, the
development board, and Ama-Afrika. Not a single respondent named a UDF-affiliated organization. These local level political orientations carry over to the national
level. When asked which national political movements help to solve the problems
that black people face, 98 percent of the sample indicated the UDF, and 95 percent
the ANC. In contrast, only 2 percent considered the government of South Africa
helpful, while 91 percent thought it didn't help at all.[87]

The security regime's inability to shift the political orientations of the black
populace affected Pretoria's ability to elicit cooperation from even the so-called
moderate "leadership" whose creation its policies had facilitated. The most dramatic manifestation of this was the failure to get any of the homeland leaders to accept
membership on the National Statutory Council. By early in 1989 the heads of all six
"self-governing homelands" had publicly announced that they would not participate
in the council in the form in which it was being presented by the government.[88] In a
joint statement, the chief ministers of the QwaQwa and Lebowa homelands declared
that the council would "come to naught unless democracy is unshackled through the
release of all political prisoners and the unbanning of all political organisations."
They rejected "the notion that SA is a country of minorities," and undertook "not to
participate in negotiations aimed at making the country's minorities building blocks
of a future constitution."[89] A similar reluctance to be drawn into Pretoria's structures of cooptation was also noticeable among municipal mayors and councillors.
The Urban Councils Association of South Africa, the community councillors' professional association, was split on the issue of participation in the National Statutory
Council, with younger members demanding the release of Nelson Mandela and
other political prisoners as a precondition for participating.[90] Sensing the political
climate of the townships to which they had returned under cover of the security
regime, local authorities sought to stake out a position independent of Pretoria so as
to avoid the collaborator tag that had been so politically costly a short time earlier.
Nelson Botile, mayor of Soweto, told a Soweto council meeting in September of
1988 that he was opposed to participation on the National Council because Africans
had "long passed the situation where they could only make recommendations. . . .
We want to be in Parliament."[91]

The emergent black commercial bourgeoisie also assumed a public stance at
odds with the expectations of the securocrats. The National African Federated
Chambers of Commerce (NAFCOC) at its twenty-fourth annual conference in August 1988, took its most radical political line ever. It encouraged black business to
support community-based anti-apartheid struggles and appointed a delegation to the

state president to demand the release of political prisoners. It expressed opposition to the municipal elections to be held in October, called for the release of political prisoners, and declared that negotiations for a new constitutional order could take place only if detainees were active participants in the process. That a group that was the backbone of Pretoria's vision of a politically "moderate" future would make such a public call indicated the extent of the security regime's failure to shift "rightward" the political center of gravity of black politics.

To the securocrats, the fact that the security regime had not, by the time of its third anniversary in 1989, achieved its major goals was a reason to extend its existence. Housing and unemployment problems had to be resolved before the emergency could be lifted, and these were long-term tasks.[92] Adriaan Vlok, the minister in charge, told a briefing of foreign journalists in mid-May 1989 that "the revolutionary climate was very high and in many instances still rising." He said it would still take time and a great deal of effort before the "climate in South Africa returned to normality and stability."[93] The securocrats' open-ended approach to repression, however, confronted certain unaccommodating economic realities. These presented the South African state with a "catch-22" situation. On one hand, the state's ability to successfully pursue its counterrevolutionary strategy required resources. These resources could only come from an expanding economy. As we have observed, by mid-1988 resource constraints were already imposing themselves on the securocrats' plans for solving the problems of unemployment, education, and housing. On the other hand, continuing with the repressive strategy threatened future economic growth. Not only would this rob the state of resources to feed the security regime, but it also threatened to alienate the business community and the white populace more generally, as economic decline translated into reduced profits and declining material welfare. Pretoria was forced to face this uncomfortable "catch-22" because the limitations of repression corresponded with parallel limitations of inward industrialization.

Infeasibility of Inward Industrialization

As I noted earlier, 1987 was a year of considerable confidence and optimism in South African business and government circles. The insurrection had been stopped; inward industrialization offered a means to break the stranglehold of sanctions; and the modest but real turnabout in economic growth rates during 1986 and 1987 indicated that this strategy was working. But by mid-1988 the growth potential of inward industrialization was revealed as more apparent than real, and the long-term economic prognosis from South African business as well as from Pretoria turned decidedly gloomy. Relatedly, and most significantly, there occurred a nearly complete reversal on the subject of the costs of international economic sanctions. An array of influential economic actors for the first time publically acknowledged that sanctions had extracted a significant price and that a sanctions-filled future was one of economic decline. Thus, in August 1988 Henri de Villiers, chairman of the Standard Bank Investment Corporation, warned the South African public and government:

In this day and age there is no such thing as economic self-sufficiency and we delude ourselves if we think we are different. . . . *South Africa needs the world. It needs markets, it needs skills, it needs technology, and above all it needs capital.*[94]

At about the same time Chris van Wyk, managing director of the Trust Bank of Africa Ltd., echoed de Villiers' caveat: "I'm fed up with the feeling that we can go it alone. . . . We can't ignore what sanctions and disinvestment have done." According to van Wyk, as a result of sanctions-induced capital outflows and a loss of export earnings of nearly $5 billion, "South Africans will be 5–10% poorer by 1990."[95] This type of analysis also found its way into the annual reports for 1988 of a number of South Africa's largest financial and industrial institutions. The report of First National Bank declared:

The economic penalty of the apartheid era has been its opportunity cost; the size of the national cake, the Gross Domestic Product, is well below what it might and should have been by now, and the difference would have contributed to solving many of our problems. The outflow of capital from our country compounds the opportunity cost in two respects. It creates a withdrawal of scarce managerial and technical skills which move with the capital; and the substitution of investment funds from local sources creates a drawing on capital funds which might otherwise be available to support the necessary socio-political developments required by the change process in South Africa.[96]

And according to the report of Rand Mines Ltd.:

[S]anctions are beginning to have an adverse effect on the economy. . . . The expansion of the South African economy is being restricted by the continued absence of substantial capital inflows. There is a consensus that the confidence of overseas investors must be restored, before adequate funds from that source will again be available.[97]

The key to the business community's turnabout regarding sanctions lay in the collapse of the economic miniboom of 1987. Because the cause of this collapse was embedded firmly in the relationship between sanctions and the structure of the South African economy, it revealed clearly the political and economic dilemma facing Pretoria. In the late 1980s Pretoria sought to meet its foreign debt obligations by spurring economic growth and boosting exports to build its reserves of foreign exchange. But because of the economy's import dependence, economic expansion rapidly translated into increased imports and thus greater claims on foreign exchange reserves.

Inward industrialization was a strategy to escape from this reality through import substitution. Import substituting strategies, however, virtually always produce a medium-term increase in the import bill, as an economy must initially import the capital goods that will be used to produce the items previously purchased from abroad. Import substitution, in other words, has a lag effect—in order to reduce imports in the future an economy must increase imports in the present. As such, between 1986 and the end of 1988 South Africa's import bill increased 60 percent, from \$11,130 million to \$17,210 million.[98] Given that sanctions blocked South Africa's access to the international banking system, the additional import costs of inward industrialization could not be financed by foreign borrowing. This put a crushing burden on foreign exchange reserves that were already being drained by debt service payments that had resulted from the recall of international loans in 1985. The new economic strategy introduced in 1986 therefore precipitated a balance of payments crisis. In October 1988 the government announced that foreign exchange reserves had fallen for the sixth month in a row. In the fourteen months between August 1987 and October 1988 these reserves declined by 47 percent in rand terms and 58 percent in dollar value.[99]

By mid-1988 it had become apparent that under conditions of international financial isolation and forced debt repayment the import cost of sustaining a growth rate of only 2 percent exceeded foreign exchange capability, which now was based almost entirely on export earnings. Economic expansion in the sanctions environment meant a short period of growth, followed by a balance-of-payments crisis, followed by decline. The irony of this situation as well as its political lesson was outlined by Johan Louw, chief economist for SANLAM, the largest Afrikaner financial institution and South Africa's second largest financial conglomerate:

> We can't afford a growth rate of more than two percent [because of pressure on the balance of payments]. Normally a developing country should be importing capital, but we are exporting capital in order to repay debt. *Unless we get certain reforms here we won't get foreign capital again. We have to at least show the outside world that we are moving in the right direction.*[100]

Of all the comments emerging from the economic difficulties of late 1988, the most interesting and significant were those by Pretoria's minister of finance, Barend du Plessis. Addressing the South African Parliament in his 1989 budget speech, du Plessis observed: "How ironic that we are now forced to label a modest growth rate of three percent in our economy as 'overheating.' " Sounding more like an ANC leader than Pretoria's official spokesman on financial matters, du Plessis declared that for South Africa the main question is not whether any progress can be made, but whether there can be *"economic survival in the face of an internationally organized assault on the economy. . . .* The answer for us," he stated, "clearly lies in the full-scale effort to break the isolation imposed on us, by dynamic expansion of our trade with the outside world and a restoration of our creditworthiness by means of the correct economic measures and political progress."[101]

A New President: A New Era?

The failure of repression and the realization of the related infeasibility of an autarkic economic strategy precipitated a division within the ruling elite. On one side were arrayed the securocrats—those associated with the government agencies responsible for domestic and foreign security. In frequent public statements, Minister of Law and Order Adriaan Vlok expressed the perspective of this faction. "It is very clear," he explained in March 1989, "that radical activists and convinced revolutionaries and their collaborators are still extremely active." Therefore, he continued, unless the state of emergency is extended "unrest and bloody violence would again engulf South Africa in chaos and immeasurable suffering."[102] In the assessment of the securocrats, in other words, movement away from repression and back to political reform carried too much domestic risk. P. W. Botha, although the "father" of South African reform, had been closely associated with the security apparatus since his ten-year service as minister of defense. In the late 1980s his was the cautious stance of the securocrats. On the other side of the division within the ruling group were officials associated with the economy and foreign relations. Their position was captured in the dramatic statement to parliament of Minister of Finance Barend du Plessis, which was quoted above. In contrast to Vlok, who stressed the risk of renewed insurrection and the need for continued repression to avoid it, du Plessis underscored the risk to economic survival that came from international isolation and the need for "political progress" (i.e., reform) as a means to "break the isolation." Within the governing party and cabinet, F. W. de Klerk stood on this "internationalist-reformer" side of the policy debate. Considerable support for this position came also from powerful actors outside of government, particularly in the business and financial community. They had, by mid-1988, concluded that the security regime and the strategy of inward industrialization were serving neither their nor South Africa's interests. Indicative of the political currents running at the time was a public statement from the chief economist for SANLAM, which is not only a financial giant but a major Afrikaner institution. Warning South Africans that to solve their economic problems "we have to at least show the outside world that we are moving in the right direction," he pointedly added, "Perhaps under a new state president things will get moving."[103]

The replacement of P. W. Botha, first as head of the National Party in February 1989, and then as state president in August, marked the ascendancy of the internationalist-reformers over the securocrats. The first manifestation of this shift at the policy level occurred somewhat earlier, however, and in the area of regional rather than domestic policy. The financial/economic crises confronting South Africa in mid-1988 created the political context for Pretoria's most ambitious foreign policy gambit—agreeing to the Angola/Namibia Accord in August 1988. From Pretoria's vantage point, the accord represented both a pragmatic adjustment to a gloomy economic reality and an effort to alter that reality.

The administration of Namibia was a costly drain on the South African treasury, whose burden intensified as the economy stagnated and the political need for socioeconomic amelioration became more pressing. South Africa's military involvement in Angola increased the drain and added to the burden. When Cuba in early 1988 responded to the South African siege of Angola's southern strategic town Cuito-Cuanavale by moving crack troops and sophisticated air and radar systems deep into southern Angola,* it upped the ante for continued military involvement in

---

*The Cuban military buildup included the establishment of a military headquarters at Lubango in southwestern Angola, the movement of some 16,000 Cuban troops into positions near the Namibian border, the construction of a southern air base at Xangongo, the positioning there of advanced MIG-23 and SU-22 aircraft that would be capable of strikes deep into Namibia, the upgrading of radar and air-defense systems in southernmost Angola, and cross-border reconnaissance by commando units and aircraft.

Angola.[104] With advanced Cuban and Angolan aircraft now capable of overflying northern Namibia, and with Cuban troops present in force at the border of Namibia, the South African military posture in the Namibia/Angola area was rendered untenable. Righting the situation would require the commitment of major new military and, therefore, financial resources. But with the Angolan war already costing some R4 billion in 1988 alone, and with the disappointing results of inward industrialization becoming ever clearer, the changed security situation in southern Angola highlighted the contradictions and failures of the securocrat strategy. The inability to either guarantee peace or provide the basis for sustained economic growth domestically undermined the state's capacity to sustain the military dimension of regional hegemony, while the allocation of scarce financial resources to maintain Pretoria's military hegemony regionally undermined the state's capacity to create the political foundation for cooptation by ameliorating the living conditions of black South Africans. Thus, the Cuban military escalation in Angola not only made a South African military withdrawal from the Angolan conflict an attractive option in Pretoria, but simultaneously offered the internationalist-reformers significant leverage in their effort to push aside the securocrats.

From Pretoria's vantage point a negotiated international agreement that linked military withdrawal from Angola with independence for Namibia offered more than simply a means to close off a costly and open-ended drain on its treasury; it presented an opportunity to break out of international isolation. Once before, with the Nkomati Accord of March 1984, Pretoria had entered into a diplomatic agreement to bring regional "peace and security." At that time, a South African newspaper commented that the treaty with Mozambique represented "the beginning of a new road which would, if followed . . . lead South Africa back into Africa and through Africa back into the world."[105] And the road back to the world was also presumably a road away from sanctions. The Nkomati Accord, the commentary continued, "will have a valuable spin-off benefit in the international arena by making the prospect of economic sanctions against South Africa—ever present for two decades—more remote."[106]

From Pretoria's vantage point the Angola/Namibia Accord represented "Nkomati II"; it was a replay of the 1984 scenario whereby a regional posture of diplomacy and compromise was supposed to pave the way back from international isolation and economic sanctions. Pretoria once again moved rapidly to capitalize on the spirit of international optimism and goodwill that followed the successful Angola/Namibia negotiations; an optimism that this time included not just the Western democracies but the Soviet Union, Cuba, and countries of sub-Saharan Africa. Within two months of the signing of the accord, South African diplomatic personnel were traveling in Europe spreading the word about Pretoria's commitment to peace, negotiation, and compromise. During one such trip Pik Botha, the South African foreign minister, told his Belgian counterpart that the South African government "was determined to continue to resolve regional disputes and differences through negotiations."[107] That same week Glen Babb, South Africa's deputy director of foreign affairs, told an audience of British MPs, businessmen, and journalists specially invited to the London embassy that "South Africa wants nothing more than to live in peace with its neighbors, work together for regional co-operation and prosperity, and put its house in order."[108] The Angola/Namibia Accord also produced a flurry of diplomatic activity, with the South African head of state and foreign minister traveling to Mozambique, Zaire, and Zambia to discuss regional issues.

While Nkomati provided a model that Pretoria replayed four years later, it also indicated the limits of regional and foreign policy in achieving the international acceptance that Pretoria requires. The "road back to the world" that South African's believed Nkomati represented turned out to be a *cul de sac*, for Western governments were attuned primarily to South Africa's domestic situation rather than to its foreign policy. When in September 1984 insurrection erupted in the townships of the Vaal Triangle the Nkomati strategy was foiled, and the stage was set for further international isolation and increased sanctions.

The 1984 experience indicated that in order for Pretoria to benefit from the 1988 Angola/Namibia Accord it would have to match its regional overture with some dramatic domestic policy change. This much was generally realized by the faction of the South African political elite that supported F. W. de Klerk's successful effort to replace P. W. Botha as party leader and state president. While those concerned primarily with security deemed a new domestic political initiative to be too risky, the internationalist-reformers viewed the risks of doing nothing as far greater. De Klerk made this assessment:

> We have decided to try and preserve [fundamental values] by taking the initiative— even if we have to take some risks in the process. . . . When we follow new methods and strategies . . . it does not mean that we have forsaken our quest to create a . . . society in which minorities can feel safe. But we must also create a South Africa that enjoys the loyalty of the majority of its people. Unless we achieve this, the future will not be safe. Unless we achieve this, there is no hope for our children and grandchildren. . . . Do we want them to inherit a stagnant situation that has made no progress toward solution, where revolution continues to brew and bubble under the surface? Do we want them to inherit new sanctions and boycotts?[109]

By the beginning of 1989, then, there was considerable support both inside and outside government for some dramatic new gesture to the black majority. A signal that a major policy shift away from the security regime was in the offing was provided by the new state president when, in his inaugural speech, he declared: "The time has come for South Africa to restore its pride and to lift itself out of the doldrums of growing international isolation, economic decline and increasing polarization."[110] A newly dominant faction within the ruling party had now joined the private business establishment in recognizing that continued international isolation meant permanent economic decline, further deterioration in white standards of living, and a lack of resources to upgrade the townships, portending even greater levels of black political alienation.

Into the 1990s

Laying the Foundation for Negotiations

The combined realization that an end to international isolation was a critical necessity, and that *political* change was essential for its achievement, led the internationalist-reformers to a focus on negotiations as a means to resolve South Africa's endemic crisis. In itself this was nothing new. The NP elite had learned from the fiasco that accompanied the introduction of the 1983 constitution that a new political dispensation imposed unilaterally by the white minority would serve neither the government's domestic nor its international purposes. Hence P. W. Botha announced in early 1985 that a search had begun for yet a new constitutional dispensation, but this time its particulars would be negotiated with representatives of South Africa's black population. The National Statutory Council, established in 1986, was to be the forum for these negotiations. The prominent blacks considered by Pretoria to be appropriate participants in the council were the homeland leaders and township council members. These were presumed to be amenable to the government's notion of "power sharing" within a consociational/federal scheme. But the insurrectionary conditions that existed in the mid-1980s ensured that Pretoria's new negotiations forum was stillborn. The "culture of liberation" that characterized township society rendered the black participants in official structures irrelevant, legitimized instead the ANC/UDF leadership, and rejected power sharing in favor of majority rule. Even the councillors and homeland leaders, seeking to salvage some political credibility, refused to accept membership on the national council unless ANC political prisoners were released, and proclaimed Pretoria's vision of an ethnic/racial consociation unacceptable.

In large measure the security regime, and the counterrevolutionary strategy that it implemented, was directed at destroying the liberatory culture of the townships and the mass organizations of radical opposition so as to make possible negotiations on Pretoria's own terms. Once the UDF and ANC were eliminated, the way would be cleared for the ascendance of councillors, mayors, and homeland officials. The negotiation of a power-sharing arrangement endorsed by "credible" black leaders, and thus acceptable internationally as well as domestically, could then proceed.

What was new about the commitment to negotiations of F. W. de Klerk and his associates was the recognition that a viable political solution to South Africa's crises required the participation of the ANC. Recognizing both that the security regime had failed to substantially alter the "culture of liberation," and that waiting much longer for it to do so would be economically disastrous, the internationalist-reformers faced up to the reality that for any political reform to have domestic and international credibility the ANC and its UDF-affiliated allies had to play a major role in negotiating it. Hence Pretoria, under the new leadership of de Klerk, set out to draw into negotiations the very organizations and leaders that it had previously sought to destroy.

Several steps followed logically as prerequisites to this task, and these were quickly taken. The participation of the ANC/UDF leadership in negotiations could only be accomplished by creating an environment in which black leadership and organizations were free to function with some semblance of normalcy. Hence the need to relax the state of emergency, unban the ANC and its allies, lift the restrictions on opposition organizations and activists, free long-term ANC political prisoners, especially Nelson Mandela, and reduce other restrictions on public political activity. The path was cleared for achieving these things when, four months after assuming the post of state president, de Klerk dismantled the organizational infrastructure of the security regime, the National Security Management System. The intention of the new administration to move down this path was indicated by the freeing of life-term ANC political prisoners in October 1989. But the concrete steps to creating a climate for negotiations were laid when de Klerk, in his dramatic speech to the opening session of the 1990 parliament, announced that the bans on the ANC and South African Communist Party would immediately be lifted, that Nelson Mandela would be released, and that much of the state of emergency would be relaxed. Although these edicts took many observers by surprise, the legalization of what had come to be called the Mass Democratic Movement (MDM)* and the freeing of the preeminent black political figure in South Africa were an inescapable part of the internationalist-reformers' strategic choice to seek a breakthrough via negotiations with their domestic opponents.

Understanding that de Klerk's bold policy alterations were an end product of a decade-long process of political conflict and change—what I have termed the trialectical process—does not reduce their significance in respect to the future. The unconditional lifting of legal prohibitions against opposition organizations, the release of Nelson Mandela, and the invitation to the ANC to join in negotiations for a new constitutional order had an electrifying effect on South African politics. The ANC and UDF leadership perceived that a major breakthrough had occurred. Although skeptical about the government's claim that it was committed to a "totally new and just constitutional dispensation [based upon] equal rights, treatment, and opportunity in every sphere of endeavor," and hugely distrustful of Pretoria's motives, the MDM leadership would probably have agreed with de Klerk's assessment that his actions had "placed [South Africa] on the road of drastic change."[111] Anti-apartheid activists differed in their enthusiasm for imminent negotiations, with some fearing a strategic trap that might allow Pretoria to regain the political initiative. But there was almost unanimous agreement within the movement that the ANC and its MDM allies would in fact soon be engaged in talks with Pretoria that would set the stage for serious negotiations about a future political order. The nearly total absorption of the MDM leadership with questions of how, what, and with whom to negotiate, as well as preparations made by ANC exiles for a return to South Africa, were testaments to the seriousness with which the opposition movement greeted the new government initiatives. Following the legalization of political organizations and the release of Mandela in February 1990, a perception took hold within the MDM that South Africa would have a government representative of the majority, if not by the end of 1990 or even 1991, then certainly within the decade. Not since the height of insurrectionary euphoria in mid-1986 had such hope, optimism, and positive expectations gripped the black community at both mass and leadership levels.

The third "leg" of the South African trialectic—the international community—

---

*The term "mass democratic movement" gained currency in the mid-1980s as a means to distinguish that segment of the opposition or "liberation struggle" that defined itself in terms of the nonracial Charterist tradition. Sometime in 1989 the term was formalized by capitalization in spelling, and through the common use of the acronym MDM by those associated with nonracial opposition politics. The MDM has no formal organizational structure. It is an alliance of the ANC, COSATU, the UDF, and UDF-affiliated organizations, whose common bond is the demand for nonracial democracy and the recognition of the African National Congress as the leading political organization in the struggle for its attainment.

responded positively to the changed political atmosphere associated with de Klerk's presidency. Expectations were raised that the South African crisis was ripe for resolution. The key international actors—the Western industrial states, the Soviet Union, and the southern African frontline states—sought to nudge the South African adversaries toward the negotiating table. The entire global political environment of 1989–90 seemed conducive to a fundamental political breakthrough. The rapid collapse of the cold war and the dramatic political changes and realignment within the Soviet Union and Eastern Europe made it difficult to resist the notion that South Africa was part of a global transition toward conflict resolution and democratization. These utterly unexpected and improbable global changes thus lent a certain air of inevitability to the notion of an imminent political settlement in South Africa.

Notes

1. "Pressuring South Africa—American Sanctions: Only a First Step," *New York Times*, August 11, 1985, III, p. 2.

2. See "Reform," *Monitor* (Journal of the Human Rights Trust of Port Elizabeth), June 1988, pp. 18–27; see also "The Republic of South Africa," *Journal of Defense & Diplomacy*, Study Series no. 1, appendix 1.

3. Robert McFarlane quoted in "McFarlane's No-Nonsense Message," *Washington Post*, August 14, 1985, p. A23.

4. *The Citizen*, June 9, 1986, reprinted in *South African Digest*, June 13, 1986, p. 531 (emphasis added).

5. *The Citizen*, October 3, 1986, reprinted in *South African Digest*, October 10, 1986, p. 937 (emphasis added).

6. Keynote address, Biennial Conference, Political Science Association of South Africa, Rand Afrikaans University, Johannesburg, September 17, 1981, p. 13; reprinted in "Reform and Stability in a Modernizing, Multi-Ethnic Society," *Politikon: South African Journal of Political Science*, vol. 8, no. 2 (December 1981), pp. 8–26.

7. Ibid.

8. "Politicians Debate SADF Role in Townships," Johannesburg Television Service in Afrikaans, 1830 GMT, September 14, 1987, translated and reproduced in FBIS-AFR-179-87, September 16, 1987, p. 10.

9. Quoted in Mark Swilling, "Whamming the Radicals," *Weekly Mail*, May 20–26, 1988, p. 15.

10. *The Art of Counter-Revolutionary War*, quoted in ibid.

11. Ibid.

12. Ibid.

13. Quoted in Anton Harber, "The Uniformed Web that Sprawls Across the Country," *Weekly Mail*, October 3–8, 1986, p. 12.

14. Confidential briefing for South African businessmen, March 1987, reported from notes in *Southscan*, January 13, 1988.

15. Adriaan Vlok, interview in *Washington Post*, October 15, 1987, p. 36.

16. See "Excerpts from New Restrictions in South Africa," *New York Times*, December 14, 1986, I, p. 27.

17. Ibid.

18. Ibid.

19. Quoted in *Washington Post*, October 15, 1987.

20. Interview with P. W. Botha, *Washington Times*, March 14, 1988, p. B8.

21. See *The Citizen*, June 21, 1988.

22. See "Excerpts from New Restrictions," *New York Times*, December 14, 1986.

23. Ibid.

24. Adriaan Volk, quoted in, "South Africa to Maintain Emergency Rule," *International Herald Tribune*, November 16, 1987 (emphasis added).

25. See Patrick Laurence, "Swabbing Out the Township Past," *Weekly Mail*, January 16–22, 1987, p. 5.

26. Quoted in *Financial Mail*, March 18, 1988.

27. See David Beresford, "A Township called Alex," *Guardian* (Br), May 1, 1989, p. 8.

28. Ibid.

29. Ibid.

30. Franz Kruger, "Speak Softly and Carry a Big Stick," *Weekly Mail*, December 24–January 14, 1987, p. 6.

31. Ibid., (emphasis added).

32. See *Weekly Mail*, May 22–28, 1987, p. 7.

33. See *Weekly Mail*, August 1–7, 1986, p. 1.

34. Ibid.

35. Ibid.

36. South African Institute of Race Relations (SAIRR), *Race Relations Survey, 1986* (Johannesburg: Institute of Race Relations, 1987), pp. 810–12.

37. See Patrick Laurence, "The Day the State Learnt it Could Not Take Black Police for Granted," *Weekly Mail*, December 18–23, 1987, p. 5.

38. See Arlene Getz, "Black Leaders Warn of Growing Resentment against Kitscops," *Natal Mercury*, February 21, 1988.

39. See, *Weekly Mail*, February 6, 1987, p. 3; see also *S.A. Barometer*, vol. 2, no. 3 (February 26, 1988), pp. 36–39.

40. Ibid.

41. See *Weekly Mail*, December 24–January 14, 1987, p. 7.

42. See *The Citizen*, February 25, 1988.

43. Ibid.

44. Quoted in *Sowetan*, February 25, 1988.

45. Interview in *Leadership*, vol. 6, no. 1 (1987), p. 32 (emphasis added).

46. Interview in *Leadership*, vol. 6, no. 5 (1987), p. 24.

47. See SAIRR, *Quarterly Countdown Nine* (Johannesburg: Institute of Race Relations, 1988), p. 52.

48. See Karen Evans and Edyth Bulbring, "Another Break-in. Another Wrecked Car. Another Fire-bomb. Another Co-incidence?" *Weekly Mail*, May 20–26, 1988, p. 9.

49. Quoted in Swilling, "Whamming the Radicals," p. 15.

50. Quoted in *Weekly Mail*, February 13–19, 1987, p. 7.

51. *Monitor*, journal of the Human Rights Trust, Port Elizabeth, June 1988, p. 56.

52. Tony Weaver, "I Watched as Police Stand By as the Vigilantes Torch the Zolani Centre," *Weekly Mail*, June 13–29, 1986, pp. 4–5.

53. *Monitor*, June 1988, p. 47.

54. See Steven Friedman, "Natal's Violence: Easily Deplored, Harder to End," *Weekly Mail*, November 6–12, 1987, p. 14; see also Philip Van Niekerk, "A Court Relives the Murderous Reign of the Village Warlords," *Weekly Mail*, November 6–12, 1987, pp. 16–17.

55. David Dison, "Tightening the Screw," *Leadership*, vol. 6, no. 5 (1987), p. 19.

56. See ibid., pp. 15–19.

57. See Robert M. Price, "Security Versus Growth: The International Factor in South African Policy," *Annals of the American Academy of Political and Social Sciences*, January 1987, pp. 116–22.

58. "The Gun-Point Election," *Weekly Mail*, October 28–November 3, 1988, p. 2.

59. Ibid.

60. Ibid.

61. See *Sunday Star*, October 30, 1988.

62. Tony Allen-Mills, "Soweto Ballot Draws the Old, Meek and Bewildered," *Independent* (Br), October 27, 1988.

63. See *Star*, December 4, 1988.

64. SAIRR, *Race Relations Survey, 1988/89* (Johannesburg: Institute of Race Relations, 1989), p. xxxiii.

65. See *S.A. Barometer*, vol. 2, no. 13 (July 15, 1988), p. 194.

66. *Weekly Mail*, February 17–23, 1989, p. 4.

67. See *City Press*, December 4, 1988.

68. See *S.A. Barometer*, vol. 2, no. 9 (May 20, 1988), p. 137.

69. *S.A. Barometer*, vol. 2, no. 11 (June 17, 1988), pp. 163–66.

70. See *Weekly Mail*, March 23–30, 1989, p. 3.

71. See *South*, March 22, 1989.

72. See SAIRR, *Race Relations Survey, 1988/89*, pp. 555–56.

73. Ibid., p. 556.

74. Ibid., p. xxxi.

75. See *Weekly Mail*, December 9–15, 1988, p. 12.

76. See *Daily Dispatch*, March 20, 1989.

77. Pieter Le Roux, "The Economics of Conflict and Negotiation," in Berger and Godsell, *A Future South Africa* (Boulder: Westview Press, 1988), p. 228.

78. See *Weekly Mail*, June 24–30, 1988, p. 4.

79. See *Weekly Mail*, February 17–23, 1989, p. 7.

80. See Shaun Johnson, "Vast Budget Cutbacks—A Schoolyard Explosion Looms," *Weekly Mail*, April 28–May 4, 1989, p. 8.

81. See Franz Kruger, "Sculpting the Landscape in Their Own Image," *Weekly Mail*, November 28–December 4, 1986, p. 10.

82. See Steven Friedman, "To Participate or Not, The Black Political Dilemma," *Monitor*, October 1988, p. 35.

83. See Steven Friedman, "Rates Rise. The State May Pay the Price," *Weekly Mail*, January 20, 1989, p. 14.

84. Surveys conducted by the Human Rights Trust of Port Elizabeth. Interviews were conducted in African townships in April–May and October–December 1987. There is no appreciable difference in the responses between the early and later interviews. See *Monitor*, June 1988, pp. 69–79; and *Monitor*, October 1988, pp. 56–64.

85. See *Monitor*, June 1988, p. 70.

86. Ibid., p. 71.

87. Ibid., p. 72.

88. See *Star*, April 25, 1989.

89. See *Star*, February 15, 1988; see also SAIRR, *Quarterly Countdown Nine*, 1988, p. 10.

90. See "Feuding Councils Group Set to Split Down Middle," *Weekly Mail*, December 12–18, 1986, p. 4.

91. SAIRR, *Quarterly Countdown Eleven* (Johannesburg: Institute of Race Relations, 1988), p. 9.

92. See, Andrew Forrest "Anatomy of Repression," *Weekly Mail*, Special Supplement, December 9–15, 1988, p. 2.

93. Quoted in *Weekly Mail*, March 17–22, 1989, p. 5.

94. Quoted by Roger Thurow, "South Africa is Facing a No-Growth Future," *Wall Street Journal*, July 26, 1988, p. 31 (emphasis added).

95. Ibid.

96. See Annual Report of First National Bank for 1988, printed in *Leadership*, vol. 7, no. 6 (1988).

97. Annual Report, Rand Mines Ltd., 1988, reprinted in *Leadership*, vol. 7, no. 6 (1988). See also, Annual Report of NEDBANK, also reprinted in *Leadership*, same issue.

98. International Monetary Fund, *International Financial Statistics, Yearbook, 1988*, p. 641; and IMF, *International Financial Statistics*, vol. 42, no. 7 (July 1989), p. 478.

99. See *Financial Mail*, November 11, 1988.

100. See *Weekly Mail*, March 17–22, 1989, p. 16 (emphasis added).

101. Quoted in ibid. (emphasis added).

102. Quoted in Southern Africa Report, March 24, 1989, reprinted in *Facts and Reports*, vol. 19, no. G (April 8, 1989), p. 4.

103. Johan Louw, quoted in *Weekly Mail*, March 17–22, 1989, p. 16.

104. See *Frontfile*, vol. 2, no. 2 (August 1988), p. 4; *Citizen*, June 9, 1988; *Star*, June 6, 1988; *Weekly Mail*, March 3, 1989, p. 13.

105. *Sunday Times* (Johannesburg), March 18, 1984, reprinted in *South African Digest*, March 23, 1984, p. 19.

106. Ibid.

107. *Daily Dispatch*, March 14, 1989.

108. *Financial Times* (UK), March 17, 1989, p. 4.

109. From a speech by F. W. de Klerk to South Africa's 500 highest-ranking police officers in January 1990, printed in *Harper's Magazine*, May 1990, pp. 23–24.

110. Quoted in the *New York Times*, September 21, 1989, p. 5.

111. Quotes from F. W. de Klerk's speech to Parliament, February 2, 1990 (Pretoria: Bureau for Information, 1990), p. 1.

9

An End to White Supremacy?

From Transformation to Transition

Developments in South Africa during the early months of 1990 suggested that the country was poised on the threshold of genuine political change away from white minority rule. During the previous fifteen years the foundations of white power had been eroded by the trialectical interaction of popular resistance, state policy, and international pressure. That erosion constituted a transformation in the means available to the state for maintaining its effective domination of society. While much had been altered in this erosion process, the formal political order whose defining characteristic was a monopoly of power by a racial minority had remained essentially intact. In other words, a disjunction had developed between the foundation, or substructure of political power, and the formal arrangement for its expression, or constitutional superstructure. Symptomatic of this disjunction were the conditions of social anger and political alienation, endemic unrest and incipient insurrection, and international isolation and economic pressure. So too was F. W. de Klerk's understanding that without political change South Africa's future would be one in which "there is no hope, . . . a stagnant situation . . . where revolution continues to brew and bubble under the surface," where "sanctions and boycotts" define economic life.[1] The actions of the new state president, clearing the path for negotiations, and the response of the African National Congress, indicating that it intended to move down that path, ushered South Africa into a new phase in the process of political change. We can think of this phase as one of *transition,* in which through the mechanism of negotiation the superstructure of political power is brought into alignment with the altered substructure of domination. There is nothing inevitable, however, about the transition phase reaching a successful or quick culmination. It may take a period, or periods of further erosion of the foundations of power—a return to transformation— before transition reaches successful closure. Simply reaching agreement about who should be "seated" at negotiations is often a difficult and time-consuming task. In South Africa, despite their considerable sense of optimism, both government and opposition agree that the negotiations process could well stretch over several or more years, for the stakes at issue are profound and the distance that separates both sides is substantial. Of course, positions shift during the process of negotiations, both as a consequence of the negotiations process itself and as a result of the political process that continues to unfold away from the negotiating table. The latter affects the relative positions of power of the protagonists, and therefore the outcome of the negotiation itself. Consequently, the process whereby the parties to negotiations compromise their original position sufficiently to be able to strike a deal is both complex and indeterminate. It does not lend itself to precise predictions in respect to either the timing of an agreement or its specifics.

Negotiations: The Stakes

Discussions about an appropriate constitutional order for a future South Africa, whether they are conducted by South African protagonists themselves or outside observers, tend to focus on disagreements over matters that appear to be purely political in nature—majority rule vs. minority rights, group vs. individual representation, unitary vs. federal state, centralized authority vs. devolution of power, consensus decision-making, proportional representation. Consequently, successful negotiations between Pretoria and its opponents are usually seen to require compromise over abstract principles derived from political philosophy and constitutional law. But this type of philosophic and constitutional discourse masks a very significant, indeed dominant, subtext to the dispute over the proper political structures for a future South Africa. That subtext in its essentials involves a conflict over *social* revolution; it is ultimately about how the resources of South African society, which have historically flowed in great disproportion to the minority racial caste, will in the future be distributed and redistributed.

The demand for political inclusion by South Africa's black majority is not driven by some philosophic desire for democracy in the abstract—for the right to vote "for its own sake"—but rather by the realization that access to political power provides a basis, perhaps the only basis, for achieving access to the kinds of social and material values previously enjoyed only by the empowered white minority. In South Africa the social revolution has driven the political revolution. Hence the ANC and the other elements of the black opposition seek a constitutional arrangement that will allow them to use state power to harness economic growth and distribution to the purpose of rapidly improving the black majority's material standard of living.

Forms of democracy that fail to facilitate the goals of the social revolution, however elegantly they can be justified on grounds of political philosophy or constitutional law, are not likely to garner the interest or approval of the Mass Democratic Movement. Its preference, embodied in the slogan "one-person, one-vote in a unitary state," is for the same type of political system that existed in South Africa from the time of Union in 1910 until the introduction of the tricameral constitution in 1983, with the obvious difference that the adult black population would be enfranchised. This is a system modeled on the English Westminster model of democracy; a system characterized by "parliamentary sovereignty." The great attraction of this model for the MDM, in comparison with the continental European parliamentary forms, lies in two areas. First, it facilitates the formation of an electoral and parliamentary majority through an electoral system based upon single-member constituencies. Second, it allows the governing party unfettered latitude in policymaking so long as it maintains the support of a majority in parliament. Hence the Westminster model contains no constitutional proscriptions or structural constraints that would inhibit the state in pursuing the MDM's redistributive goals.

While the MDM's political/constitutional agenda is driven by its desire to further the social revolution, the constitutional preferences of white South Africans in general and the National Party in particular is just the opposite. The overriding interest of whites is to maintain the standard and quality of living that their historical monopoly of political power has provided, and which the MDM's socioeconomic redistributive agenda potentially threatens.* Consequently, the National Party, and indeed virtually all other predominately white political groupings, reject the Westminster parliamentary model for the same basic reason that the MDM prefers it: it places power in the hands of the governing party to pursue an agenda of socioeconomic change. The preference of the National Party, as well as white liberals, is for constitutional mechanisms that will place constraints on governmental action in the socioeconomic arena.

There is considerable historical irony in white objections to British-style parliamentary democracy and to the idea of using state policies to achieve economic and social upliftment. Throughout modern South African history there was little significant criticism of the Westminster model that had been inherited from British colonialism. Only when black South Africans had attained enough leverage to force their inclusion in the political system did concerns about the supposed democratic shortcomings of this model become salient. Indeed, it was the power available in the Westminster parliamentary system that gave the National Party the opportunity to elevate Afrikaners through statist economic policies of regulation, allocation, and public ownership. The extent of state intervention was such that the South African economy was characterized by one expert as "about as interventionist and centrally directed a policy regime as could be found in the world."[2] Not only was this redistributive project a resounding success, but the Afrikaner advance relative to English-speakers was coupled with high levels of general economic growth. Ironically, the possibility that the ANC might pursue a similar statist strategy in respect to the black majority is denounced by the National Party leadership as irrational and

---

*A decline in white standards of living is not an inevitable consequence of improved material conditions for the black populace. It is possible that a redistribution in the flow of resources will be accomplished with the proceeds of future economic growth. In that case both blacks and whites would benefit in absolute terms from majority rule, while the improvements for blacks would be proportionately greater. This is precisely what occurred between Afrikaners and English-speaking whites when the National Party used its control of the state to improve the lot of the Afrikaner during the 1950s and 1960s. During that period the material standard of all whites advanced, and at the same time the Afrikaner community moved into a position of greater parity with English speakers. This type of result may occur under conditions of majority rule, but in 1990 relatively few South African whites wanted to risk that it would.

economically ruinous. Under these circumstances, it is not surprising that white demands for constitutional limits on state action, made in the name of perfecting democracy, are considered disingenuous and self-serving by black South Africans.

Negotiations: The Positions

As they consolidated their position within the National Party, the internationalist-reformers indicated a preference for a South African state possessing two cardinal features: (1) it should be a state in which all people regardless of race have full and equal access; and (2) it should be a weak state, highly constrained in its ability to pursue major alterations in the economic and social system. The first feature reflects the internationalist-reformers' ultimate acceptance, slowly arrived at, that only a constitutional arrangement which appeared to fully include the African majority on an equal footing could achieve legitimacy domestically and internationally. The second reflects a desire to prevent the enfranchisement of the black majority from threatening what are considered vital "white interests," or what the reformers of the 1990s refer to as "reasonable standards of public life and civilisation."[3] This new conception of a future South African state involved a modification of the concept of "power sharing." In the mid-1980s, the Botha administration viewed a consociational constitutional arrangement as a "democratic" means of sharing power while simultaneously guaranteeing white control of the government. As South Africa entered the 1990s, the National Party elite became willing to risk a loss of government control; it began to contemplate an acceptable constitutional future in which blacks might be in a position to form the government, and white political parties, including the National Party, would move into the role of opposition. Having backed away from its historic objection to government elected through a universal franchise, it instead focused its attention on ways to limit governmental control of the economy and society.

In the NP's effort to design a constitution for an inclusive but weak state, consociational concepts continue to have a key role. However, in keeping with F. W. de Klerk's political initiatives, the National Party's commitment to consociationalism has been modified in several respects. First, the complete rejection of majoritarianism has been tempered to allow for a political system that combines both majoritarian and consociational elements. Second, group "self-determination" and "own affairs" have been de-emphasized. And third, statutorily prescribed racial group membership has been recognized as politically nonviable in the contemporary South African context. In this last area, however, the NP leadership faces what may be an intractable problem: how to avoid prescribing racially specific political groups and at the same time protect the interests of a racial minority. In an interview with the *New York Times* Gerrit Viljoen, South Africa's minister of constitutional planning, talked about this dilemma. Viljoen explained that the NP's constitutional conception included the notion that racial groups would elect their own representatives. But, he added, a new method had to be found for defining racial groups. The existing system of prescription would have to be replaced by one in which "each person chose his or her racial group, or chose to be in none. . . . Freedom of association would be a dominant factor."[4] But if free association was to be the dominant factor, how could race-group cohesiveness be maintained and the interests of racial minorities be protected? The answer apparently lies in the NP elite's conception that "freedom of association" includes the freedom to exclude. Thus, while race group membership would not be prescribed by the legal system, groups could still form based upon race and they could maintain their racial "identity" by themselves excluding those deemed racial outsiders. Such groups could then become the basis for race-group political representation and for the drawing up of separate racial voting rolls.

Various planning documents, as well as public statements by key officials, indicate that the National Party was preparing in 1990 to propose a constitutional dispensation with the following elements:

> 1. A two-chamber legislature combining majoritarian and consociational elements. Majoritarianism would characterize a lower house elected on a common voters roll, in which the allocation of seats would correspond to the proportion of the popular vote received by a candidate or party. An upper house would be consociational in nature, providing equal representation to geographically, ethnically, and racially constituted groups. Election to the upper house would be on the basis of separate voter rolls.[5]

> 2. The upper, or consociational, legislative chamber would operate according to the principle of "consensus decision-making." As such, each minority group would be able to veto legislation dealing with "important political issues," such as cultural, language, and religious practices, and "the nature of the economic system."[6]

> 3. An executive cabinet in which ministries are divided among political parties and groups according to their proportion of seats in the two legislative houses. The head of government could come from the majority party, or a majority coalition, in the lower house.

> 4. A bill of rights incorporating guarantees of individual liberties, group rights, and the rights of property.

> 5. An independent judiciary with the power to enforce constitutional prescriptions against the executive and legislative branches.

What is significant about these various constitutional specifics is that their common logic reveals Pretoria's goal orientation as it prepares to enter negotiations. All of the structural specifics work to weaken the central state, either through making the formation of majorities difficult and thus facilitating government immobilism, or through blocking mechanisms on government action. In addition to designing constitutional mechanisms, Pretoria under the leadership of F. W. de Klerk prepared for an altered political future by restructuring the existing relationship between state and economy. A policy of "privatization" was accelerated whereby the South African state is selling off its substantial economic assets to individuals and private businesses. Having, since 1948, brought an estimated 57 percent of the economy's fixed assets under state ownership,[7] the National Party in 1990 began divesting the state of its economic holdings in preparation for turning the state over to a government that might be controlled by the black majority.

At the outset of the decade of the 1990s, the highly divergent constitutional preferences of the ANC and the National Party, rooted as they are in fundamentally
different interests, did not represent much of a basis for negotiating a settlement.
Only when, and if, the positions of the protagonists shift significantly will there
develop a "zone of agreement" within which a compromise can be reached. Notwithstanding their considerable differences, however, there are some similar elements in the prenegotiation positions of the protagonists that do provide common
ground upon which divergent stances can converge. Both Pretoria and the ANC
favor the concepts of a bill of rights and an independent judiciary. These items are
found in the ANC's "Constitutional Guidelines for a Democratic South Africa,"
published in 1988,[8] and have been reiterated since and with increasing emphasis in
many ANC discussions of a future constitutional order.[9] There is more significance
here than mere agreement about constitutional structures. The ANC's acceptance of
a bill of rights and an independent judiciary indicates that it is willing to place limits
on the parliamentary sovereignty normally associated with the British-type Westminster model. In this respect, it would probably be receptive to bill of rights
guarantees of freedom of religious, linguistic, and cultural expression.[10] This would
be consistent with the Freedom Charter declaration that "All people shall have equal
rights to use their own languages and to develop their own folk culture and
customs."[11] The right to ethnically and culturally separate schools, a major concern
of Afrikaners, can be accommodated within this perspective. A guarantee of state
subsidies for such educational efforts, however, is more problematic.

The two areas of most difficulty, and where the National Party will have to
demonstrate the most movement if a negotiated settlement is to be achieved, are
racial/ethnic representation and socioeconomic policy. National Party efforts to
maintain race and ethnic group exclusivity, even if presented under the guise of
some apparently "neutral" criteria, will meet stiff resistance from the ANC and its
MDM allies. And while the ANC might accept some bill of rights protection of
private property, it is likely to be far more resistant to NP stipulations that the South
African economy be "capitalist" or based on the "free market." Likewise, the ANC
will have great difficulty accepting substantial constitutional limits on the economic
policies of a future government.

The Politics of Transition

How far each of the South African protagonists shifts its initial bargaining position,
and whether or not they shift significantly enough for agreement to be reached and
political transition to take place, is itself a function of a dynamic political process.
That process can be conceived of as containing three interrelated dimensions: the
negotiation itself (the bargaining process between the main protagonists); the international environment (the manner in which international reactions to the negotiation
process affects the relative power of the protagonists); and domestic politics (the
latitude or limitations that the South African domestic political situation places on
the flexibility of the protagonists). Each dimension contains forces that both pull the
protagonists apart and push them together. The broad outlines of these can be

comprehended. But whether the outcome of their complex interactions will be a successful political transition or a breakdown of negotiations cannot be predicted.

The main protagonists in the South African conflict—the National Party and the ANC along with its MDM allies—bring to negotiations histories, ideologies, and political identities that will inhibit their finding sufficient common ground for substantial agreement. The National Party embodies a political tradition, going back to the seventeenth century, whose central tenet is that white "survival" requires the political exclusion of the more numerous black populace. This remains the essential core of National Party thinking about the future even though *total* exclusion has been deemed politically inviable. "If we accept a new constitution in which there is a simple majority on a common voters' register," explained Gerrit Viljoen in March 1990, "that would be the end [for the white man]. . . . But we won't accept that."[12] The ANC, for its part, has struggled and sacrificed over the past three decades for precisely what the NP rejects: a nonracial form of majority rule. That has likewise been the rallying-cry of the mass movement of political opposition that formed in the 1980s and is embodied in the MDM. The notion that majority rule is inappropriate for South Africa because it is a country split among racial and ethnic minorities who lack a genuine basis for common action is as anathema to the ANC as majority rule is to the NP. "In justifying their proposed system," the National Party is "claiming that South Africa is a country of 'minorities' " that need protection, stated ANC leader Ahmed Kathrada: "[But] stripped of all the nice phrases they are simply once again changing their language and style to perpetuate white domination. . . . We reject the concept of group rights because we believe that it is simply another way of perpetuating white domination."[13]

Although their histories and self-identities keep the South African protagonists apart, there is one element which they share that does push them toward compromising their differences. That element, which can be termed the "psychology of transition," made its appearance with the ascendancy of F. W. de Klerk and particularly with the dramatic legalization of the ANC and release of Nelson Mandela. Both the governing group and its opponents came to hold the belief that a new situation had developed in which through negotiations a viable political transition could be achieved. Once adopted, this essentially optimistic psychological orientation, the expectation of resolution, raised the perceived costs of failure. For de Klerk and his associates these costs involved a future in which "there is no hope for our children and grandchildren";[14] for the ANC they involved a return to exile and the political wilderness. The combination of optimistic expectations, and the real and perceived costs of failure to achieve a political resolution, constitutes a powerful psychological factor keeping the South African protagonists locked into the process of negotiation and pushing them toward compromise.

International isolation, especially its economic manifestation, was a key element in bringing Pretoria to the point at which it was willing to accept the risks attendant upon negotiating an end to white rule. The history of the 1980s provides strong evidence that the willingness of Pretoria to move in the direction of full black political participation and to seek agreement with the ANC is directly related to the amount of international economic pressure it feels. Correlatively, the 1980's experience suggests that should international isolation and economic pressure diminish before a settlement, a major incentive for Pretoria to reach agreement with its opponents will have been eliminated. As a result, we can expect that during negotiations both Pretoria and its opponents will be addressing an international audience; the one seeking to have economic sanctions maintained and the other to have them lifted.

Pretoria will seek international support by trying to show that its conception of qualified majority rule is democratic and reasonable, and that the ANC's insistence on unconstrained nonracial majority rule is both intransigent and dangerous. For Pretoria, a situation in which international economic pressures ease and negotiations stall or break down is a second-best yet quite favorable outcome. The ANC will attempt to advance its own bargaining position by campaigning internationally for the maintenance of sanctions. It's message to the world will be that Pretoria's qualified version of political inclusion is merely another form of institutionalized racism, that is, apartheid with a new face.

Initially, Pretoria possessed considerable advantages in this duel for international support. De Klerk's bold moves in February 1990 enabled the South African government to regain some of the credibility that had been lost during the Botha years. The Western political establishment is predisposed to accept Pretoria's constitutional design because the consociational elements it contains are present in a number of European countries that are considered bona fide democracies. In any case this establishment is very unlikely to identify with the MDM's redistributive goals. Moreover, the international environment of 1990 was one especially receptive to Pretoria's demand that limits be placed on the state's economic role. The collapse of socialist economies in Europe, the disastrous performance of state-centric African economies, and the related global enthusiasm for market-oriented economic strategies all provided a solid foundation for Pretoria to present the ANC's preference for a strong state role as both irrational and ruinous. Finally, Pretoria's southern African strategy, although it was very costly, did succeed in forcing the governing elites of southern African states to recognize that their economic survival was tied to a rapid resolution of South Africa's internal political crisis. There thus exists a distinct possibility that other African nations will attempt to force the ANC to accede to less than unqualified majority rule. Such was the fate of the nationalists in Zimbabwe in 1979.

The ANC also has advantages that can be used in a campaign to maintain international economic pressure on Pretoria. The two most important are its acknowledged position as the leading organization of black opposition and the stature of its preeminent leader, Nelson Mandela. The mass insurrection of the mid-1980s galvanized international attention and generated bonds of identification and sympathy with the plight of black South Africans. In the 1990s, the ANC is in a position to use those bonds in an appeal to Western industrial countries to "stay the course" for the final push to genuine nonracial democracy. In the person of Nelson Mandela the ANC has someone ideally placed to carry its message to the international audience. Ironically, it was Pretoria's own treatment of Mandela—his long incarceration and the drawn-out process of his release—that focused extraordinary global attention on him, turning his release into an international drama and imparting to him the aura of an elder statesman. Whether economic sanctions will be maintained until an agreement on majority rule is reached will depend on the ANC's skill in using its global reservoir of sympathy and the moral authority of Mandela. The first major test came with Mandela's tour of Europe and America in June–July 1990, and indicated the ANC's ability to counter Pretoria's new international thrust. Greeted everywhere with respect bordering on reverence, Mandela was received in the United States with a level of enthusiasm never before seen for a foreign political figure and beyond living memory for any domestic one. By creating a political atmosphere in which a decision to lift sanctions would generate massive political fallout, the Mandela visit served to check any such inclination by the Bush administration. In Europe, the European Community, which had appeared ready to ease sanctions after President de Klerk had toured the continent in May, voted to maintain its economic pressure.

The most significant and complex dimension of South Africa's politics of transition is the domestic one. Three significant aspects can be distinguished. First is the role of the collaborationist black elite. When F. W. de Klerk announced in his February 2 speech that homeland leaders and township councillors would be guaranteed a place at the negotiating table, he indicated that the National Party would continue its decades-long strategy of legitimating its political designs through the collaboration of black "leaders." Pretoria's hope was that bringing potential black allies into the negotiations would not only improve its chances of a favorable settlement, but that such a settlement would be positively received internationally.

The collaborationist legitimation strategy, however, remains a dubious enterprise. Homeland leaders and township councillors have not gained any semblance of legitimacy, and they are still the focus of a simmering popular anger. In the euphoria that followed Nelson Mandela's release, townships in the Transvaal erupted in mass protests against township conditions and council rule. As the situation evolved in a pattern reminiscent of the urban protest politics of the early 1980s, seven councils in the Transvaal collapsed, as did thirteen in the Cape Province. Fifty-eight councillors in Cape townships resigned between January and April of 1990.[15] When governments in two of the four nominally independent homelands were overthrown by military officers who indicated sympathy with the ANC, and when mass protests erupted in a third, nearly bringing down its government, it appeared that the utter collapse of Pretoria's structures of indirect rule might precede the beginning of negotiations. Would any surviving members of the collaborationist elite be willing to take a seat at the negotiating table? Doing so would call attention to their lack of popular mandate and thus increase their vulnerability to mass opposition. To in addition align themselves with Pretoria and against the MDM might well be an act of political suicide, at the least.

Gatsha Buthelezi, the head of the KwaZulu homeland, remained the only black political figure who might offer significant assistance to Pretoria's legitimation strategy. With his independent base of support in rural Zululand and his own personal preference for consociationalism, he has both credibility and a predisposition toward Pretoria's constitutional design.* Yet Buthelezi's utility as an ally for

---

*In 1986 a commission appointed by Buthelezi recommended a constitutional design for a regional government (encompassing KwaZulu and the Natal Province) that was heavily consociational in form. A year later a "great *indaba*" (negotiation) between Natal white liberal political organizations and

Pretoria was increasingly limited. Both his support and organizational reach were limited to the Zulu-speaking areas of Natal Province—and even there his situation was precarious. His Inkatha political movement was locked into an intra-Zulu civil war, within which better educated and urban Zulu-speakers have allied themselves with the ANC/UDF. By mid-1990 security officials were estimating that in Natal's townships, where ten years earlier Inkatha's political sway was uncontested, up to 70 percent of the residents supported the MDM alliance.[16] Outside Natal popular backing for Buthelezi was, in the wake of Mandela's release, approaching the insignificant. An opinion survey conducted between April and June 1990 in the country's other three provinces found only 2 percent support for Inkatha among adult black South Africans.[17] Based upon a random sample of 2,281 respondents, the survey also revealed the dominant position of MDM within the black community: some 84 percent of black adults residing outside Natal voiced primary allegiance to the MDM or one of its constituent political organizations (ANC = 38%, UDF = 19%, MDM = 15%, SACP = 12%).[18]

The political marginalization of Buthelezi coincided with an increased use of violence by his supporters. Between June and October 1990 Inkatha, utilizing ethnic appeals and forced recruitment, organized "war bands" among Zulu-speaking migrant laborers within the large urban townships of the Transvaal. Operating from the barrackslike hostels in which migrant laborers are housed, the Inkatha bands launched random terrorist attacks against the more permanently settled township residents, setting off a kind of civil war between Inkatha "warriors" and ANC-supporting youth in the industrial townships of the central Transvaal.[19] With his mass support dwindling to insignificance, and with the domestic and international political spotlight firmly focused on Mandela, Buthelezi apparently decided to guarantee himself a central role in negotiations over South Africa's future by deomonstrating that unless he is taken into account there will be no peace. He implied as much in a statement issued after three days of particularly savage clashes between his supporters and ANC youth in the black townships around Johannesburg: "Active attempts to isolate Inkatha and [me] . . . have resulted in unnecessary conflict. Until respect for one another is observed, it will be difficult to obtain peace."[20]

Buthelezi's strategy of violence is likely to exacerbate an already tense township environment and may potentially introduce intrablack ethnic conflict—which has hitherto been largely absent—into South African politics. However, as a way of leveraging the homeland leader into a pivotal role in the negotiations process, the strategy's prospects are dubious. Lacking a social base outside of Natal, it is doubtful that Inkatha can sustain its war against the MDM in the Transvaal. Consequently, the strategy of violence will likely fall short of demonstrating the necessary disruptive power to "muscle" Buthelezi into a central role in negotiations.

A second aspect of the domestic politics of transition involves "constituency constraints" on the main South African protagonists. Students of negotiations point

---

Buthelezi's Inkatha movement incorporated the Buthelezi Commission's recommendations into a consociational constitutional blueprint for a KwaZulu/Natal regional government. Rejected by Pretoria at the time, this scheme is very similar to what National Party officials apparently plan to propose in negotiations with the ANC.

out that more is involved in successful outcomes than simply obtaining compromise from the parties at the bargaining table. The protagonists in a negotiation usually have external constituencies that must be "brought along" if the negotiated compromise is to hold.[21] This aspect of negotiations is given institutional expression in the U.S. Constitution, which specifies that the Senate must ratify all international treaties. As such, agreements worked out by negotiators must have political support outside the negotiating room if they are to have a lasting impact. This knowledge is a powerful limiting factor on U.S. diplomats engaged in treaty negotiations.

In the South African case, observers are usually sensitive to the constituency problem of the National Party. They generally acknowledge that both the extent and pace of reform that the NP can accept is significantly constrained by the existence of a large and very conservative "white right." Much less awareness exists of the constituency constraints that face the ANC "on the left." But these are substantial, and represent a counterweight to any internal inclinations to accept substantial qualifications to majority rule. In part the constraints are a product of the ANC's own making. It defined the litmus test of genuine change as "one-person, one-vote in a unitary state" and a "nonracial" constitutional order. During the 1980s these canons became part of the "culture of liberation" that dominated black political life. But the general political beliefs of the black populace are not the only constraints that keep the ANC from moving toward acceptance of Pretoria's constitutional designs. More important, the township youth and the trade unions, the two most organized and politically active elements in domestic black politics, would likely oppose a compromise that rendered the new South African state powerless to undertake the task of socioeconomic redistribution. The real possibility that accepting significant limits on majority rule could split the MDM will powerfully affect the ANC's ability to compromise on matters like consociational structures.

The ANC's problems with potential defections from its ranks are exacerbated by political competition among opposition organizations. With South Africa moving into an era of negotiations and possible compromise, the Pan Africanist Congress and the Black Consciousness Movement (BCM) have moved to outflank the ANC on the left. Emphasizing their commitment to socialism and revolution, and accusing the ANC of preparing to "sell out" in a compromise deal with the whites, both organizations saw an opportunity to regain ground they had lost during the 1980s when the ANC and Charterism came to dominate the politics of black South Africa. In a situation in which the ANC will have to make some compromises and in which mass political culture continues to be highly charged with militancy and liberatory expectations, the PAC and BCM rhetoric, with its mix of revolution, socialism, and racial solidarity, could have considerable appeal.

On balance the ANC may have less latitude to compromise than the National Party. The latter, if it were willing to abandon its exclusive Afrikaner identity, would certainly be able obtain support from much of the English-speaking community. In contrast, the ANC has no alternative base of support if youthful activists and trade unionists defect to the PAC or BCM. The dynamics of constituency politics in South Africa suggest, therefore, that if there is to be a negotiated settlement between Pretoria and the ANC, then the government will have to abandon much of its preferred consociational apparatus for qualifying majority rule.

The negotiations process will also be affected by the continuing thrust toward populist mobilization among the black population. As already noted, the period following F. W. de Klerk's assumption of the state presidency, with the relaxation of the state of emergency and the release of Nelson Mandela, saw many black townships return to a state of affairs reminiscent of the early 1980s. Urban grievances gave rise to mass protests, often focused on the role of township councils. The protests turned violent when police moved to disperse crowds. Township councils again collapsed and the political funeral made a reappearance. A new element in the situation was the extension of populist mobilization politics to some of the smallest rural towns—areas that had existed outside the arena of insurrection during 1984–86.

The significance of renewed popular mobilization for the process of negotiations is complex. It has been argued, on the one hand, that Pretoria will not be able to proceed with negotiations under conditions of disorder and violence. The presumption is that with renewed unrest white perceptions of risk will escalate, making compromise with the ANC more difficult for the government. On the other hand, the popular mobilization of the 1980s was instrumental in forcing Pretoria to accept political change. The continued state of mobilization in black society is an indication, a reminder, of what the future will hold unless an agreement is reached that the ANC can sell to its constituents. As such the renewed unrest, although not actually controlled by the ANC, represents leverage for the ANC in pushing Pretoria toward acceptance of genuine majority rule.

At a more general level, the heightened popular mobilization that has accompanied the move toward the bargaining table indicates that negotiations are only part of a larger process of political change. F. W. de Klerk's actions and promises raised expectations and introduced an atmosphere of extraordinary optimism, as did the reformist actions and promises of P. W. Botha some ten years earlier. The lesson that the 1980s offers for South Africa of the 1990s is that this mix of expectations and optimism is a volatile one. Should expectations prove to be illusory, optimism will rapidly turn into alienation and anger. If Pretoria's willingness to accept significant political change proves to be far less in action than in promise, and as a result negotiations stall or break off, then South Africa could find itself back on the path to insurrection and intensified international pressure. The process of change that began in the mid-1970s would not necessarily be terminated. But a negotiated settlement would await the day when white power was sufficiently eroded to convince the ruling group that maintaining minority control entails greater risks than a transition to genuine majority rule.

Conclusion: The Dynamics of Political Change

The consequences of two structural incompatibilities built into its system of racial rule have, in the last quarter of the twentieth century, come to dominate South Africa's social, economic, and, most of all, its political life. The economic inclusion of the black majority as an industrial work force and its concomitant exclusion from the political community, in combination with the anomaly of official white racism in a racially heterogenous global system, gave rise to a "trialectical" conflict. The South African state, seeking to maintain white minority rule, found itself squeezed between a more unified and effective opposition and an international community gradually but increasingly willing to impose costs upon a state whose official racism rendered it a pariah. This trialectic struggle involving government, its black opposition, and the international community took on a particular dynamic that constitutes for Pretoria a fundamental and irreconcilable "security contradiction."

Pretoria's Security Contradiction

In its efforts to maintain white minority rule, the government of South Africa is confronted by a fundamental contradiction between its international and domestic requirements. Figure 9.1 presents the key elements of this security contradiction and their interaction. Internationally, South Africa requires access to markets for the export of its minerals and manufactured goods, and it depends upon the importation of vital capital, technology, and producer goods. These are prerequisites for the growth and development of its modern industrial economy. But the nature of South Africa's domestic system of white supremacy and Pretoria's repressive efforts to maintain it threaten the country's access to global markets and thus jeopardize economic health.

The contradiction between domestic and international requirements is a dynamic one: the greater the domestic black opposition and the more manifest the govern-

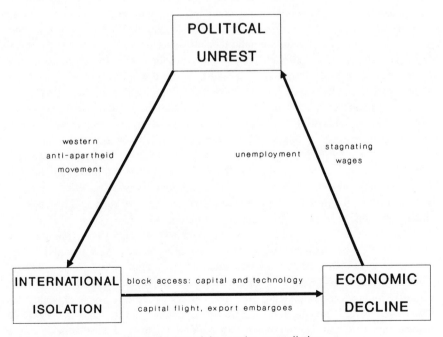

FIG. 9.1. Pretoria's security contradiction

ment's repressive response to it, the greater its problems with its international environment. Active political pressure by the majority and its counterpoint, repressive action by the minority government, render the nature of the South African system visible to the world and thus serve as a catalyst for international reactions. Conversely, in periods of relative political quiescence, Pretoria's international problem recedes. It is when the majority makes its political opposition felt and visible, and thus when the need of the white government to make its authority manifest is greatest, that the international threat becomes substantial.

In this dynamic the domestic dialectic is the active element, but the international reaction in respect to constraints on the South African economy is both real and consequential. Moreover, the internationally imposed economic constraints have a "boosting effect" on the domestic political dialectic. They contribute to material conditions of life that produce intense political alienation, they deny government resources that could be used for policies of cooptation; and they make the financing of repression more politically painful. The international constraints thus increase the likelihood of repeated episodes of intense internal political opposition.

South Africa's security contradiction has manifest itself in an especially intense form since 1976. Isolated internationally because of its system of racial rule, Pretoria has found that when its domestic situation is characterized by visible black resistance, western governments are unwilling or unable to resist taking steps against it. Likewise, under these circumstances, multinational corporations, and international banks came to recognize that an expanded, or even continued, presence in or relationship with South Africa entailed significant costs. International isolation has been transposed into capital flight from South Africa and blocked access to markets for new capital and technology. Difficulty in obtaining new direct investment from abroad, in importing the latest technology, in finding export markets, and in gaining access to international bank loans threatens South Africa's long-term economic growth. Without economic growth, the prospects for domestic tranquility and security decline, for unemployment and downward pressure on wages serve to increase black anger and to make militant political responses more likely.

A violent and seemingly unstable domestic situation, in circumstances of diplomatic isolation and hostility, serves to undermine South Africa's economic relations further by increasing the likelihood of sanctions and by reducing the attractiveness of South Africa's investment climate. Such developments, in turn, threaten economic growth, jobs, and income, producing more alienation and threats to domestic peace. In other words, the dynamic elements in South Africa's security contradiction have since the mid-1970s generated a continuing downward spiral of international isolation, political unrest, and economic decline.

The downward spiral produced by the trialetic of change is not a smooth one. Rather, it is characterized by a series of episodes and plateaus. As depicted in Figure 9.2, since World War II the security contradiction has manifested itself in a series of "peak episodes," as upsurges in militant domestic opposition are followed in short order by intensified international pressure. Observing the three peak episodes that South Africa has thus far experienced—Sharpeville, Soweto, and the 1984–86 insurrection—we can see an interesting pattern. Each successive episode had a larger mass base, was more politically radical, lasted for a longer period, and

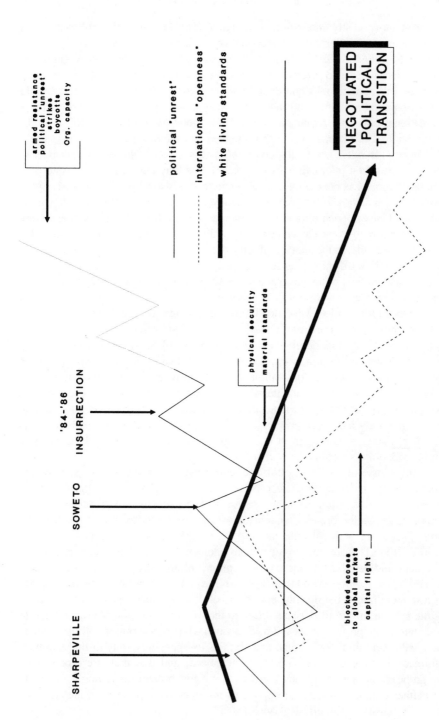

FIG. 9.2. Path to negotiations

produced more costly international isolation. The episodes also followed more quickly upon each other: sixteen years between Sharpeville and Soweto; eight years between Soweto and the 1984 insurrection. And, while political unrest and international isolation receded after each peak episode, South Africa's internal political order and its international situation did not return to the status quo ante. Instead, the level of political militancy and radical political organization, as well as the level of international pressure, remained higher than prior to the previous peak episode, creating a kind of plateau from which the next episode of unrest and isolation took off. There is, in other words, a kind of cumulation effect to the various episodes of political unrest and international isolation. That is why the time lag between peak periods of unrest has been progressively shorter. It is also why each successive peak episode is characterized by greater militancy and organizational capability on the part of the black opposition and more intense pressure from the international community. For South Africa's white minority this process has meant a gradual but continuous decline in the quality of life—a reduction in the material standard of living, and with it a diminishing sense of physical safety and psychological security.

For the South African government seeking to maintain minority control, the security contradiction within which it is locked has created a sisyphean reality of continuous failure. In an effort to defuse black opposition at home and prevent costly economic pressure from abroad, it has shifted policy and changed significantly the mode of white domination. But the irreconcilable nature of the contradictions within which Pretoria is trapped have meant that each policy shift and each alteration in the mode of domination has had the reverse of the intended effect. Black opposition has, with each iteration of government strategy, become more not less militant, better not less organized, stronger not weaker. In parallel the international community has given progressively less credence to Pretoria's solutions and more legitimacy to even its most radical opponents, and has imposed increasingly painful economic sanctions.

In the course of its failed efforts to secure white supremacy domestically and internationally, the relative power of the state in relationship to the organized expression of black opposition has declined. The once solid Afrikaner unity has crumbled, as has the broader white acquiescence in the leadership of the National Party. The white political elite has lost its cohesiveness and its sense of moral purpose. It shifts from one policy tact to another: from regional militarization to diplomacy and then back to the military option, followed by a return to diplomacy; from reform to repression and then back to reform. The government and ruling party has also unwillingly, but nonetheless effectively, relinquished the initiative in defining the agenda for South Africa's future to the Mass Democratic Movement and to prominent white professionals and businessmen who operate outside official circles. The government imprisons, bans, and restricts its opponents, only to find that their legitimacy in their own community is enhanced, and that they are received by foreign heads of state as if they constituted a "government-in-waiting." The state can neither eliminate its radical opponents nor effectively protect the material and security interests of the privileged whites.

In 1970 the South African state appeared utterly invincible; the National Party completely dominated white politics and seemed capable of choking off any space for autonomous political organization among the black majority. Twenty years later, although the formal structure of power, the constitutional order, had not changed significantly, the foundation of that formal power had been profoundly eroded. As South Africa entered the 1990s, the actions of F. W. de Klerk raised several basic questions: Has the erosion in the foundation of state power that took place during the 1980s created the conditions for a genuine transition in the formal system of power? Or will Pretoria's efforts to qualify the terms of black political inclusion lead to a breakdown in negotiations and an aborted transition process? If so, rather than a pivotal decade in South African history, the 1990s will probably be a replay of the 1980s as the trialectical process of transformation continues in a more devastating form. F. W. de Klerk will then end up looking much like his predecessor—a new state president offering change, arousing expectations and enthusiasm, but producing insurrection and economic decline. Alternatively, the experience —and recollection—of the 1980s may be the very things that lead de Klerk and his associates from replaying it. In that case the new decade will witness rapid movement toward a negotiated settlement as a result of which a form of majority rule acceptable to the MDM will result, and the establishment of a nonracial and democratic South Africa will become a real possibility.

Notes

1. *Harper's,* May 1990, pp. 23–24.

2. See Stephen R. Lewis, Jr., *Apartheid's Economics* (New York: Council on Foreign Relations, 1989), manuscript, chapter 2, p. 54.

3. See interview with Minister of Constitutional Planning Gerrit Viljoen, *Star,* March 17, 1990, p. 11.

4. See Anthony Lewis, "The New South Africa," *New York Times,* March 27, 1990, p. A15.

5. See ibid.; and *Star,* April 20, 1990. See also Daily Dispatch, June 30, 1990.

6. Gerrit Viljoen, quoted in Anthony Lewis, p. A15.

7. See Stephen R. Lewis, *Apartheid's Economics,* p. 53.

8. South African Institute of Race Relations (SAIRR), *Race Relations Survey, 1988/89* (Johannesburg: Institute of Race Relations, 1990), p. 642.

9. See for example Albie Sachs, "White South Africans in a Non-Racial Democracy," *Sechaba,* vol. 24, no. 7 (July 1990), p. 15.

10. See ibid., p. 16.

11. Reprinted in Nelson Mandela, *The Struggle Is My Life* (New York: Pathfinder Press, 1986), p. 51.

12. *Star,* March 17, 1990, p. 11.

13. Quoted in *Weekly Mail,* November 3–9, 1989, p. 11.

14. See *Harper's,* May 1990, p. 24.

15. BBC Monitoring Service, April 18, 1990, printed in *ANC Newsbriefing,* April 22, 1990, p. 25.

16. See Star, July 20, 1990, printed in *ANC Newsbriefing,* July 29, 1990, p. 5.

17. See "ANC Heads the Field," *Front File,* vol. 4, no. 11, extra (August 1990), p. 3.

18. Ibid.

19. See "Vigilante Terror Spreads," Star, August 9, 1990, printed in *ANC Newsbriefing,*

August 11, 1990, pp. 4–5; "South Africa's Week of the Long Knives," *Observer* [London], August 19, 1990, printed in *ANC Newsbriefing*, August 18, 1990, pp. 7–8; Allister Sparks, "Township Fighting Has Roots in Natal," *Washington Post*, August 19, 1990, p. A34; "Roots of the Reef War," *New Nation*, August 24–August 30, 1990, printed in *ANC Newsbriefing*, August 25, 1990, p. 15; Mondli Makhanya, "Soweto's Killing Fields," *Weekly Mail*, September 24, 1990, p. 13; Themba Khoza, "Lord of the Rooidoeke," *Weekly Mail*, September 7–13, 1990, pp. 1–2.

20. Quoted in Allister Sparks, "Township Fighting Has Roots in Natal," p. A34.

21. See Robert Putnam, "Diplomacy and Domestic Politics," *International Organization*, vol. 42, no. 3 (Summer 1988), pp. 427–60.

Index